How to Prepare for the

STATE TROOPER EXAMINATIONS

Including Highway Patrol Officer

by

Donald J. Schroeder, Ph.D.

Adjunct Professor
JOHN JAY COLLEGE OF CRIMINAL JUSTICE

Senior Instructor
REMS TUTORIAL, EXAM PREPARATION SPECIALISTS

Former Commanding Officer
81ST POLICE PRECINCT, NEW YORK CITY POLICE DEPARTMENT

Frank A. Lombardo

Deputy Inspector (retired)
NEW YORK CITY POLICE DEPARTMENT

Adjunct Professor
JOHN JAY COLLEGE OF CRIMINAL JUSTICE

Former Commanding Officer
30TH POLICE PRECINCT, NEW YORK CITY POLICE DEPARTMENT

BARRON'S

All inquiries should be addressed to:

Barron's Educational Series, Inc.
250 Wireless Boulevard
Hauppauge, New York 11788

Library of Congress Catalog Card No.: 95-50924

International Standard Book No. 0-8120-9371-2

Library of Congress Cataloging-in-Publication Data

Schroeder, Donald J.
    How to prepare for the state trooper examinations : including
highway patrol officer / by Donald J. Schroeder, Frank A. Lombardo.
        p.   cm.
    ISBN 0-8120-9371-2
    1. Police, State—United States—Examinations, questions, etc.
2. Traffic police—United States—Examinations, questions, etc.
I. Lombardo, Frank A.   II. Title.
HV8143.S342   1996
363.2'3'076—dc20
                                                                    95-50924
                                                                    CIP

PRINTED IN THE UNITED STATES OF AMERICA
987654321

Contents

Preface

This book was written to help the men and women who seek careers as highway patrol and state police officers do well on the entrance-level examinations. The questions in this book are typical of those found on these examinations. *How to Prepare for the State Trooper Examinations* also contains test-taking strategies designed to simplify the question types that are found in these examinations. By following these strategies, candidates will be able to answer questions quickly and accurately.

The many, many questions included in this book will allow candidates to develop speed and accuracy in answering questions, which is the key to success in civil service examinations of this type. The diagnostic chart found after each practice examination will help a candidate find where his or her particular strengths and weaknesses may lie.

The knowledge and experience gained by us in our many years of police work, and the test-taking expertise we have developed from the many years of tutoring candidates have been joined together in writing this book. If you work hard and allow this book to help and guide you in your efforts, you should be successful and a step closer toward realizing your goals. Good luck!

Donald J. Schroeder
Frank A. Lombardo

Acknowledgments

We would like to thank Alicia Schroeder and Dan DiCampli for their help in assisting us with much of the artwork appearing in this book. We also would like to thank Linda and Lizette for their patient and supportive roles as understanding wives while we toiled with our manuscript.

CHAPTER 1

About the State Trooper Examination

What You Should Know About the Entrance Test

The type of state trooper or highway patrol officer examination that is administered throughout the country to select qualified men and women for careers as state troopers has been modified greatly over the past decade. As a result of a Supreme Court decision a number of years ago, test writers are not permitted to use certain kinds of questions. For example, it is against the law to ask questions that require prior knowledge of the law or the specific duties and responsibilities of a state trooper. As a candidate, you are not required to know what procedure a state trooper should follow under certain circumstances, such as when he or she witnesses the commission of a crime. That is the kind of knowledge you acquire after you become a trooper and are trained by the state police agency involved. Therefore, it is a waste of time to prepare for the state trooper examination by learning the law or by memorizing actual state police procedures. The proper way to prepare is to learn how to deal with the types of questions contained in this book. Please note that because of the great similarity of the jobs involved, those preparing to take either a state traffic officer or highway patrol officer examination can also prepare effectively by using this book. Therefore, whenever in this text we use the term *trooper* or otherwise refer to the job of a state trooper, whatever is said is applicable to the job of a highway patrol officer or a state traffic officer.

The material presented in this book, including the hundreds and hundreds of practice questions, was written after a careful analysis of recent major state trooper and highway patrol officer examinations and court decisions relating to entrance level testing procedures. All the questions in the book are related to the job of a state trooper and highway patrol officer. This is important because you will see these kinds of questions when you take the official state trooper examination. Therefore, we are confident that using this book will help you achieve your goal of becoming a state trooper, a highway patrol officer, or a state traffic officer.

The rest of this chapter is devoted to explaining the job of a state trooper and outlining the steps you need to take to become one.

What a State Trooper Does

Before discussing the typical duties of a state trooper, we would like to point out that these duties vary from state to state. In some states, troopers are required to enforce laws dealing with a wide variety of crimes, while in others their responsibility is limited to the enforcement of vehicle and traffic regulations. Bear in mind, however, that the knowledge and abilities needed to perform as a law enforcement officer, such as a state trooper, are basically the same regardless of the scope of the laws they enforce. For this reason, this book can be used by trooper candidates from all states.

THE HEADQUARTERS COMPLEX

The majority of state police agencies are organized on a geographical basis. The basic organizational unit is a *troop,* although some states use the term *post.* The term *trooper,* however, is used almost exclusively to refer to the entry-level position in a state police agency. Most troops, or posts, occupy barracks that are located in a complex that usually also serves as troop headquarters. Typically, the staff and administrative units needed to support the work of the troop, such as the communications unit, the forensic unit, the firearms unit, and the jail unit, are also located within the headquarters complex.

THE WORK DAY

State troopers usually work 8-hour shifts, which are often referred to as *tours.* But because emergencies invariably occur in police work, troopers are often required to work overtime, for which they are compensated.

And, because police are needed 24 hours a day, most state police agencies use a three shift work day: a day shift, an evening shift, and a night shift. In some agencies troopers work steady shifts, whereas in others they work rotating shifts.

Troopers usually report to the headquarters complex prior to the start of their work day for what is generally known as *roll call*. Typically, roll call involves such things as receiving the day's assignment, standing inspection, and obtaining updates on current situations.

The great majority of troopers work in uniform in a conspicuously marked, specially equipped patrol vehicle, although some troopers work in civilian clothes and perform investigatory or crime prevention work in unmarked vehicles. The automobile is the most commonly used patrol vehicle, but some troopers patrol on motorcycles, and still others use helicopters, airplanes, or boats. Because of the large areas that are patrolled, most troopers work the majority of their shift without direct supervision.

THE DUTIES OF STATE TROOPERS

The following listing of duties details the most common responsibilities of state troopers.

The Enforcement of Vehicle and Traffic Laws.   The enforcement of vehicle and traffic laws is one duty that is common to all state police agencies. To the uninformed person, enforcement of such laws might seem to be an easy task. In reality, however, it is a very difficult undertaking involving knowledge of the law, courtesy, caution, tact, and the exercise of discretion. In most cases, enforcement action, when needed, involves the issuance of warnings or citations, but in certain cases arrests are required.

The Enforcement of Criminal Laws.   In many states, the trooper is the only law enforcement officer working in certain areas of the state. In those areas, because of the absence of local police agencies, troopers enforce criminal laws as well as traffic laws. In other words, some troopers perform the job of city or county police officers, and these responsibilities include such things as maintaining the peace, responding to crimes in progress, and investigating past crimes.

Accident Prevention and Investigation.   The prevention and investigation of vehicle accidents is a major duty of the state police. Prevention is achieved via such things as conspicuous patrol, traffic engineering, motor vehicle inspections, and safety lectures. Accident investigation includes such things as rendering first aid, securing medical assistance, determining the cause of the accident, and completing required forms.

Rendering Emergency Assistance.   The state police are very often the first on the scene of such disasters as fires, floods, and airplane crashes. At such scenes they are responsible for rescuing victims caught in life-threatening situations and for controlling vehicular and pedestrian traffic. The state police perform similar functions at the scenes of civil disorders and riots.

Community and Public Relations. State troopers render assistance to the public in wide-ranging matters. They furnish directions, supply general information, assist stranded motorists, search for lost children, help to locate lost property, and perform a host of other activities intended to assist those in need.

Case Preparation and Courtroom Testimony. State troopers are trained to assist in the prosecution of criminals and are often called upon to testify in court.

Preparation of Written Reports. Report writing is a very important duty of state troopers. These reports are used as the basis for such things as the compilation of official police statistics, the unearthing of faulty highway design, the prosecution of criminals in criminal court, and the settling of disputes in civil court.

Job Opportunities

State police agencies are at the heart of each state's law enforcement effort. There has been great pressure in recent times to eliminate or merge many local police departments. Most of these proposals are based on the ability of the state police to perform the duties of these local police agencies. Consequently, job opportunities in state police agencies are as plentiful as ever, and, in many states, they are better than ever. There is no reason to believe this situation will change in the foreseeable future.

The Benefits of a Career As a State Trooper

The many material benefits typically associated with the position of state trooper follow.

Job Security. State troopers, like most other police and fire officers, are civil servants. Their employment is regulated by Civil Service Law. They have the same solid job security as all other civil servants.

Salary. While salary rates for state troopers vary from one state to another, it is safe to say that state troopers all over the nation are always among some of the highest paid entry-level civil servants.

Insurance Benefits.   Most state troopers are, as part of their compensation, covered by health, dental, prescription drug, optical, and life insurance.

Leave Benefits.   State troopers have very liberal leave benefits, which include such things as time off at full pay for annual leave, personal leave, bereavement leave, workers' compensation leave, and sick leave.

Retirement Benefits.   State troopers are part of the employee's retirement system in the state where they are employed. Normal retirement age in many state systems is 62 years old. However, in most cases, state troopers are allowed to retire after 20 or 25 years of service regardless of their age. This means that early retirement is the norm for state troopers.

Promotional Opportunities.   Civil service promotion examinations are very seldom open to the general public. Promotion is from within the employing agency. For this reason, promotional opportunity is one of the most attractive features of the state trooper's job. Entering officers can realistically aspire to be sergeants, lieutenants, captains, and majors, based almost exclusively on their ability to compete with their peers on written promotion examinations.

Other Benefits.   State troopers, depending on where they work, often receive such other benefits as credit union membership, consumer buying power, uniform allowances, education and training incentives, and disability insurance.

General Job Requirements

Because an overwhelming number of state trooper jobs are civil service positions, the minimum requirements for such jobs are established by the Civil Service Law in the state involved. This, of course, makes it impossible to list one definitive set of job requirements. To get the specific information for the job you are seeking, you must contact the civil service agency that is offering the job. However, we have compiled the following set of typical job requirements to give you a general idea of the most commonly accepted standards of employment used by state police agencies. If you believe you may have a problem meeting any of these standards, you should be especially alert for them and specifically inquire about any such standard when you apply for the position of state trooper. Such questions should be resolved before you spend a lot of time and effort attempting to become a state trooper.
  These standards follow.

Age.   There are two age considerations: the minimum age one must be to hold a job as a state trooper and the maximum age limit. Minimum age is much more uniform. Very rarely are persons who are less than 20 years old eligible for appointment as a state trooper, and in some states the minimum age for appointment could be as high as 22 years of age. This does not mean that persons under 20 cannot take a state trooper examination, rather it means that such persons cannot be appointed prior to their attaining the minimum age. Candidates who are too young for appointment when they otherwise become eligible are put on a special list and are appointed when they reach the minimum age unless the entire list is terminated prior to that time. For this reason we always encourage students to take the entrance examination at their earliest opportunity.

Maximum age is not nearly as standard, and such maximum standards are in a state of flux because of a series of nationwide law suits based on age discrimination. As a general rule, the maximum age standard at the present time is somewhere between 29 and 40 years of age.

Character. Proof of good character is absolutely essential for all state trooper positions. However, what is considered to be "good character" varies from state to state and once again is determined by the Civil Service Law in effect in that state. As a general rule, however, any of the following circumstances would typically be cause for disqualification:

- A criminal conviction for a felony

- A series of criminal convictions regardless of the seriousness of the underlying charges

- Previous suspension or revocation of driver's license or conviction of a serious traffic offense, such as driving while intoxicated or impaired

- Evidence that indicates a propensity for violence

- A history of repeated firings from jobs or long periods of unexplained unemployment

- Dishonorable discharge from the Armed Services

The background investigation that is conducted to determine if candidates meet the character requirements is usually quite thorough and somewhat time consuming, and it always includes the taking of the candidate's fingerprints. Candidates who are preparing to undergo a background investigation can speed up the process by having ready for the investigator originals or certified copies of such documents as birth certificates, diplomas, military discharge papers, drivers licenses, and naturalization papers, if appropriate. If a candidate has one or more arrests, then complete documentation of the details involved are essential. Candidates who are awaiting a background investigation should also prepare a chronological listing of employment from the day they finished attending school on a full-time basis to the present time.

Education. A minimum of a high school diploma or its equivalent, a General Education Development (GED) diploma is, by far, the most prevalent educational requirement. It should be noted that the diploma or its equivalent usually must be obtained prior to the date of appointment.

Citizenship. United States citizenship at the time of appointment is a universal standard for employment as a state trooper.

Medical and Psychological Standards. Prior to appointment, eligible candidates must meet the medical and psychological standards set by the hiring agency. Any candidate who has a medical or psychological problem that would impair his or her ability to carry out the duties of a state trooper will be disqualified. Candidates are required to reveal their medical history to the doctors who perform the medical examination. It is strongly suggested that those candidates who have had a medical problem that resulted in hospitalization obtain, if possible, a letter from their personal physicians stating that they are now fit to do the job of a state trooper. This letter should then be shown to the doctors from the employing agency along with the other pertinent information about the specific medical problem involved.

Another important consideration concerning the medical and psychological component of the entry process is the appeals process. The Civil Service Law in almost every jurisdiction allows candidates to appeal the findings of the medical and psychological board of the hiring agency. However, such appeals always have to be made on a timely basis. If you must appeal, make sure that you do so in accordance with the time frames set forth in the law.

Here is one final word in this area. Most civil service hiring rules require state trooper eligibles to pass an eyesight examination, including a color vision test. As a general rule, a minimum uncorrected vision of 20/50 is acceptable if it is correctable to 20/20 vision with lenses. If you have poor unaided vision, however, you should investigate the eyesight requirement before you make a significant commitment of time and effort to determine if you will be able to meet the standards of the job you are seeking.

Height and Weight Requirements. In the great majority of cases, there is no minimum height requirements prescribed as a requisite for employment as a state trooper. But, there are usually weight requirements. Such weight requirements are usually determined by a candidate's height and body frame. In other words, to be eligible for appointment, a candidate's weight must be proportionate to the candidate's height and frame. Body frame is usually categorized into small frame, medium frame, and large frame. The examining doctor from the hiring agency determines the applicable frame size of a candidate. Exceptions are generally made in those cases where excess weight is deemed by the examining doctor to be lean body mass and not fat. For those of you who think you might be overweight, we recommend that you seek a doctor's opinion and then, if necessary, initiate a weight reduction program under medical supervision prior to their official medical examination.

Drug Screening Test. Eligibles for the position of state trooper are subject to drug-screening tests. It is universally true that state police agencies are not interested in hiring those with illegal drug-use habits.

Probationary Period. Virtually every state police agency requires newly hired officers to successfully complete a probationary period prior to their becoming fully tenured civil service employees with all the rights and privileges that accompany such tenure. The average length of such probationary periods is about 18 months. During this time, probationary state troopers are required to successfully complete a training course that has academic, physical fitness, and firearms proficiency components. Many agencies also require probationary officers to pass another full medical examination at the very end of the probationary period.

Candidates must understand that during their probationary period they can be dismissed by an agency and such dismissals are not subject to court review. It is a term of employment. Therefore, the conduct of candidates who are serving probationary periods must be exemplary both on and off duty. Serious off-duty indiscretions are cause for dismissals. Although this is also true for tenured employees (those who are not on probation), tenured employees usually have many avenues to appeal such decisions. This is not true for those who are on probation.

Residency Requirements. Civil Service Law typically imposes residency requirements on state troopers. Usually, such requirements must be met on the date of appointment, not on test day. However, some states require candidates to be a resident of that state for a period of time, usually 1 year, prior to the taking of the written examination. It is strongly suggested that you be certain that you meet the residency requirements in your area before you spend a considerable amount of time and effort pursuing such employment only to find out afterwards that you are ineligible for appointment.

Physical Fitness Test. At some point prior to becoming a tenured state trooper, candidates are required to pass a physical fitness test. This is done in two ways. In some cases the test is administered prior to appointment as part of the hiring process. In other cases, the physical fitness test is administered after hiring as part of the probationary process. Of all the components of the hiring and probationary processes, none is more varied from jurisdiction to jurisdiction than the physical fitness component. However, successful completion of some sort of obstacle course, during which candidates must demonstrate an ability to run, push weighted objects, jump over hurdles, and lift and carry weighted dummies, all within a certain time period, is a very common requirement. Our experience with the physical fitness test has convinced us that, with proper preparation, most candidates can successfully pass it. The key phrase is, "with proper preparation." When the test is administered as part of the probationary period, this proper preparation is built into the physical fitness component of the official training curriculum. The physical fitness component is more of a problem when it is administered as part of the hiring process. When this is the case, we always strongly advise candidates to find out the specifics of the physical fitness test and to prepare for it. In many cases, the hiring agencies offer interested candidates the opportunity to prepare for the physical fitness test at no cost. If this is the case in your jurisdiction, we strongly urge you to take advantage of the opportunity.

Driver's License.   All state police agencies require candidates to possess a valid driver's license at the date of appointment. We are often asked by candidates whether a history of traffic or parking violations would have an impact on their eligibility to become state troopers. We tell them that one of the major considerations in this area is whether or not there are any outstanding violations that they have neglected to respond to. Ignoring official citations would definitely have a negative impact on your character investigation. Therefore, should you have any outstanding traffic or parking citations, you should clear them up before your background investigation.

Sample Test Announcement

As you can see, there is not just one standard set of requirements for the position of state trooper. Your task is to find out the specific requirements for the position you are seeking. The first step toward obtaining this information is to obtain the test announcement for that position. This announcement will supply you with general information about that job, the requirements for that job, and the steps to follow to obtain that job. To assist you, we have included a sample test announcement, also referred to as a *job announcement* or a *notice of examination,* so that you can read and become familiar with what typically appears on such announcements. You must understand, however, that the information included on our sample announcement is general information and does not relate specifically to any one state police or highway patrol agency. Once again, you must get the test announcement for the position to learn the specific information about the job you are seeking. We also remind you that the specifics listed on a test announcement very often change from test to test, so it is a mistake to believe that the requirements for the last examination will definitely be the same as the requirements for an upcoming examination.

APPLICATION INFORMATION

APPLICATION FEE: There is a nonrefundable application fee of $15.00, payable by money order only. Money orders must be made payable to the Commissioner of the Department of Personnel. The name and number of the test as well as the applicant's social security number must be included on the money order. This application fee will be waived for applicants receiving public assistance who submit proof of this status along with their application.

APPLICATION PERIOD: From May 3rd through June 30th. Completed applications may be submitted by mail or in person to the Hiring Unit of the Department of Personnel, State Capital Building, 300 Broadway, Metropolis. Applications must be postmarked no later than midnight on June 30th of this year.

TESTING LOCATIONS: The examination will be conducted in the state capital and in certain other cities around the state. The specific location of the test sites will be determined after a review of the applications, and all candidates will then be notified via the U.S. mail.

SALARY: Annual salary of $46,000.00 after 5 years of service. In addition, there is paid health insurance, holiday pay, an annuity plan, 21 days paid vacation, unlimited sick leave, life insurance, a uniform allowance, tuition reimbursement for higher education, and participation in the state retirement system.

LIFE OF THE LIST: The eligible list established as a result of State Trooper Examination # 007 shall be at least 1 year but not more than 4 years. However, the list shall be automatically terminated upon the promulgation of a subsequent list for the position of State Trooper.

REQUIREMENTS TO QUALIFY

MAXIMUM AGE STANDARDS: Candidates must not have reached their 36th birthday by the last day of the filing period, June 30th. However, veterans of the U.S. Armed Services who have not reached their 42nd birthday by June 30th are eligible. Proof of such military service must be produced upon demand during the background investigation discussed below.

MINIMUM AGE STANDARDS: Applicants must have reached their 21st birthday before they are appointed. Those who are too young when they are called for appointment shall go on a special list and become eligible for appointment upon attaining the age of 21.

EDUCATION STANDARDS: By the date of appointment, either (a) a standard high school diploma or (b) a high school equivalency diploma is required.

DRIVER'S LICENSE: By the date of appointment, possession of a valid driver's license is required.

RESIDENCY STANDARDS: There are no residence requirements for participation in the examination. By the date of appointment, applicants must reside within the boundaries of the state.

CITIZENSHIP: By the date of appointment, U.S. citizenship is required.

MEDICAL STANDARDS: Eligibles will be refused employment should they have a medical condition that significantly limits their ability to perform the tasks required of a state trooper. Details on medical requirements, including eyesight requirements, are posted at the Medical Unit of the Department of Personnel and are available upon request.

PSYCHOLOGICAL STANDARDS: Candidates are required to pass a battery of standard psychological tests and may also be required to appear for personal psychological evaluation.

PHYSICAL FITNESS STANDARDS: Candidates are required to pass a job-related physical agility test at a yet undetermined date after the written test. Details of this physical fitness test are posted at the Medical Unit of the Department of Personnel and are available upon request. Prior to the administration of this test, all eligibles will be offered an opportunity to train for the physical agility test at a site yet to be selected. Details concerning this no-cost training and the actual physical agility test will be sent to all eligibles via United States mail.

BACKGROUND STANDARDS: Prior to hiring, each eligible will be fingerprinted and subject to an intensive background investigation and a criminal history search, which is to be conducted by the State Police Agency Applicant Investigation Unit. Conviction of any felony will be an absolute bar to appointment. All other convictions will be considered on a case by case basis.

As part of the background investigation, all eligibles will be required to participate in substance-abuse testing prior to appointment and thereafter at any time during the probationary period. Candidates whose overall background is not deemed suitable as determined by the appointing authority shall be rejected. Candidates who fail to cooperate fully with their assigned investigators or who fail to present required documents are also subject to rejection.

LANGUAGE STANDARDS: All candidates must be proficient in the English language so as to be able to communicate orally and in writing at a level established by the State Police Commissioner. Candidates may be required to pass a communications test at any time prior to the completion of their probationary period.

JOB INFORMATION

PROBATIONARY PERIOD: Each appointed eligible will be required to successfully complete an 18-month probationary period during which they shall have the title of Probationary State Trooper. Candidates must understand that the probationary period is an extension of the selection process and that they are subject to continuous evaluation during their entire period of probation. Those who do not successfully complete the probationary period shall be rejected with no right to appeal.

TRAINING REQUIREMENTS: Upon appointment and prior to assignment, each probationary state trooper must successfully complete a 24-week training program at the State Police Academy. Those who successfully complete this training will receive full police officer status.

STATE TROOPER DUTIES AND RESPONSIBILITIES: As a state trooper you will be expected to be available to work on an around-the-clock basis and on weekends and holidays. At times you will be required to work overtime. The nature of the job requires you to work out of doors in all kinds of weather conditions. Your primary duties and responsibilities follow.

Traffic Patrol. The major purpose of traffic patrol is to expedite the movement of vehicular and pedestrian traffic in the safest possible manner. This is accomplished via the deterrent effect of visible patrol in conspicuously marked patrol vehicles as well as through the issuance of warnings and citations and the making of arrests.

Preventive Patrol. State troopers are required at times to perform general preventive patrol in those areas not patrolled by local police. The major purpose of this preventive patrol is to protect life and property. It involves such things as inspecting buildings in commercial and residential areas, responding to alarms, and engaging in constant conspicuous patrol to deter street crime.

Responding to Calls for Assistance. State troopers quite often are called upon to assist those in need. Typically, troopers assist lost or stranded persons, those in need of medical assistance, and even those with problems of a civil nature.

Conducting Investigations. As a state trooper you will be required to conduct investigations of incidents, such as fatal vehicle accidents, that quite often culminate in criminal or civil prosecution.

WRITTEN TEST INFORMATION

TEST DATE: To be announced. All candidates will receive notification via the U.S. mail as to the date and time of the examination. Such notification will be given at least 2 weeks in advance of the test date.

ADMISSION CARD: Applicants will not be admitted to the test site without an admission card. Such cards will be sent to candidates via U.S. mail. Those candidates who do not receive an admission card at least 5 days prior to the announced test date must appear personally at the Admissions Unit of the Department of Personnel between 9:00 A.M. and 5:00 P.M. on one of the 5 days preceding the test to obtain their admission card.

TEST DESCRIPTION: The written test will be of the multiple-choice type and will consist of 100 questions to be answered in a 3½-hour period. It will contain questions to test your memory; your verbal and mathematical ability; your ability to comprehend written material; your ability to complete and interpret forms, charts, and tables; your ability to apply procedures; your reasoning ability; your ability to understand legal definitions; your ability to identify faces; and your ability to interpret traffic maps.

PASSING SCORE: The passing score will be determined and announced after statistical analysis of the results of the test.

APPEALS: Within 60 days after the administration of the test, a tentative scoring key will be published. Candidates who petition the Department of Personnel to do so will be allowed to appeal this tentative key providing they do so within 30 days of the publication of the tentative scoring key.

> **NOTIFICATION OF RESULTS:** All applicants who actually take the test will receive notification via the U.S. mail of their final test score and, if appropriate, their place on the eligible list within 60 days of the end of the appeals period.

The Steps to Becoming a State Trooper

1. Determine the date of the next test. This can be done by watching the civil service newspaper that services the area where you are seeking employment. Or, you can contact the civil service agency that administers the test. A third option is to call the training unit of the state police agency you are interested in joining. The bottom line is— do not be afraid to ask. State police agencies want good people. You are taking the time to prepare yourself for the examination and, therefore, have begun to qualify as one of the candidates that the state police want.

2. Obtain a test announcement.

3. File an application.

4. Prepare for and pass the written test.

5. Prepare for and take the physical agility test, if required prior to appointment.

6. Take the medical examination.

7. Take the psychological examination.

8. Prepare for and undergo the background investigation.
   (Note that steps 5–8 may occur in a different sequence.)

9. Get appointed.

10. Attend and successfully complete a training school.

11. Successfully complete your probationary period.

A Note From Your Authors

Don't be discouraged by the apparent complexity of the required steps you must take to become a state trooper. Such a job is both rewarding and satisfying. It offers financial security and promotional opportunities plus a liberal retirement benefit. Pursue the job. Make it your goal. Use this book to help you. Remember that all state troopers were once in the position you are in right now. They did it, and you can too!

CHAPTER 2

How to Maximize Your Test Score

This chapter contains information you need to get the best return from your test preparation efforts so that you can achieve the highest possible score on your official state trooper examination. Too many students approach test preparation in a slipshod manner. Consequently, they waste time and do not achieve their potential. The guidelines presented in this chapter are designed to help you avoid such wasted effort.

The first part of this chapter provides guidelines to help you develop good study habits. Until you are quite familiar with the rules for effective studying that are contained in this section, you should review them prior to each study session.

The second part of this chapter provides a specific strategy to deal with multiple-choice questions, with material distributed in advance of the test, and with tests that contain a video component. Understanding and mastering these strategies is vitally important. Concerning the strategy to deal with multiple-choice questions, make sure that you review it prior to taking each of the full-length examinations included in this book. Finally, make sure that you practice this strategy while taking these examinations.

Please note that some of the practice questions in this book are based on laws, rules, policies, and procedures that are typical of those that might be found in a state police or highway patrol agency. Do not assume, however, that they are the exact laws, rules, policies, and procedures that are actually in use in any specific state trooper or highway patrol agency.

Also note that the difficulty level of the practice questions appearing in this book is in most cases higher than those questions you may encounter on your official examination. *This is a very important point for you to understand.* If you can learn to master the questions in this book, you should have great success on your official test. Therefore, do not get discouraged if you miss some questions. Instead, learn why you missed them, and avoid such errors in the future.

Good Study Habits—The Key to Success

Many students incorrectly believe that the amount of time spent studying is the most important factor in test preparation. Of course, all else being equal, the amount of time you devote to your studies is a critical factor. But spending time reading is not necessarily studying. If you want to learn what you read, you must develop a system. For example, a student who devotes 60 minutes a day to uninterrupted study in a quiet, private setting will generally learn more than someone who puts in twice that time by studying five or six times a day for 15–20 minutes at a time.

Ten Rules for Studying More Effectively

We list ten rules for you to follow to increase study-time efficiency. If you follow these rules, you will get the most out of this book as well as similar study efforts that you might undertake.

1. **Make sure that you understand the meaning of every word you read.** Your ability to understand what you read is the most important skill needed to pass your official examination. Therefore, starting immediately, every time you see a word that you don't fully understand, make certain that you write it down and make note of where you saw it. Then, when you have a chance, look up the meaning of the word in the dictionary. When you think you know what the word means, apply the meaning of the word to the written material that contained the word and make certain that you fully understand its meaning as well as the written material that contained the word. Keep a list of all words you didn't know the first time you saw them and periodically review the meaning of these words. Also, try to use these words whenever you can in conversation. If you do this faithfully, you will quickly build an extensive vocabulary that will help you not only when you take your official examination but also for the rest of your life.

2. **Study uninterrupted for at least 30 minutes.** Unless you can study for at least an uninterrupted period of 30 minutes, you should not bother to study at all. It is essential that you learn to concentrate for extended periods of time. Remember that the official examination usually takes anywhere from 3 to 5 hours to complete. You must be prepared to concentrate just as hard in the final hour of the test as you did in the first hour. Therefore, as the examination date approaches, study for more extended periods of time without interruption. When you take the full-length practice examinations in this book, do a complete examination in one sitting, just as you must do at the actual examination. Remember that not being prepared to concentrate effectively throughout the entire examination is a major reason why many candidates fail! Don't let that happen to you.

3. **Simulate examination conditions when studying.** Insofar as possible you should study under the same conditions as those of the examination. Eliminate as many outside interferences as you can. If you are a smoker, refrain from smoking when you study because you will not be allowed to smoke in the test room on the day of the examination.

4. **Study alone.** Studying alone is the best way to prepare for your official test. However, if possible, form a study group of from three to five serious students and meet with them for 2–3 hours periodically, perhaps every other week. At each such meeting, the group should be prepared to discuss one area that will probably appear on the examination. In addition, everyone in the group should keep a list of items they are confused about; these items should be discussed at the study-group meetings. Items that no one is certain of should be referred to an outside source, such as a teacher or a criminal justice practitioner. Extensive debate or, worse, arguing in a study group defeats the purpose of the group and must be avoided at all costs.

5. **Make sure that you understand the answers to every question in this book.** Every multiple-choice question in this book has an explained answer. Don't overlook the tremendous value of this feature. Whenever you get a question wrong, be sure to understand why you missed it so that you won't make the same mistake again. However, it is equally important to make certain that you have answered a question correctly for the right reason. Therefore, study the answer explanation to every multiple-choice question in this book as carefully as you study the question itself.

6. **Always follow our recommended strategy for answering multiple-choice questions.** In the following section of this chapter, we provide an invaluable strategy for answering multiple-choice questions. Use this strategy every time you take a series of multiple-choice questions.

7. **Always time yourself when doing practice questions.** Running out of time on a multiple-choice examination is a tragic error that is easily avoided. Learn, through practice, to move to the next question after you spend a reasonable period of time on any one question. This technique is explained in greater detail in the following strategy for taking multiple-choice questions. The bottom line is this: When you are doing practice questions, always time yourself and always try to stay within recommended time limits. In the absence of such time limits, allow yourself 2 minutes per question, since that is the standard often used by test writers on entry-level multiple-choice examinations.

8. **Concentrate your study time in the areas of your greatest weakness.** The diagnostic procedures we use for every practice test in this book will give you an idea of the most difficult question types for you. Even though you should spend most of your study time improving yourself in these areas, do not ignore the other question types.

9. **Exercise regularly and stay in good physical condition.** Students who are in good physical condition have an advantage over those who are not. It is a well-established principle that good physical health improves the ability of the mind to function smoothly and efficiently, especially when taking examinations of extended duration, such as the state trooper or highway patrol officer examination.

10. **Establish a schedule for studying and stick to it.** Do not put off studying to those times when you have nothing else to do. Schedule your study time and try not to let anything else interfere with that schedule. If you feel yourself weakening, review Chapter 1 and remind yourself of why you would like to become a state trooper or a highway patrol officer.

Strategies for Handling Multiple-Choice Questions

A very specific test-taking strategy valuable for a multiple-choice examination follows. This strategy not only will serve you well on the state trooper or highway patrol officer examination but also is valid for any multiple-choice exam you may take. Study the strategy and practice it; then study it again until you have mastered it.

1. **Read the instructions.** Do not assume that you know what the instructions are without reading them. Make sure that you read and understand them. There are test instructions and question instructions. Test instructions are a set of general instructions that govern

the entire examination and are to be read prior to the start of the exam. Question instructions are found throughout the test prior to each series of questions that require specific instructions. They govern the taking of each such series of questions. On the day of your official examination, if you are unsure about the instructions, ask questions when given the opportunity.

2. **Make sure that you have the complete examination.** As soon as your official examination starts, check the test booklet page by page. Because these booklets have numbered pages, simply make certain that you have all the pages. If you do not have a complete examination, inform a test monitor immediately.

3. **Take a close look at the answer sheet.** Some answer sheets are numbered vertically and some, horizontally. This numbering system is used to discourage cheating. The answer sheets used in this book for the practice examinations are typical of what you will see on your exam. However, do not take anything for granted. Review the instructions on the answer sheet carefully and familiarize yourself with its format.

4. **Be extremely careful when marking your answers.** Be sure to mark your answers in accordance with the official instructions. Be absolutely certain that

   ● you mark only one answer for each question, unless the instructions specifically indicate the possibility of multiple answers.

   ● you do not make extraneous markings on your answer sheet.

   ● you completely darken the allotted space for the answer you choose.

   ● you erase completely any answer that you wish to change.

   Please note that a distinction must be made between making extraneous markings on your answer sheet and making notes in your test booklet, which is the booklet that contains the test questions. As you will see, good test-taking strategy demands that you make certain notations in your test booklet. The only exception would be in the very rare instance where the test instructions prohibit writing in the test booklet.

5. **Make absolutely certain that you are marking the answer to the right question.** Many candidates have failed multiple-choice tests because they have been careless in this area. All it takes is one mistake. If, for example, you mark an answer to question 10 in the space for question 11, you probably will continue the mistake for a number of questions until you realize your error. To prevent some-

thing like this from happening, we recommend that you use the following procedure when marking your answer sheet.

● Select the choice you believe is the answer, circle that choice on the test booklet, and remind yourself what question number you are working on.

● If you, for example, select choice C as the answer for question 11, circle choice C on the test booklet, and say to yourself, "C is the answer to question 11."

● Then find the space on your answer sheet for question 11, and again say "C is the answer to question 11" as you mark the answer.

Although this procedure may seem rather elementary and repetitive, after a while it becomes automatic. If followed properly, it guarantees that you will not fail the examination because of this type of careless mistake.

6. **Make certain that you understand what the question is asking.** Test takers often choose wrong answers because they fail to read the question carefully enough. Read the stem of the question (the part before the choices) very carefully to make certain that you know what the examiner is asking. If necessary, read it twice. Be certain to read every word in the question. If you do not, you could select a wrong answer to a very simple question.

7. **Always read all the choices before you select an answer.** Distractors are what test writers call incorrect choices. Every multiple-choice question usually has one best distractor, which is very close to being correct. Many times this best distractor comes before the correct choice. Therefore, don't select the first choice that looks good. Read all the choices!

8. **Be aware of key words that often tip off the correct and incorrect answers.** When you are stuck on a question and have to guess at the answer, you can often select the correct choice by understanding that absolute words tend to appear more often in incorrect choices and that limiting words tend to appear more often in correct choices. Absolute words are very broad and do not allow for any exceptions. Limiting words are not all inclusive and allow for exceptions.

Absolute Words

never	always	only	none
must	all	nothing	any
every	everyone	everything	sole

Limiting Words

usually	sometimes	generally	many
occasionally	possible	some	often
may	could	probably	might

9. **Never make a choice based on frequency of previous answers.** Some students inappropriately pay attention to the pattern of answers when taking an exam. Multiple-choice exams are not designed to have an equal number of A, B, C, and D choices as the answers. Always answer the question without regard to what the letter designations of the previous choices have been.

10. **Use a systematic and uniform approach for each question.** Start with the individual choices. As you consider the various choices to each question, put an X in the test booklet to cross out the letter designation of any choice you know for sure is not the answer. If you cross out all but one of the choices, the remaining choice should be your answer. Read that choice one more time to satisfy yourself, put a circle around its letter designation (if you still feel it is the correct answer), and transpose it to your answer sheet using strategy 5. Spend no more time on this question.

    If, however, after your initial review of the choices, you are left with more than one possible answer, you need to reread only those choices that you did not cross out the first time. Many times, the second time you read the remaining choices, the answer is clear. If that happens, cross out the wrong choice, circle the correct one, and transpose the answer to the answer sheet. If, after the second reading, you still have not selected an answer, reread the stem of the question and make certain that you understand the question. The stem is that part of the question that precedes the choices. Then review those choices that you did not initially eliminate by putting an X through them. Keep in mind the absolute words and limiting words mentioned in strategy 8, which may give you a hint of the correct answer.

    When you answer a question that gave you trouble, put an asterisk or star in the margin of the test booklet next to that question. Then, if after answering all the questions on the test you still have time remaining, return to these questions one more time. Very often, now that the pressure of finishing the examination is over, you can deal with the question more easily.

11. **Skip over questions that give you trouble.** During the first time through the examination, be certain not to dwell too long on any one question. Spending too much time on a question is a common cause of running out of time. It is an error that you must avoid. Simply skip these tough questions after putting a circle around the question number in the test booklet and go on to the next question. The circle around the question number in the test booklet is to help you find unanswered questions the second time through the examination, as explained in strategy 12.

Keep in mind that when you skip a question you must skip the appropriate space on the answer sheet.

12. **Return to the questions you skipped after you finish the rest of the examination.** Once you answer all the questions you were sure of, check the time remaining. If time permits (it should if you follow our recommendations), return to each question you did not answer and reread the stem of these questions and any of the choices that are not crossed out. It should be easy to find the questions you have not yet answered because, if you are following our recommended strategy, all of them will have their number designation circled on the test booklet. Many times the correct answer will now be easy to determine. If, however, the answer is still not clear and you are running out of time, then make an "educated guess" from among those choices that you have not already eliminated. When making an educated guess, use the guidelines in strategy 15.

   If you still have time left after you have answered every question, go back and reread those questions that gave you trouble when you originally answered them. You will find them easily if you put a star or asterisk in the margin as we suggested. Reread each of these questions and reconsider your answer. Many times you will discover a careless mistake. If you do, you should, of course, change your answer.

13. **Never leave questions unanswered unless the instructions indicate a penalty for wrong answers.** In most state trooper or highway patrol officer examinations, you will not have points subtracted from your final score for wrong answers. In other words, there is no penalty for guessing. If this is the case on your examination, guess at any question you are not sure of.

   However, in rare instances, a penalty is assessed for wrong answers on multiple-choice examinations. Because this would have to be explained in the test instructions, be sure, as already recommended, to read all your instructions very carefully. If there is a penalty for wrong answers on your examination, decide how strongly you feel about each individual question before answering it. Note again that this rarely happens on entry-level examinations such as the one you are planning to take.

14. **Develop a time management plan.** It is extremely important for you to have a time management plan when you take your examination. Not to systematically monitor the passage of time on an examination is similar to inviting failure. The mechanics of developing a time management plan are presented later in this chapter.

15. **Rules for making an educated guess.** Your chances of selecting the correct answers to questions you are not sure of will be significantly increased if you use the following rules:

- Never consider answer choices you have already positively eliminated.

- Be aware of key words that give you clues as to which answer might be right or wrong.

- Always eliminate choices that are very close in meaning to each other.

EXAMPLE

Alicia's complaint about the weather was that
(A) it was too hot.
(B) it was too cold.
(C) it varied too much.
(D) it was unpredictable.

In this example, choices C and D are so close together in meaning that neither is likely to be the correct answer. Choices A and B, on the other hand, are quite opposite each other, and one of them is most likely the correct answer.

- If two choices are worded so that combined they encompass all the possibilities, one of them has to be the correct choice.

EXAMPLE

How old is John?
(A) John is 7 years old or less.
(B) John is over 7 years of age.
(C) John is 6 years old.
(D) John is 14 years old.

In this example, it should be clear to you that the correct answer has to be either A or B, because if John is not 7 years old or less (choice A), then he must be over 7 years of age (choice B).

- An answer choice that has significantly more or significantly fewer words in it is very often the correct choice.

16. **Be very reluctant to change answers.** Unless you have a very good reason, do not change an answer once you have chosen it. Experience have shown us that all too often people change their answer from the right one to the wrong one. This doesn't mean that you should never change an answer. If you discover an obvious mistake, for example, you should most certainly change your answer.

17. **Understand that there are specific strategies for dealing with different question types.** On every entry-level examination you will encounter different question types. For example, some questions

might test your ability to understand what you read, others might test your verbal or mathematical ability, and still others might test your memory or your ability to interpret graphs, charts, or tables. If you are to maximize your test score, you must understand that it is wrong to approach the answering of all question types on the test with the same strategy. Instead, your strategy or approach should change based on the type of question you are answering at any given time. Included in Chapters 4–13 of this book is a discussion of each of the most common question types used on most state trooper and highway patrol officer examinations throughout the country. Included in each discussion is an explanation of a strategy to follow for the question type being considered. Learn to recognize the various question types and learn the specific strategies for answering each one of them. Then, as you take the practice examinations in Chapters 14–18, use these strategies.

Developing and Using a Time Management Plan

The primary goal of a time management plan is to determine the average number of minutes you should spend on each multiple-choice question on the test and then to use that information throughout the test to guard against running out of time. In order to develop a time management plan you must know (1) the number of questions on the exam and (2) the amount of time allowed to complete the test. Many times you will not have this information until the day of the test. But, because it is a relatively simple task, the development of your time management plan can easily be done on test day before you begin to answer any questions.

The following step-by-step explanation details how a time management plan is developed. For the purposes of this explanation, assume that you are taking an examination that has 100 questions and has a time limit of 4 hours.

Step 1.   Convert the time allowed to minutes and put 30 minutes aside or, as we say, in the bank. This 30 minutes is to be used when you have finished the examination to go back to the questions you have skipped and to otherwise review your exam. Using our example, convert 4 hours to 240 minutes and subtract 30 minutes, which leaves you with 210 minutes to answer 100 questions. Remember that this also leaves you with 30 minutes in the bank to use at the end of the test.

Step 2.   Divide the time allowed to answer the questions by the number of questions to determine the average amount of time you should spend on each question. In our example, this means that you would divide 210 minutes by 100 questions and thus determine that you should spend approximately 2 minutes per question.

Step 3. This step involves the use of your time management plan. Knowing that you should spend approximately 2 minutes per question is of little value unless you then proceed to monitor your time usage from the start of the exam. On a 100 question test we recommend that you specifically check your time every 10 questions. Using our example, at the end of the first 10 questions, no more than 20 minutes should have passed (2 minutes per question); after completing 20 questions, no more than 40 minutes should have passed; and so forth.

By developing and using a time management plan, you will find out early in the test if you are falling behind. This is quite beneficial because you will still be able to do something about it. Contrast that situation with one where you realize much too late that you have been using too much time. Clearly the former is the preferable situation.

Test Material Distributed in Advance

In some jurisdictions, material about entrance examinations is distributed in advance of the test. This material typically takes the form of a test preparation and orientation booklet. Included in this advance material may be general information about the examination, a description of the types of questions that will appear on the examination, specific suggestions or hints for you to follow when taking the examination, and sample questions. In addition, you might also be given accompanying reference material containing information that you should study to prepare for the examination.

The rule to follow when dealing with advance material is both simple and obvious. You should read the material carefully and use it to prepare for the examination. Your score on the examination will, in all probability, be in direct proportion to your understanding of the advance material.

SPECIAL CONSIDERATIONS FOR REFERENCE MATERIALS DISTRIBUTED IN ADVANCE

By *reference material* we mean material that actual test questions might be based on. Concerning reference material distributed in advance, there are generally three possibilities. The way you deal with this reference material is predicated on which of the three possibilities apply to your particular examination, if indeed your examination involves the use of advance material.

The first possibility is that the advance reference material may be similar to but not identical with the reference material you will be using on the day of the test. In that case, you should familiarize yourself with the format and structure of the material, but you do not have to learn it.

The second possibility is that the advance reference material may be identical to the actual reference material to be distributed on the day of the test. In that case you should become very familiar with the advance material because the questions you will be asked will be based on that material, but it is not necessary to memorize the material because you will have it at your disposal on test day.

The third possibility is that the advance reference material will be used on the day of the test but you will not be able to refer to it even though the questions will test your knowledge of it. In that case, you must commit the information involved to memory prior to test day. Failure to do so will result in almost certain failure.

Dealing with Tests Presented On Video

Occasionally another practice used in entrance level examinations is the use of video simulations. Should a video be used on your official examination, you can expect the following. On the day of the test, you will be shown a video presentation and then asked questions about what you have heard and seen on the video tape. In some cases, the questions you are asked are designed to measure your ability to understand by observing and listening. Other questions are designed to test your ability to apply written material to the situations shown in each scenario.

In many tests that include a video component, candidates are shown a sample video tape prior to the day of the examination. If your test is structured in that way, it is absolutely essential that you view the sample video.

STRATEGY FOR TAKING A VIDEO TEST

1. The general rule about the importance of reading and understanding test instructions and directions must be followed if you are to be successful on a video test. If, after reading the instructions, you are unsure about their exact meaning, ask questions when given the opportunity. Make sure that you know what to expect before the video begins because most video tests prohibit the asking of questions once the video begins.

2. Unless specifically prohibited by the test instructions, take notes as the video presentation unfolds. However, you should not try to record the scene verbatim. Make your notes as brief as possible. Use key words and phrases and not complete sentences. Use abbreviations

whenever possible, keeping in mind that your notes are useless if you cannot interpret them later. Also keep in mind that candidates who get overly engrossed in taking lengthy notes often miss critical information.

3. Concentrate. You must not let your mind wander. You must pay strict attention to what you are seeing and what you are hearing. Completely ignore the actions of those around you. Please note that you can hone your note-taking skills and concentration ability through practice. Simply watch a news show on television (video tape it if possible). Make notes of what you hear and see. After the show, see how many of the important points you have captured.

4. Pay particular attention to errors as you see or hear them occur. Note what appears to be inappropriate actions on the part of the actors in the video.

5. Note times, dates, and locations when given. Understanding the time frames and locations involved are often the subject of questions.

How to Use This Book Most Effectively

To obtain maximum benefit from the use of this book, we recommend the following approach.

1. Learn the strategies for handling multiple-choice questions, which appear earlier in this chapter.

2. Take the Diagnostic Test in Chapter 3. After completing this examination and reviewing the explained answers, fill out the diagnostic chart that follows the explained answers. This will indicate your strengths and weaknesses. You should then devote most of your study time to correcting your weaknesses.

3. Study Chapters 4–13. As mentioned previously, concentrate your study efforts in your weak areas but make certain to cover each chapter. Note that each of these chapters deals with a different type of question and that a specific test-taking strategy is offered for each question type. As mentioned previously, make a special effort to learn these different strategies and then practice them when you take the exams in Chapters 14–18.

   Also, when studying Chapters 4–13, be sure to follow the ten rules for studying more effectively, which appear earlier in this chapter. Also, make sure to apply the strategies for handling multiple-choice questions when doing the practice exercises at the end of Chapters 4–13.

4. After you have completed Chapters 4–13, take Practice Examination One in one sitting. When you have finished this examination and have reviewed the explained answers, complete the diagnostic chart that follows the explained answers. Then restudy the appropriate chapters in accordance with the directions on the bottom of the diagnostic chart.

5. In the order they appear, take Practice Examinations Two through Five. After you have finished each examination, follow the same procedure that you followed after finishing Practice Examination One.

6. When your actual examination is a week away, read Chapter 19. Be sure to follow the recommended strategy contained in this chapter for the 7 days immediately preceding the examination.

DIAGNOSE YOUR PROBLEM

CHAPTER 3

A Diagnostic Examination

There are 100 questions on this diagnostic examination and you should finish the entire examination in 3½ hours. For maximum benefit, it is strongly recommended that you take this examination in one sitting as if it were the actual official test.

The answers to this examination, their explanations, and a diagnostic chart are included in this chapter after the last test question. By completing the diagnostic chart, you can get an idea of which question types give you the most difficulty. You can then devote most of your time to studying those areas.

Before You Take the Examination

Before taking this examination, you should have read Chapters 1 and 2. Be certain that you employ the recommended test-taking strategies outlined in Chapter 2 while taking the examination.

Remember to read each question and related material carefully before choosing your answers. Select the choice you believe to be the answer and make your answers on the appropriate answer sheet. This answer sheet is similar to the one used on the actual examination. The answer key, diagnostic chart, and answer explanations appear at the end of this chapter.

Answer Sheet
Diagnostic Examination

Follow the instructions given in the test. Mark only your answers in the circles below.

WARNING: Be sure that the circle you fill is in the same row as the question you are answering. Use a No. 2 pencil (soft pencil).

BE SURE YOUR PENCIL MARKS ARE HEAVY AND BLACK. ERASE COMPLETELY ANY ANSWER YOU WISH TO CHANGE.

DO NOT make stray pencil dots, dashes or marks.

1. Ⓐ Ⓑ Ⓒ Ⓓ	2. Ⓐ Ⓑ Ⓒ Ⓓ	3. Ⓐ Ⓑ Ⓒ Ⓓ	4. Ⓐ Ⓑ Ⓒ Ⓓ
5. Ⓐ Ⓑ Ⓒ Ⓓ	6. Ⓐ Ⓑ Ⓒ Ⓓ	7. Ⓐ Ⓑ Ⓒ Ⓓ	8. Ⓐ Ⓑ Ⓒ Ⓓ
9. Ⓐ Ⓑ Ⓒ Ⓓ	10. Ⓐ Ⓑ Ⓒ Ⓓ	11. Ⓐ Ⓑ Ⓒ Ⓓ	12. Ⓐ Ⓑ Ⓒ Ⓓ
13. Ⓐ Ⓑ Ⓒ Ⓓ	14. Ⓐ Ⓑ Ⓒ Ⓓ	15. Ⓐ Ⓑ Ⓒ Ⓓ	16. Ⓐ Ⓑ Ⓒ Ⓓ
17. Ⓐ Ⓑ Ⓒ Ⓓ	18. Ⓐ Ⓑ Ⓒ Ⓓ	19. Ⓐ Ⓑ Ⓒ Ⓓ	20. Ⓐ Ⓑ Ⓒ Ⓓ
21. Ⓐ Ⓑ Ⓒ Ⓓ	22. Ⓐ Ⓑ Ⓒ Ⓓ	23. Ⓐ Ⓑ Ⓒ Ⓓ	24. Ⓐ Ⓑ Ⓒ Ⓓ
25. Ⓐ Ⓑ Ⓒ Ⓓ	26. Ⓐ Ⓑ Ⓒ Ⓓ	27. Ⓐ Ⓑ Ⓒ Ⓓ	28. Ⓐ Ⓑ Ⓒ Ⓓ
29. Ⓐ Ⓑ Ⓒ Ⓓ	30. Ⓐ Ⓑ Ⓒ Ⓓ	31. Ⓐ Ⓑ Ⓒ Ⓓ	32. Ⓐ Ⓑ Ⓒ Ⓓ
33. Ⓐ Ⓑ Ⓒ Ⓓ	34. Ⓐ Ⓑ Ⓒ Ⓓ	35. Ⓐ Ⓑ Ⓒ Ⓓ	36. Ⓐ Ⓑ Ⓒ Ⓓ
37. Ⓐ Ⓑ Ⓒ Ⓓ	38. Ⓐ Ⓑ Ⓒ Ⓓ	39. Ⓐ Ⓑ Ⓒ Ⓓ	40. Ⓐ Ⓑ Ⓒ Ⓓ
41. Ⓐ Ⓑ Ⓒ Ⓓ	42. Ⓐ Ⓑ Ⓒ Ⓓ	43. Ⓐ Ⓑ Ⓒ Ⓓ	44. Ⓐ Ⓑ Ⓒ Ⓓ
45. Ⓐ Ⓑ Ⓒ Ⓓ	46. Ⓐ Ⓑ Ⓒ Ⓓ	47. Ⓐ Ⓑ Ⓒ Ⓓ	48. Ⓐ Ⓑ Ⓒ Ⓓ
49. Ⓐ Ⓑ Ⓒ Ⓓ	50. Ⓐ Ⓑ Ⓒ Ⓓ	51. Ⓐ Ⓑ Ⓒ Ⓓ	52. Ⓐ Ⓑ Ⓒ Ⓓ
53. Ⓐ Ⓑ Ⓒ Ⓓ	54. Ⓐ Ⓑ Ⓒ Ⓓ	55. Ⓐ Ⓑ Ⓒ Ⓓ	56. Ⓐ Ⓑ Ⓒ Ⓓ
57. Ⓐ Ⓑ Ⓒ Ⓓ	58. Ⓐ Ⓑ Ⓒ Ⓓ	59. Ⓐ Ⓑ Ⓒ Ⓓ	60. Ⓐ Ⓑ Ⓒ Ⓓ
61. Ⓐ Ⓑ Ⓒ Ⓓ	62. Ⓐ Ⓑ Ⓒ Ⓓ	63. Ⓐ Ⓑ Ⓒ Ⓓ	64. Ⓐ Ⓑ Ⓒ Ⓓ
65. Ⓐ Ⓑ Ⓒ Ⓓ	66. Ⓐ Ⓑ Ⓒ Ⓓ	67. Ⓐ Ⓑ Ⓒ Ⓓ	68. Ⓐ Ⓑ Ⓒ Ⓓ
69. Ⓐ Ⓑ Ⓒ Ⓓ	70. Ⓐ Ⓑ Ⓒ Ⓓ	71. Ⓐ Ⓑ Ⓒ Ⓓ	72. Ⓐ Ⓑ Ⓒ Ⓓ
73. Ⓐ Ⓑ Ⓒ Ⓓ	74. Ⓐ Ⓑ Ⓒ Ⓓ	75. Ⓐ Ⓑ Ⓒ Ⓓ	76. Ⓐ Ⓑ Ⓒ Ⓓ
77. Ⓐ Ⓑ Ⓒ Ⓓ	78. Ⓐ Ⓑ Ⓒ Ⓓ	79. Ⓐ Ⓑ Ⓒ Ⓓ	80. Ⓐ Ⓑ Ⓒ Ⓓ
81. Ⓐ Ⓑ Ⓒ Ⓓ	82. Ⓐ Ⓑ Ⓒ Ⓓ	83. Ⓐ Ⓑ Ⓒ Ⓓ	84. Ⓐ Ⓑ Ⓒ Ⓓ
85. Ⓐ Ⓑ Ⓒ Ⓓ	86. Ⓐ Ⓑ Ⓒ Ⓓ	87. Ⓐ Ⓑ Ⓒ Ⓓ	88. Ⓐ Ⓑ Ⓒ Ⓓ
89. Ⓐ Ⓑ Ⓒ Ⓓ	90. Ⓐ Ⓑ Ⓒ Ⓓ	91. Ⓐ Ⓑ Ⓒ Ⓓ	92. Ⓐ Ⓑ Ⓒ Ⓓ
93. Ⓐ Ⓑ Ⓒ Ⓓ	94. Ⓐ Ⓑ Ⓒ Ⓓ	95. Ⓐ Ⓑ Ⓒ Ⓓ	96. Ⓐ Ⓑ Ⓒ Ⓓ
97. Ⓐ Ⓑ Ⓒ Ⓓ	98. Ⓐ Ⓑ Ⓒ Ⓓ	99. Ⓐ Ⓑ Ⓒ Ⓓ	100. Ⓐ Ⓑ Ⓒ Ⓓ

The Diagnostic Test
Time Allowed: 3½ hours

INSTRUCTIONS FOR QUESTIONS 1–8: Before answering questions 1–8, take 5 minutes to examine the following four wanted posters with the information that accompanies each poster. Do not look ahead to the questions until 5 minutes have passed and then do not look back at the posters while answering the questions.

STATE POLICE WANTED POSTER

Joseph Kelly

Age:	19	Race:	White
Height:	5' 6"	Weight:	140 pounds
Eyes:	Blue	Hair:	Reddish Brown
Scars:	Pockmarked Face	Tattoos:	None

Subject is a convicted murderer who escaped from State Prison. Is believed to be armed and should be considered extremely dangerous. Is known to carry firearms. Uses the alias "Big Jake."

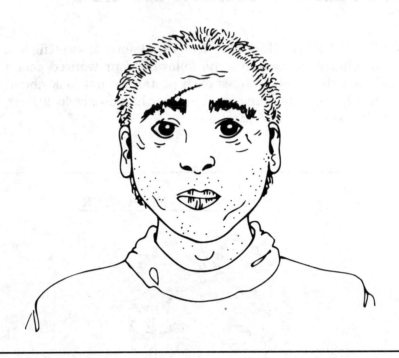

STATE POLICE WANTED POSTER

Rob Monchall

Age:	39	Race:	White
Height:	5' 10"	Weight:	175 pounds
Eyes:	Brown	Hair:	Brown
Scars:	6" scar above right eye	Tattoos:	None

Subject, who is wanted for manslaughter, is an international terrorist who is known to carry explosives on his person. Must be approached with caution.

STATE POLICE WANTED POSTER

Josephine Aponte

Age:	58	Race:	Hispanic
Height:	5' 3"	Weight:	125 pounds
Eyes:	Brown	Hair:	Dark Brown
Scars:	None	Tattoos:	None

Subject is an acknowledged tax expert and specializes in schemes to defraud the government. Has been charged with five counts of grand larceny and forgery.

STATE POLICE WANTED POSTER

Fred Kruger

Age:	43	Race:	Black
Height:	6' 4"	Weight:	250 pounds
Eyes:	Brown	Hair:	Black
Scars:	None	Tattoos:	None

Subject, who escaped from prison while serving a 20-year sentence for felonious assault, must be approached with caution. Is an expert knife fighter and is usually armed with a switchblade knife.

DO NOT PROCEED UNTIL 5 MINUTES HAVE PASSED.

INSTRUCTIONS: Answer questions 1–8 solely on the basis of the wanted posters on the preceding pages.

1. Which of the wanted persons illustrated in the following posters is not usually armed with a weapon or explosives?

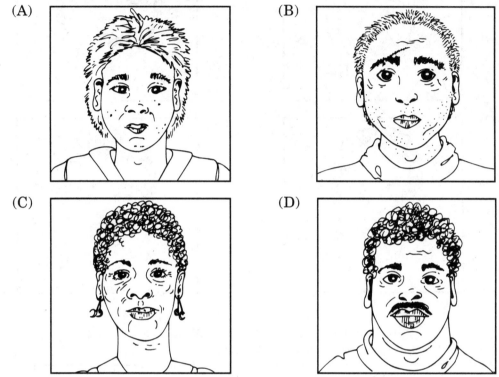

(A)

(B)

(C)

(D)

2. Which of the wanted persons illustrated in the following posters is a convicted murderer?

(A) (B)

(C) (D)

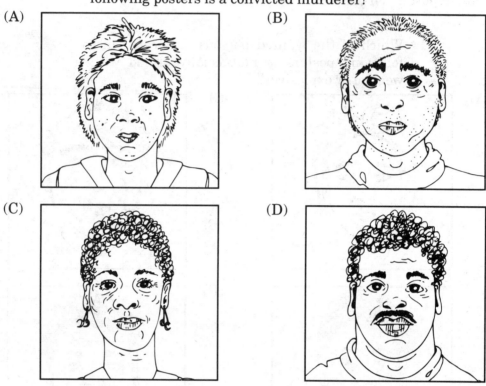

3. Which of the wanted persons illustrated in the following posters is the heaviest?

(A) (B)

(C) (D)

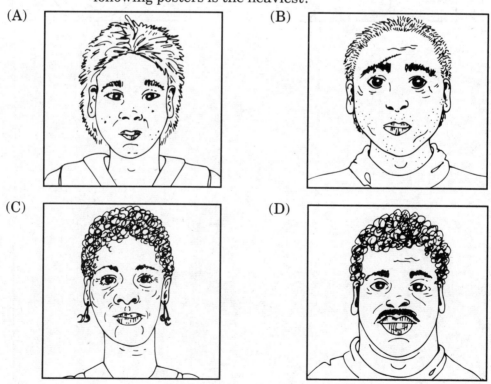

4. Which of the wanted persons illustrated in the following posters is the oldest?

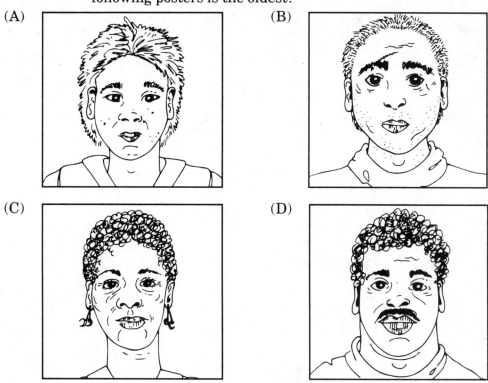

(A)　(B)　(C)　(D)

5. Which of the wanted persons illustrated in the following posters has blue eyes?

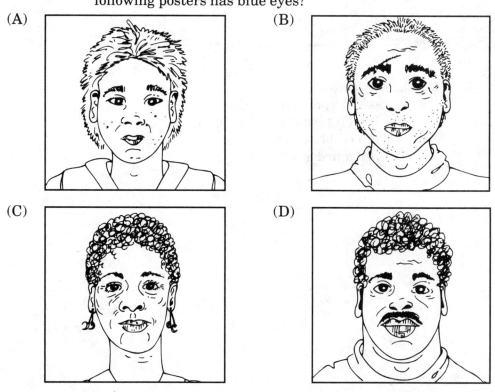

(A)　(B)　(C)　(D)

6. The subject illustrated in the wanted poster directly above
    (A) is an expert knife fighter.
    (B) is a forger.
    (C) is a child abuser.
    (D) is a murderer.

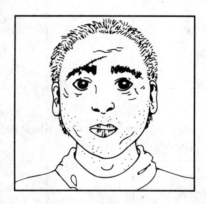

7. The subject illustrated in the wanted poster directly above
    (A) is an expert knife fighter.
    (B) is an international terrorist.
    (C) is a child abuser.
    (D) is a murderer.

8. The subject illustrated in the wanted poster directly above
   (A) is an expert knife fighter.
   (B) is an international terrorist.
   (C) is a tax expert.
   (D) is a murderer.

Answer questions 9–14 based solely on the information contained in the following passage.

On June 1st, at about 8:30 P.M., Trooper Frank Role, shield 333, observed a male, white, on foot on Center Street in the town of Pleasantville. The male white was later identified as Bob Smith of 2020 Vision Avenue.

Fifteen minutes prior to his observing Mr. Smith, Trooper Role had been notified by Sam Ash, an owner of a store located at 240 Center Street, that a man wearing a red cap, a white shirt, and tennis shorts had just robbed him at the corner of Center and Canal Streets. Mr. Ash said that the thief, who was white and looked to be from 30 to 35 years of age, had taken a white-handled pistol from his waistband and demanded money. Mr. Ash gave the thief $75.00 in U.S. currency in a yellow pay envelope, and then the robber fled the scene.

Trooper Role noticed that the white male he was observing was acting suspiciously so he decided to stop and question him. Therefore, exactly 10 minutes after he first observed Mr. Smith, the trooper stopped Smith at the corner of Center and Worth Streets. Almost immediately the trooper realized that his suspect fit the description of the perpetrator in the robbery of Mr. Ash. Trooper Role asked the suspect to identify himself and to give an explanation of his actions. After remarking, "Why are you hassling me?" the male identified himself as Bob Smith. While listening to Mr. Smith identify himself, Trooper Role noticed a bulge in the suspect's waistband. Remembering Mr. Ash's story and believing his life to be in danger, Trooper Role then frisked the outer garments of Mr. Smith in the vicinity of the bulge in his clothing at his waistline. As he performed the frisk, the bulge felt like the handle of a pistol to the trooper. The trooper then lifted Mr. Smith's shirt and removed a white-handled pistol from his waistband. After ascertaining that Mr. Smith had no legal authority to carry a handgun, at 8:50 P.M., Trooper Role placed Smith under arrest for illegal possession of a firearm. A further search of the prisoner yielded a yellow pay envelope that contained $75 in cash. At that point, the trooper informed Mr. Smith that he was also being charged with robbery.

Trooper Role then brought his prisoner to the State Police Headquarters. They arrived at the headquarters about 20 minutes after the arrest was made. The desk officer at the headquarters was Lieutenant Eagle. Trooper Role explained to the lieutenant that, while he was on routine patrol in Sector Four, which was his assignment for that tour, he stopped, frisked, and then arrested Mr. Smith. After hearing the story, Lieutenant Eagle said that the arrest number of the case will be 1245 and reminded the trooper that a notification has to be made to Mr. Ash to come to the barracks to view Mr. Smith in a lineup. That notification was made 30 minutes after Trooper Role arrived at headquarters.

9. The robbery of Mr. Ash took place at
   (A) about 8:30 P.M.
   (B) 8:45 P.M.
   (C) about 8:15 P.M.
   (D) an undetermined time.

10. The reason why Trooper Role stopped Mr. Smith was that
    (A) Smith fit the description of the robbery suspect.
    (B) Smith was acting suspiciously.
    (C) it looked like Smith had a weapon on his person.
    (D) it seemed as if Smith was looking for robbery victims.

11. Trooper Role stopped the suspect
    (A) at 8:15 P.M.
    (B) at 8:30 P.M.
    (C) at 8:40 P.M.
    (D) at 9:00 P.M.

12. Trooper Role noticed the bulge in the suspect's shirt
    (A) immediately upon stopping him.
    (B) as the suspect was identifying himself.
    (C) after the arrest was made.
    (D) as he approached the suspect.

13. The charge of robbery against Mr. Smith was made
    (A) when the Trooper discovered the white-handled pistol.
    (B) at the same time that the weapons charge was made.
    (C) immediately after the yellow pay envelope was found.
    (D) when Mr. Ash identified the suspect.

14. At what time was Mr. Ash notified to come to the headquarters?
    (A) 8:50 P.M.
    (B) 9:10 P.M.
    (C) 9:40 P.M.
    (D) not given

Answer questions 15–21 solely on the basis of the following information.

On November 10th, defendant Myers and three other people were traveling north on the state thruway when their car was stopped by a state trooper for speeding. Approaching the vehicle the trooper smelled marijuana coming from within the vehicle and observed on the floor of the vehicle an envelope, which he recognized as a type commonly used in selling marijuana. The trooper then ordered the occupants out of the vehicle, frisked each one, removed the envelope from the floor, and determined that it contained a small amount of marijuana.

After the marijuana was found, Myers and the three other people standing outside the car were placed under arrest for the illegal possession of marijuana. The trooper reentered the vehicle, searched portions of it likely to conceal drugs, and searched the pockets of five jackets lying on the back seat. He opened the zippered pocket of one of the jackets and discovered a small amount of cocaine. The trooper placed an additional charge against the prisoners for illegally possessing cocaine. All four prisoners were then removed to the State Police Headquarters where they were interrogated for 20 minutes.

Myers and his three accomplices engaged in plea bargaining with respect to the possession of marijuana, but Myers elected to go to trial with respect to the charge concerning possession of cocaine. Myers was convicted by the Trial Court, and a unanimous Appellate Division Court affirmed, holding that the warrantless search of the jacket was lawful as incident to the defendant's arrest.

Myers appealed to the Court of Appeals. In arriving at its decision, the Court of Appeals discussed the right of privacy and the area that might be searched when an arrest is made. The court held that when a person is placed under arrest, there is always a danger that he/she may seek to use a weapon to effect an escape or to destroy or conceal evidence of a crime or other contraband. Accordingly, it would be reasonable for the arresting trooper to conduct a prompt warrantless search of the arrestee's person and the area within his/her immediate control in order for the trooper to protect himself/herself and others and to prevent loss of evidence. The area within the arrestee's immediate control would mean any area from which he/she might reach a weapon or evidence that could be destroyed.

Both the Trial Court and the Appellate Division Court concluded that as a factual matter, the jacket was not within the exclusive control of the police nor were the arrestees effectively neutralized. Therefore, they ruled that the search of the jacket was a constitutionally valid one. The Court of Appeals disagreed, holding that once the defendant Myers was arrested and removed from the vehicle, he was incapable, as were his confederates, of reentering the vehicle to attempt to obtain a weapon or destroy evidence.

15. The Court of Appeals held that it is reasonable for the arresting trooper to search the person of an arrestee and the area under the arrestee's immediate control. The court defined immediate control as including
   (A) the area within reach of the arrested person's arms.
   (B) the entire area inside the car, but not including the inside of jacket pockets.
   (C) any area from which the arrested person might reach a weapon.
   (D) any area from which the arrested person might reach evidence of any kind.

16. Which of the following can accurately be concluded from the facts in the case?
   (A) Myers is a male.
   (B) The jacket with the cocaine belonged to Myers.
   (C) Myers was questioned alone for 20 minutes.
   (D) None of the defendants were sentenced to prison.

17. Which of the following courts rendered a decision that was favorable to Myers?
   (A) Trial Court
   (B) Appellate Division Court
   (C) Court of Appeals
   (D) all three courts involved

18. Which of the following statements is most accurate concerning actual ownership of the cocaine?
    (A) Myers was the owner of the cocaine.
    (B) One of Myers' three accomplices owned the cocaine.
    (C) Someone other than Myers and his three accomplices owned the cocaine.
    (D) It is not clear who owned the cocaine.

19. The Court of Appeals based its findings primarily upon which of the following?
    (A) The trooper smelled marijuana upon approaching the car.
    (B) None of the defendants could have reentered the vehicle after they were arrested.
    (C) The jacket in the car belonged to Myers.
    (D) The other three defendants engaged in plea bargaining.

20. What was the offense that led to the stopping of the car that Myers was traveling in?
    (A) possession of marijuana
    (B) speeding
    (C) possession of cocaine
    (D) unlicensed operator

21. Which event occurred first?
    (A) the discovery of the cocaine
    (B) the discovery of marijuana
    (C) the search of the jacket
    (D) the removal of the occupants from the car

Answer questions 22–27 solely on the basis of the following passage.

At 12:55 P.M. State Trooper Smith was on foot patrol on Court Street between 2nd and 4th Avenue, which is located on the grounds of the state capital complex. While standing on the southeast corner of Court Street and 3rd Avenue, the trooper heard a scream coming from the direction of the State's Administration Building on the opposite side of the street. When he looked in that direction he saw a young white male running on Court Street toward 2nd Avenue, followed by a woman yelling "Stop that man." Trooper Smith joined in the pursuit, but by the time he caught up with the woman, she had fallen over some debris on the sidewalk. The woman was quite upset and appeared to have injured her head. Trooper Smith decided that, because the young white male had disappeared from sight, he should stay with the injured woman and call for an ambulance. While awaiting the arrival of the ambulance, the injured woman, Ms. Cramdon, told Trooper Smith that she was the manager of the Administration Building and that the young white male had taken approximately

$35.00 from the petty cash draw while she was trying to find a job application for him. She also mentioned that the Administration Building was unattended at the time because her two helpers had not come to work that day.

Trooper Smith called for backup assistance at 1:20 P.M. and asked the radio dispatcher to send someone to the Administration Building located at 4241 Court Street to safeguard the premises. As a result, State Troopers Jones and Brown arrived at the Administration Building at 1:35 P.M. and confirmed that the premises were unattended. When Trooper Smith arrived at the Administration Building at 1:55 P.M., Trooper Brown told him that it would be impossible to determine what items had been taken from the building because there was no listing of the building's equipment readily available.

At 2:10 P.M., a young woman entered the building and identified herself as Ms. Martin, a part-time helper at the building whose shift started at 2:00 P.M. On seeing the situation in the building, she asked the troopers what had occurred. After telling her, they asked her where the equipment list for the building was kept, and she stated that Administrative Assistant Connors kept that information. She was told to call the state police dispatcher when the list was available.

22. Where was Trooper Smith when he heard a scream?
   (A) on Court Street and 4th Avenue
   (B) at 4241 Court Street
   (C) at the intersection of Court Street and 3rd Avenue
   (D) in front of the Administration Building

23. Which one of the following is the most exact address of the Administration Office?
   (A) 4241 3rd Avenue
   (B) 3rd Avenue and Court Street
   (C) 4241 Court Street
   (D) Court Street and 4th Avenue

24. At what time did Trooper Smith meet Troopers Jones and Brown at the Administration Building?
   (A) 12:55 P.M.
   (B) 1:20 P.M.
   (C) 1:35 P.M.
   (D) 1:55 P.M.

25. Which one of the following people manage the Administration Building?
   (A) Ms. Cramdon
   (B) Ms. Martin
   (C) Mr. Connors
   (D) Ms. Smith

26. What is Ms. Martin's scheduled starting time at the Administration Building?
    (A) 1:35 P.M.
    (B) 1:55 P.M.
    (C) 2:00 P.M.
    (D) 2:10 P.M.

27. Keeping the equipment list is the responsibility of
    (A) Ms. Martin.
    (B) Administrative Assistant Connors.
    (C) Ms. Cramdon.
    (D) the radio dispatcher.

Answer question 28 based solely on the following rule.

State troopers may apply for an interview with the State Police Superintendent, in writing, either direct or through official channels.

28. State troopers
    (A) can telephone and ask for an interview with the superintendent.
    (B) can forward a written request for an interview with the superintendent through their supervisors.
    (C) must have a good reason for requesting an interview with the superintendent.
    (D) must inform their supervisors when they want to have an interview with the superintendent.

Answer questions 29–36 solely on the basis of the following information.

In order to determine the necessity of commencing a vehicle pursuit and the method to be employed in conducting such a pursuit, a highway patrol officer shall adhere to the following procedure.

DEFINITIONS
PRIMARY VEHICLE—the vehicle that initiated the pursuit
SECONDARY VEHICLE—first additional vehicle unit assisting in the pursuit

Upon observing that there is a likelihood that a vehicle pursuit may be imminent, the highway patrol officer concerned shall

1. Initiate the vehicle stop when feasible.

2. Determine the necessity for commencing and continuing a vehicle pursuit by considering the following:

    a. Nature of offense
    b. Time of day
    c. Weather conditions
    d. Location and population density
    e. Capability of highway patrol vehicle
    f. Familiarity with the area by the officer

NOTE: AGENCY POLICY MANDATES THAT A VEHICLE PURSUIT BE TERMINATED WHENEVER THE RISKS TO MEMBERS OF THE AGENCY AND THE PUBLIC OUTWEIGH THE DANGER TO THE COMMUNITY IF THE SUSPECT IS NOT IMMEDIATELY CAUGHT. IF THE CHASE IS TERMINATED, MEMBERS WILL ATTEMPT TO OBTAIN SUFFICIENT INFORMATION TO EFFECT THE APPREHENSION OF THE SUSPECT.

3. Notify radio dispatcher at start of pursuit and provide the following information:

    a. Location of the highway patrol vehicle
    b. Type and color of vehicle pursued and direction of travel
    c. Nature of offense
    d. Registration number and state of registration
    e. Occupants of pursued vehicle

4. Maintain contact with the radio dispatcher.

    a. DO NOT depress the transmitter key unnecessarily and keep all radio transmissions brief while speaking in normal tones

5. Utilize the vehicle's emergency signaling devices but

    a. DO NOT use the constant position on siren because it distorts transmissions and blots out the sound of approaching vehicles.

6. Inform radio dispatcher if vehicle changes direction by giving the last location of the pursued vehicle, its speed, and its direction of travel.

7. Notify the radio dispatcher if the pursued vehicle is lost or the pursuit is terminated.

NOTE: VEHICLES SHALL NOT CARAVAN BEHIND PURSUING VEHICLES. Instead they shall

    a. Allow at least five (5) car lengths distance from primary pursuit vehicle.
    b. NOT pass the primary vehicle unless requested by that unit,

or if other circumstances exist such as an accident, or mechanical malfunction.

The following tactics are prohibited and WILL NOT BE used in an attempt to stop a vehicle:

    a. Ramming the pursued vehicle
    b. Placing a highway patrol vehicle in a position to be struck by the pursued vehicle
    c. Driving alongside the pursued vehicle
    d. Setting up roadblocks (unless specifically directed by supervisory personnel)

8. Unmarked highway patrol vehicles will limit pursuits.

9. Highway patrol vans and scooters (2 and 3 wheel) WILL NOT be used in pursuits.

10. Two (2)-wheel motorcycles will limit pursuits and terminate pursuit when four (4)-wheel highway patrol vehicle has joined pursuit.

29. Highway Patrol Officer Don Green is considering starting a vehicle pursuit. According to procedure, Officer Green would be least correct if he considered which of the following factors?
    (A) nature of offense
    (B) weather conditions
    (C) time of day
    (D) year, make, and model of the pursued vehicle

30. Highway Patrol Officer April Bays is instructing a newly assigned officer concerning vehicle pursuits. Regarding the use of a vehicle's emergency signaling devices, Officer Bays indicates that the constant position of the siren should not be used. In such an instance Officer Bays' comment was
    (A) proper, mainly because extended use of the constant position of the siren drains the battery.
    (B) improper, mainly because it is the best way to warn oncoming traffic.
    (C) proper, mainly because use of the constant position of the siren distorts transmissions and blots out the sound of approaching vehicles.
    (D) improper, mainly because it serves as a notice to pedestrians in the area.

31. While pursuing a vehicle, Highway Patrol Officer Marks is about to inform the radio dispatcher that the pursued vehicle is about to change direction. As such the officer should do all the following except
    (A) notify the radio dispatcher of the speed of the pursued vehicle.
    (B) give the last location of the pursued vehicle.
    (C) identify the direction of travel of the pursued vehicle.
    (D) advise the radio dispatcher of the suspected destination of the pursued vehicle.

32. Vehicles are not permitted to caravan behind a pursued vehicle. Actually the distance that a secondary vehicle should allow from the primary pursuit vehicle is at least
    (A) 500 feet.
    (B) 5 yards.
    (C) 5 blocks.
    (D) 5 car lengths.

33. Under certain circumstances, a highway patrol officer could, in connection with a vehicle pursuit, engage in which of the following tactics?
    (A) driving alongside the pursued vehicle
    (B) placing a moving highway patrol vehicle in a position to be struck by the pursued vehicle
    (C) setting up roadblocks
    (D) ramming the pursued vehicle

34. Which of the following statements is least accurate?
    (A) Unmarked highway patrol vehicles will be used as much as possible in pursuits because of their ability to blend in with their surroundings.
    (B) Highway patrol van vehicles are not to be used in connection with vehicle pursuits.
    (C) Three-wheel scooters may not be used in vehicle pursuits.
    (D) Two-wheel motorcycles will limit pursuits and terminate the pursuit as soon as a four-wheel highway patrol vehicle has joined the pursuit.

35. Which of the following most accurately represents the factor that decides whether a vehicle pursuit should be terminated?
    (A) the driving record of the officer in the primary vehicle
    (B) the driving record of the officer in the secondary vehicle
    (C) if the person in the pursued vehicle has been positively identified
    (D) whether the risks to members of the agency and the public outweigh the danger to the community if the subject is not immediately caught

36. Highway Patrol Officer Ray Block, while in his patrol car, observes the driver of a vehicle commit an offense. The officer unsuccessfully attempts to pull the vehicle over as the vehicle roars away. Officer Block is about to begin pursuit of a vehicle. In this instance, the officer is required to notify the radio dispatcher of all the following except
    (A) the location of the highway patrol vehicle.
    (B) the type and color of vehicle pursued and the direction of travel of the pursued vehicle.
    (C) the nature of the offense that initiated the pursuit.
    (D) the number of occupants in the highway patrol vehicle.

Answer questions 37 and 38 solely on the basis of the following information.

TO ALL TROOPER COMMANDS
SUBJECT: AIRCRAFT INCIDENTS
    If an aircraft makes an emergency landing at other than an airport, the trooper on the scene shall inform the pilot to personally report the landing to the post desk officer within 8 hours of the incident. The trooper shall also inform the pilot that failure to do so is a misdemeanor. In the event that the pilot is incapacitated, then the owner of the aircraft shall assume the pilot's responsibilities.
    When an airport or seaplane base is discovered by a trooper to be operating without a license, the trooper concerned shall verbally notify the patrol supervisor and notify the post commander in writing.

37. Trooper Marks responds to a deserted stretch of highway where a single-engine plane has made an emergency landing. Luckily no one is injured. In such an instance it would be most correct for Trooper Marks to advise the pilot
    (A) to notify the post commander in writing within 24 hours of the incident.
    (B) to notify the patrol supervisor within 10 hours of the incident.
    (C) to notify the post desk officer within 8 hours of the incident.
    (D) to notify the owner to appear at the post command within 8 hours of the incident.

38. Trooper Bays discovers an airport operating without any license. In this instance the most correct action for the trooper to take is
    (A) to only verbally notify the patrol supervisor.
    (B) to verbally notify the post commander and notify the patrol supervisor in writing.
    (C) to verbally notify the patrol supervisor and notify the post commander in writing.
    (D) to notify both the patrol supervisor and post commander in writing.

Answer questions 39–45 solely on the basis of the following information.

To protect life and property and assist local fire departments responding to a fire, a trooper shall, in this order:
UPON ARRIVING AT THE SCENE OF A FIRE:

1. Send an alarm or make sure one has been sent.

2. Direct a responsible person to remain at the alarm box to direct fire apparatus if the fire is not in view.

3. Park the patrol car to prevent interference with the fire-fighting operation.

4. Warn and assist occupants in evacuation of buildings.

5. Prevent looting.

UPON ARRIVAL OF FIRE APPARATUS:

6. Establish police lines beyond the fire apparatus and hydrants in use.

   a. Also establish police lines behind the building beyond the fire lines

7. Notify the radio dispatcher if the fire is suspicious and, through the radio dispatcher, request the detectives.

8. Permit only the following persons or vehicles to enter fire lines:

   a. Local officials such as the mayor
   b. Members of governmental agencies in the performance of duty
   c. Employees of public service corporations in the performance of emergency duties
   d. Persons holding unexpired:
      1. Working press cards
      2. Fire line cards signed by a local fire commissioner

   e. Police and Fire Department vehicles
   f. Ambulances
   g. Public service corporation vehicles for duty in connection with the fire
   h. U.S. Mail vehicles
   i. Prison vans transporting prisoners

9. Record the following information in the Trooper Activity Log:

   a. Time and date of fire
   b. Part of premises in which fire occurred
   c. Type of building and number of stories
   d. Address of building
   e. Name and address of building owner
   f. Name and address of premises occupant
   g. Number of persons injured, if any
   h. Cause of fire, extent of damage, and any suspicion of arson (obtained from fire officer in charge)
   i. Any dangerous condition resulting from the fire.

10. Prepare a Complaint Report if the fire is suspicious.

11. Send a telephone message of fire report to the division command and the Operations Unit if

    a. Injury or death occurs
    b. Three alarms or more are sent
    c. Unusual type of fire occurs
    d. Cause of fire is suspicious
    e. Forced entry is effected by the Fire Department
    f. Relocation of tenants is required

39. Trooper Walls responds to the scene of a fire in her patrol car. The actual site of the fire is difficult to see from the street. After making sure that an alarm has been sent, the trooper should next
   (A) warn and assist occupants in evacuation of buildings.
   (B) prevent looting.
   (C) direct a responsible person to remain at the alarm box to direct fire apparatus.
   (D) park the patrol car to prevent interference with the fire-fighting operation.

40. After fire apparatus arrives at the scene of a fire, and the fire has officially been classified as suspicious, the trooper concerned should request the detectives through
   (A) the operations unit.
   (B) the radio dispatcher.
   (C) the patrol supervisor.
   (D) the division command.

41. Trooper Wills is at the scene of the fire. If the trooper wishes to determine the cause of the fire, the trooper should
   (A) ask the patrol supervisor.
   (B) obtain the information from the fire officer in charge.
   (C) conduct an independent investigation.
   (D) ask the radio dispatcher to send the detectives to determine the cause of the fire.

42. Trooper Hall observes that fire lines have been established around the scene of a fire. A correction officer driving a prison van transporting correction officers back to their facility asks the officer if he might pass through the fire lines and continue on to the correctional facility. Trooper Hall refuses. In this instance Trooper Hall was
   (A) correct, mainly because no vehicles other than fire vehicles should be allowed to pass through fire lines at the scene of a fire.
   (B) incorrect, mainly because correction officers are officials and should be allowed to drive through fire lines.
   (C) correct, mainly because no prisoners were in the van.
   (D) incorrect, mainly because the trooper's action probably interferes with the correction officers who are performing their duties.

43. At the scene of a fire, a trooper should prepare a Complaint Report if
   (A) the damage is more than $500.
   (B) the patrol supervisor responds to the scene.
   (C) the fire is suspicious.
   (D) a fire officer is overcome by smoke.

44. In which of the following instances would a trooper at the scene of a fire be least correct in notifying the operations unit?
   (A) if an injury occurred
   (B) if two alarms of fire were sent
   (C) if forced entry by the Fire Department occurred
   (D) if relocation of tenants is needed

45. A trooper at the scene of a fire would be most correct if the trooper did not permit which of the following to enter fire lines?
   (A) members of governmental agencies in the performance of duty
   (B) employees of public service corporations in the performance of emergency duties
   (C) any persons holding working press cards
   (D) ambulances

Answer questions 46–48 solely on the basis of the following information.

In order to record instances when nonmembers of the State Troopers are transported in state trooper vehicles the following procedure will be followed.

DEFINITION: A nonmember includes prisoners, complainants, witnesses, abandoned children, lost persons, and mentally ill persons.
   Therefore when it is necessary to transport a nonmember in a patrol car, the operator of the vehicle shall

1. Obtain permission, if possible, from the patrol supervisor and desk officer.

2. Notify the radio dispatcher at the start and conclusion of the trip.

3. Search the passenger area of the vehicle for contraband, weapons, or other property immediately upon the conclusion of the trip.

4. Enter the following information in the TROOPER ACTIVITY LOG:

   a. Time trip starts
   b. Identity of persons transported

     c. Place of beginning and end of trip
     d. Purpose of trip
     e. Time trip ends
     f. Results of vehicle inspection

5. Inform the member on telephone switchboard duty of the trip.

46. In connection with the procedure dealing with the transporting of nonmembers in state trooper vehicles, which of the following statements is least correct?
    (A) Permission must always be obtained from the patrol supervisor.
    (B) Permission should be obtained from the desk officer, if possible.
    (C) The radio dispatcher should be notified at the start of the trip.
    (D) The radio dispatcher should be notified at the end of the trip.

47. At the conclusion of a trip transporting a nonmember, Trooper Frank Hanks would be required to enter all the following in his TROOPER ACTIVITY LOG except
    (A) the place where the trip began.
    (B) the time the trip starts.
    (C) the name of the member on telephone switchboard duty who was notified of the trip.
    (D) the identity of the person transported.

48. According to procedure, a trooper transporting a nonmember is required to search the passenger compartment
    (A) only at the start of the trip.
    (B) only at the end of the trip.
    (C) neither at the start nor at the end of the trip.
    (D) at both the start and at the end of the trip.

INSTRUCTIONS: In each of questions 49–53 you will be given four choices. Three of the choices, A, B, and C, contain a written statement. You are to evaluate the statement in each choice and select the statement that is most accurately and clearly written. If all or none of the three written statements is accurately and clearly written, you are to select choice D.

49. According to the instructions, evaluate the following statements.
    - (A) A continuous enforcement effort is required to deal with what seems like a never-ending supply of illicit drugs.
    - (B) In the academy you learn how to tackle you're own problems.
    - (C) Most troopers drive very good.
    - (D) All or none of the choices is accurate.

50. According to the instructions, evaluate the following statements.
    - (A) The desk officer's post is a fixed stationery post.
    - (B) The officers were certain of their facts.
    - (C) The bomb threat was written on company stationary.
    - (D) All or none of the choices is accurate.

51. According to the instructions, evaluate the following statements.
    - (A) June was married twice and killed both her father-in-laws.
    - (B) Pat is the suspect who was previously convicted of shooting at several passer-bys from his car.
    - (C) If anyone tries to sell narcotics, they will be arrested.
    - (D) All or none of the choices is accurate.

52. According to the instructions, evaluate the following statements.
    - (A) The trooper immigrated to the United States from Guyana.
    - (B) The highway patrol officer wants to emigrate from the United States to France, his country of birth, after he retires.
    - (C) The trooper implied to the captain that he did not want a transfer to the warrant squad.
    - (D) All or none of the choices is accurate.

53. According to the instructions, evaluate the following statements.
    - (A) After doing the exercises, the trooper felt accelerated.
    - (B) I hate to loose to him.
    - (C) The trooper was so tired after work yesterday that the trooper had to lay down.
    - (D) All or none of the choices is accurate.

54. On a certain map ¼ inch represents 10 miles. If two cities are 3½ inches apart on this map, the actual distance in miles between the two cities is
   (A)   100 miles.
   (B)   120 miles.
   (C)   140 miles.
   (D)   160 miles.

55. A highway patrol officer's patrol car is able to get 21 miles to a gallon of gasoline. How many gallons of gasoline would be used if the officer traveled 147 miles?
   (A)   6 gallons
   (B)   7 gallons
   (C)   8 gallons
   (D)   9 gallons

56. While booking a prisoner, Trooper Sands states that he removed the following U.S. currency from the prisoner: one $50 bill, two $20 bills, one $5 bill, 3 quarters, and 17 nickels. The prisoner later indicates that when he was booked, he had exactly $100. In this instance, regarding what the trooper states and what the prisoner indicates
   (A)   there is a difference of $4.30.
   (B)   there is a difference of $3.40.
   (C)   there is a difference of $4.40.
   (D)   there is no difference.

57. A burglary complainant reports to Trooper May Bell that a burglar took $280 in cash, a tape recorder worth $400, three collectible dolls each appraised at $188, and a fur coat valued at $2850. The total value of what was reported stolen was
   (A) $3718.
   (B) $4094.
   (C) $4022.
   (D) $4059.

INSTRUCTIONS: Answer questions 58–65 SOLELY on the basis of the information recorded on the following AIDED REPORT.

STATE HIGHWAY PATROL—WATERS DIVISION
AIDED REPORT

DATE OF OCCURRENCE	AIDED SURNAME	FIRST
MAR. 18–19XX	HALL	JEFF

SEX	COLOR	AGE	TIME OF OCCURRENCE
M	B	28	1530 HOURS

ADDRESS	APT NO.	AIDED #
51–37 SUN AVENUE	3E	899

PLACE OF OCCURRENCE
In the bathroom of Rest Area of Route 19 North at exit 23 North in the vicinity of the entrance door.

check one ( ) Dead ( ) Sick (x) Injured ( ) Mentally Ill

NATURE OF ILLNESS OR INJURY	REMOVED TO
Broken Ankle	Fillton Hospital

DOCTOR	HOSPITAL ADMISSION NUMBER
Marris	3919

LOCAL TOWN POLICE NOTIFIED	RELATIVES NOTIFIED
2nd Pct. Detective Belles	The aided's sister Frances was present and notified

Details

At the time and place of occurrence, during an altercation, aided, Jeff Hall, a visitor to the area fell to the floor of the bathroom of the Rest Area of Route 19 North at exit 23 North in the vicinity of the entrance door after being struck in the head by Luis Parkers, also a visitor. While both males were using the same bathroom, an argument developed over the use of the hand-drying machine. Highway Patrol Officer Rays was called to the scene and immediately arrested Parkers for assault. Arrest number 3232.

The aided's sister Frances Tang was present and notified. The aided lives with his sister and their phone number is 555-0009.

NAME AND ADDRESS OF WITNESSES
Neil Bailes - 518 Boston Road - Tel. No. 555-1000
          APT. 39E   or 555-1001

REPORTED BY HIGHWAY PATROL OFFICER	SHIELD NO.	COMMAND
John Sexton	1889	Waters Division

58. The name of the doctor who treated the aided was
    (A) Sexton.
    (B) Bailes.
    (C) Belles.
    (D) Marris.

59. The person who made the arrest was
    (A) Detective Belles.
    (B) Highway Patrol Officer Sexton.
    (C) Highway Patrol Officer Rays.
    (D) the sister of the person aided.

60. The telephone number of the person aided is
    (A) 555-1000.
    (B) 555-0009.
    (C) 555-1001.
    (D) not available.

61. The hospital admission number is
    (A) 1530.
    (B) 899.
    (C) 3919.
    (D) 1889.

62. Who lives in apartment 3E?
    (A) the prisoner
    (B) the aided
    (C) the witness
    (D) the officer making out the report

63. Which of the following is the most accurate state-
    ment about Mr. Luis Parkers?
    (A) He is a bully.
    (B) He is a visitor to the area.
    (C) He has been arrested before.
    (D) He was accompanied by his sister.

64. The number 3232 is
    (A) an officer's badge number.
    (B) the aided number.
    (C) the arrest number.
    (D) part of an address of one of the persons in-
        volved in the incident.

65. Which of the following statements is least accurate?
    (A) The aided is 28 years old.
    (B) A female named Frances lives at 51–37 Sun Avenue.
    (C) The officer who made the arrest is assigned to the Waters Division.
    (D) An arrest was made for assault.

Answer questions 66–73 based on the following data.

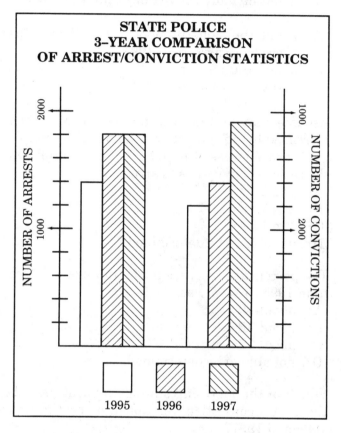

Answer questions 66–73 based on the above data.

66. Which of the following is the most accurate statement concerning the number of arrests during the 3-year period shown in the data?
    (A) The number of arrests increased each year of the 3-year period.
    (B) The number of arrests decreased each year of the 3-year period.
    (C) The number of arrests increased after the first year of the 3-year period and remained about the same for the next 2 years.
    (D) The number of arrests was the greatest during the second year of the 3-year period.

67. In 1995 what was the ratio of convictions to arrests?
    (A) about 1 to 1.6
    (B) about 1 to 0.8
    (C) about 1.6 to 1
    (D) It cannot be determined.

68. In 1997 there were
    (A) about the same number of convictions as there were in 1995.
    (B) about 50 more convictions than there were in 1996.
    (C) about the same number of convictions than there were arrests in 1997.
    (D) about 150 more convictions than there were arrests in 1995.

69. Assume that in 1998 the number of convictions increased by 50 convictions, whereas the number of arrests increased by 600. At the end of 1998, the ratio of convictions to arrests is
    (A) 1 to 2.
    (B) 2 to 1.
    (C) 1 to 1.5.
    (D) not able to be determined.

70. The percentage increase in the number of arrests from 1995 to 1997 was
    (A) about 10%.
    (B) about 40%.
    (C) about 75%.
    (D) not able to be determined.

71. Which of the following statements best describes the arrest/conviction relationship for the years 1996 and 1997?
    (A) Arrests and convictions increased.
    (B) Arrests and convictions remained the same.
    (C) Arrests remained about the same, and convictions increased.
    (D) Convictions remained the same, and arrests increased.

72. On any given day in 1996, how many arrests are made?
    (A) 1400
    (B) 4
    (C) 14
    (D) It cannot be determined.

73. Exactly how many persons were convicted of a crime during May of 1996?
    (A) 700
    (B) 58
    (C) 2
    (D) It cannot be determined.

74. Troopers may have to evacuate people from a building when a dangerous condition occurs. Under which of the following circumstances would it be most appropriate for an evacuation to take place in accordance with this rule?
    (A) A domestic argument is occurring in the lobby of the building.
    (B) A building employee is trapped in an elevator.
    (C) An asbestos fire is burning in the boiler room.
    (D) A deranged person is observed entering the building.

75. Troopers often must administer first aid when people require medical assistance in life-threatening situations. In which one of the following cases should a trooper administer first aid pending the arrival of medical assistance?
    (A) A person is bleeding profusely from the stomach area.
    (B) A person is experiencing cramps in his stomach.
    (C) A person is complaining of a pain in his back.
    (D) A person has a headache.

76. When investigating a reported crime, state troopers are trained to always determine if an automobile was involved in the commission of the crime and, if so, to obtain as much information about the car as possible. The primary reason for this training is that information about automobiles used by criminals
    (A) often leads to the identification of the criminals.
    (B) often helps to eliminate the commission of similar crimes.
    (C) is needed in order to establish roadblocks to prevent the escape of criminals.
    (D) is needed to complete the required forms that must be prepared when crimes are committed.

77. To remain safe in a dangerous environment and to most effectively accomplish the goals of the state police, troopers must function together as a team. The most important characteristic of teamwork is
    (A) individual accomplishment.
    (B) cooperation.
    (C) aggressiveness.
    (D) rigidity.

78. When engaged in preventive patrol, a trooper should try to create an impression of omnipresence while on patrol. This means that street criminals should be made to believe that
    (A) they are always being watched by ever-present troopers.
    (B) it is wrong to break the law.
    (C) a trooper will be coming by on a regularly scheduled basis.
    (D) they should behave even when they are not being watched.

79. Troopers are sometimes required to request emergency transportation for seriously injured persons. In which of the following situations would it be most appropriate for a trooper to request emergency transportation?
    (A) An elderly person falls down on the sidewalk and suffers an abrasion of the knee.
    (B) A young person falls down a flight of stairs and is knocked unconscious.
    (C) A fellow trooper complains of feeling faint.
    (D) An elected official who is a chronic complainer says that he is experiencing difficulty eating.

80. A complaint is an allegation of an improper or unlawful act by a trooper that relates to the business of a state police agency. Which of the following is not an example of a complaint?
    (A) A citizen states that a trooper used excessive force on him.
    (B) A prisoner claims that his court-appointed lawyer did not properly represent him.
    (C) A prisoner contends that the trooper who arrested him acted in a discriminatory manner.
    (D) A recently arrested person reports that a trooper stole property from him.

81. State troopers are prohibited from going through the wallet of a stopped motorist to find the motorist's driver's license. Instead, troopers are instructed to tell motorists to remove the license themselves. The primary reason for this rule is to
(A) determine if motorists are sober enough to find the license.
(B) establish who is in charge of the situation.
(C) avoid charges that troopers removed valuables from the wallets of stopped motorists.
(D) ensure the safety of troopers.

Answer questions 82–89 SOLELY on the basis of the following legal definitions. Do not base your answers on any other knowledge of the law you may have. You may refer to the definitions when answering the questions.

An offense is either a felony, a misdemeanor, or a violation.

A violation is an offense for which a person upon conviction shall receive a sentence of imprisonment of no more than 15 days.

A misdemeanor is an offense for which a person upon conviction shall receive a sentence of imprisonment of no less than 16 days and up to and including 1 year.

A felony is an offense for which a person upon conviction shall receive a sentence of imprisonment of more than 1 year. Felonies are classified as A, B, C, D, or E felonies. The most serious felonies, which receive the most severe penalties, are A felonies, followed by B felonies, and so on.

A crime is either a misdemeanor or a felony.

A deadly weapon is any loaded gun, capable of firing a shot that can cause death or other serious physical injury, or a billy, blackjack, metal knuckles, dagger, switchblade knife, gravity knife, or pilum ballistic knife.

A dangerous instrument is any article or substance (including a vehicle) that, depending on how it is used, attempted to be used or threatened to be used, is capable of causing death or serious physical injury.

A physical injury is an injury that causes substantial pain or physical impairment.

A serious physical injury is a physical injury that causes a substantial risk of death, a protracted injury or disfigurement, or an impairment of an organ.

82. Which of the following felonies is most likely to have the least severe penalty?
(A) A felony
(B) B felony
(C) C felony
(D) D felony

83. An offense is
    (A) always a felony.
    (B) always a misdemeanor.
    (C) always a violation.
    (D) either a felony, a misdemeanor, or a violation.

84. If a certain criminal act is a misdemeanor, then
    the act
    (A) is more serious than a felony and will receive
        a greater penalty than a felony.
    (B) will receive a lesser punishment than a vio-
        lation.
    (C) is always a crime.
    (D) will be punished according to the age of the
        defendant and the defendant's past criminal
        record.

85. Concerning felonies, misdemeanors, and viola-
    tions, it would be most accurate to state that
    (A) they are all crimes.
    (B) they are all offenses.
    (C) they all have a maximum punishment stated
        in their respective definitions.
    (D) they all have a minimum punishment stated
        in their respective definitions.

86. Which of the following is most likely to be consid-
    ered a deadly weapon?
    (A) every loaded gun
    (B) any gun that is operable
    (C) a razor
    (D) a dagger

87. Don attempts to run over Pat with his motor vehi-
    cle. In this instance Don's motor vehicle is
    (A) a deadly weapon.
    (B) a dangerous instrument.
    (C) both a deadly weapon and dangerous instru-
        ment.
    (D) neither a deadly weapon nor a dangerous in-
        strument.

88. If Frank kicks Pat and causes Pat to experience
    substantial pain, Frank has inflicted upon Pat
    (A) a serious physical injury.
    (B) a physical injury.
    (C) a serious physical injury if Pat receives any
        medical attention.
    (D) a physical injury but only if it can be shown
        that Pat experienced substantial pain.

89. Tom strikes Pat over the head with an unloaded gun. Tom has used
    (A) a deadly weapon.
    (B) a dangerous instrument.
    (C) no weapon.
    (D) a deadly weapon but only if the gun is operable.

INSTRUCTIONS: Answer questions 90–94 solely on the basis of the following map. The flow of traffic is as shown by the arrows. Where there is only one arrow, then the traffic flows only in the direction indicated by the arrow. You must follow the flow of traffic when moving from one location to another.

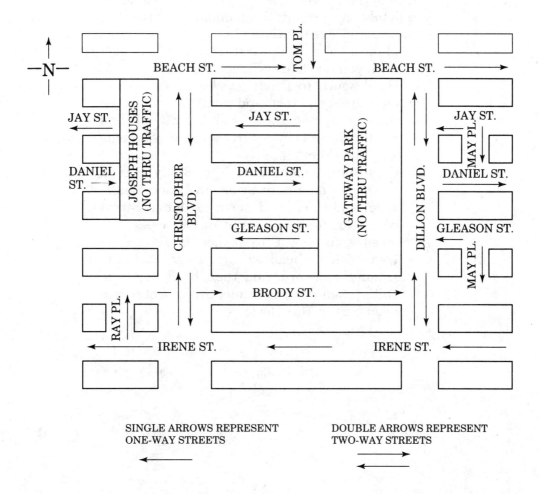

SINGLE ARROWS REPRESENT
ONE-WAY STREETS

DOUBLE ARROWS REPRESENT
TWO-WAY STREETS

90. You are in your patrol car proceeding west on Gleason Street toward Gateway Park. You proceed to the next street where you are able to make a right turn and do so. You continue straight ahead for three blocks and then make a left turn and continue straight ahead. At that point you would be
(A) heading east.
(B) going against traffic.
(C) traveling on a two-way street.
(D) heading north.

91. You are in your patrol car, legally parked facing south in front of the Joseph Houses at Daniel Street. You receive an assignment to meet the patrol supervisor at May Place and Daniel Street. Which of the following is the most direct route for you to take in your patrol car, making sure to obey all of the traffic regulations?
(A) Make a left onto Daniel Street and head east until you reach May Place.
(B) Head south to Brody Street, make a right onto Brody Street and continue to Dillon Boulevard, and then head north on Dillon Boulevard to Daniel Street where you make a right to May Place.
(C) Continue straight ahead to Brody Street, head east on Brody Street to Dillon Boulevard, and then head north to Daniel Street where you make a right to May Place.
(D) Head south on Christopher Boulevard to Irene Street, head east on Irene Street to Dillon Boulevard, and then head north on Dillon Boulevard to Daniel Street where you head east to May Place.

92. While you are in your patrol car, legally parked facing the Joseph Houses at the intersection of Jay Street and Christopher Boulevard, you are directed to respond to a past larceny at Irene Street and Dillon Boulevard. Which of the following is the most direct route for you to take in your patrol car, making sure to obey all of the traffic regulations?

(A) Turn south and continue on Christopher Boulevard to Brody Street, head east on Brody Street to Dillon Boulevard, and then head south on Dillon Boulevard to Irene Street.

(B) Turn north and continue on Christopher Boulevard to Beach Street, head east on Beach Street to Dillon Boulevard, and then head south on Dillon Boulevard to Irene Street.

(C) Turn south and continue on Christopher Boulevard to Irene Street; then head east on Irene Street to Dillon Boulevard.

(D) Turn south and continue on Christopher Boulevard to Brody Street; then make a right and continue to Dillon Boulevard where you should make another right to Irene Street.

93. While at Tom Place and Beach Street, you are directed to respond to the Joseph Houses. Which of the following is the most direct route for you to take in your patrol car, making sure to obey all of the traffic regulations?

(A) Head west on Beach Street to Christopher Boulevard; then head south on Christopher Boulevard to the Joseph Houses.

(B) Head east on Beach Street to Dillon Boulevard, head south on Dillon Boulevard to Jay Street, and then head west on Jay Street to the Joseph Houses.

(C) Make a left onto Beach Street and head east to Dillon Boulevard, go south on Dillon Boulevard to Gleason Street, head west on Gleason Street to Christopher Boulevard, and then head north on Christopher Boulevard to the Joseph Houses.

(D) Head east on Beach Street to Dillon Boulevard, head south on Dillon Boulevard to Irene Street, and then head west on Irene Street to Christopher Boulevard and then head north on Christopher Boulevard to the Joseph Houses.

94. If you were traveling in your patrol car on May Place and arrived at Brody Street, which of the following actions would be permitted according to the traffic regulations?
(A) head north
(B) make a right
(C) head directly south for another two blocks
(D) make a left

DIRECTIONS: Answer questions 95–100 on the basis of the following sketches. The model face, the one appearing above the dotted line, is a sketch of a person who is wanted. Of the four comparison faces, the ones appearing below the dotted line, one of them is the way the model face looked after changing appearance. You are to assume that no surgical alteration of the wanted person's face has occurred. You are to select the face that is most likely that of the wanted person.

95.

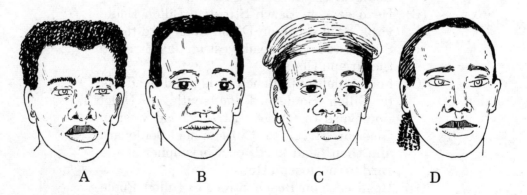

A   B   C   D

96.

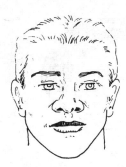

A   B   C   D

97.

A   B   C   D

98.

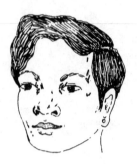

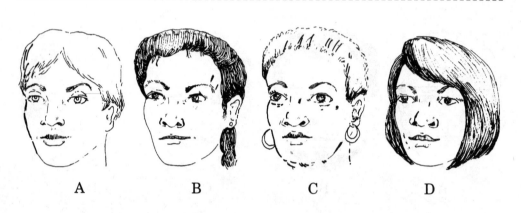

A   B   C   D

99.

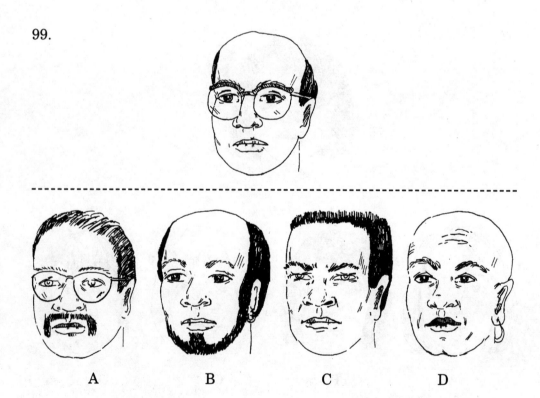

A   B   C   D

100.

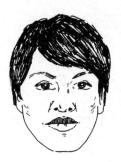

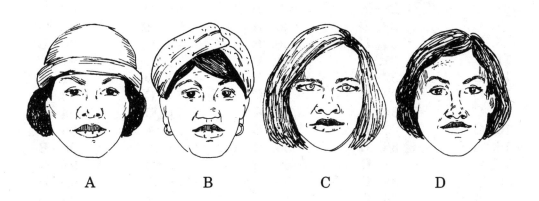

A   B   C   D

ANSWER KEY

1. C	21. D	41. B	61. C	81. C
2. A	22. C	42. C	62. B	82. D
3. D	23. C	43. C	63. B	83. D
4. C	24. D	44. B	64. C	84. C
5. A	25. A	45. C	65. C	85. B
6. A	26. C	46. A	66. C	86. D
7. B	27. B	47. C	67. A	87. B
8. C	28. B	48. B	68. D	88. B
9. C	29. D	49. A	69. A	89. B
10. B	30. C	50. B	70. C	90. B
11. C	31. D	51. D	71. C	91. C
12. B	32. D	52. D	72. D	92. A
13. C	33. C	53. C	73. D	93. D
14. C	34. A	54. C	74. C	94. D
15. C	35. D	55. B	75. A	95. C
16. A	36. D	56. B	76. A	96. B
17. C	37. C	57. B	77. B	97. C
18. D	38. C	58. D	78. A	98. D
19. B	39. C	59. C	79. B	99. B
20. B	40. B	60. B	80. B	100. A

Diagnostic Chart

INSTRUCTIONS: After you score your test, complete the following chart by inserting in the column captioned "Your Number Correct" the number of questions you answered correctly in each of the ten sections of the test. Then compare your score in each section with the ratings in the column captioned "Scale." Finally, to correct your weaknesses follow the instructions found after the chart.

SECTION	QUESTION NUMBER	AREA	YOUR NUMBER CORRECT	SCALE
1	1–8	Memory (8 questions)		8 Right—Excellent 6–7 Right—Good 5 Right—Fair Under 5 Right—Poor
2	9–28	Reading Comprehension (20 questions)		20 Right—Excellent 18–19 Right—Good 16–17 Right—Fair Under 16 Right—Poor
3	29–48	Applying State Police Procedures (20 questions)		20 Right—Excellent 18–19 Right—Good 16–17 Right—Fair Under 16 Right—Poor
4	49–57	Verbal and Math (9 questions)		9 Right—Excellent 7–8 Right—Good 6 Right—Fair Under 6 Right—Poor
5	58–65	State Police Forms (8 questions)		8 Right—Excellent 6–7 Right—Good 5 Right—Fair Under 5 Right—Poor
6	66–73	Interpreting Data (8 questions)		8 Right—Excellent 6–7 Right—Good 5 Right—Fair Under 5 Right—Poor
7	74–81	Judgment and Reasoning (8 questions)		8 Right—Excellent 6–7 Right—Good 5 Right—Fair Under 5 Right—Poor
8	82–89	Legal Definitions (8 questions)		8 Right—Excellent 6–7 Right—Good 5 Right—Fair Under 5 Right—Poor
9	90–94	Traffic Directions (5 questions)		5 Right—Excellent 4 Right—Good 3 Right—Fair Under 3 Right—Poor
10	95–100	Matching Sketches (6 questions)		6 Right—Excellent 5 Right—Good 4 Right—Fair Under 4 Right—Poor

How to correct weaknesses:

1. If you are weak in Section 1, concentrate on Chapter 6.
2. If you are weak in Section 2, concentrate on Chapter 4.
3. If you are weak in Section 3, concentrate on Chapter 9.
4. If you are weak in Section 4, concentrate on Chapter 5.
5. If you are weak in Section 5, concentrate on Chapter 7.
6. If you are weak in Section 6, concentrate on Chapter 8.
7. If you are weak in Section 7, concentrate on Chapter 10.
8. If you are weak in Section 8, concentrate on Chapter 11.
9. If you are weak in Section 9, concentrate on Chapter 13.
10. If you are weak in Section 10, concentrate on Chapter 12.

Note: Consider yourself weak in a section if you receive other than an excellent rating in it.

Answer Explanations

1. **C** Kelly carries firearms, Monchall carries explosives, and Kruger carries a switchblade knife. Please note that many wanted-poster questions involve comparisons among the various wanted persons.

2. **A** Kelly is a convicted murderer who escaped from State Prison.

3. **D** Kruger is 250 pounds. None of the others are even 200 pounds. Note that the difference in weight involved is not a slight one. When differences in physical appearance are the subject of the question, the differences are usually pronounced ones.

4. **C** Josephine Aponte is the only wanted person over 50 years of age. Please note that such things as weight and age are good question areas since physical descriptions often lead to the capture of wanted persons.

5. **A** Kelly has blue eyes. The other three have brown eyes.

6. **A** Kruger is an expert knife fighter who is usually armed with a switchblade knife.

7. **B** Monchall is an international terrorist who is known to carry explosives on his person.

8. **C** Aponte is an acknowledged tax expert and specializes in schemes to defraud the government.

9. **C** Smith was first observed by Trooper Role at 8:30 P.M. The robbery happened 15 minutes prior to that time. Time is often the subject of a question when the passage is a narrative of a police incident. Quite often the times are not given directly in the question, as in this case. A point of reference time (like the time of observation in this question) is given, and the test taker must determine

times from that point of reference. This series of questions emphasizes the determination of time from a point of reference.

10. **B** This is a typical trick question. Many untrained students will select choice A as the answer because the story centers around the robbery. But, the passage clearly states that the stop was made because Smith was acting suspiciously. It was after the stop that the trooper made the connection between the suspect and the robbery of Mr. Ash.

11. **C** The stop was made exactly 10 minutes after the trooper initially observed the suspect, which was at 8:30 P.M. That was the point of reference time. At 8:40 P.M., or 10 minutes after the point of reference time, the stop was made.

12. **B** The trooper noticed the bulge as he was listening to the suspect identify himself.

13. **C** According to the passage, a further search of the prisoner yielded a yellow pay envelope, which contained $75 in cash. At that point the trooper informed Mr. Smith that he was also being charged with robbery.

14. **C** The arrest was made at 8:50 P.M.; 20 minutes later they were at headquarters; and 30 minutes after that the notification was made. Therefore, the notification was made at 9:40 P.M.

15. **C** Choice D is wrong because it talks of evidence of any kind; the passage limits evidence to that which could be destroyed.

16. **A** Myers is never specifically designated in the paragraph as a male, but in the last paragraph the masculine form of pronouns is used when referring to Myers. This question emphasizes the importance of concentration when taking test questions.

17. **C** The Trial Court and the Appellate Division Court ruled against Myers when they held that the search of the jacket was constitutional. The Court of Appeals reversed both courts and held that the cocaine was unconstitutionally obtained.

18. **D** The passage does not make it clear who owned the cocaine. Just because it was Myers who went to trial does not prove anything about ownership of the cocaine. Remember that all four individuals were arrested for possession of the cocaine.

19. **B** It was made clear in the last sentence of the passage that the Court of Appeals felt that once the defendant Myers was arrested and removed from the vehicle, he was incapable, as were his confederates, of reentering the vehicle to attempt to obtain a weapon or destroy evidence.

20. B The whole matter began when the car Myers was traveling in was stopped for speeding.

21. D After the occupants were out of the car, the marijuana was found, and the arrests were made.

22. C While standing on the southeast corner of Court Street and 3rd Avenue, the trooper heard a scream. This means, of course, that the trooper was at the intersection of Court Street and 3rd Avenue. The exact same language used in the passage does not have to appear in the choices.

23. C Note the similarity between choices A and C. To be successful, you must maintain a high level of concentration throughout the entire examination.

24. D Troopers Jones and Brown arrived at the building at 1:35 P.M., but Trooper Smith did not join them until 1:55 P.M.

25. A The injured woman who went to the hospital, Ms. Cramdon, identified herself to the trooper as the manager of the Administration Building.

26. C Although Ms. Martin arrived for work at 2:10 P.M., she was 10 minutes late. Her shift started at 2:00 P.M.

27. B Ms. Martin told the troopers that Administrative Assistant Connors kept the equipment list.

28. B According to the rule, requests must be in writing, and they can be made directly to the superintendent, or they may be sent through official channels (up the chain of command). Nothing in the rule mentions the reason for the request. Even though C is a logical answer, it is not supported in the rule.

29. D The nature of offense, the weather conditions, and the time of day are all to be considered according to the procedure. The year, make, and model of the pursued vehicle is not mentioned in the procedure upon which the instructions clearly direct that the answer must be based.

30. C As the procedure states, constant use of the siren makes radio transmissions difficult to hear and also makes it difficult to hear other civilian and emergency vehicles that may be in the area.

31. D Advising the radio dispatcher of the suspected destination of the pursued vehicle is not mentioned in the procedure.

32. D A candidate should always pay close attention to numbers when they appear in a procedure.

33. C Setting up roadblocks of pursued vehicles are permissible if specifically directed by supervisory personnel. The other actions are what we refer to as absolutes. When you are scanning a procedure, pay particular attention to absolutes. They often become the focus of a procedures type question.

34. A Unmarked highway patrol vehicles will limit pursuits. The statements found in choices B, C, and D can be found in the procedure.

35. D Choices A, B, and C are strictly made up. Only choice D may be found in the procedure.

36. D The information required regarding vehicle occupants is in connection with the pursued vehicle, not the highway patrol vehicle.

37. C Whenever notifications are part of a procedure, you should pay particular attention to that part of a procedure, especially when they are joined to time requirements.

38. C Any trooper who discovers an airport operating without a license should verbally notify the patrol supervisor and notify the post commander in writing.

39. C The procedure indicated that certain steps must be taken in a certain order. When you see that in a procedure, it is highly probable that you will be asked a question about the order of the steps a trooper or highway patrol officer has taken. In this question, the trooper should do as indicated by choice C because the stem of the question tells you that the fire is difficult to see from the street.

40. B The trooper should notify the radio dispatcher and request the detectives.

41. B One of the Trooper Activity Log entries is whether the fire was suspicious, and that information is to be obtained from the fire officer in charge.

42. C In order for a prison van to be allowed to pass through fire lines at the scene of a fire, the prison van must be transporting prisoners.

43. C The trooper is required to prepare a Complaint Report if the fire is suspicious.

44. B A trooper is required to notify the operations unit and the division command if there are three, not just two, alarms of fire.

45. C Persons holding unexpired working press cards are permitted to pass through fire lines. The use of the word any in choice C should have alerted you to look extra carefully at that choice.

46. **A** If possible, permission must be obtained from the patrol supervisor.

47. **C** The information contained in choices A, B, and D would be required, but the information suggested in choice C is not required by the procedure.

48. **B** The procedure requires that the passenger compartment be searched by the trooper at the end of the trip.

49. **A** Choice B should state, ". . . your own problems." Choice C should state, ". . . quite well," and choice A is correctly stated.

50. **B** *Stationary* means placed in a fixed position, whereas *stationery* means writing supplies such as envelopes and writing paper. Choices A and C are therefore incorrect. Choice B is stated correctly.

51. **D** All the choices contain incorrect statements. Choices A and B are incorrect because compound words are not made plural by adding the letter *s* to the end of the word. They are made plural by adding the *s* to the first word making up the compound word. For example, *passers-by* and *fathers-in-law* would be correct plurals. Choice C is incorrect because *anyone* indicates one person, but more than one person is indicated by the word *they*.

52. **D** All are accurately and clearly written. Choice A is correct because *immigrate* means to enter a country. Choice B is correct because *emigrate* means to leave the country in which you are presently. Because *imply* means to hint, choice C is also correct.

53. **C** Choice A is incorrect because *accelerate* means to speed up. Clearly the intent here was to communicate that the exercise stimulated or *exhilarated* the trooper. Choice B is incorrect because *loose,* which means not firm, was used; use *lose,* which means to fail to win. Choice C is correct because the word *lay* was properly used to show resting by the trooper in the past.

54. **C** First find out how many ¼ inches there are in 3½ inches. To do this, divide 3½ by ¼, which can be expressed as

$$\frac{3\frac{1}{2}}{\frac{1}{4}}$$

or expressing 3½ as an improper fraction

$$\frac{\frac{7}{2}}{\frac{1}{4}}$$

To divide, invert the number on the bottom of the fraction and multiply. Thus we get

$$\frac{7}{2} \times \frac{4}{1} = \frac{28}{2} = 14.$$

If there are fourteen ¼-inch segments in a distance of 3½ inches and each ¼ inch represents an actual distance of 10 miles, simply multiply 14 times 10 miles to arrive at an actual distance between the two cities of 140 miles.

55. B The question actually asks how many groups of 21 are in the number 147, because said another way, each 21 miles traveled represents 1 gallon of gasoline used. Therefore, simply divide 147 by 21, which yields 7.

56. B The trooper states that he removed the following:

$$
\begin{aligned}
1 \times 50 &= \$50.00 \\
2 \times 20 &= 40.00 \\
1 \times 5 &= 5.00 \\
3 \times 0.25 &= 0.75 \\
17 \times 0.05 &= \underline{.85} \\
&\quad \$96.60
\end{aligned}
$$

The difference between $100.00 and 96.60 is $3.40.

57. B The complainant reported that the following items were stolen:

cash	$280.00
tape recorder	$400.00
three dolls appraised at $188 (3 × 188)	$564.00
fur coat valued at	$2,850.00
	$4,094.00

Choice A is incorrect because it accounts for only one doll being stolen. Choice C incorrectly reflects the cash stolen as $208 instead of the reported amount of $280. Choice D would be selected if the value of the fur coat was incorrectly added as $2815 instead of $2850. In this type of question, you must take care to ensure that you add the right amounts to arrive at the correct answer.

58. D The aided was treated by Dr. Marris. By now it should be clear that quickly reviewing the stem of the question before studying a completed form helps in identifying what information on the form should receive special attention.

59. C The details of the report indicate that Officer Rays made the arrest.

60. B The aided, Jeff Hall, lives with his sister and their telephone number according to the details of the report is 555-0009.

61. **C** Numbers are a favorite area for examiners to ask questions about when dealing with forms.

62. **B** The aided is the person who received assistance from the Highway Patrol Officer. That person is Jeff Hall who lives at 51-37 Sun Avenue, Apartment 3E.

63. **B** Luis Parkers is a visitor to the area, as is Jeff Hall. None of the other choices can be documented by the form. Remember to base your answers solely on the basis of the information recorded on the Aided Report.

64. **C** If you scanned the stems of the questions before studying the form, you should have focused on 3232, the arrest number.

65. **C** The command of the Highway Patrol Officer who reported the incident is the Waters Division. But the command of Officer Rays, the arresting officer, was never mentioned. Do not assume. When answering forms questions, base your answers only on what you can document.

66. **C** To answer this whole series of questions correctly, you had to recognize that the scale used on the *Y*-axis was different. Each mark on the left *Y*-axis represented 200 arrests, but each mark on the right *Y*-axis represented 100 convictions. In 1995 there were approximately 800 arrests; in 1996 and 1997 there were approximately 1400 arrests.

67. **A** In 1995 there were about 500 convictions and 800 arrests. By dividing 500 into 800 it is determined that there were about 1.6 arrests for every conviction. Choice C is wrong because it shows the ratio of arrests to convictions. The question asked for the ratio of convictions to arrests.

68. **D** In 1997 there were about 950 convictions (each increment equals 100 convictions). In 1995 there were about 800 arrests (each increment equals 200 arrests).

69. **A** In 1997 there were about 950 convictions and 1,400 arrests. That means that in 1998 there are about 1,000 convictions (an increase of 50) and 2,000 arrests (an increase of 600). By dividing 1,000 convictions into 2,000 arrests, you can determine that in 1998 the ratio of convictions to arrests is 1 to 2.

70. **C** In 1995 there were about 800 arrests. In 1997 there were about 1,400 arrests. The number of arrests increased by 600. As explained in a later chapter, by dividing 800 into 600 it is determined that the percentage increase was about 75%.

71. **C** During the time periods stated, arrests remained at about the 1,400 level while convictions went up to about 950.

72. **D** Questions 72 and 73 are asked to make you aware of the limitations of graphs. Graphs can show only approximate numbers and are used primarily to show trends. Tables are used to show specific numbers. You must understand that you cannot obtain specific data from graphs.

73. **D** There is no way that you could determine the answer to this question from the data shown. The word in the question that should have alerted you to this fact is *exactly*.

74. **C** Remember that fire is a threat to many people. The fire makes the entire area a dangerous one. Evacuation should take place. The situation described in choice B is unquestionably a dangerous condition but would not require evacuation. Make sure that you understand the rule before you answer the question.

75. **A** *Profuse* means a lot. Significant loss of blood always amounts to a life-threatening situation.

76. **A** Included, of course, in information about a car is the vehicle's plate number, which is of tremendous value when attempting to identify criminals who use automobiles.

77. **B** In police work, cooperation among troopers (teamwork) is essential. Aggressiveness and rigidity are not characteristics of teamwork.

78. **A** The word *omnipresence* means always present. Troopers on patrol create this feeling by passing the same location frequently but on an irregular basis. You must remember that preventive patrol should NOT be predictable; it must be unpredictable to be effective.

79. **B** Unconsciousness should always be treated as a serious matter. Note that, according to the rule, the age or status of a person is not a factor to consider.

80. **B** The allegation in choice B does not relate to the business of the state police but to the business of the courts.

81. **C** Once it is established that a trooper had a motorist's wallet in his/her possession, it is easy to claim that the trooper removed property from the wallet.

82. **D** The most serious felonies, which receive the most severe penalties, are A felonies, followed by B felonies, and so on. Therefore, of the choices given, a Class D felony would receive the least severe penalty.

83. D   An offense can be either a felony, a misdemeanor, or a violation.

84. C   The punishment for a misdemeanor is less than a felony and more than a violation; so choices A and B are incorrect. Choice D sounds good, but you are to base your answers solely on the legal definitions that were given. Choice C is correct because a crime is always either a felony or a misdemeanor.

85. B   Only misdemeanors and felonies are crimes; a violation does not have a minimum punishment stated in its definition, and the definition of a felony does not state a maximum punishment. The correct choice is B because all three are considered offenses.

86. D   Every loaded gun is not necessarily a deadly weapon. It must also be operable. Every operable gun is not necessarily a deadly weapon. It must also be loaded. A dagger is mentioned in the definition of deadly weapon. A razor is not.

87. B   A vehicle is never a deadly weapon; however, when it is used to cause serious physical injury, it would be considered a dangerous instrument.

88. B   Either substantial pain or physical impairment must occur for a physical injury to have taken place. Thus choice B is correct, and choice D is incorrect. Note the importance of the word *or*. Choice A is incorrect because there must be more than just substantial pain for a serious physical injury to have taken place. Choice C is not found anywhere in the definitions.

89. B   A dangerous instrument is any article that, depending on how it is used, attempted to be used, or threatened to be used, is capable of causing death or serious physical injury. If this gun were operable, it still would not be a deadly weapon because it is unloaded.

90. B   When you turned right from Gleason Street, you would be heading north on Dillon Boulevard, which is a two-way street. After continuing straight ahead for three blocks, you would be at Beach Street, which is a one-way street heading east. Our suggestion for counting blocks is to count from one intersection to another. If you made a left turn at this point, you would be going west on Beach Street and as such heading against traffic.

91. C   Choice A can be eliminated because heading east on Daniel Street is blocked by Gateway Park, which prohibits thru traffic. Choice B is incorrect because making a right on Brody Street would have you heading west on Brody Street, which not only is an eastbound street but also would have you heading away from the required destination of Daniel Street and May Place. Choice D is incorrect because heading east on westbound Irene Street would be against the flow of traffic.

92. **A** Although choice A is the most appropriate, in this type of question you must examine all the choices. Following choice B will get you to the correct destination, but it is not as direct as following the directions given in choice A. Choice C is incorrect because it directs you to head east on Irene Street, which is a westbound street. Choice D is incorrect because it directs you to make a right at Brody Street after heading south on Christopher Boulevard. This would cause you to go against traffic on Brody Street as well as head off the map.

93. **D** Choice A is incorrect because you are required to head west on Beach Street, which is an eastbound street. Choice B and C are incorrect because they both require that you go through Gateway Park, an area that does not permit thru traffic.

94. **D** Under such circumstances the only action that would be in keeping with the traffic regulations would be to make a left and thus head east on Brody Street. Remember that when you are given directions that require you to make right or left turns or to head north, south, east, or west, you must imagine yourself in the driver's seat of the patrol car.

95. **C** The nose and eyes of choice A, the nose of choice B, and the eyes and nose of choice D leave choice C as the only possible answer.

96. **B** The chin line of choice A, the eyes and lips of choice C, and the eyes, nose, and lips of choice D leave choice B as the only possible answer.

97. **C** The nose of choices A and B and the lips and facial mark on the chin of choice D leave choice C as the only possible answer.

98. **D** The missing facial line on the cheek of choices A, B, and C leave choice D as the only possible answer. Also note the different nose and eyes of choice A, the different lips of choice B, and the different facial lines of choice C. These differences highlight the fact that there is often more than one reason for eliminating a particular choice. Remember, however, that all you need is one good reason. Do not eliminate a choice based on slight differences.

99. **B** The eyes of choices A and C and the lips of choice D leave choice B as the only possible answer.

100. **A** The nose of choice B, the eyes of choice C, and the nose of choice D leave choice A as the only possible answer.

CORRECT YOUR WEAKNESSES

CHAPTER 4

Reading Comprehension Questions

Reading comprehension questions are designed, as the name implies, to measure the candidate's ability to comprehend or understand written material. In effect, reading comprehension questions on a state trooper examination measure a candidate's ability to read and understand the type of written material that is used by state troopers and other state law enforcement officers in the performance of their everyday duties. For example, the written material could be a narrative or story about an incident, or it could be in the form of a rule or procedure that a state trooper is supposed to follow.

Reading comprehension questions appear on virtually all state trooper examinations, and they are usually the question type that accounts for the greatest number of questions. In addition, most of the other question types used also require good reading comprehension ability. Therefore, you should improve your reading comprehension skills through diligent practice and make certain that you master the strategy presented in this chapter for handling reading comprehension questions.

The Importance of Concentration

How often do you "read" something by looking at the words without concentrating on what they mean. This is the biggest roadblock to overcome if you want to become a good reader. Actually, letting your mind wander is not bad for light reading. However, for the kind of reading that is essential to master almost any examination, *you must learn how to concentrate on the material totally*. One way to accomplish this task is to continuously ask yourself questions about what you are reading. Another way is to use your imagination and create mental impressions about what you are reading. Above all, don't let your mind wander! You must learn to concentrate exclusively on what you are reading.

A simple way to practice concentration is to read an article from the newspaper. As you read, have a pencil in your hand and underline or circle key points. After reading the article, write down the key points you remember; then return to the passage and see how well you did. You will become better with practice. Remember that the key to reading comprehension is *concentration*.

Increase Your Vocabulary

Concentration alone will not help if a reading passage contains a significant number of words that you don't understand. Therefore, follow these suggestions to increase your vocabulary.

1. When you read a word you don't fully understand, make a note of it along with a reminder of where you read it. Keep a special notebook for this purpose. It is especially important for you to jot down any word that you do not understand in this book because the words in this book are typical of the ones you will see on the official examination.

2. Look up the meaning of the word in the dictionary as soon as possible.

3. Return to the material where you read the word and make sure that you now understand its meaning and how it fits into the material.

4. Try to use the new words in your everyday conversation.

5. Review these words periodically until you have mastered them.

6. Ask a friend or another student to test you on the meanings of these words.

Strategies for Handling Reading Comprehension Questions

Please note that some students do not completely understand our recommended test-taking strategies until they practice using them. It is vital, therefore, that you study each strategy and then practice using it. Throughout this book we give you practice questions with explained answers. These explanations, when appropriate, include a review of the strategy you should have used. Our experience is that, with practice, our strategies result in candidates achieving a high degree of accuracy in a minimum amount of time. However, you must practice using the strategies to benefit from them. The strategy for reading comprehension questions is as follows.

1. **Read the instructions.** As mentioned previously, state trooper examinations contain general instructions at the beginning of the examination along with specific instructions preceding certain question types. Be sure to read all instructions carefully before doing the questions. When the instructions tell you to answer one or more questions based *solely* (or only) on the information contained in a reading passage, you should recognize the fact that you are dealing with a reading comprehension question.

2. **Use only that information contained in the passage to answer the questions.** You must understand that the answers to reading comprehension questions are contained in the written passage that comes before the questions. Do not introduce personal knowledge into a reading comprehension question. As the instructions state, the question is to be answered solely (or only) on the basis of the information contained in the written material that appears before the question(s).

3. **Read the stem of each question pertaining to the passage.** It is a mistake to read the passage first and then look at the choices. It's too time consuming. Instead, read the stem of each question before reading the passage. Also take a quick look at the choices. The stem of the question is the part of the question that comes before the choices. It tells you what information is needed to answer the question. When you use this strategy, you know what information you need to answer the question before you read the passage. This practice enables you to disregard unimportant information when you read the passage and saves you time.

4. **Read the passage carefully.** Because you already have read the question stems, you know what information you need to answer the

questions. The next step is to read the passage very carefully. As you come across the information needed to answer a question, circle that information. If necessary, stop reading periodically and refresh your memory concerning the information you are looking for by rereading the question stems. Once you have located the information needed to answer all the questions involved, you can quickly answer the questions.

5. **Answer the questions.** As mentioned previously, once you have located all the information needed to answer the questions, answer the questions. Simply use the information you located and circled in the passage and select the answer choice that contains that information.

Practice Exercises

It is now time for you to take some practice reading comprehension questions. Remember to use the recommended strategies when taking these questions. Also remember that the practice questions we use throughout this book have a high level of difficulty.

GROUP ONE
10 QUESTIONS—
TIME ALLOWED 20 MINUTES

Answer questions 1–3 solely on the basis of the following passage.

State Troopers Harris and Green, working an 8:00 A.M. to 4:00 P.M. shift at the Orange County State Fair, receive a call at 11:01 A.M. over their portable radio to investigate a theft from an automobile that was parked in the public parking lot on the southeast corner of Fairground Row and Fourth Street. Trooper Harris explains to his partner, Trooper Green, who is a newly appointed state trooper, that thefts from automobiles that are parked in the county fair's public parking lot are an ongoing problem that requires much of their attention. He tells Trooper Green that most of the thefts from the parking lot at Fairground Row and Fourth Street occur between 10:00 A.M. and 11:30 A.M. He adds that the time periods between 2:00 P.M. and 3:30 P.M. and between 7:00 P.M. and 9:00 P.M. are also times when many thefts occur. Trooper Harris then tells Trooper Green that most of the thefts from automobiles parked in the private parking lot for county fair employees, which is located at Fairground Row and Fourteenth Street, occur between 10:00 P.M. and 11:30 P.M.

Turning into the public parking lot at Fairground Row and Fourth Street, the troopers see a female waving to them. They park their patrol vehicle and approach the female. After identifying herself to the troopers as Gloria Swanson, she tells them that at 9:45 A.M. she parked her car and went to see the livestock contest at the fair. At 10:45 A.M., when she returned to her car, a brand new white Buick Riviera, she discovered that the right front vent window had been smashed and that her car radio had been stolen. She stated that the radio was worth $300. She stated that the thieves also stole $15 worth of tokens she had in her glove compartment. No other property was taken.

After obtaining the required information from Ms. Swanson, the troopers officially reported the theft, and at 11:22 A.M. they resumed their normal duties.

1. Most of the thefts from automobiles parked in the private parking lot for employees at Fairground Row and Fourteenth Street occur
   (A) between 10:00 A.M. and 11:30 A.M.
   (B) between 2:00 P.M. and 3:30 P.M.
   (C) between 7:00 P.M. and 9:00 P.M.
   (D) between 10:00 P.M. and 11:30 P.M.

A B C D
1 ||||||||

2. The property was stolen from Ms. Swanson's car
   (A) at 11:01 A.M.
   (B) before 9:45 A.M.
   (C) after 10:45 A.M.
   (D) sometime between 9:45 A.M. and 10:45 A.M.

A B C D
2 ||||||||

3. The total value of the property reported stolen from Ms. Swanson's car was
   (A) $300.
   (B) $15.
   (C) $315.
   (D) not given.

A B C D
3 ||||||||

Answer questions 4–7 solely on the basis of the following passage.

State vehicle and traffic laws outline the basic restrictions on owning and operating motor vehicles throughout the entire state. Counties, cities, and towns have the authority to enact local laws that are more restrictive than state law, but such laws do not have statewide applicability.

When enforcing vehicle and traffic laws, state troopers must always remember that the primary purpose of such laws is to protect life and property. A secondary purpose of vehicle and traffic laws is to promote the efficient use of public roadways and public parking areas. While the assessment of monetary fines is a necessary element of traffic law enforcement, the collection of revenue from such fines is not either a primary or a secondary goal of traffic law enforcement, nor should it be the sole responsibility of the state police.

Insofar as possible, all state troopers should engage in uniform enforcement of vehicle and traffic laws. This is not to say, however, that every traffic violation should be handled in exactly the same manner. It is not true that every violator should be given a traffic citation. State troopers have the authority on a case-by-case basis to exercise discretion when deciding how to best handle each traffic stop they make. However, all state police agencies should have written guidelines concerning the exercise of such discretion as well as a policy that requires troopers to know and follow those guidelines.

State troopers should always make a written record of each traffic stop they make. Such a written record must contain justification for the course of action that was taken to best handle that stop.

4. The primary purpose of vehicle and traffic laws is to
   (A) achieve efficient use of public roadways.
   (B) increase the availability of parking space.
   (C) protect life and property.
   (D) reduce traffic violations.

   A B C D
   4 || || || ||

5. The assessment of monetary fines is
   (A) a necessary element of traffic law enforcement.
   (B) a primary goal of traffic law enforcement.
   (C) a secondary goal of traffic law enforcement.
   (D) an exclusive responsibility of the state police.

   A B C D
   5 || || || ||

6. State troopers should
   (A) issue a traffic citation to every motorist they stop.
   (B) handle every traffic violation in exactly the same manner.
   (C) make a written record of every traffic stop they make.
   (D) stop every vehicle they observe in violation of the traffic laws.

   A B C D
   6 || || || ||

7. When deciding how to handle a traffic stop, a state trooper should
   (A) always consult a supervisor.
   (B) be required to follow written guidelines.
   (C) be free to apply their own guidelines.
   (D) never exercise judgment.

   A B C D
   7 || || || ||

Answer questions 8–10 solely on the basis of the following passage.

Auto thefts fall into three general categories. The first, often referred to as joyriding, is auto theft that is committed for the pleasure of the experience. The second is auto theft committed for transportation purposes, and the third and final category is auto theft that is committed for profit.

Most auto thefts are committed by joyriding teenagers. The teenagers who steal cars for joyriding purposes usually abandon the stolen cars within a few hours of the theft, and, in most cases, they abandon them in the vicinity where the cars were stolen. Although the rate of recovery of cars stolen for joyriding purposes is high, in many cases the recovered cars are damaged.

Auto thefts committed for transportation purposes usually involve transients, runaways, military personnel on leave, or criminals who use the vehicles while committing other crimes. Cars stolen for transportation purposes are generally abandoned far from where they were stolen when the thief reaches his or her destination or when the car runs out of gas. Quite often, the thief will steal another auto in the area where the first one was abandoned. Cars stolen for transportation purposes are seldom damaged.

Auto thefts that are committed for profit pose the greatest theft enforcement problem. Cars that are stolen for profit are seldom recovered. In most instances, they are dismantled in what is known as chop shops within hours of their being stolen. Auto thefts for profit have been fueled in recent years by the rising costs of auto parts. The thief who steals a car for profit poses a definite threat to the safety of the general motoring population.

Carjacking, or the use of force to steal a car when the owner is present, is the form of auto theft that causes the greatest number of injuries and deaths. Most carjackers are drug addicts who sell stolen vehicles at a fraction of their actual value.

8. Most automobile thieves are
   (A) teenagers.
   (B) drug addicts.
   (C) transients.
   (C) professional criminals.

   A B C D
   8 ||||||||

9. A stolen car is least likely to be damaged if it is stolen
   (A) by a joyrider.
   (B) for transportation purposes.
   (C) for profit.
   (D) by a teenager.

   A B C D
   9 ||||||||

10. Which of the following is the most accurate statement?
    (A) Most thieves who steal cars for transportation purposes are runaways.
    (B) Most carjackers are drug addicts.
    (C) Most cars stolen for profit are recovered.
    (D) Most cars stolen for transportation purposes are recovered in the area where they were stolen.

    A B C D
    10 ||||||||

GROUP TWO
10 QUESTIONS—
TIME ALLOWED 20 MINUTES

Answer questions 11–15 solely on the basis of the following paragraph.

On May 31st, at approximately 10:05 A.M., State Troopers May Smith, shield #314, and Pat Stone, shield #413, assigned to general patrol duty in car #7990, received a radio call to respond to a report of a burglary at 1492 Beach Avenue, apartment 128. The two troopers arrived at that location at 10:10 A.M. and were met by Mr. Don Green, a white male, date of birth 02/12/32. Mr. Green stated to the troopers that his apartment had been broken into and that some of his property had been stolen.

Mr. Green told Trooper Smith that he left his home at 8:30 A.M. that morning to do some food shopping. When he returned to his apartment at about 9:45 A.M., he observed that the cylinder to his apartment doorknob was removed. Mr. Green further stated that he did not go into his apartment at that time. Instead, he asked a neighbor, one Mike Short, to call the state police, which he did. After hearing Mr. Green's story, Troopers Smith and Stone entered apartment 128 and found the living room to be ransacked. Trooper Stone asked Mr. Green if he noticed any suspicious individuals in his building when he went shopping at 8:30 A.M. Mr. Green stated that he did not observe any suspicious persons at that time.

Trooper Smith then questioned some of the other tenants in Mr. Green's building. Those questioned were Ms. Aponte, an Hispanic female, age 30, who lives in apartment 126, and Mr. Bob Wolf, a black male, age 23, who lives in apartment 124. Trooper Smith asked both tenants if they observed or heard anything unusual that morning. Neither tenant had anything to report.

At 11:20 A.M., Trooper Green requested the dispatcher via his portable radio to have a trooper from the Crime Scene Unit respond to Mr. Green's apartment to search for fingerprints. Mr. Green was requested not to touch anything in the living room until the fingerprint search was completed. Mr. Green was also informed to inventory his property after the Crime Scene Unit completed their fingerprint search to determine what, if anything, was stolen.

Trooper Smith then completed Incident Report #1490 and at 11:40 A.M., the two troopers resumed patrol.

11. When was the radio call originally dispatched to car #7990?
(A) 8:30 A.M.
(B) 10:05 A.M.
(C) 9:45 A.M.
(D) 11:20 A.M.

A B C D
11 ||||||||

12. Who called the state police?
    (A) Mr. Green
    (B) Mr. Short
    (C) Ms. Aponte
    (D) Mr. Wolf

13. Mr. Green's date of birth is
    (A) 02/12/32.
    (B) 02/21/32.
    (C) 02/12/23.
    (D) 02/21/23.

14. Who lives in apartment #126?
    (A) Mr. Green
    (B) Ms. Aponte
    (C) Mr. Wolf
    (D) Mr. Short

15. How was Mr. Green's apartment apparently entered by the burglar?
    (A) through the door
    (B) through the window
    (C) through the ceiling
    (D) through the wall

Answer questions 16–20 based only on the information contained in the following passage.

There are times when the taking of photographs is a vital component of the effort to gather evidence when a crime has been committed. In other instances, the taking of photographs would be nothing more than a waste of time and effort. Therefore, whether or not to take photographs as part of the evidence-gathering process is a decision that is made by the crime scene investigator on a case-by-case basis.

When photography is used as part of the collection and care of evidence, photographs should be taken of each separate piece of evidence before it is examined by the trooper performing the crime scene search. Once the photograph has been taken, the trooper can then examine the piece of evidence involved.

Another very important responsibility of the trooper performing the crime scene search is to mark each piece of evidence. The standard method for marking evidence is for the trooper to place his initials, shield number, and the date of the examination on the article of evidence. When this cannot be done because of the size or nature of the evidence, the article of evidence is marked by being placed in an envelope or container that must then be tape sealed. The trooper involved should then write his name across the tape in such a way that any future opening of the envelope or container would be immediately apparent.

An unbroken and fully documented chain of custody for evidence that is to be used in court is a legal requirement. This means that there must be a witnessed, written record of all persons who had control over an article of evidence from the time it came into the custody of the state police until its introduction in court. If the chain of custody for an article of evidence is deemed by the court to be faulty, the article will be suppressed. That means that it will not be admissible as evidence.

Maintaining the chain of custody of evidence is but one task of an investigator who is responsible for the collection and care of evidence. Other such responsibilities include being able to identify each article of evidence even years after it was collected, being able to describe the condition of each article of evidence when it was initially located, and being able to state where each article of evidence was initially discovered.

16. When an article of evidence is going to be photographed, the photographs should be taken
   (A) before it is examined.
   (B) as soon as it is discovered.
   (C) after it is examined.
   (D) either before or after it is examined.

   A B C D
   16 || || || ||

17. The chain of custody for evidence that is going to be used in court
   (A) must be lengthy.
   (B) must be documented in writing.
   (C) does not have to be witnessed.
   (D) does not have to satisfy the court.

   A B C D
   17 || || || ||

18. If the court believes that an article of evidence has a faulty chain of custody, then
   (A) the article will not be admissible as evidence.
   (B) the trooper involved will be disciplined.
   (C) the defendant will be found not guilty.
   (D) the fault must be corrected.

   A B C D
   18 || || || ||

19. Every piece of evidence must be
   (A) initialed by the trooper involved.
   (B) marked.
   (C) placed in a sealed envelope.
   (D) photographed.

   A B C D
   19 || || || ||

20. There are times when taking photographs of evidence
   (A) is not legally permissible.
   (B) is a waste of time and effort.
   (C) is unconstitutional.
   (D) is prohibited by agency policy.

   A B C D
   20 || || || ||

GROUP THREE
10 QUESTIONS—
TIME ALLOWED 20 MINUTES

Answer Questions 21–26 based solely on the following information.

A person named Pat Stone was descending the front steps of his house as state troopers were about to execute a warrant to search the house for narcotics. The troopers requested his assistance in gaining entry to the house, and they detained him while they searched the premises. After finding narcotics in the basement and ascertaining that he owned the house, Stone was arrested and searched. The narcotic, heroin, was found in his coat pocket. Stone moved to suppress the heroin found on his person as the product of an illegal search in violation of the Fourth Amendment of the Constitution of the United States. This means that he wanted to prevent the police from using the heroin against him as evidence during his criminal trial. The trial court granted the motion and suppressed the heroin, and the State Appellate Court affirmed. The U.S. Supreme Court agreed to review the case and subsequently reversed the decision of both lower courts.

The Supreme Court, in its decision, noted that the initial detention constituted a seizure within the meaning of the Fourth Amendment. Stone was not free to leave the premises while the troopers were searching his home. The issue was whether the state police had the necessary authority to detain Stone while the search was being conducted.

In making its decision, the Supreme Court restated its often-used general rule that Fourth Amendment seizures are reasonable only if they are based on probable cause. Probable cause is defined as the level of information that has to be present in order for the police to arrest or otherwise detain suspects. However, the court recognized that there are exceptions to this general rule for limited intrusions that may be justified by special law enforcement interests. The Supreme Court stated:

> These cases recognize that some seizures admittedly covered by the Fourth Amendment constitute such limited intrusion on the security of those detained and are justified by such substantial law enforcement interests that they may be made on less than probable cause, as long as the police have an articulable basis for suspecting criminal activity.

In analyzing the character of the intrusion and its justification, the Court noted that the fact that the police had obtained a search warrant was of prime importance. Since the house search had already been authorized by the courts, the limited detention of one of the residents at the premises, while it was being searched, was not unreasonable.

The rule established by this case is that state troopers, when executing search warrants of premises, may detain occupants therein while the search is being conducted. Should the search of the premises uncover contraband that is illegally possessed property, the occupant in control of the premises can be arrested and charged with the possession of the contraband.

21. As a general rule, Fourth Amendment seizures are reasonable when
   (A) they are based on probable cause.
   (B) they are made on the authority of a warrant.
   (C) the safety of troopers is involved.
   (D) they are accomplished by a search.

   A B C D
   21 ‖ ‖ ‖ ‖

22. Who can be arrested if a house search pursuant to a warrant uncovers contraband?
   (A) only the owner of the house
   (B) the occupant in control of the house
   (C) everyone present in the house
   (D) no one present in the house

   A B C D
   22 ‖ ‖ ‖ ‖

23. Which of the following is the most accurate statement concerning the opinions of the various courts involved in this case?
   (A) The trial court was in agreement with the Appellate Court.
   (B) The U.S. Supreme Court was in agreement with the Appellate Court.
   (C) All the courts involved were in agreement.
   (D) None of the courts involved were in agreement.

   A B C D
   23 ‖ ‖ ‖ ‖

24. According to the facts in this case, narcotics were found
   (A) only in the basement of the house.
   (B) only in the defendant's pocket.
   (C) in the basement and in the house owner's pocket.
   (D) in at least three different locations.

   A B C D
   24 ‖ ‖ ‖ ‖

25. A factor that the Supreme Court found to be of extreme significance in this case was that
   (A) heroin was discovered.
   (B) Stone owned the house.
   (C) there are exceptions to all judicial rules.
   (D) the police had already obtained a search warrant.

   A B C D
   25 ‖ ‖ ‖ ‖

26. When evidence is suppressed by the courts then
    (A) it cannot be used at a criminal trial.
    (B) it has received the approval of the courts.
    (C) the defendant is always found not guilty.
    (D) that evidence has to be destroyed.

A B C D
26 |||||||

Answer question 27 based solely on the following rule.

A state trooper should not sleep while on duty. He or she shall not engage in games of chance of any kind while on duty. Except in the line of duty, he or she shall not bring cards or dice into a state police facility.

27. While working, a state trooper is sometimes permitted to
    (A) sleep.
    (B) play cards.
    (C) play dice.
    (D) bring a deck of cards into a state police facility.

A B C D
27 |||||||

Answer question 28 based solely on the following rule.

Personal telephone calls by on-duty state troopers, which are made without prior authorization, are prohibited.

28. According to the rule, state troopers
    (A) can never make personal telephone calls while on duty.
    (B) can always make personal telephone calls while on duty.
    (C) can make personal telephone calls while on duty if they obtain permission immediately after the call.
    (D) can make personal telephone calls while on duty if they obtain permission before making the call.

A B C D
28 |||||||

Answer question 29 based solely on the following rule.

State troopers, while in uniform, are not allowed to smoke while performing any duties that require them to be in contact with the general public. For the purpose of this rule, prisoners are not considered to be part of the general public.

29. State troopers
    (A) cannot smoke while on duty.
    (B) cannot smoke when processing arrested persons.
    (C) can sometimes smoke while in uniform.
    (D) can smoke anytime they want.

A B C D
29 ||||||||

Answer question 30 based solely on the following rule.

Off-duty state troopers have the option to carry their firearms or to leave their firearms in a safe and secure location at their residence or at their barracks. It is strongly suggested that off-duty troopers who are planning to consume alcoholic beverages do so while unarmed. When unarmed, troopers should not attempt to enforce the law.

30. Off-duty state troopers
    (A) must be armed at all times.
    (B) must leave their guns at work.
    (C) must be unarmed when consuming alcohol.
    (D) must be armed when enforcing the law.

A B C D
30 ||||||||

Answer Key and Explanations

ANSWER KEY

1. **D**	7. **B**	13. **A**	19. **B**	25. **D**
2. **D**	8. **A**	14. **B**	20. **B**	26. **A**
3. **C**	9. **B**	15. **A**	21. **A**	27. **D**
4. **C**	10. **B**	16. **A**	22. **B**	28. **D**
5. **A**	11. **B**	17. **B**	23. **A**	29. **C**
6. **C**	12. **B**	18. **A**	24. **C**	30. **D**

ANSWER EXPLANATIONS

GROUP ONE

NOTE: If you followed our recommended strategy, you should have recognized from the instructions—especially the use of the word *solely*—that you were taking reading comprehension questions. Then, for questions 1–3, you should have first read the stem of the three questions and understood that you needed the following information to answer the questions:

1. The time when most thefts occur from cars parked in the employee's parking lot, located at Fairground Row and Fourteenth Street.

2. The time when the theft from Ms. Swanson's car took place.

3. The total value of property stolen from Ms. Swanson's car.

Once you knew the three pieces of information you were looking for, you should have then read the passage. As you found the information needed to answer each of the three questions, you should have circled that information in the test booklet. Once you had located the information needed to answer all three questions, you should have immediately answered the questions.

1. **D**   If you selected choice A you picked the time when most thefts occur in the public parking lot at Fairground Row and Fourth Street. This is a common distractor used to confuse test takers. Make sure that you understand what information the question is asking for. In this case it was stated in the last sentence in the first paragraph that most thefts in the private parking lot for employee's occur between 10:00 P.M. and 11:30 P.M. Also note the numerical similarity between choices A and D. You must be careful when choosing answers.

2. **D**   Note that all the times listed in the choices appeared somewhere in the paragraph. But, since Ms. Swanson left her car at 9:45 A.M. and returned at 10:45 A.M., the theft occurred sometime between those two times as indicated in Choice D.

3. **C**   The key word in the question was the word *total*. Because the radio was worth $300 and the tokens were worth $15, and because no other property was taken, the total value of property stolen was $315.

4. **C**   Note that choices A and B are secondary purposes of vehicle and traffic laws. The key word in the question was the word *primary*. Also note that although choice D sounds good, it is not mentioned anywhere in the passage and, therefore, cannot be the answer.

5. **A** According to the passage, even though the assessment of monetary fines is a necessary element of traffic law enforcement, the collection of revenue from such fines is not either a primary or a secondary goal of traffic law enforcement, nor should it be the sole responsibility of the state police.

6. **C** Choices A and B are specifically contradicted in the passage. Choice D can't be correct because it is not mentioned in the passage.

7. **B** The passage clearly states that state police agencies should have written guidelines concerning the exercise of discretion and that each trooper should be required to know and apply these guidelines.

8. **A** The passage states that "most auto thefts are committed by joyriding teenagers." The fact that the answer left out the descriptive term *joyriding* does not change the fact that it is teenagers who commit most auto thefts.

9. **B** Cars stolen for transportation purposes are seldom damaged. Cars stolen by joyriders are often damaged, and those stolen for profit are often dismantled completely.

10. **B** The passage very clearly states that most carjackers are drug addicts.

GROUP TWO

NOTE: Remember that you should have looked at the questions before you read the passage to determine what information you needed to answer them. Then, as you found that information, you should have circled it in the passage.

11. **B** Whenever a story contains various times, you can be sure that time will be the subject of a question. In this case, the original call was dispatched at 10:05 A.M. Also note that the times stated in choices A, C, and D all appeared in the story.

12. **B** It was the neighbor, Mike Short, who called the state police.

13. **A** For careful students this is an easy question. But, the numbers in the wrong choices are so close to the answer that making a careless mistake is a distinct possibility. Be careful!

14. **B** Ms. Aponte lives in apartment 126. Once again, you should see that answering these question types can be easy if you are careful.

15. **A** When he returned after shopping, Mr. Green noticed that the cylinder to the knob of his apartment door was missing.

16. **A** A good test taker would recognize that the answer to this question must be either choice A or C because together they encompass all the possibilities. In this case, because the paragraph states that photographs should be taken of each separate piece of evidence before it is examined, the answer is choice A.

17. **B** The chain of custody must be written and witnessed, and it must satisfy the court. The answer is choice B. Note that the paragraph does not mention the length of the chain of custody, so choice A cannot be the answer.

18. **A** If the chain of custody for an article of evidence is deemed by the court to be faulty, the article will be suppressed. That means that it will not be admissible as evidence.

19. **B** One very important responsibility of the trooper performing the crime scene search is to mark each piece of evidence.

20. **B** The passage clearly states that in some instances the taking of photographs is nothing more than a waste of time and effort.

GROUP THREE

21. **A** In making its decision, the Supreme Court restated its often-used general rule that Fourth Amendment seizures are reasonable only if they are based on probable cause.

22. **B** Should the search of the premises uncover contraband that is illegally possessed property, the occupant in control of the premises can be arrested and charged with the possession of the contraband. Note that this person may or may not be the owner of the premises.

23. **A** In this case, the Trial Court and the Appellate Court agreed that the heroin should be suppressed. The Supreme Court disagreed with both of these lower courts and reversed their decision.

24. **C** This question could have been answered quickly and accurately if you followed our strategy of scanning the stems of the questions and the choices prior to reading the passage thoroughly.

25. **D** Being of prime importance and being of extreme significance are two ways of saying the same thing. Note once again the importance of a good vocabulary. We hope that you are looking up and learning the meaning of every word in these questions that you do not fully understand.

26. **A** Stone wanted the court to suppress the evidence against him, which was heroin. According to the passage, "this means that he wanted to prevent the police from using the heroin against him as

evidence during his criminal trial." Note that you are not responsible for having this kind of technical knowledge prior to taking your test. The information was in the passage. That is why it can be the basis of a question.

Please note that questions 27 through 30 are what we call rule interpretation questions. They are sometimes used as reading comprehension questions and sometimes classified as procedure questions.

27. **D** Bringing cards or dice into a state police facility is permitted in the line of duty.

28. **D** Prior authorization means getting permission ahead of time.

29. **C** The whole thrust of the rule is to regulate when troopers in uniform are allowed to smoke.

30. **D** When unarmed, troopers should not attempt to enforce the law. Therefore, they must be armed when enforcing the law.

CHAPTER 5 ▬▬▬▬▬▬▬

Verbal and Mathematical Ability Questions

▬▬▬▬▬▬▬▬▬▬▬▬▬▬▬▬▬▬▬

Verbal Skills

State troopers and highway patrol officers are called upon to communicate information clearly and accurately. Verbal ability is a talent that such officers must certainly possess. This talent must be especially demonstrated when they are called upon to clearly and accurately prepare reports. Report writing requires proper word usage.

For this reason, the ability to use words properly is often tested in state trooper and highway patrol officer entry-level examinations. The best way to test such word usage would be to have candidates actually write a report and then have the report examined and scored by a qualified expert examiner. However, because of the large number of candidates taking the examination, such a procedure would be unwieldy and too time-consuming. Also a large number of examiners would be needed, which, in addition to making the process expensive, would create the potential for a great deal of subjectivity caused by the large number of examiners who would be required.

Therefore, proper word usage, which is required to prepare reports clearly and accurately, is tested by presenting the candidate with written material and requiring the candidate to indicate if the material has been written clearly and accurately with proper word usage. The candidate makes such indications by answering multiple-choice questions about the written material. The belief is that if a candidate can recognize proper word usage then the candidate can use words properly to communicate information clearly and accurately.

The pages that follow highlight and review word usage often tested by examiners.

1. **Accelerate/Exhilarate**
   Accelerate means to speed up.
      Good study habits can accelerate learning.
   Exhilarate means to stimulate.
      Exercise can exhilarate the heart rate.

2. **Accept/Except**
   Accept means to take what is offered.
      I accept the promotion.
   Except means to exclude.
      The troopers excepted Don from their association.

3. **Adapt/Adopt**
   Adapt means to fit or adjust as needed.
      The new trooper adapted to barracks life.
   Adopt means to take as one's own.
      Because of his prior conviction for child abuse, John could not legally adopt a child.

4. **Affect/Effect**
   Affect as an action word or a verb means to influence something.
      The new law will affect all motorists.
   Effect as an action word or a verb means to produce a result.
      The new speed limit will effect a change in the number of injuries on the highway.

5. **All ready/Already**
   All ready means totally prepared.
      The troopers are all ready to execute the search warrant.
   Already means occurring before a specific time period.
      The trooper already had been instructed in the new law.

6. **All together/Altogether**
   All together means in a group.
      The highway patrol officers will sit all together during the ceremonies.
   Altogether means totally or wholly.
      It is altogether too dangerous to storm the farmhouse.

7. **Allusion/Illusion**
   Allusion means a casual mentioning or a hint.
      During his speech he made an allusion to the arrest of his opponent.

Illusion means a misleading appearance.

> She gave the illusion of being much taller.

8. **Among/Between**

Between is used when referring to two persons or two things.

> He was stabbed between his shoulder blades.

Among is used when referring to more than two people or more than two things.

> She stood out among the twenty academy students.

9. **Beside/Besides**

Beside means next to or at the side of.

> The dog stood beside the trooper.

Besides means in addition to.

> No one entered the location besides the suspect.

10. **Casual/Causal**

Casual means by chance or informal.

> Her dress was very casual.

Causal means caused by a certain action.

> There was a causal connection between her heart attack and the fight with her son.

11. **Complement/Compliment**

Complement means to make complete.

> His personality really complements hers.

Compliment means to praise someone.

> He saw her remarks as a great compliment to him.

12. **Council/Counsel**

Council means an advisory or legislative body.

> The council met last week.

Counsel means advice.

> He provided me with excellent counsel.

13. **Envelop/Envelope**

Envelop means to surround.

> The mother could not wait to envelop her baby in her arms.

Envelope means a container for a letter or similar document.

> The motorist put the summons in an envelope.

14. **Formally/Formerly**

Formally means to do something according to a rule.

> He formally retired from the department.

Formerly refers to something that occurred in the past.

> She was formerly a state trooper.

15. **Good/Well**

Good is an adjective and as such usually modifies or describes names of persons, places, or things.

Because the trooper had a good arrest record, she was given a choice assignment.

Well is an adverb and as such usually modifies or describes action words or verbs or adjectives or other adverbs.

Because he writes well, he also speaks well.

16. **I/Me**

I should be used when the intent is to describe the doer of an action.

I wanted to be a highway patrol officer as soon as I learned about the job.

Me should be used when the intent is to describe the receiver of an action.

After chasing me through traffic, the trooper arrested me.

17. **Imply/Infer**

Imply means to suggest or hint.

The witness tried to imply to the trooper that he was tired.

Infer means to conclude by reasoning.

Because of the clues, the officer was able to infer who committed the crime.

18. **In/Into**

In means a location, place, or situation.

The highway patrol officer sat in his car.

Into means movement toward a place.

The trooper ran into the burning barn.

19. **Its/It's**

Its means possession.

The barracks has maintained its bright appearance.

It's means it is.

It's too risky to rush the robber.

20. **Later/Latter**

Later means that something is more late in time.

Troopers Roe and Wall were both late, but Officer Wall arrived later.

Latter means the second of two things that were mentioned.

I like May and June, but I prefer the latter.

21. **Lie/Lay**

Lie means to recline.

I like to lie in the shade.

Lay means to put or place something.

Lay your guns on the ground.

Note: The problem with *lie* and *lay* arises when different time frames are involved with the use of these two words. For example, concerning the word *lie* meaning to recline:

In the present tense:

To lie or lie—I lie down when I'm sleepy.

In the past tense:
Lay—I lay down last night.
Using the past participle with words like *have* or *has:*
Lain—When tired, I have lain down on the bed.
Concerning the word *lay* meaning to put or place something:
In the present tense:
To lay or lay—Lay down your guns right now.
In the past tense:
Laid—The suspects laid down their weapons.
Using the past participle with words like *have* or *has:*
Laid—The suspect has agreed and has laid down his gun.

22. **Learn/Teach**
Learn means to get knowledge
   I learn something every time I attend roll call training.
Teach means to give knowledge.
   My supervisor teaches me something every time he conducts roll call training.

23. **Loose/Lose**
Loose means not tight or not firm.
   Because the handcuffs were loose, the prisoner escaped.
Lose means to fail to win or keep.
   If you don't keep your prisoner properly handcuffed, you could lose your prisoner.

24. **Moral/Morale**
Moral means good or virtuous conduct.
   Returning the old lady's purse was a very moral act.
Morale means spirit or the mood of an individual or an organization.
   The morale among the highway patrol officers was high.

25. **Practical/Practicable**
Practical means useful, workable, sensible, not theoretical.
   Keeping a spare set of keys to the patrol car is a practical idea.
Practicable means that something is possible or feasible. It is capable of being put into practice.
   The plan to execute the search warrant was practicable.

26. **Principal/Principle**
Principal means the main idea or chief person.
   The principal result of the increased patrol should be a safer environment.
Principle means a basic truth or rule.
   It is an accepted principle that criminals desire to commit crime.

27. **Their/They're/There**
Their shows possession relating to the word *they.*
   They sat in their barracks.

They're means they are.

They're very tired.

There means a location.

The officers never searched there.

28. **To/Too/Two**

To means in a certain direction.

The trooper went to the house.

Too means also or more than.

Trooper Marks wanted to go too, but it was too late.

Two is a number.

There are two troopers in a patrol car.

29. **Whose/Who's**

Whose shows possession relating to the word *who*.

The trooper could not identify whose voice he had heard.

Who's means who is.

Who's going to search the kitchen?

30. **Your/You're**

Your shows possession relating to the word *you*.

You had better bring your weapon.

You're means you are.

You're under arrest.

In addition to the areas of word usage explained here, there are practice exercises toward the end of the chapter. These exercises along with the practice tests found in this book also will address even more areas of word usage commonly tested by examiners.

Math Skills

State troopers and highway patrol officers use basic math skills such as adding, subtracting, multiplying and dividing in their everyday duties. These officers are also called upon to use these skills in working with fractions and decimals to determine averages, ratios, and percentage increases and decreases. Examiners who prepare entry-level state trooper and highway patrol officer examinations recognize the need for such skills and often include questions that test these skills. To quickly and accurately answer these types of questions, which appear on these entry-level examinations, a candidate must develop and practice such skills. Let's review these basic skills.

ADDITION

Addition is finding the sum of numbers, and it requires two specific actions.

1. Properly line up or align the numbers to be added.

   EXAMPLE:

Add 837.68, 47, 4922.7, and 8.039.
Remember that, when aligning numbers, 47 is the same as 47.000. So make sure that decimal points are correctly lined up. When properly aligned the numbers look like this:

$$837.680$$
$$47.000$$
$$4922.700$$
$$8.039$$

Adding from the top down we get $\overline{5815.419}$

2. After you find the sum, in this case 5815.419, check the answer by adding again but this time from the bottom to the top.

SUBTRACTION

Subtraction is finding the difference between two numbers. It requires two specific actions.

1. Use the decimal point to properly align the numbers.

   EXAMPLE:

Subtract 876.9 from 1289.42.
Remember that 876.9 is the same as 876.90. When properly aligned the numbers look like this:

$$1289.42$$
$$-876.90$$
$$\overline{412.52}$$

2. Check your subtraction by adding. To do this, add your answer 412.52 to the bottom number in your subtraction 876.90 and the sum should be 1289.42.

MULTIPLICATION

Multiplication is adding a number to itself several times. For example, $4 \times 3 = 12$ is the same as adding $4 + 4 + 4 = 12$ or $3 + 3 + 3 + 3 = 12$.

The two specific actions required by multiplication follow.

1. Align the products as you arrive at them.

2. If there are decimals in the numbers you are multiplying, add up the number of places to the decimal point from right to left and then count off an equal number in the answer from right to left and insert a decimal point there.

EXAMPLE:

Multiply 86.2×196.47.

$$
\begin{array}{r}
196.47 \\
\times\, 86.2 \\
\hline
39294 \\
117882 \\
157176 \\
\hline
16935714
\end{array}
$$

Note how each of the numbers being multiplied were aligned. Now count in both numbers being multiplied, from right to left, the total number of places to the decimal point. The total number of places to the decimal point is three. Next count three places from right to left in the final product and insert a decimal in this final product. Thus the number 16935714, becomes 16935.714, our answer.

To check a multiplication answer, divide the final product by one of the numbers used in the multiplication, and you should get the other number originally used in the multiplication. For example, $9 \times 4 = 36$. To check the multiplication divide 36 by 4 and you get 9.

DIVISION

Division is separating a number into a certain number of equal parts. The statement 30 divided by 5 is the same as asking how many equal parts consisting of 5 are there in 30? The answer would be 6.

The two specific actions required by division follow.

1. Make sure that you are dividing by the right number. When asked to divide 144 by 12 that means you must divide 12 into 144. The question is asking how many equal parts of 12 are in 144.

2. If the number you are dividing by has a decimal in it such as 18.37, you must first move the decimal point as many places to the right as possible. That number now becomes 1837. If the number you are dividing into is, for example, 238.81, then you must move the decimal in the number you are dividing into an equal number of places to the right. When you divide 1837 into 23881, the answer is 13.

To check a division problem, simply multiply the answer by the number you divided by. If you divided correctly, you will get the number you divided into. For example, 36 divided by 3 is 12. To check it, multiply 12×3, and you get 36.

FINDING AVERAGES

To find an average number of a group of numbers:

1. Find the sum of all the items in the group.

2. Divide by the number of items in the group.

EXAMPLE:

The weights in pounds of all the prisoners in the state police van are 178, 196, 231, 242, and 143. What is the average weight of the prisoners? Add 178, 196, 231, 242, and 143; the sum is 990. Then divide by 5, the number of prisoners, to determine the average weight, which in this case is 198 pounds.

RATIOS

A ratio is a relationship between two numbers of the same kind. When expressing a ratio, take care to compare the same kind of items.

EXAMPLE:

To remove blood stains, 8 quarts of bleach were used along with 18 gallons of water. What is the ratio of bleach to water used to remove the blood stain?

To find the ratio or relationship between the same kind of items, the number of quarts must be converted to gallons so that we can compare gallons to gallons. After converting the 8 quarts to 2 gallons (there are 4 quarts to 1 gallon), we now have 2 gallons of bleach used for every 18 gallons of water. Expressed as a ratio, we would have the fraction $\frac{2}{18}$. Note that a ratio maintains its value if you multiply or divide both numbers in a ratio by the same number. In our ratio of $\frac{2}{18}$ if we divide both numbers in the ratio $\frac{2}{18}$ by 2, we get a ratio of $\frac{1}{9}$, which is the same value as $\frac{2}{18}$.

A kind of question involving ratios known as a proportion question is often asked by examiners.

EXAMPLE:

If 3 troopers must be assigned for every 50 demonstrators, how many troopers must be assigned for 200 demonstrators?

Immediately set up your ratios: 3 troopers are needed for 50 demonstrators as an unknown number of troopers are needed for 200 demonstrator, or

$$\frac{3}{50} = \frac{X}{200}$$

The solution calls for cross multiplying and dividing.

First cross multiply the $3 \times 200 = 600$.

Then cross multiply the $50 \times X = 50X$.

We now have the equation $50X = 600$.

We can divide by 50, as long as we do it to both sides of our equation.

$$\frac{50X}{50} = \frac{300}{50}$$

We are left with:

$$X = 6.$$

PERCENTAGE INCREASE OR PERCENTAGE DECREASE

Candidates are often asked to examine a situation that has occurred and correctly indicate what has been the percentage increase or decrease.

EXAMPLE:

Last year the number of state troopers who were injured was 150. This year 225 officers were injured. What was the percentage increase in the number of troopers who were injured?

1. Find the distance or space between the numbers being compared. In this case, it is $225 - 150 = 75$.

2. Divide the number you just calculated, in this case 75, by the older number (that is, the number that previously existed), in this case 150. So we now have $\frac{75}{150}$ or $\frac{1}{2}$, which is 50%.

The numbers increased from 150 to 225 so there has been a percentage increase of 50%. Remember that, in setting up this fraction, the denominator will always be the older number (that is, the number that previously existed).

FINDING PERCENTAGES

Occasionally examiners ask candidates to determine what percent one number is of another number. In answering this type of question, you should form a fraction. Just remember that the number that immediately follows the word *of* will be your denominator, or the number on the bottom, and the remaining number is the numerator, or the number on the top.

EXAMPLE:

What percent of 100 is 25?

The number that immediately follows the word *of* (that is 100) goes on the bottom and the other number (that is 25) goes on the top, $^{25}/_{100}$, which 0.25 or 25%.

At other times examiners ask candidates to simply find a percentage of a given number. In such an instance, immediately convert the percentage to a decimal and then multiply by that decimal.

EXAMPLE:

What is 43% of 105?

Convert the percentage to a decimal by moving the decimal point in the percentage two places to the left. Thus 43% becomes 0.43 as a decimal. Then multiply $0.43 \times 105 = 45.15$.

Practice Exercises

Try to answer the following practice questions in the time allotted. After answering all the questions in a group, turn to the answers and check your work. Also make sure to review the answer explanations to help you understand why you are correct or incorrect in your choice of answers.

GROUP ONE
10 QUESTIONS—
TIME ALLOWED 20 MINUTES

DIRECTIONS: In each of questions 1–10 you will be given four choices. Three of the choices, A, B, and C, contain a written statement. You are to evaluate the statement in each choice and select the statement that is most accurately and clearly written. If all or none of the three written statements is accurately and clearly written, you are to select choice D.

1. According to the instructions, evaluate the following statements.
   (A) She was always interested in climactic discussions about the amount of snow in winter.
   (B) The trooper had to device his own plan.
   (C) The ball hit both Bob and I.
   (D) All or none is accurate.

   A B C D
   1 ‖ ‖ ‖ ‖

2. According to the instructions, evaluate the following statements.
   (A) She to should make two trips.
   (B) The following list of items are to be carried by the trooper.
   (C) I never liked him singing.
   (D) All or none is accurate.

   A B C D
   2 ‖ ‖ ‖ ‖

3. According to the instructions, evaluate the following statements.
   (A) I hid the gun in my pocket that I intended to use on her.
   (B) After being arrested, the trooper put handcuffs on the prisoner.
   (C) I have seen that too many times.
   (D) All or none is accurate.

   A B C D
   3 ‖ ‖ ‖ ‖

4. According to the instructions, evaluate the following statements.
   (A) That lawyer hated to loose that case.
   (B) The trooper was not able to adopt to life in a barracks.
   (C) It's already too late to register your car.
   (D) All or none is accurate.

   A B C D
   4 ‖ ‖ ‖ ‖

5. According to the instructions, evaluate the following statements.
   (A) Its a different world on the road.
   (B) Golf and tennis are great, but I prefer the latter.
   (C) Their getting away.
   (D) All or none is accurate.

   A B C D
   5 ‖ ‖ ‖ ‖

6. According to the instructions, evaluate the following statements.
   (A) Trick photography can create an allusion.
   (B) The principal motive was greed.
   (C) Your being too stubborn.
   (D) All or none is accurate.

   A B C D
   6 ‖ ‖ ‖ ‖

7. According to the instructions, evaluate the following statements.
    (A) Keeping a daily log is a very practicable idea.
    (B) She likes to lie on a couch.
    (C) The captain disciplined her and I.
    (D) All or none is accurate.

    A B C D
    7 | | | | | | |

8. According to the instructions, evaluate the following statements.
    (A) Keep your advise to yourself.
    (B) He did it to her and myself.
    (C) My dad always helped me with his counsel.
    (D) All or none is accurate.

    A B C D
    8 | | | | | | |

9. According to the instructions, evaluate the following statements.
    (A) When you attend the firing range, your dress must be causal.
    (B) In connection with that robbery, no witnesses ever came fourth.
    (C) It's easy to hit a stationery target.
    (D) All or none is accurate.

    A B C D
    9 | | | | | | |

10. According to the instructions, evaluate the following statements.
    (A) I haven't never used one of those.
    (B) Drinking alcohol affects his driving.
    (C) The trooper was so overbearing in his directions that he actually became very official.
    (D) All or none is accurate.

    A B C D
    10 | | | | | | |

GROUP TWO
TEN QUESTIONS—
TIME ALLOWED 20 MINUTES

11. Trooper Ted Bars arrests Bob Wilson for burglary. During the arrest processing, he removes, counts, and vouchers $485. Sometime thereafter Wilson makes bail and is released after having his money returned. He is given two $50 bills, sixteen $20 bills, two $10 bills, and six $5 bills. In this instance the prisoner received

(A) exactly the same amount that Trooper Bars vouchered.

(B) $25 less than the amount that Trooper Bars vouchered.

(C) $15 less than the amount that Trooper Bars vouchered.

(D) $10 more than the amount that Trooper Bars vouchered.

A B C D
11 ||||||||

12. In addition to his other duties, Trooper Mark Rivers has performed nine crime prevention surveys in 6 months. Assuming a continuing similar workload and production level, how many crime prevention surveys could he do in 2 years?

(A) 3 surveys
(B) 16 surveys
(C) 27 surveys
(D) 36 surveys

A B C D
12 ||||||||

13. After many years of studying the relationship between the issuance of traffic summonses and vehicular accidents, it has become apparent that for every 75 summonses given, 1.5 accidents are prevented. Assuming a continuance of this relationship between the issuance of summonses and the prevention of vehicular accidents, how many summonses must be given to prevent 50 such accidents?

(A) 2000 summonses
(B) 2250 summonses
(C) 2500 summonses
(D) 3000 summonses

A B C D
13 ||||||||

14. The standard patrol car assigned to the highway patrol has a gas mileage of 23 miles per gallon of fuel. If the same standard patrol car has a fuel tank with a capacity of 22 gallons, how far can such a car travel on 2½ tanks full?
    (A) 1155 miles
    (B) 1265 miles
    (C) 1380 miles
    (D) 1435 miles

A B C D
14 ||||||||

15. The base pay for a clerical assistant working in the post command is $8.58 per hour with time and one half overtime pay for each hour worked in excess of 40 hours. If the clerical assistant worked and is paid for 48½ hours then the gross salary for this employee would be
    (A) exactly $450.
    (B) between $451 and $452.
    (C) between $452 and $453.
    (D) exactly $454.

A B C D
15 ||||||||

16. If 125 troopers qualified as sharpshooters during firearms training in the month of November and 140 qualified as sharpshooters in December, then in connection with the number of troopers qualifying as sharpshooters
    (A) there has been between a 10% and 11% increase.
    (B) there was a 12% increase.
    (C) there has been between a 10% and 11% decrease.
    (D) there was a 12% decrease.

A B C D
16 ||||||||

17. In purchasing uniform items during the current year, Trooper Roe spends $14.83 on neckties, $125.85 on trousers, $169.84 on shoes, $73.26 on shirts, and $47.84 on hats. If the trooper receives $475 in uniform allowance, then the trooper's uniform allowance was
    (A) between $43 and $44 more than was spent.
    (B) between $43 and $44 less than was spent.
    (C) between $48 and $49 more than was spent.
    (D) between $48 and $49 less than was spent.

A B C D
17 ||||||||

Answer questions 18 and 19 based on the following information.

In a certain highway patrol training academy class, there are 67 males and 13 females. Of the members of the class, 8 females and 12 males achieved a perfect score in a law exam.

18. Of the females who took the class, what is the percentage of females who received a perfect score?
    (A) approximately 62%
    (B) approximately 12%
    (C) approximately 67%
    (D) approximately 10%

A B C D
18 || | | ||||

19. Of the male officers who took the class, what percent did not receive a perfect score?
    (A) approximately 18%
    (B) approximately 82%
    (C) approximately 15%
    (D) approximately 69%

A B C D
19 || | | ||||

20. The following amounts of a controlled substance were seized in connection with undercover drug buys by troopers assigned to the Star Mountain post command: 2 pounds, ⅜ ounce, ¼ ounce, 2½ ounces, and ⁵⁄₁₆ ounce. The total weight of the controlled substances seized was
    (A) 34½ ounces.
    (B) 35⁷⁄₁₆ ounces.
    (C) 36⅓ ounces.
    (D) 37⁹⁄₁₆ ounces.

A B C D
20 || | | ||||

Answer Key and Explanations

ANSWER KEY

1. **D**	6. **B**	11. **C**	16. **B**
2. **D**	7. **B**	12. **D**	17. **A**
3. **C**	8. **C**	13. **C**	18. **A**
4. **C**	9. **D**	14. **B**	19. **B**
5. **B**	10. **B**	15. **C**	20. **B**

ANSWER EXPLANATIONS

GROUP ONE

1. **D** Choice A is incorrect because *climatic*, having to do with climate, should have been used in place of *climactic*, which means related to a climax or the highest point. Choice B is incorrect because *devise*, meaning to invent, should be used instead of *device*, which means an apparatus. Choice C is incorrect because *me* should be used in place of *I*. Choice C is easily seen as incorrect when the words *both Bob and* are removed and the sentence becomes "The ball hit I," which is obviously incorrect.

2. **D** Choice A is incorrect because *too*, meaning also, should be used in place of *to*, which means in a certain direction. Choice B is incorrect because the following list *is to be carried*, not *are to be carried*, because it is the list (singular) that is to be carried. When arriving at the correct choice, the words *of items* should not be considered when deciding whether *is* or *are* should be used. Choice C is incorrect because *his*, which is a pronoun showing possession, should be used in place of *him*. Action words ending in *ing*, such as *running*, *dancing*, and *fighting*, when accompanied by a pronoun should be accompanied by a pronoun that shows possession. For example, it would be incorrect to state, "I hate them arguing." Correctly stated it becomes, "I hate their arguing." Note the proper use of the pronoun showing possession, namely *their*.

3. **C** Choice A is incorrect because it seems as if the pocket was intended to be used on her. More clearly stated it becomes, "I hid the gun I intended to use on her in my pocket." Choice B is incorrect because it seems as if the trooper was arrested. More clearly stated it becomes, "After arresting the prisoner, the trooper put handcuffs on the prisoner."

4. **C** Choice A is incorrect because *lose*, meaning failing to win, should have been used instead of *loose*, which means not firm. Choice B is incorrect because *adapt* should have been used in place of *adopt*.

5. **B** Choice A is incorrect because *it's*, meaning it is, should be used instead of *its*, which means belonging to it and shows possession. Choice C is incorrect because *they're*, which means they are, should be used instead of *their*, which indicates possession and means of them.

6. **B** Choice A is incorrect because *illusion*, which means a misleading appearance, should be used in place of *allusion*, which means a casual mentioning or a hint. Choice C is incorrect because *you're*, which means you are, should be used instead of *your*, which indicates possession and means of you.

7. **B** Choice A is incorrect because *practical,* which means useful, should have been used instead of *practicable,* which means that something is possible. Choice C is incorrect because it should be stated as "her and me." Remember to remove the first pronoun, in this case *her,* and then reread the sentence. In this instance it would become, "the captain disciplined I," which is obviously incorrect.

8. **C** Choice A is incorrect because *advice,* which means help or counsel, should be used instead of *advise,* which means to notify. Choice B is incorrect because it should state, "to her and me." Words like *myself, yourself, himself, herself,* and *themselves* are used to reflect back to pronouns such as *I, you, he* or *she,* and *they.* For example, I hurt myself while lifting weights.

9. **D** Choice A is incorrect because *causal,* which means caused by a certain action, should not be used; instead, *casual,* which means informal, should have been used. Choice B is incorrect because *forth,* which means forward, should have been used instead of *fourth,* which refers to a numerical position. *Stationery* means writing material and should not have been used in choice C. Instead, *stationary,* which means in a fixed location, should have been used.

10. **B** Choice A is incorrect because of the double negative, *haven't* and *never.* Such double negatives are not correct because their use actually creates a positive statement when a negative statement is intended. In this instance, choice A when taken literally, actually means that I have used one of these. Choice C is incorrect because *officious,* which means self important or rude, should have been used instead of *official,* which indicates legitimate authority.

GROUP TWO

11. **C** In this type of question, we recommend that you be especially organized. Here the prisoner received

$$
\begin{array}{rcl}
2 \times 50 &=& \$100 \\
16 \times 20 &=& \$320 \\
2 \times 10 &=& \$\ 20 \\
6 \times 5 &=& \$\ 30 \\
\hline
& & \$470, \text{ which is } \$15 \text{ less than } \$485.
\end{array}
$$

12. **D** The ratio of crime prevention surveys to months is 9 surveys to 6 months or %. We can now construct a proportion by stating that 9 surveys is to 6 months as an unknown number (X) of surveys is to 2 years. However, when constructing a proportion all units of measure must be the same. For example, in this instance we must compare months to months. To do that we simply convert 2 years to 24 months (12 months in each year). Thus we have the proportion

$$
\frac{9}{6} = \frac{X}{24}
$$

Now cross multiply and get $6X = 216$. Dividing each side of the equation by 6, we arrive at X, or the number of months = 24. If you selected choice A, it is probably because you failed to convert 2 years to 24 months. If you selected choice B it is probably because you incorrectly constructed the proportion of $\% = \frac{X}{24}$. If you did that then you forgot that, when constructing a proportion made up of two ratios, the kind of item you put on the top of one ratio, in this case either months or surveys, you must put that same kind of item on the top of the other ratio.

13. **C** Immediately constructing a proportion, we arrive at 75 summonses is to 1.5 accidents prevented as

X amount of summonses is to 50 accidents prevented or

$$\frac{75}{1.5} = \frac{X}{50}$$

When we cross multiply, we get $1.5X = 3750$. Dividing both sides of the equation by 1.5, we get $X = 2500$ summonses.

14. **B** First, find the number of gallons used. Each tank full of fuel represents 22 gallons and we have 2½ tanks full, so we multiply $2\frac{1}{2} \times 22$ by first changing 2½ to a fraction or $\frac{5}{2}$. Now,

$$\frac{5}{2} \times 22 = 55 \text{ gallons}$$

If the car can travel 23 miles for each gallon of fuel used, then to find how far the car can travel on 55 gallons, simply multiply

$$55 \times 23 = 1265 \text{ miles.}$$

15. **C** Multiplying 40 hours × \$8.58 (regular pay) = \$343.20. Then, \$8.58 (the normal wage) × 1.5 (time and one half for overtime) = \$12.87 (the overtime pay rate) × 8½ hours or 8.5 hours (the number of overtime hours performed) equals \$109.395:

$$\$8.58 \times 1.5 = \$12.87 \times 8.5 = \$109.395$$

Combining the base pay and the overtime pay:
$$\begin{array}{r} \$343.20 \\ + 109.395 \\ \hline \$452.595 \end{array}$$

Rounding off we get \$452.60.

16. **B** First, find the distance or space between the numbers given. When considering 125 and 140, we see that there is a space of 15. Place that number 15 over the older or previously existing number

of 125 and create the fraction of $^{15}/_{125}$. Then simply divide to get 0.12 or 12%. The numbers increased so it is a percentage increase.

17. **A** The monies spent were

$$
\begin{array}{r}
\$ \ 14.83 \\
125.85 \\
169.84 \\
73.26 \\
47.84 \\
\hline
\$431.62
\end{array}
$$

which is $43.38 less than the $475 the trooper received. Thus the trooper's allowance was $43.38 more than what was spent.

18. **A** When asked what percentage one number is of another, you should form a fraction. Just remember that the number that immediately follows the word *of* is the denominator, the number on the bottom, and the remaining number is the numerator, the number on the top. In this instance, the number of females who took the class follows the word *of* and will be the denominator: the number of females who received a perfect score will be the numerator. This gives us $^{8}/_{13}$ = 0.615, which becomes 0.62 or 62%. If you selected choice B, you constructed the fraction improperly by using the number of males in the class as the denominator, so $^{8}/_{67}$ = .119, which is 11.9% or, as rounded off, 12%. If you selected choice C, the fraction you improperly constructed was $^{8}/_{12}$, where 12 is the number of males in the class who received a perfect score; $^{8}/_{12}$ equals 0.666 or 66.6% or 67% when rounded off. If you selected choice D, the fraction you improperly constructed was $^{8}/_{80}$, where 80 is the total number of students in the class both male and female; that equals 0.1 or 10%.

19. **B** We know 67 males took the class and only 12 received a perfect score. Therefore, 55 (67 − 12) did not receive a perfect score. Constructing our fraction, we arrive at $^{55}/_{67}$ = 0.82 or 82%. If you selected choice D, you probably improperly constructed the fraction $^{55}/_{80}$, which is the total number of students in the class, both male and female combined, and that equals 0.69 or 69%.

20. **B** First, changing the 2 pounds to ounces, we get 32 ounces (16×2). Then we change all fractions to sixteenths and add:

$$
\begin{array}{rcl}
^{3}/_{8} & = & ^{6}/_{16} \\
^{1}/_{4} & = & ^{4}/_{16} \\
2^{1}/_{2} & = & 2^{8}/_{16} \\
^{5}/_{16} & = & ^{5}/_{16} \\
\hline
& & 2^{23}/_{16}
\end{array}
$$

We now have 2 ounces and $^{23}/_{16}$ ounces, which is the same as $3^{7}/_{16}$ ounces. Add 3 $^{7}/_{16}$ ounces to 32 ounces and get 35 $^{7}/_{16}$ ounces.

CHAPTER 6

Memory Questions

In Chapter 4 we provided strategies for reading comprehension questions, which, as you now know, are questions that measure whether you understand written information that may be referred to while actually answering such questions.

In this chapter we go one step farther. Now you will learn to answer questions that measure whether you can understand and remember written or pictorial information that is given to you to study for a period of time and then taken away while you answer questions about it. This is why we call these questions memory questions. To answer these questions correctly, you must be able to commit information to memory and then retain that information long enough to answer the questions.

The Importance of Memory Questions

In our opinion, memory questions are especially important. We feel this way for two reasons. The first is that memory questions are typically the question type that causes the greatest difficulty for test takers. In fact, statistics that we have gathered over the years indicate that the average untrained test taker misses about 50 percent of these questions. This means that test takers who do well on memory questions have a distinct advantage over most of the other candidates taking the test.

The second factor contributing to the importance of memory-type questions is that such questions almost always appear at the beginning of the test. When test takers experience difficulty answering these questions, it almost always has a negative impact on their performance for the rest of the examination. Conversely, those test takers who have no trouble answering memory questions tend to develop a high level of confidence, which carries over to the remainder of the test.

The bottom line is this: If you master the technique for answering memory questions and do well with them on the official test, you will be taking a giant step toward reaching your goal of becoming a state trooper.

Two Widely Used Types of Memory Questions

There are two widely used memory-question formats in general use on state trooper examinations. We call the first type pictorial memory questions, and the second type we refer to as narrative memory questions.

PICTORIAL MEMORY QUESTIONS

In pictorial memory questions, you are given a drawing, sketch, or some other form of illustrated material and are permitted to study it for a specified time period, usually between 5 and 10 minutes. In the great majority of cases, the illustration you are given to study has some relationship to the job of a state trooper. You are then asked a series of questions based on information that is contained in the illustration you were given to study. In most cases, the test instructions make it clear that you are not permitted to make notes while studying the pictorial material, and you cannot refer back to it when answering the questions. In fact, the pictorial material is usually collected before the questions are started.

NARRATIVE MEMORY QUESTIONS

In narrative memory questions, which are really quite similar to the pictorial memory questions, you are given written material, which you are permitted to study for a specified time period, usually about 10 minutes. As is the case with pictorial memory questions, the written material you are given to study should have some relationship to the job of a state trooper. You are then asked a series of questions based on information that is contained in the narrative material you were given to study. In most cases, the question instructions make it clear that you are not permitted to make notes while studying the material and that you cannot refer to it when answering the questions. In fact, as is the case with pictorial material, the narrative material is usually collected before the questions are started.

Please note that in some cases the written material you must commit to memory is distributed well in advance of the day of the test. Then, on the day of the test, a series of questions about this material is asked. As is the case with all memory questions, candidates are not allowed to refer to the material when answering the questions. As you might expect, when the narrative material that is used as the basis for memory questions is distributed in advance of test day, it is always more lengthy and somewhat more complicated than narrative material that is distributed on the day of the test.

Using "Associations" — The Key to Success

Unless you are one of those very rare individuals who has a photographic memory, you should not rely strictly on brute memory to remember either narrative or pictorial material. Instead, we strongly recommend that you use a memory technique that we refer to as association. Interestingly, if you learn and master the association technique, it will not only help you to be quite successful when answering memory questions on any examination, but it will also help you to remember important matters in your everyday life.

Proving Our Point

In the many classroom sessions we have conducted to assist students who are preparing to take memory questions, we have learned that it is important to convince those students of the value of using associations as a memory aide. That is what we intend to do with you right now by asking you to work through two practice exercises. It is important that you take these two exercises before reading the rest of this chapter.

PRACTICE EXERCISES

PRACTICE EXERCISE ONE

A list of 20 common words follows. Take 5 minutes to study and commit these words to memory. At the end of 5 minutes, stop studying these words, let 10 minutes pass, and then write down as many of these words as you can to see how many you can remember. Do not take notes during your 5 minute studying period and do not refer back to the list when you are attempting to write all the words down. When you cannot remember any more of the 20 words, record the number of words you were able to remember and resume reading this chapter starting with the next paragraph.

1.	peach	2.	ring
3.	razor	4.	champion
5.	lettuce	6.	universe
7.	final	8.	teacher
9.	justice	10.	prisoner
11.	automobile	12.	camp
13.	missile	14.	lamp
15.	children	16.	balance
17.	listen	18.	jump
19.	speak	20.	tank

PRACTICE EXERCISE TWO

In all probability you were able to remember about 10–12 of the words from Practice Exercise One after studying them for 5 minutes. We now want you to take a similar exercise with one big difference. This time we will give you the following associations to help you remember the 20 words that appear in this exercise.

1. When you are studying the 20 words, be aware that there is one word in the list that begins with the letter *a*, one word that begins with the letter *b*, and so forth. For example, the *a* word is *apple*, the *b* word is *bread*, and so forth. As you study each word in the list, make sure that you take note of the first letter of each word and associate it with the alphabet. Then, later on when you are trying to remember the words, you will easily remember the first letter of each word you cannot readily recall.

2. An *elephant* (word 7 — the *e* word) is *gigantic* (word 17 — the *g* word) and usually travels in a *herd* (word 6—the *h* word). He has an occasional fight with a *lion* (word 12—the *l* word), who is the *king* (word 10—the *k* word) of the jungle, and has a *queen* (word 9—the *q* word).

3. *Twenty* (word 2—the *t* word) rhymes with *plenty* (word 14—the *p* word), and is a number that is used in *mathematics* (word 8—the *m* word).

4. *Apple* (word 1—the *a* word) *jelly* (word 19—the *j* word) is *sweet* (word 15—the *s* word) and can be spread on *bread* (word 4—the *b* word.

Now take the same amount of time, 5 minutes, that you used in Practice Exercise One and study the following list of 20 words remembering to use the suggested associations. Then, as you did for Practice Exercise One, let 10 minutes pass and see how many of the words from Practice Exercise Two you can remember. Remember that you should not make notes when studying the words and should not refer back to the list when you are trying to remember its contents. Instead, use the suggested associations to help you remember.

1.	apple	2.	twenty
3.	run	4.	bread
5.	candle	6.	herd
7.	elephant	8.	mathematics
9.	queen	10.	king
11.	dark	12.	lion
13.	office	14.	plenty
15.	sweet	16.	nonsense
17.	gigantic	18.	idle
19.	jelly	20.	finish

LEARN TO DEVELOP AND MAKE YOUR OWN ASSOCIATIONS

In all probability, you were much more successful in Practice Exercise Two and you are now convinced of the benefit of using associations as a memory aide. You probably also understand that when we say making associations we mean associating (or connecting) the information you want to remember with some other information so that it is easier to recall the information you want to commit to memory. Association is a necessary process because trying to remember things by brute memory alone is very difficult.

The type of associations made by different people varies tremendously from individual to individual, depending upon background, interests, and imagination. This is where practice will help you the most. The technique involves associating or relating what you are trying to remember with something you already know or with something else you are trying to remember. Let's try another example. Some facts that you might want to remember about a story and some suggested associations to help you remember them follow. You must remember, however, that these are only suggestions offered to give you an idea of how the technique of association works.

Facts	Possible Associations
* The prisoner is 25 years old.	* You or someone you know well is 25 years old.
* Altogether ten inmates reported sick.	* They could have had a full-court basketball game (10 players).
* One inmate was 42 and the other was 24.	* The reverse of one age equals the other age.
* The escaped prisoner, Michael Murphy, is wanted for murder.	* <u>M</u>ike <u>M</u>urphy is <u>m</u>issing and wanted for <u>m</u>urder. This is an alphabetical association—note all the <u>m</u> words.

These examples should help you understand how to use associations to aid memory. Bear in mind, however, that your degree of success with this technique depends upon practice. Incidentally, you do not need state police material to practice. Your daily newspaper will do just fine. Study a news story for about 5–10 minutes while developing associations to remember the details of the story; then put the paper down and see how many details you can remember.

Focusing on the Key Facts

Every state trooper is taught during his or her entry-level training how to capture the key facts in a story in order to write an accurate report. More often than not, the code word *NEOTWY* has been part of this training. This code word is derived by taking the last letter from each of the six key facts that must be contained in any thorough narrative report of an occurrence.

The Key Facts
wheN
wherE
whO
whaT
hoW
whY

If you answer these questions when you are investigating an occurrence (e.g., When did it happen?, Where did it happen?, Who was involved?, What happened?, How did it happen?, and Why did it happen?), you have captured all the key information. Therefore, when you are answering memory questions, either pictorial or narrative, concentrate on remembering the information that answers these questions. To help you, we list and explain the most common kinds of information to be found in each of the six categories.

1. **When.** Times and dates are favorite targets of test writers. Remember that there can be a number of times involved in a police incident. The most common are

   ● time of occurrence,

   ● time of reporting, and

   ● time of arrest.

   The best way to remember these times is in chronological order. Keep asking yourself, "When did this happen?" When dealing with times, do not neglect the dates. Don't assume everything is happening on the same date.

2. **Where.** A critical element in any police incident is where the incident took place. If more than one incident took place, make sure that you can relate each incident to its location. When you are taking a pictorial memory-type question, a favorite where question involves the placement of items in relation to one another. Incidentally, if a narrative or a pictorial representation mentions or shows any kind of weapon, you can be certain that you will be asked a question about that weapon, such as "Where is it located?" If the story mentions directions such as north, east, south, or west, be alert because this is a very fruitful question area. This is especially true if the story involves a vehicle accident.

3. **Who.** There are a number of who's in every police story, including

   ● perpetrators (those who commit crimes),

   ● victims,

   ● witnesses, and

   ● accomplices.

   Physical descriptions of the various who's in the story or illustration are fair game for questions. Things such as beards, glasses, scars, and clothing are often the subject of questions. Or, if there is a vehicle of some sort involved, then it is a sure bet that you will see a question or two about the vehicle, especially its license plate number.

4. **What.** Key questions are

   ● What happened?

   ● What did the perpetrators do?

   ● What did the police do?

   ● What was the scene of the incident like?

5. **How.** How many? is a question that is almost always asked. For example, how many weapons or how much money is depicted in the picture? How things happened is also a favorite question area.

6. **Why.** Motive is the primary why question. Always look for indications of motive when reading a story or looking at a picture. A very common why in pictorial formats involves things that are unusual. When something unusual is shown, you will be asked about it and/or the reason why the unusual condition exists (e.g., "Why was the old man running?").

Strategies for Recalling Pictorial Details

The illustration you are given to study is never very complicated. Therefore, all you need to become proficient at answering these questions based on the picture is a strategy, concentration, and practice. The concentration must be developed through practice. You can practice every time you look at a picture or read a story. The strategy follows:

1. **Develop a standardized method of studying the material.** If you want to remember all the details in a pictorial representation, you must look at the picture in an organized fashion. You cannot stare at it with the mistaken belief that your mind is recording all the details. You must look at the picture methodically. You must start looking in one certain place, proceed through the picture carefully, work yourself back to the starting place, begin again, and repeat the process. You continue in this manner until your entire amount of allotted time has been used.

2. **Focus on the key facts.** As you observe the details shown in the illustration, you should focus on the NEOTWY key facts.

3. **Observe all readable matter.** If there is information in the picture that can be read, then you probably will be asked about it.

4. **Search for oddities.** Test writers do not write questions about things that appear usual; they write questions about things that are unusual. They do this because state troopers on patrol are expected to notice things that are unusual or out of the ordinary. The following are some of the unusual things to look for when you are studying memory pictures:

   ● Weapons

   ● Contraband

   ● Things that are out of place in the scene

   ● Injuries

   ● Crimes taking place

   ● Dangerous conditions

5. **Use associations to remember.** Earlier we spoke a great deal about the use of associations to help you remember things. Now, as you observe key facts, you can apply the association technique to them.

6. **Count objects.** If there are fewer than a dozen separate items in the picture, count them. Examiners often frame questions based on the number of objects. Similarly, if there are more than one of the same type of objects, count them. Finally, if money is pictured, count the money.

7. **Do not break your concentration.** Do not stop concentrating until you have answered all the memory questions. And do not try to observe everything the first time through the picture. Go over it in a methodical way again and again.

8. **Don't stop concentrating when your time to observe the material has elapsed.** The time between the closing of the memory booklet and the answering of the questions is the most critical time of all. It is imperative that you maintain your concentration during this time. This is the time when untrained candidates let their minds wander. And they forget some of what they observed.

Strategies for Recalling Narrative Material

Narrative memory questions are not as difficult as you may think because the written story is never a complicated one to understand. Perhaps more than any other test area, this area can be improved upon significantly by practice. So, if you work hard and adhere to the following guidelines, you will be able to do very well on this part of your examination.

1. **Do not just read the story; become part of it!** When you are reading the story, you must clear your head of everything else except what you are reading. You must concentrate. The kind of intense concentration that is needed is best achieved by putting yourself in the story. Create a mental picture of what is happening.

2. **Relate the unknown to the known.** You will find that it is easier to put yourself into the story if you create mental images involving persons, places, and things that you know and with which you are familiar. For example, if the story involves people, try to associate each person in the story with someone you know. If the story is about a street incident, such as a vehicle accident, try to associate the location with one that you know.

3. **Do not try to memorize the entire narrative.** Some students attempt to memorize the entire story verbatim. For most of us, this is an impossible task. The trick is to identify the key facts in the story and to remember them. And, don't be concerned if the story seems incomplete; it will not necessarily have a conclusion. All the test writer

is interested in is giving you enough information to test your memory.

4. **Use associations to remember.** As with the pictorial format, do not try to use brute memory. Instead, use the association techniques we discussed previously.

5. **Do not break your concentration.** Do not stop concentrating until you have answered all the memory questions. Do not try to remember everything the first time you read the story. Go over it in a methodical way again and again.

6. **Do not stop concentrating when your time to observe the material has elapsed.** As already mentioned, the time between the closing of the memory booklet and the answering of the questions is the most critical time of all. It is imperative that you maintain your concentration during this time. This is the time when untrained candidates let their minds wander with the result that they forget some of what they have read.

Practice Exercises

GROUP ONE

10 Questions—Time Allowed 25 Minutes

DIRECTIONS: The following story is about an occurrence involving state troopers. You are allowed 10 minutes to read it and commit to memory as much about it as you can. You are not allowed to make any written notes during the time you are reading. At the end of 10 minutes, you are to stop reading the material and answer 10 questions about the story without referring back to it. You have 15 minutes to answer the 10 questions.

MEMORY STORY—10-MINUTE TIME LIMIT

You are state trooper Frank Money, shield #3232 of Troop 3. You are assigned for today, May 19th, as the operator of patrol car 3220, Sector One. The tour you are working is 4:00 P.M. to 12:00 P.M., and your partner is trooper Mike Prince, shield #3331, also of Troop 3. Your immediate supervisor is Sergeant Sam Smith, shield #13. The time is now 5:20 P.M.

A radio call from the dispatcher has just been directed to your unit. You are to respond to the Interboro Highway, eastbound, near Metropolitan Street. There has just been a three-car accident at that location, and personal injury is involved. Two ambulances have also been dispatched to the scene.

You attempt to enter the highway at the eastbound entrance at Grant

Street, which is just west of Metropolitan Street, but the traffic has become impassable. You notify Sergeant Smith of the traffic jam on the highway. He instructs you to respond to the accident scene by entering the highway westbound at York Avenue, which is just east of the accident, and to approach the accident from the westbound side of the highway. The sergeant also directs another unit, patrol car 711, Sector Two, to respond to the eastbound exit at Grant Street to detour traffic off the highway. Furthermore, he directs the dispatcher to inform the responding ambulances to approach the accident by using the westbound lane of the highway.

Upon arrival at the accident location approximately 10 minutes after you received the call, you determine that additional assistance is needed for traffic control. You inform Sergeant Smith, and he directs the dispatcher to send patrol car #99, Sector Three, to assist you. Sector Three arrives approximately 5 minutes later and proceeds to direct traffic around the three disabled vehicles. In the meantime, you and your partner determine that there are four injured persons, the driver of Vehicle One and a passenger of that vehicle, the driver of Vehicle Two, and a passenger from Vehicle Three. You then gather the following information:

1. Vehicle One: A late model red Datsun, two-door sedan, registration #16 DBF, owned and operated by Joe Doyle of 1543 Eastern Avenue.

2. Vehicle Two: A white Ford, four-door sedan, registration #212 FFN, owned and operated by Harvey Friend of 54-31 Metropolitan Street.

3. Vehicle Three: A blue Plymouth, four-door sedan, registration #303 PPP, owned and operated by James Kirk of 4321 Sky Street.

Just as you finish obtaining the information, the two ambulances arrive—one from Bayside Hospital and the other from Flushing Hospital. The two injured parties from Vehicle One are put into the Bayside Hospital ambulance, and the other two injured parties are placed in the Flushing Hospital ambulance.

According to accounts obtained from uninjured participants in the accident and from two impartial eye witnesses, the accident occurred when Vehicle One made an unsafe lane change, causing Vehicle Two to brake hard to avoid hitting Vehicle One in the rear. Vehicle Three then slammed Vehicle Two in the rear, which caused Vehicle Two to pile into the rear of Vehicle One.

DO NOT PROCEED UNTIL 10 MINUTES HAVE PASSED.

INSTRUCTIONS: Answer questions 1–10 solely on the basis of the preceding story. Do not refer back to the story when answering these questions. You have 15 minutes to complete all 10 questions.

1. Your partner's shield number is
   (A) 3232.
   (B) 3220.
   (C) 3331.
   (D) 3241.

2. Your supervisor's name is
   (A) Money.
   (B) Prince.
   (C) Smith.
   (D) Grant.

3. You arrived at the scene of the accident at approximately
   (A) 5:20 P.M.
   (B) 5:30 P.M.
   (C) 6:00 P.M.
   (D) 6:30 P.M.

4. Which unit did your supervisor assign to respond to the Grant Street exit of the highway?
   (A) Sector One
   (B) Sector Two
   (C) Sector Three
   (D) Sector Four

5. What unit was dispatched to the accident scene to assist with traffic direction?
   (A) Sector One
   (B) Sector Two
   (C) Sector Three
   (D) Sector Four

6. The driver of which vehicle was uninjured in the accident?
   (A) Vehicle One
   (B) Vehicle Two
   (C) Vehicle Three
   (D) All three of the drivers were injured.

7. The registration number of the Datsun was
   (A) 16 DBF.
   (B) 212 FFN.
   (C) 303 PPP.
   (D) not given.

8. Your partner's name is
   (A) Money.
   (B) Prince.
   (C) Smith.
   (D) Grant.

9. Who lives on Sky Street?
   (A) James Kirk
   (B) Harvey Friend
   (C) Joe Doyle
   (D) Mike Prince

10. Which vehicle caused the accident?
    (A) Vehicle One
    (B) Vehicle Two
    (C) Vehicle Three
    (D) That information was not given.

GROUP TWO

10 Questions—Time Allowed 20 Minutes

INSTRUCTIONS: Study for 5 minutes the following illustration, which depicts items taken from two prisoners immediately after they were arrested. Try to remember as many details as possible. Do not make written notes of any kind during this 5-minute period. After the 5 minutes are up, you have an additional 15 minutes to answer the 10 questions that follow immediately. When answering the questions, do NOT refer back to the illustration.

DO NOT PROCEED UNTIL 5 MINUTES HAVE PASSED.

Answer questions 11–20 solely on the basis of the preceding illustration. Do not refer back to the illustration when answering these questions. You have 15 minutes to complete all 10 questions.

11. Where does John Brown live?
    (A) 246 Main Street   (B) 31 7th Avenue
    (C) 731 Main Street   (D) 642 7th Avenue

    A B C D
    11 ||||||||

12. What is John Brown's driver's license number?
    (A) 642   (B) 246
    (C) 731   (D) 317

    A B C D
    12 ||||||||

13. How many keys were removed from the prisoners?
    (A) 2   (B) 3   (C) 4   (D) 5

    A B C D
    13 ||||||||

14. How much money was removed from Ann Smith?
    (A) $5.60   (B) $6.00
    (C) $10.60   (D) $16.60

    A B C D
    14 ||||||||

15. Which of the two prisoners most likely smoked cigarettes?
    (A) John Brown.   (B) Ann Smith.
    (C) both John Brown   (D) neither John Brown
        and Ann Smith.   nor Ann Smith.

    A B C D
    15 ||||||||

16. Perfume was taken from
    (A) John Brown.   (B) Ann Smith.
    (C) both John Brown   (D) neither John Brown
        and Ann Smith.   nor Ann Smith.

    A B C D
    16 ||||||||

17. A knife was taken from
    (A) John Brown.   (B) Ann Smith.
    (C) both John Brown   (D) neither John Brown
        and Ann Smith.   nor Ann Smith.

    A B C D
    17 ||||||||

18. A gun was taken from
    (A) John Brown.   (B) Ann Smith.
    (C) both John Brown   (D) neither John Brown
        and Ann Smith.   nor Ann Smith.

    A B C D
    18 ||||||||

19. A writing implement was taken from
    (A) John Brown.   (B) Ann Smith.
    (C) both John Brown   (D) neither John Brown
        and Ann Smith.   nor Ann Smith.

    A B C D
    19 ||||||||

20. Both prisoners had
    (A) aspirins.   (B) a 50¢ piece.
    (C) a comb.   (D) a $50 bill.

    A B C D
    20 ||||||||

GROUP THREE

10 Questions—Time Allowed 25 Minutes

INSTRUCTIONS: You are allowed 10 minutes to read the following information about four wanted persons and commit to memory as much about it as you can. You are not allowed to make any written notes during the time you are reading. At the end of 10 minutes, you are to stop reading the material and answer 10 questions about the story without referring back to it. You have 15 minutes to answer the 10 questions.

MEMORY STORY—10-MINUTE TIME LIMIT

Trooper Don Ginty is assigned to Troop 68. During roll call training he is given the following information about four wanted persons.

Wanted Person #1: Larry Ash, male, white, 45 years old, 185 pounds, 6'4", black hair, and blue eyes. He walks with a limp as a result of an automobile accident when he was 12 years old. Larry Ash is wanted for arson. On May 31st of this year, he set fire to the unoccupied automobile of his former girl friend, Pat Swan. He is an avid fan of country music and frequents country music clubs. He has no previous convictions.

Wanted Person #2: Don Smart, male, white, 25 years old, 180 pounds, 5'7", brown hair, and brown eyes. He has a 5-inch scar over his right eye as a result of a bar fight when he was 19 years old. Smart is wanted for armed robbery. He is known to carry a handgun and is considered extremely dangerous. He has a lengthy arrest record with many previous convictions. He is a college graduate with a degree in accounting. He is a life-long sports fan and often attends professional sports events, especially basketball games.

Wanted Person #3: Pat Wall, male, white, 32 years old, 225 pounds, 5'9", brown hair, and brown eyes. He has a speech impediment. He is wanted for the murder of the husband of his ex-wife. He is an expert knife fighter with a reputation for being armed and dangerous. He has spent time in prison as a result of a previous assault conviction. He is an expert chef who specializes in cooking Italian food.

Wanted Person #4: Art Champion, male, white, 24 years old, 175 pounds, 5'9", brown hair, and brown eyes. He is wanted for the sexual abuse of an 11-year-old girl. He is known to be an extremely violent person who is often armed with some sort of deadly weapon and should be considered dangerous. He has four previous convictions for various sex offenses. He is known to loiter in the vicinity of elementary schools and often poses as a law enforcement officer when approaching his young victims.

DO NOT PROCEED UNTIL 10 MINUTES HAVE PASSED.

INSTRUCTIONS: Answer questions 21–30 solely on the basis of the preceding information. Do not refer back to the information when answering these questions. You have 15 minutes to complete all 10 questions.

21. Which of the wanted persons has a college degree?
(A) Larry Ash
(B) Don Smart
(C) Pat Wall
(D) Art Champion

A B C D
21 || || || ||

22. The wanted person who walks with a limp is
(A) Larry Ash.
(B) Don Smart.
(C) Pat Wall.
(D) Art Champion.

A B C D
22 || || || ||

23. Which of the following wanted persons is an expert knife fighter?
(A) Larry Ash
(B) Don Smart
(C) Pat Wall
(D) Art Champion

A B C D
23 || || || ||

24. The tallest of the wanted persons is
(A) Larry Ash.
(B) Don Smart.
(C) Pat Wall.
(D) Art Champion.

A B C D
24 || || || ||

25. Which of the wanted persons is known to loiter in the vicinity of elementary schools?
(A) Larry Ash
(B) Don Smart
(C) Pat Wall
(D) Art Champion

A B C D
25 || || || ||

26. Larry Ash is wanted for
(A) armed robbery.
(B) murder.
(C) sexual abuse.
(D) arson.

A B C D
26 || || || ||

27. Pat Wall
(A) is a college graduate.
(B) is a country music fan.
(C) is an expert chef.
(D) impersonates law enforcement officers.

A B C D
27 || || || ||

28. Don Smart
(A) likes to attend professional basketball games.
(B) loiters in the vicinity of schools.
(C) enjoys going to country music clubs.
(D) is an expert knife fighter.

A B C D
28 || || || ||

29. Which of the wanted persons has a facial scar?
      (A) Larry Ash   (B) Don Smart
      (C) Pat Wall   (D) Art Champion

30. The heaviest of the wanted persons is
      (A) Larry Ash.   (B) Don Smart.
      (C) Pat Wall.   (D) Art Champion.

Answer Key and Explanations

ANSWER KEY

1. **C**	7. **A**	13. **D**	19. **C**	25. **D**
2. **C**	8. **B**	14. **C**	20. **C**	26. **D**
3. **B**	9. **A**	15. **B**	21. **B**	27. **C**
4. **B**	10. **A**	16. **A**	22. **A**	28. **A**
5. **C**	11. **A**	17. **A**	23. **C**	29. **B**
6. **C**	12. **A**	18. **D**	24. **A**	30. **C**

ANSWER EXPLANATIONS

GROUP ONE

Please note that in giving the answers we will suggest associations that could have been made to recall the information needed to answer the questions. But our associations are only suggestions to help give you an idea of how associations can be made. You must remember that the development of associations is a personal matter. What works best for you is what you should follow.

1. **C** If a memory story gives shield numbers, it is highly likely that they will be the subject of a question. Note the similarity of the numbers in the four choices offered. Hopefully you made associations to remember the various numbers in the story.

2. **C** Your supervisor's name was Sergeant Smith. Alphabetical associations are among the easiest to make, and they are very effective. Practice making them.

3. **B** The radio call was dispatched at 5:20 P.M., and you arrived at

the scene of the accident about 10 minutes later, or at approximately 5:30 P.M. Always try to remember times chronologically.

4. **B** You are Sector One and the first assigned vehicle. Sector Two was the second assigned vehicle and was dispatched to Grant Street.

5. **C** Sector Three was the third assigned vehicle and was sent to the scene of the accident.

6. **C** A passenger from Vehicle Three was injured. The drivers of Vehicles One and Two were also injured.

7. **A** If you noticed that the plate number for the Datsun had a D in it, the one for the Ford had an F in it, and the one for the Plymouth had a P in it, then you would have had no trouble with this question.

8. **B** Your partner's name was <u>P</u>rince. Many students report back to us that alphabetical associations are the easiest ones for them to make. Try them.

9. **A** James Kirk lives on Sky Street. For Star Trek fans, the association here is obvious.

10. **A** The accident occurred when Vehicle One made an unsafe lane change.

GROUP TWO

11. **A** Note that all the numbers in the choices appear somewhere in the illustration. Hopefully you created an association to help you remember that John Brown lives at 246 Main Street.

12. **A** If you recognized that John Brown's address and driver's license number are the reverse of each other, you would have had no trouble with this question.

13. **D** John Brown had three keys, and Ann Smith had two keys. Remember to count similar items.

14. **C** Always count money if it is depicted in a memory scene. Ann Smith had a $10 bill and 60 cents in coin.

15. **B** This question emphasizes the point that assumptions can be made to answer memory questions if they are based on facts. The fact is that Ann Smith was in possession of cigarettes. Therefore, it is likely that she smoked.

16. **A** Surprisingly, it was the male, John Brown, who had the perfume. This is how you might have remembered it.

17. **A** Anytime a weapon is in a memory picture, you can be sure that you will be asked about it.

18. **D** It is not uncommon for a question like this one to be asked. There was no gun depicted anywhere in the scene.

19. **C** John Brown had a pen, and Ann Smith had a pencil.

20. **C** Both prisoners had a comb. Always try to remember similarities and differences.

GROUP THREE

21. **B** Don Smart has a college degree. The association, we hope, was obvious to you. Note that questions using this format rely heavily on the differences among the wanted persons.

22. **A** An alphabetical association, Larry Ash walks with a limp would have guaranteed your answering this question correctly.

23. **C** Pat Wall is an expert knife fighter with a reputation for being armed and dangerous.

24. **A** Once again, the question involved differences among the four wanted persons. Note that the differences are usually pronounced ones. Larry Ash is the only wanted person over 6 feet tall.

25. **D** Art is a subject one takes in school and Art Champion loiters around schools.

26. **D** Arson causes ashes, and Larry Ash is wanted for arson.

27. **C** Pat Wall is an expert chef who specializes in cooking Italian food.

28. **A** Smart is a life-long sports fan who enjoys attending professional sporting events, especially basketball games.

29. **B** Don Smart has a 5-inch scar over his right eye.

30. **C** Pat Wall is the only wanted person over 200 pounds. As mentioned earlier, the questions are quite often keyed into the differences among the wanted persons.

CHAPTER 7

Handling State Police Forms

An important responsibility of both a state trooper and a highway patrol officer is to

● properly complete standard forms and

● to retrieve information from already completed forms.

The importance of such actions is particularly evident when

1. these completed forms are offered as evidence in both criminal and civil hearings. The information recorded on such forms is examined and relied on by both prosecutors and defense counsels. This recorded information even serves as the basis of many decisions made by judges.

2. the information that must be entered on such forms helps troopers and highway patrol officers conduct thorough and appropriate investigations, which in turn ensure that the rights of the citizens involved are protected. For example, a trooper gathering information concerning a traffic accident is guided while conducting the investigation by the information required by accident-reporting forms.

3. information gathered from completed forms serves as the basis for administrative decisions concerning equipment and personnel.

4. property previously reported lost or stolen is returned to its rightful owner.

5. missing children and adults are identified and located.

6. serious crimes are solved. A serial killer was once apprehended because of the information recorded in connection with the issuance of a traffic ticket.

Because state troopers and highway patrol officers must be able to both enter information onto a form and extract information from an already completed form, questions measuring these abilities appear on entrance examinations for the positions of state trooper and highway patrol officer.

Reporting from Completed Forms

In the first type of forms-type question—reporting from completed forms—you are given a completed form and asked questions about the information appearing on the completed form. For example, such a question might ask who the victim is, when the accident occurred, or where the incident occurred? In a sense you are being required to reconstruct the incident and tell the story, all from the already completed form.

Filling Out Forms and Reports

In the second type of forms question—filling out forms and reports—you are given a completed story describing an incident and in addition a blank form related to the incident. The story may be an account of a crime that has taken place or an accident that has occurred. The questions will require you to fill out the form. You will be asked to select the correct information that should be placed, for example, in box 13, caption c, and so on. Here you are already given a completed story and are not required to reconstruct the story. Instead, you are to select or extract important information about the story, which is often referred to as a narrative.

WHAT KIND OF INFORMATION IS IMPORTANT?

The kind of information that is important when answering forms-type questions can be easily remembered by *NEOTWY*, an acronym that is comprised of the last letter of six basic questions.

N	WHE**N**?
E	WHER**E**?
O	WH**O**?
T	WHA**T**?
W	HO**W**?
Y	WH**Y**?

The answers to these six questions comprise most of the information on state trooper and highway patrol officer forms.

Whe**N** did it happen? This type of question includes

● when it actually happened,

● when it was discovered,

● when it was reported to the trooper,

● when the trooper arrived at the scene, and

● when it was officially reported by the troopers.

Wher**E** did it happen? Often there is more than one location involved in an incident.

> *EXAMPLE:* A crazed gunman shoots and wounds several pedestrians at a suburban mall after robbing a store at the mall. Finally the gunman is shot and killed after a trooper fires six shots and strikes the gunman twice.

● Where was the store that was robbed?

● Where was the first pedestrian wounded?

● Where was the last pedestrian wounded?

● Where was the trooper when the trooper shot the crazed gunman?

Also there could be other important locations involved in this example.

- Where were the wounded pedestrians taken?

- Where did the shots fired by the trooper and missing the gunman strike?

There are obviously many important locations in incidents handled by troopers and highway patrol officers.

WhO are the people involved? This basic question includes:

- Who is the trooper reporting the incident?

- Who is the victim?

- Who is the person making the complaint (i.e., the complainant)?

- Who is the suspect?

- Who is the highway patrol officer making the arrest?

- Who witnessed the incident?

It should quickly become apparent that in a typical incident that a trooper or highway patrol officer might become involved with, there are numerous persons who must be identified. Therefore, when answering questions dealing with forms, a candidate must be constantly aware of the different characters involved and be able to identify each one accurately.

WhaT happened? This basic question includes:

- What injuries were suffered?

- What property was damaged?

- What property was stolen?

Regarding property, note that when a trooper takes property into custody, meticulous records are kept so that in the future it can be shown who was in possession of the property at any given point in time. This record keeping involves being able to accurately and positively describe property using such things as specific identification marks and serial numbers.

- What actually occurred?

Was the incident a criminal offense or was it an accident? In describing an incident, troopers and highway patrol officers must differentiate between what was observed personally and what was reported to them. It is the officer's job to develop what actually happened from the statements of those involved and from the officer's personal observations. However, the report must separate what is known to be fact from what is alleged. Consider the following example, which illustrates the correct and incorrect methods of recording information:

● Mr. Parks told Trooper Banks that Mr. Gray stole Mr. Parks's car.

Incorrect: Mr. Gray stole Mr. Parks's car.

Correct: Mr. Parks reported to Trooper Banks that Mr. Gray stole Mr. Parks's car.

● While at the scene of a traffic accident, Highway Patrol Officer Marks observed Mr. Rays, who was arguing with Mr. Kegs, strike Mr. Kegs.

Incorrect: Highway Patrol Officer Marks observed Mr. Kegs strike Mr. Rays because of a traffic accident.

Correct: Highway Patrol Officer Marks observed Mr. Rays strike Mr. Kegs at the scene of a traffic accident.

When reporting facts that indicate what happened, only the facts and not assumptions are to be reported.

Ho**W** did the incident occur? This basic question includes:

● How did the injury occur?

● How did the suspect escape?

● How was entry gained to the building?

● How was the property damaged?

Wh**Y** did the incident occur? This basic question includes:

● Why was the victim assaulted?

● Why did the trooper fall?

● Why did the trooper follow the car?

● Why did the victim not report the incident?

Strategies for Answering Questions Dealing with State Police and Highway Patrol Officer Forms

The following strategies are designed to assist a candidate in answering the type of questions that requires a candidate to properly complete standard state police and highway patrol forms and reports and to retrieve information from such already completed forms.

In answering either type of forms question:

1. Quickly determine the basic purpose of the form. Ask yourself, Is this form reporting an accident? Is it describing stolen property? Usually the title of the form will identify its purpose.

2. Establish what kind of forms question it is. Are you being asked to complete a form or to retrieve information from a completed form or report?

If you are being asked to complete a form based on an accompanying narrative, follow these steps.

1. Take a quick look at the blank form and determine its purpose. This will also give you a hint regarding the kind of situation the accompanying narrative is about.

2. Read the stem of the question, which is the part of the question appearing before the choices. This is done to determine which pieces of information appearing in the narrative will be needed to answer the question.

3. Carefully read the narrative accompanying the form. Look for pieces of information that you know, will be needed to answer the question based on your earlier reading of the stem of the question. Get a clear understanding of the situation by asking such questions as:

● When did the incident take place?

● Where did the incident take place?

● Who is the victim?

● Who is the complainant?

● Who is the suspect?

- Who is the trooper making the report?

- What actually happened?

- How did it happen?

- Why did it happen?

4. Answer the questions. Remember in this type of question the form and narrative are available. So refer to them whenever necessary.

If you are being asked to retrieve information from a completed form, follow these steps.

1. Quickly read the stem of the question to determine what information on the completed form will be needed to answer the question.

2. Carefully review the completed form and confirm its purpose. As you review the form, ask yourself questions to make sure that you understand the information on the form. Pay particular attention to the pieces of information that, based on your earlier reading of the stem of the question, will be needed to answer the question.

3. Answer the question by referring to the form as often as needed.

Common Errors to Avoid

1. Do not assume. If an injury to Mrs. Woods is reported to Trooper Bends, do not assume that Mrs. Woods reported the injury. Base your answer on facts that are contained in what is in front of you.

2. Do not assume that the captions and boxes on the form are numbered in strict sequential order. This is not always the case. Caption 5 could appear on the form before caption 4.

3. Do not confuse the identities of officers involved in the incident. Trooper Adams could be the arresting officer, Highway Patrol Officer Grant could be the first officer on the scene, and Trooper Winds could be the reporting officer.

4. Do not confuse different locations. The crime may have taken place at one location, but an arrest could have been made at a different location.

5. Do not confuse different times and dates. Because this kind of information involves numbers, it is a favorite question area for examiners. Therefore, understand, for example, that the time an incident

occurred is not necessarily the same time that it was reported to the authorities.

6. Do not mix up the description of suspects.

7. Do not assume that the victim and the complainant are always the same person. For example, a child may be the victim of a crime for which a parent is the complainant, or the actual person making the complaint.

8. Do not assume that information required to answer each question is always available. At times the correct entry to be inserted in a caption on a form could be unknown or not available.

9. Do not confuse descriptions and serial numbers of lost or stolen property.

10. Do not mix up badge or shield numbers of officers involved. Part of what is being tested here is the ability to pay attention to detail while following directions. Therefore, another favorite question area of examiners when asking this type of question concerns the shield numbers of the officers involved.

Practice Exercises

GROUP ONE

10 Questions—Time Allowed 20 Minutes

INSTRUCTIONS: Answer questions 1–10 solely on the basis of the following narrative and the following USE OF FORCE/ASSAULT REPORT. Some of the boxes on the USE OF FORCE/ASSAULT REPORT form are numbered; some are not. The boxes are not necessarily consecutively numbered.

On August 30, State Trooper Mark Best, Shield Number 7068, assigned to post Sector Adam, of Troop B was injured while participating in a road block by a person subsequently arrested and identified as Don Kinder of 335 Court Street, Dodge City. The details are as follows:

At about 0930 hours, in Moon County on Route 26 northbound, at approximately 500 feet south of the intersection with Interstate 37, Trooper Best was participating in a road block accompanied by Trooper Harps, Shield Number 6078, assigned to post Sector Baker, of Troop B. The purpose of the roadblock was to assist in the search for a perpetrator of an armed bank robbery occurring an hour earlier at the Gotham Bank located at 553 Marshall Avenue in Holster City. As Trooper Best was in the process of stopping a late-model gray Ford sedan, the driver of the vehicle suddenly drove the vehicle into a fence, jumped from the vehicle, and ran south on Route 26 with Trooper Best in pursuit on foot. Trooper Best quickly overtook the driver who, during the course of an ensuing struggle, struck Trooper Best in the right eye with a closed fist. In order to subdue the driver, Trooper Best struck the driver in the right elbow with the regulation baton. The driver was identified as Don Kinder of 207 West 158 Street of Big Town, telephone number 555 1234, and was arrested for Assaulting a Police Officer along with other traffic violations. Examination of his driver's license revealed the license number to be K104305633.

At about the time Trooper Best was subduing Mr. Kinder, Trooper Harps found a passenger hiding in the back of the Ford sedan. Protruding from the waistband of the passenger was a loaded .45 caliber pistol. The passenger was identified as Mark Chamber, a male white, 31 years old, of 3105 Park Avenue also of Big Town. He was placed under arrest, arrest number 2356, for possession of a loaded weapon.

Trooper Best and Mr. Kinder were taken to Mercy Hospital and treated by Dr. Bones. Mr. Kinder was admitted for a broken right elbow. Trooper Best received two stitches over the right eye and was released.

1. Which of the following should be inserted in caption number 4?
    (A) August 30
    (B) August 31
    (C) July 30
    (D) cannot be determined

    A B C D
    1 | | | | | | |

2. If violator A refers to Don Kinder, then the words broken right elbow should appear in the caption numbered
    (A) 21.
    (B) 38.
    (C) 51.
    (D) 55.

    A B C D
    2 | | | | | | |

DEPARTMENT OF PUBLIC SAFETY
USE OF FORCE/ASSAULT REPORT

INCIDENT INFORMATION: TROOPER ASSAULTED: (7)   Yes ☐   No ☐

Post: ____(1)____County: ____(2)____ Location: _____(3)_____
Date: ____(4)____Day of Week: ____(5)____Time: ____(8)____ A.M. ☐ P.M. ☐
Light Conditions: Daylight ☐   Dawn ☐   Weather Conditions: Clear ☐ Overcast ☐
      (9)   Dusk ☐   Night ☐   Rain ☐   Snow ☐   Fog ☐
Specify Assignment: (10)   Routine Traffic Patrol ☐   Serving Process ☐   Processing DUI Suspect ☐
Road Block ☐   Transporting Prisoner ☐   Civil Disorder ☐   Other: _____

VIOLATOR(S):

A) NAME: _____(11)_____ Race/Sex __(12)__ Age ____(13)____ Height ____(14)____ Weight ____(15)____
Address: _____(16)_____ Phone No. _____(17)_____
Occupation: _____(18)_____ Driver's License No. _____(19)_____
Violator Intoxicated: Yes ☐ No ☐   Alcohol ☐ Drugs ☐   Alone ☐ Accompanied ☐
Weapon (s) Used by Violator: _____(20)_____
Injuries Sustained: _____(21)_____
      (22) Hospitalized ☐   (23) Treated & Released ☐   (24) Refused ☐
Where Treated: _____(25)_____
ARREST No. _____(26)_____ Charge(s)_____(27)_____

B) NAME: _____(28)_____ Race/Sex __(29)__ Age ____(30)____ Height ____(31)____ Weight ____(32)____
Address: _____(33)_____ Phone No. _____(34)_____
Occupation: _____(35)_____ Driver's License No. _____(36)_____
Violator Intoxicated: Yes ☐ No ☐   Alcohol ☐ Drugs ☐   Alone ☐ Accompanied ☐
Weapon (s) Used by Violator: _____(37)_____
Injuries Sustained _____(38)_____
      (39) Hospitalized ☐   (40) Treated & Released ☐   (41) Refused ☐
Where Treated: _____(42)_____
      Attach Copy of Citation(s) ☐
ARREST No._____(43)_____ Charge(s)_____(44)_____

TROOPER:

Rank/Name:_____(45)_____ Height _____(46)_____ Weight _____(47)_____ Post/Troop ____(48)___
      Alone (49) ☐   Accompanied by: _____(50)_____
Injuries Sustained: ____·_____(51)_____
      Hospitalized (52) ☐   Treated & Released (53) ☐
Where Treated: _____(54)_____
Defensive Weapon(s):   Used ☐   Displayed Only ☐   Hands ☐   OC Spray ☐
      (55) Baton ☐   Flashlight ☐   Firearms ☐   Other: _____
Witnesses and Officers:
Name: _____(56)_____ Address: _____(57)_____
      (57a) Phone No: (H) _____ (W) _____
Name: _____(58)_____ Address: _____(59)_____
      (59a) Phone No: (H) _____ (W) _____

3. Assuming that the information relating to violator A refers to Mr. Don Kinder, then the words *Mercy Hospital* should be inserted
   (A) only in caption 25.
   (B) only in caption 42.
   (C) in both captions 25 and 42.
   (D) both in captions 25 and 54.

   A B C D
   3 || || ||| ||

4. If violator A refers to Don Kinder, which of the following would be most correct to enter in caption number 19?
   (A) 104305633
   (B) K104305633
   (C) K104305336
   (D) 104303356

   A B C D
   4 || || ||| ||

5. Assuming that the information relating to violator A refers to Mr. Don Kinder, then the number 2356 should be inserted
   (A) only in caption 26.
   (B) only in caption 43.
   (C) either in caption 26 or 43.
   (D) in both captions 26 and 43.

   A B C D
   5 || || ||| ||

6. The most accurate entry for caption 3 is
   (A) 3105 Park Avenue.
   (B) 207 West 158 Street.
   (C) Route 26.
   (D) Interstate 37.

   A B C D
   6 || || ||| ||

7. The name Harps would be most appropriately entered in which of the following captions?
   (A) 8
   (B) 11
   (C) 28
   (D) 50

   A B C D
   7 || || ||| ||

8. Assuming that the information relating to violator A refers to Mr. Don Kinder, then the most appropriate entry for caption 20 is
   (A) a .45 caliber pistol.
   (B) a baton.
   (C) none.
   (D) not able to be determined.

   A B C D
   8 || || ||| ||

9. It would be most correct to insert the word *Moon* in which of the following captions?
   - (A) 2
   - (B) 11
   - (C) 42
   - (D) 54

   A B C D
   9 | | | | | | |

10. The caption *roadblock* would be most appropriately checked in connection with caption number
   - (A) 3.
   - (B) 10.
   - (C) 21.
   - (D) 37.

   A B C D
   10 | | | | | | |

GROUP TWO

10 Questions—Time Allowed 15 Minutes

INSTRUCTIONS: Answer questions 11–20 solely on the basis of information recorded on the following Found Property Report form.

FOUND PROPERTY REPORT

1. Date property found   January 10, 19xx

2. Location where property found   Rear of 702 Ray St.

3. Owner of property   Don King

   Address   720 Day Avenue Apartment 2E

   Telephone number 1 555 555 1987

4. Name of who lost the property   Frank King

   Address   720 Day Avenue Apartment 2E

   Telephone number 1 555 555 1987

5. Finder of property   Ray Burns

   Address   702 Terrace Street Apartment E2

   Telephone number 1 555 555 1897

---

6. Nature of Property   Simco laptop computer

7. Estimated value $1200.00

8. Officer receiving the property

   Name   Trooper Neil Bailes   Shield number   748
   Command   Bass Creek Troop   Division   Carter

9. Distinguishing marks of property

   Manufacturer serial number 014333356

10. Trooper property number   013453336

11. Property movement records:

    January 10th property received into department custody by
    Trooper Bailes

    January 11th from Bass Creek Troop barracks to Central
    Property Unit by Trooper Cash

    January 12th owner Don King picks up property from Cen-
    tral Property Unit

---

11. The day the property was lost
    (A) was January 10.
    (B) was January 11.
    (C) was January 12.
    (D) cannot be determined from the information.

    A B C D
    11 ||||||||

12. Which of the following is most correct?
    (A) The owner lost the property.
    (B) The owner and the loser of the property are
        related.
    (C) The property is worth over $1000 dollars.
    (D) The finder of the property is not related to
        the owner of the property.

    A B C D
    12 ||||||||

13. It would be most correct to state that Trooper
    Cash
    (A) found the property.
    (B) handed the property over to the owner.
    (C) delivered the property to the Central Prop-
        erty Unit.
    (D) is the first trooper to handle the property.

    A B C D
    13 ||||||||

14. It would be most correct to state that the telephone number 1 555 555 1987 belongs to
   (A) only the owner of the property.
   (B) only the loser of the property.
   (C) only the finder of the property.
   (D) Mr. Don King.

15. The location where the property was found was
   (A) 702 Day Avenue.
   (B) 720 Day Avenue.
   (C) 702 Ray Street.
   (D) 702 Terrace Street.

16. Which of the following statements is most correct?
   (A) Mr. Don King and Mr. Ray Burns both live in an apartment numbered 2E.
   (B) The person who lost the property last saw the property in the rear of 702 Ray Street.
   (C) The property was returned to its owner 2 days after it was lost.
   (D) The property had a manufacturer serial number.

17. The property that was lost was
   (A) a ring.
   (B) a watch.
   (C) a laptop computer.
   (D) a calculator.

18. The number 013453336 represents
   (A) the manufacturer serial number.
   (B) the trooper property number.
   (C) the social security number of the property owner.
   (D) the complaint number assigned to the case.

19. Trooper Bailes's shield number is
   (A) 749.
   (B) 748.
   (C) 847.
   (D) 784.

20. The address 702 Terrace Avenue belongs to
   (A) the owner of the property.
   (B) Mr. Frank King.
   (C) Mr. Ray Burns.
   (D) the Bass Creek Trooper Barracks.

Answer Key and Explanations

ANSWER KEY

1. **A**	5. **B**	9. **A**	13. **C**	17. **C**
2. **A**	6. **C**	10. **B**	14. **D**	18. **B**
3. **D**	7. **D**	11. **D**	15. **C**	19. **B**
4. **B**	8. **C**	12. **C**	16. **D**	20. **C**

ANSWER EXPLANATIONS

GROUP ONE

1. **A** Caption 4, which is in the Incident Information area, calls for the date of the incident, which is August 30.

2. **A** There are spaces on the form for information relating to violators A and B. If violator A refers to Don Kinder, who we know sustained a broken right elbow, then such information should appear in caption 21, the "Injuries Sustained" caption.

3. **D** Captions 25 and 54 refer to "where treated" in connection with violator A, Mr. Kinder, and the injured trooper. The use of the word *only* makes choice A incorrect. Choices B and C are incorrect because caption 42 refers to violator B, Mr. Mark Chamber.

4. **B** Caption 19 calls for a driver's license number of violator A, Mr. Kinder, whose driver's license number is K104305633. Choice A is only partially correct because the letter *K* was omitted. In choices C and D the numbers were incorrectly presented. Often examiners change a series of numbers slightly to see if you can maintain your concentration for extended periods of time. This is why practice exams and questions help to develop your concentration.

5. **B** The number 2356 is the arrest number assigned to Mr. Don Chamber who according to this question is not violator A but is violator B. Caption 43, which is in the information area relating to violator B, relates to Mr. Chamber's arrest number of 2356.

6. **C** Caption 3 calls for the location of the incident, which was on Route 26, the location where Trooper Best quickly overtook Mr. Kinder.

7. **D** Caption 50 asks whom was the injured trooper accompanied by, and that person is Trooper Harps.

8. **C** No weapon was used by Mr. Kinder. He struck the officer with his fist. Choice D is incorrect because an entry can be determined.

9. **A** The incident took place in Moon County, which is the appropriate entry for caption 2. In this type of question, you should look only at the captions that are suggested by the choices.

10. **B** Caption 10 asks for the specific assignment at the time of the incident, which was the conducting of a roadblock.

GROUP TWO

11. **D** The date the property was found is provided, but nothing is said about when the property was lost. Always follow the instructions, which in this case direct you to base your answers solely on the information recorded on the form.

12. **C** Only the information suggested in choice C can be found on the form. Choice A is incorrect because the owner did not lose the property. There is nothing to support choices B and D. Do not assume that just because people do or do not have the same last name that they may or may not be related. When answering forms questions, base your answer solely on the information provided.

13. **C** Under the information contained in line 11, it is indicated that Trooper Cash brought the property from the Bass Creek Troop Barracks to the Central Property Unit. By now it should be obvious that the kind of forms question you are dealing with in this section is what we refer to as reporting from completed forms, where there is no narrative, only a completed form.

14. **D** Mr. Don King is the owner of the property and his telephone, and not that of the finder of the property, is 1 555 555 1987. Choices A and B are incorrect; both Don and Frank King have the same telephone number.

15. **C** As stated in line 2 of the form. Notice the similarity in all the address choices. The question sought to find out if you could continue your concentration and not allow yourself to be distracted by similar choices.

16. **D** As stated in line 9, the property had a manufacturer serial number. Choice A is incorrect because Mr. Ray Burns lives in apartment E2. Choice B is incorrect because nothing on the form indicates where the property was last seen by the person who lost the

property. Choice C is incorrect because the property was returned to its owner 2 days after it was found, not lost.

17. **C**   As stated in line 6, the nature of the property is a laptop computer.

18. **B**   As stated on line 10, the number is the trooper property number. Remember that one of the ways troopers and highway patrol officers use forms is to retrieve information from already completed forms, which is exactly what this type of question seeks to do.

19. **B**   Shield numbers are important pieces of information because they assist in identifying the troopers involved.

20. **C**   The information on line 5 of the form clearly indicates that Mr. Ray Burns, who is the finder of the property, resides at 702 Terrace Avenue.

CHAPTER 8

Data Interpretation Questions

State police officers often work with data from graphs and tables. For this reason, questions about how to interpret graphs, and tables appear on many state trooper examinations. Such questions are called data interpretation questions. When we mention this to students who are preparing to take such tests, many of them become uneasy. They erroneously believe that they must be a combination of engineer and mathematician to handle this type of question. Once we show them how simple such questions can be, they actually gain confidence in their ability to deal with them. This is what we intend to do in this chapter. We will strip away the mask of difficulty that seems to surround these questions and help you develop the level of skill needed to answer them quickly and accurately.

The Cardinal Rule

Before discussing the major types of data interpretation questions, we discuss the cardinal rule for dealing with all such questions. The rule follows:

The answers are somewhere in the data. Your task is to make sure that you know what the data represent and exactly what data you are looking for.

In a way, data interpretation questions are like reading comprehension questions. This is what we mean by the first half of the cardinal rule, "the answers are somewhere in the data." Just as the answers to reading comprehension questions are found solely in the written information given as part of the question, so are the answers to data interpretation questions found in the information that supports these questions. Let's explore this a little further with a simple example.

A SAMPLE QUESTION

Suppose that you encountered the following question on a state trooper examination:

> Q1. The percentage of illiterate persons arrested for driving while intoxicated is 15%. What percentage of persons arrested for driving while intoxicated are illiterate?
> (A) 10% (B) 15% (C) 20% (D) 25%

Would such a question make you feel ill at ease? Would you find such a question to be difficult? Obviously you wouldn't. Yet, this is an example of how a data interpretation question actually works. Of course, it is not as simple as we have presented it, but that is how it works.

In actuality you will get a set of data, either in graph or table form, that contains a lot of information, most of which you do not need to answer the questions. Somewhere in that data is the fact that 15% of persons who are arrested for driving while intoxicated are illiterate. Your job in this type of question, therefore, is to sift through a lot of information to find the information you are looking for.

Graphs and Tables

The data in data interpretation questions are presented either in graph or table form. Because state troopers work much more frequently with tables than with graphs, the majority of the questions you will see on your official examination will probably involve tables. For this reason, the majority of data interpretation questions you will see in our practice examinations involves tables.

THREE TYPES OF GRAPHS

When writing data interpretation questions involving graphs, test writers generally use one of three different types of graphs:

● a line graph

● a circle graph

● a bar graph

LINE GRAPHS

A line graph similar to those typically found on state trooper examinations is pictured here.

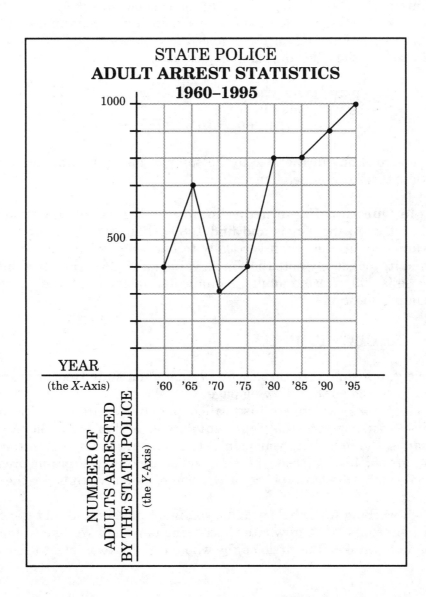

As a general rule, all graphs have a title. The title is very important because it usually tells you what the graph is about. The sample line graph shown is entitled "State Police—Adult Arrest Statistics—1960–1995." Upon reading this title, you know that the data involved in the questions have something to do with the number of adults arrested by the state police during the years 1960 to 1995.

Line graphs have what is known as an *X*-axis and a *Y*-axis. In the sample line graph, the *X*-axis shows the years 1960 to 1995. The *X*-axis extends horizontally, from left to right. The *Y*-axis shows the number of adults arrested by the state police and extends vertically from top to bottom. Although only two numbers are shown on the *Y*-axis, 500 and 1000, you must count the marked increments on the *Y*-axis to determine that each mark equals 100 arrested adults. The line graph itself is made up of a number of coordinates that are connected to each other with a line. The coordinates are usually shown as a dot or period. Each coordinate represents two values, the *X*-axis value and the *Y*-axis value. For example, the coordinate for 1960 (the *X*-axis value) corresponds to the number 400 on the *Y*-axis (the *Y*-axis value), and there is an *X*-axis coordinate for 1965 that corresponds to 700 on the *Y*-axis. Now, to see if you can read this graph, answer the following sample question.

Q2. Approximately how many adults were arrested by the state police in 1980?
(A) 500   (B) 600   (C) 700   (D) 800

Do not read any further. Go to the sample line graph and answer the question; then resume reading.

Sample Question Explained.   To answer the sample question, you must first go to the *X*-axis and find 1980. Then, once you locate 1980, you simply go up the graph vertically to find the 1980 coordinate. Once you find it, you simply note the *Y*-axis value for that coordinate, which in this case is 800 arrested adults, as indicated in choice D, the answer to our sample question.

CIRCLE GRAPHS

A circle graph similar to those typically found on state trooper examinations is pictured on the following page.

Circle graphs, which are also called pie charts, are, as their name implies, circular graphs that represent data as part of the whole. As with all graphs, the first thing you should do to understand it is read the title of the graph. In this case, the title indicates that the graph presents an analysis by the state police of the age of crime victims for the year 1996.

When working with circle graphs, you must understand that the circle itself represents 100% of whatever is being depicted. We like to tell our students to think of the circle as the whole pie. For example, the circle in

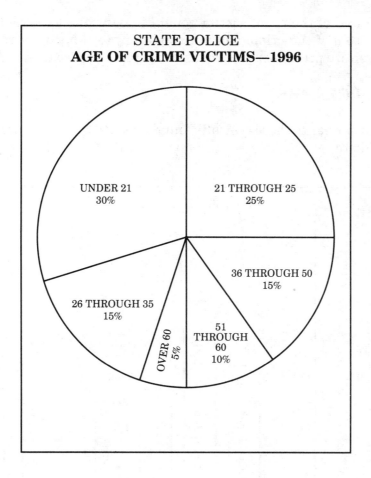

STATE POLICE
AGE OF CRIME VICTIMS—1996

UNDER 21
30%

21 THROUGH 25
25%

36 THROUGH 50
15%

26 THROUGH 35
15%

OVER 60
5%

51
THROUGH
60
10%

the sample circle graph represents all the crime victims during 1996. Each segment of the circle, or each piece of the pie, represents a certain portion of that crime victim population. For example, the age group from 21 to 25 years of age represents 25% of the entire crime victim population for the year 1996. Now, to see if you can read this graph, answer the following sample question.

Q3. Together the age groups 26–35 years of age and 36–50 years of age represent
(A) 15% of the crime victim population for 1996.
(B) 20% of the crime victim population for 1996.
(C) 30% of the crime victim population for 1996.
(D) 40% of the crime victim population for 1996.

Do not read any further. Go to the sample circle graph and answer the question; then resume reading.

Sample Question Explained. All you need to do to answer the sample question is locate the piece of the pie that represents the age group 26–35 and the one that represents the age group 36–50 and then add together the percentages for these two groups. Because the age group 26–35 represents 15% of the crime victim population and the age group 36–50 represents 15% of the crime victim population, together they represent 30% of the entire prison population, as indicated in choice C.

BAR GRAPHS

A bar graph similar to those typically found on state trooper examinations is pictured here.

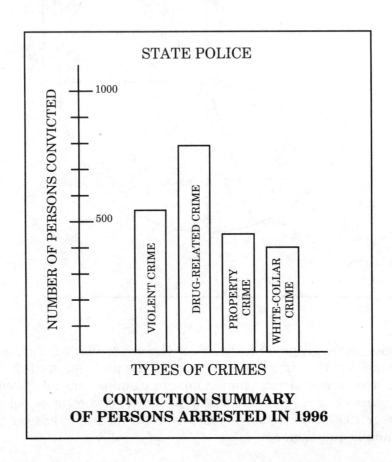

Bar graphs are, as their name implies, graphs that use bars to present data. The title of the sample bar graph reveals that it represents the conviction history of all persons arrested in 1996. A quick review of the individual bars shows that all convictions are divided into four categories: violent crime, drug-related crime, property crime, and white-collar crime. For example, the number of arrested persons who were convicted for the commission of some sort of violent crime is about 550. Now, to see if you can read this graph, answer the following sample question.

Q4. The number of persons arrested in 1996 who were convicted of property crimes is about
(A) 400.   (B) 450.
(C) 500.   (D) 600.

Do not read any further. Go to the sample bar graph and answer the question; then resume reading.

Sample Question Explained.   All that you need to do to answer our sample question is locate the bar that represents property crimes and then measure over from the top of that bar to the *Y*-axis, which represents the number of arrested persons who were convicted of a property crime. The answer is about 450, as indicated in choice B.

TABLES

There are many different ways of presenting data in table form, but the tables that are most often used on state trooper examinations have the following characteristics in common: they have titles that describe the information contained in the table, they have vertical labels, and they have horizontal labels. All three of these characteristics are shown in the following tables.

DISPOSITION OF TRAFFIC TICKETS ISSUED DURING THE CURRENT YEAR BY TROOPERS ASSIGNED TO TROOP 15

Charge	Total Issued	Guilty	Not Guilty
Unsafe lane change	123	112	11
Failure to signal	873	760	113
Following too closely	45	45	0
Failure to yield right of way	89	87	2
Speeding	1245	1201	44

As you can see, the sample table has a title that explains its contents; vertical labels, which are the various charges; and horizontal labels, which are the dispositions of the various charges. Reading the table is simple. For each charge, the vertical label, you have three pieces of information, the horizontal labels: (1) the total made, (2) the number of guilty findings and (3) the number of not guilty findings. For example, this year there were 123 tickets issued for unsafe lane changes, of which 112 were disposed of via a finding of guilty and 11 were disposed of with a finding of not guilty. Now, to see if you can read this table, answer the following sample question.

> Q5. Which of the following charges resulted in the greatest number of guilty findings?
> (A) following too closely
> (B) failure to signal
> (C) unsafe lane change
> (D) speeding

Do not read any further. Go to the sample table and answer the question; then resume reading.

Sample Question Explained. All you must do to find the answer to our sample question is look under the horizontal label guilty and then proceed down and look for the largest number, which is 1201—the number of guilty findings for speeding. Having found that number, you simply check to see if speeding is one of the choices. If, however, there were many more vertical labels, then a better strategy would be to look only at the charges suggested in the choices.

Strategies for Answering Data Interpretation Questions

When you are answering data interpretation questions, the first thing you must do is study the title of the graph or table involved and then make sure that you understand the kind of information that is presented in that graph or table. The next step is to go to the question and make sure that you know what the question is asking. After you are familiar with the graph or table and after you know what a particular question is asking, then you go to the graph or table and search for the information you need to evaluate each choice in the question. You must remain extremely careful. Attention to detail is absolutely required to maintain a high record of success when dealing with data interpretation questions. Now, compare this strategy with our cardinal rule as it was presented earlier:

> **The answers are somewhere in the data. Your task is to make sure that you know what the data represent and exactly what data you are looking for.**

We hope that this cardinal rule makes much more sense to you now after our discussion.

MATH MAY BE REQUIRED

One final word about data interpretation questions is in order before you try some practice exercises. It is highly likely that arriving at some of the answers to data interpretation questions will require you to do some basic mathematics. But the math is very similar to what we reviewed in Chapter 5.

Practice Exercises

GROUP ONE

10 Questions—Time Allowed 20 Minutes

Answer questions 1–10 based on the following data.

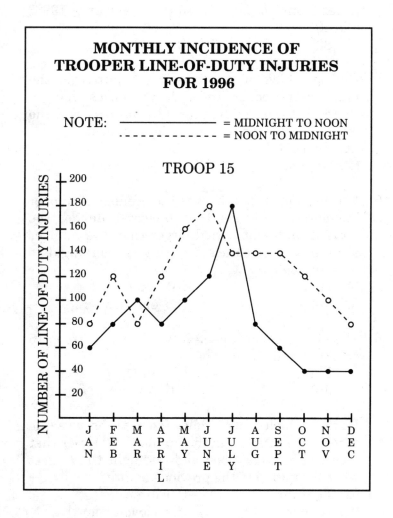

MONTHLY INCIDENCE OF TROOPER LINE-OF-DUTY INJURIES FOR 1996

NOTE: ———————— = MIDNIGHT TO NOON
- - - - - - - - - - = NOON TO MIDNIGHT

TROOP 15

1. In what three months was the number of trooper line-of-duty injuries that occurred between midnight and noon approximately the same?
   (A) July, August, and September
   (B) October, November, and December
   (C) January, February, and March
   (D) April, May, and June

A B C D
1 |||||||

2. In what month was the number of injuries that occurred from midnight to noon approximately the same as the number of injuries that occurred from noon to midnight?
   (A) April
   (B) December
   (C) May
   (D) There was no month in 1996 when this occurred.

A B C D
2 |||||||

3. Approximately how many trooper line-of-duty injuries occurred in Troop 15 in December of 1996?
   (A) 40   (B) 60
   (C) 80   (D) 120

A B C D
3 |||||||

4. During which of the following months did the number of trooper line-of-duty injuries that occurred between midnight and noon decrease the most as compared to the previous month?
   (A) February   (B) July
   (C) August   (D) November

A B C D
4 |||||||

5. For how many months was the number of trooper line-of-duty injuries that occurred during the noon to midnight period larger than the number of injuries that occurred during the midnight to noon period?
   (A) eight   (B) nine
   (C) ten   (D) eleven

A B C D
5 |||||||

6. The most trooper line-of-duty injuries in Troop 15 occurred in the month of
   (A) May.   (B) June.
   (C) July.   (D) August.

A B C D
6 |||||||

7. During which of the following months was the percentage increase in the number of injuries that occurred between noon and midnight the largest when compared to the previous month?
   (A) February   (B) June
   (C) August   (D) November

A B C D
7 |||||||

8. Which of the following 2-month periods accounted for the most trooper line-of-duty injuries in Troop 15?
   (A) from January 1st to March 1st
   (B) from May 1st to July 1st
   (C) from July 1st to September 1st
   (D) from October 1st to December 1st

   A B C D
   8 |||||||

9. Exactly how many trooper line-of-duty injuries occurred in Troop 15 on May 28th, 1996?
   (A) 100
   (B) 180
   (C) 280
   (D) cannot be determined

   A B C D
   9 |||||||

10. Which of the following is the most accurate statement concerning trooper line-of-duty injuries in Troop 15 during 1996?
   (A) They remained about the same for the entire year, although they did not remain constant.
   (B) They increased during the entire year.
   (C) They decreased during the entire year.
   (D) They reached their peak about the middle of the year and then decreased.

   A B C D
   10 |||||||

GROUP TWO

10 Questions—Time Allowed 20 Minutes

Answer questions 11–20 based on the information presented in the following table.

ACCIDENT–PRONE LOCATIONS
WITHIN JURISDICTION OF TROOP 15

Note: A location is considered to be accident prone if a minimum of five vehicle accidents have taken place at that location in the last 6 months. This list is updated on the fifth day of each month.

Location	Primary Causes*	Code**
Main Street & 14th Avenue	None	A
Elm Street & 12th Avenue	1-3-5	D
Broadway & 42nd Street	1	B
Broad Street & 10th Avenue	1	B
Park Street & 7th Avenue	1-2	E

Canal Street & 4th Avenue	1-2	C
Park Lane & 7th Avenue	6	C
Oak Street & 11th Avenue	7	D

*Primary causes are applicable only to vehicle accidents that result in the death of at least one person. They are not used for other than fatal accidents. The following are the only primary causes that apply:

1 = Speeding
2 = Driving while intoxicated
3 = Following too closely
4 = Failure to obey signal device
5 = Failure to obey stop/yield sign
6 = Unsafe lane change
7 = Other than one of the above

** A code must be entered for each accident-prone location. The code is used to classify locations according to the total number of accidents in the last 6 months. The following are the only codes that apply:

A = 5–9 accidents
B = 10–14 accidents
C = 15–19 accidents
D = 20–24 accidents
E = over 24 accidents

11. The location that has had the most vehicle accidents in the last 6 months is
    (A) Broadway & 42nd Street.
    (B) Broad Street & 10th Avenue.
    (C) Park Street & 7th Avenue.
    (D) Canal Street & 4th Avenue.

    A B C D
    11 |||||||

12. Driving while intoxicated was a causative factor in a fatal accident that occurred at
    (A) Broadway & 42nd Street.
    (B) Broad Street & 10th Avenue.
    (C) Park Street & 7th Avenue.
    (D) Main Street & 14th Avenue.

    A B C D
    12 |||||||

13. Of the following locations, the one that was the scene of the fewest accidents in the last 6 months is
    (A) Main Street & 14th Avenue.
    (B) Elm Street & 12th Avenue.
    (C) Broadway & 42nd Street.
    (D) Broad Street & 10th Avenue.

    A B C D
    13 |||||||

14. Which of the following is the most common cause of fatal accidents in the last 6 months at accident-prone locations in Troop 15?
    (A) speeding   (B) unsafe lane change
    (C) following too closely   (D) intoxicated driving

    A B C D
    14 ||||||||

15. There were no fatal accidents in the last 6 months at
    (A) Main Street & 14th Avenue.
    (B) Elm Street & 12th Avenue.
    (C) Broadway & 42nd Street.
    (D) Broad Street & 10th Avenue.

    A B C D
    15 ||||||||

16. An up-to-date listing of accident-prone locations is available
    (A) every 3 months.
    (B) on the 5th of each month.
    (C) twice a month.
    (D) every Monday.

    A B C D
    16 ||||||||

17. Which of the following is the most accurate statement concerning the number of vehicle accidents in the last 6 months at Broadway and 42nd Street and Broad Street and 10th Avenue?
    (A) There were more accidents at Broadway and 42nd Street than at Broad Street and 10th Avenue.
    (B) There were more accidents at Broad Street and 10th Avenue than at Broadway and 42nd Street.
    (C) There were an equal number of accidents at Broad Street and 10th Avenue and Broadway and 42nd Street.
    (D) There is not enough information available to make specific comparisons of the number of accidents at those locations.

    A B C D
    17 ||||||||

18. Which of the following was not a cause of at least one fatal accident in the last 6 months?
    (A) Driving while intoxicated
    (B) Following too closely
    (C) Failure to obey signal device
    (D) Failure to obey stop/yield sign

    A B C D
    18 ||||||||

19. The cause of the fatal accident at Oak Street and 11th Avenue
   (A) was speeding.
   (B) was driving while intoxicated.
   (C) was unsafe lane change.
   (D) cannot be determined from the available data.

   A B C D
   19 | | | | | | |

20. The number of accidents in the last 6 months that have occurred at Park Lane and 7th Avenue is
   (A) over 24.
   (B) between 15 and 19.
   (C) either 16, 17, or 18.
   (D) unknown.

   A B C D
   20 | | | | | | |

GROUP THREE

10 Questions—Time Allowed 20 Minutes

Answer questions 21–30 based on the following information.

CRIME STATISTICS FOR TROOP 20

Note: All reported crimes in Troop 20 are given a report number starting with the number 0001 each month. Those crimes that have been cleared by arrest are marked with an asterisk.

Report	Date	Day	Crime	Time	Location
0001	3/3	Saturday	Rape	3:00 A.M.	105 Elm St.
0005	3/7	Tuesday	Trespass	4:20 A.M.	415 Oak St.
*0009	3/7	Tuesday	Homicide	9:00 A.M.	321 Pine St.
0014	3/9	Thursday	Homicide	12:10 A.M.	203 Elm St.
0019	3/11	Saturday	Trespass	4:00 A.M.	300 Elm St.
*0023	3/11	Saturday	Rape	6:00 P.M.	439 Oak St.
0028	3/11	Saturday	Trespass	3:45 A.M.	567 Main St.
0036	3/12	Sunday	Rape	4:00 P.M.	400 Oak St.
*0043	3/16	Thursday	Rape	7:00 P.M.	387 Oak St.
0051	3/18	Saturday	Trespass	1:15 A.M.	145 Elm St.
0065	3/21	Tuesday	Homicide	7:00 A.M.	345 Pine St.
*0069	3/22	Wednesday	Homicide	1:45 A.M.	187 Elm St.
0074	3/22	Wednesday	Trespass	5:00 A.M.	535 Oak St.

0081	3/25	Saturday	Trespass	7:00 A.M.	095 Elm St.
*0083	3/26	Sunday	Rape	1:00 A.M.	310 Pine St.
0089	3/31	Saturday	Rape	4:00 P.M.	349 Pine St.

21. A trooper would most likely be able to reduce the number of trespasses by patrolling
    (A) Elm Street between 4:00 P.M. and midnight on Tuesdays.
    (B) Oak Street between 1:00 P.M. and 9:00 P.M. on Mondays.
    (C) Elm Street between midnight and 8:00 A.M. on Saturdays.
    (D) Oak Street between midnight and 8:00 A.M. on Tuesdays.

    A B C D
    21 ||||||||

22. A trooper would most likely be able to reduce the number of rapes by patrolling
    (A) Pine Street between 4:00 P.M. and midnight, Wednesday through Sunday.
    (B) Oak Street between 3:00 P.M. and 10:00 P.M., Tuesday through Saturday.
    (C) Oak Street between 4:00 P.M. and midnight, Wednesday through Sunday.
    (D) Pine Street between 1:00 P.M. and 9:00 P.M., Tuesday through Saturday.

    A B C D
    22 ||||||||

23. The day of the week that accounts for the most crime is
    (A) Saturday.   (B) Sunday.
    (C) Tuesday.   (D) Thursday.

    A B C D
    23 ||||||||

24. Which of the following is the most accurate statement?
    (A) All rapes are committed on Saturdays.
    (B) There were at least 89 crimes reported in Troop 20 during the month of March.
    (C) No homicides are committed in Troop 20 on Tuesdays.
    (D) All homicides are committed on Tuesdays.

    A B C D
    24 ||||||||

25. How many crimes in Troop 20 were committed in March at exactly 4:00 P.M.?
    (A) at least 2   (B) at least 3
    (C) at least 4   (D) more than 4

    A B C D
    25 ||||||||

26. A trooper would be most likely to reduce the number of homicides by patrolling
    (A) Elm Street between 11:00 P.M. and 7:00 A.M., Tuesday through Saturday.
    (B) Pine Street between midnight and 8:00 A.M., Tuesday through Saturday.
    (C) Oak Street between noon and 8:00 P.M., Monday through Friday.
    (D) Main Street between midnight to 8:00 A.M., Wednesday through Sunday.

    A B C D
    26 ||||||||

27. A trooper who works on Elm Street, Oak Street, Pine Street, and Main Street should know that for the month of March the combined total of rapes, trespasses, and homicides was greatest on
    (A) Elm Street.   (B) Pine Street.
    (C) Oak Street.   (D) Main Street.

    A B C D
    27 ||||||||

28. Which of the following is the most accurate statement concerning the crime statistics for Troop 20 during the month of March?
    (A) There were no rapes on Elm Street.
    (B) There were no trespasses on Pine Street.
    (C) There were no homicides on Pine Street.
    (D) There were no rapes on Oak Street.

    A B C D
    28 ||||||||

29. The day of the week with the fewest reported rapes, homicides, and trespasses is
    (A) Monday.   (B) Tuesday.
    (C) Wednesday.   (D) Thursday.

    A B C D
    29 ||||||||

30. How many of the reported homicides, trespasses, and rapes were cleared by arrest?
    (A) 2   (B) 3
    (C) 5   (D) unable to determine

    A B C D
    30 ||||||||

Answer Key and Explanations

ANSWER KEY

1. **B**	7. **A**	13. **A**	19. **D**	25. **A**
2. **D**	8. **B**	14. **A**	20. **B**	26. **A**
3. **D**	9. **D**	15. **A**	21. **C**	27. **A**
4. **C**	10. **D**	16. **B**	22. **C**	28. **B**
5. **C**	11. **C**	17. **D**	23. **A**	29. **A**
6. **C**	12. **C**	18. **C**	24. **B**	30. **C**

ANSWER EXPLANATIONS

GROUP ONE

If you followed our strategy, you would have taken some time to study the title of the graph and its contents before answering the questions. You should have recognized it as a line graph. Hopefully, the fact that it had two sets of lines did not confuse you. The note tells you that the solid line represents the time period from midnight to noon, and the dotted line represents the time period from noon to midnight. Then you should have observed that the X-axis represents the month of the year, and the Y-axis represents the number of trooper line-of-duty injuries divided into increments of 20, from 0 to 200.

1. **B** If you picked choice A, you failed to interpret the note carefully enough. The dotted line represents the time period from noon to midnight. The question involved the time period from midnight to noon.

2. **D** Graphs can also be used to indicate that something has not occurred. As indicated in choice D, there is no month, based on the graph, for which the number of injuries was the same for both time periods.

3. **D** In December of 1996 there were about 40 line-of-duty injuries during the midnight to noon period, and there were about 80 line-of-duty injuries during the noon to midnight period. This means that there were 40 plus 80 injuries, which, of course, is 120.

4. **C** There was no need to do any math to answer this question. Concerning injuries that occurred between midnight and noon, during February (choice A) injuries increased. During July (choice B) they also increased. During November they remained the same as the previous month. Only during August did they decrease.

5. **C** Only in March and July were the number of injuries that occurred during the noon to midnight period less than those that occurred during the midnight to noon period.

6. **C** In May there were about 260 injuries. In June there were about 300. In July, the answer, there were about 320. In August there were 220.

7. **A** In November there was a decrease in injuries during the noon to midnight period, and in August they remained about the same. This means that choices C and D can be eliminated. In February the number of these injuries went from about 80 in January to about 120. Referring to the formula you were shown in the math chapter, this means that there was a 50% increase, (120−80 = 40; 40 divided by 80, the old number, is 50%). In June, the noon to midnight injuries went from about 160 to about 180, which is an increase of about 12% (180 minus 160, divided by 160, or 20/160). The answer is choice A.

8. **B** Injuries reached their maximum incidence between May 1st and July 1st.

9. **D** If you missed this question you probably do not understand that one cannot determine exact statistics from line graphs such as the one we used for this series of questions. These line graphs are used to show trends and not to supply specific daily statistics. To completely understand this, ask yourself this question, How would I determine exactly from the graph the point at which May 28th is represented? The answer, of course, is that you can't. Exact numbers, as you will soon find out, are presented in questions involving tables.

10. **D** The injuries that occurred during both time periods involved started low, reached their highest levels (in other words, they reached their peak) at about the middle of the year, and then decreased.

GROUP TWO

If you followed our strategy, you would have spent some time understanding the material presented in the table prior to answering the questions. Remember that one thorough review of the table is a more efficient use of time than thoroughly reviewing it again and again prior to answering each question.

11. **C** The code for Park Street and 7th Avenue is E, and that code is used for locations that have been the scene of over 24 accidents in the last 6 months.

12. **C** Driving while intoxicated is Primary Cause #2, and it was listed as a cause of an accident that occurred at Park Street and 7th Avenue.

13. **A** Main Street and 14th Avenue is listed as a Code A location, which means that there have been no more than nine accidents at that location in the last 6 months.

14. **A** Speeding was a primary cause of five fatal accidents.

15. **A** The fact that there were no primary causes listed for Main Street and 14th Avenue means that there were no fatal accidents at that location.

16. **B** According to the note at the top of the chart, this list is updated on the fifth day of each month.

17. **D** The code for both locations is B. This means that there were between 10 and 14 accidents at both locations. More specific information is not available.

18. **C** The only primary cause that was not listed in the chart was number 4, and that corresponds to choice C, Failure to Obey Signal Device.

19. **D** The primary cause of the fatal accident at Oak Street and 11th Avenue was listed as #7, which is then given as other than one of the above. This, of course, means that the primary cause of that accident cannot be determined from the available data.

20. **B** The code for Park Lane and 7th Avenue is C, and that means that between 15 and 19 accidents have occurred at that location. If you picked choice A, you were careless and selected the number of accidents that occurred at Park Street and 7th Avenue.

GROUP THREE

21. **C** Of the six trespasses on the chart, three of them occurred on Elm Street between midnight and 8:00 A.M. on Saturdays. One trespass occurred on Tuesday on Oak Street, one occurred on Wednesday on Oak Street, and one occurred on Main Street on Saturday.

Clearly, the trooper involved would get the best return by patrolling on Elm Street on Saturdays between midnight and 8:00 A.M.

22. **C** Of the six reported rapes, three of them occurred on Oak Street between 4:00 P.M. and midnight—one on Thursday, one on Saturday, and one on Sunday.

23. **A** Of the 16 crimes listed, 7 of them were committed on Saturdays.

24. **B** According to the note, every crime reported in Troop 20 is given a report number starting with #0001 each month. The report number for the last crime shown on the chart is 0089.

25. **A** This question requires attention to detail. If you selected B, then you counted the crime that was reported at 4:00 A.M..

26. **A** Choices C and D are wrong because there were no reported homicides on Oak or Main Streets. Choice A is correct because there were two homicides on Elm Street between 11:00 P.M. and 7:00 A.M. from Tuesday through Saturday.

27. **A** Of the 16 reported crimes, 6 of them took place on Elm Street.

28. **B** Pine Street was the scene of two homicides and two rapes but no trespasses.

29. **A** Monday did not appear anywhere in the table.

30. **C** As stated in the note, those crimes that were cleared by arrest are marked with an asterisk. There were five such crimes.

CHAPTER 9

Understanding and Applying State Police Directives, Procedures, and Regulations

Troopers and highway patrol officers often work alone and find themselves in situations that call for them to use discretion while making their decisions. To help and guide them in these situations, they are given procedures to follow. These procedures, which act as guidelines, are, of course, in keeping with the overall policies of the agency. These guidelines and procedures are usually in written form and are made available to the troopers and highway patrol officers. Clearly then, part of the job of these officers is to read and understand these guidelines and policies and also to correctly apply them to job-related incidents.

For example, it may become evident that a need exists for better detection of narcotics hidden in suspicious vehicles at the scene of traffic stops. An officer would probably then receive new guidelines for searching such vehicles for narcotics. The officer would be expected to read and understand the new guidelines. However, the officer would also be expected to be able to apply these guidelines to situations involving the detection of narcotics in suspicious motor vehicles at traffic stops. Obviously no two incidents are exactly alike. Each involves a different and specific set of circumstances. This fact requires that the officer involved be able to apply the general guidelines to specific situations. The questions in this chapter will develop your ability to read, understand, and apply procedures that might be typically given to trooper and highway patrol officers.

Two Question Types

Two main types of questions used to test a candidate's ability to read, understand, and apply procedures are known as understanding procedures and applying procedures to situations.

UNDERSTANDING PROCEDURES

In this question type a candidate is given a procedure similar to what a trooper or highway patrol officer might typically receive on the job. After reading and understanding the procedure, the candidate then must answer questions about the procedure. Here a candidate's ability to understand such procedures is tested. Generally this question type requires the candidate to identify accurate or inaccurate statements about the procedure. The candidate may refer back to the procedure as often as necessary.

EXAMPLE OF AN UNDERSTANDING PROCEDURES QUESTION

When handcuffing prisoners, troopers shall always handcuff prisoners with the prisoner's hands behind his or her back. This is known as rear cuffing. However, when, in the opinion of, and with permission of, the patrol supervisor, it would be safe to handcuff a prisoner with the prisoner's hands in front, then a prisoner may be front cuffed. In those instances when authorized to front cuff prisoners, under no circumstances will troopers leave such prisoners unattended.

Q1. Based solely on the information in this procedure, which of the following statements is most appropriate?
(A) Only the patrol supervisor may front cuff a prisoner.
(B) A trooper may never front cuff a prisoner.
(C) At times a prisoner who has been front cuffed may be left unattended if the permission of the patrol supervisor is obtained.
(D) A trooper may front cuff a prisoner under certain circumstances.

STRATEGIES FOR ANSWERING UNDERSTANDING PROCEDURES QUESTIONS

1. **Scan the procedure.** The first step you should take is to read the material quickly to get an idea of what the procedure is about. A quick scan of the procedure in this example tells you that usually troopers are not allowed to front cuff prisoners. However, it also tells you when and by whose authority a trooper might be allowed to front cuff a prisoner. Finally the procedure indicates that a prisoner who has been front cuffed may never be left unattended.

2. **Scan the stem and the choices.** You should read the stem of the question and the choices quickly. By doing this for the example given, you should have been able to determine that the question concerned itself with the use of handcuffs on prisoners by troopers. The question asks you to select the most appropriate statement concerning the procedure.

3. **Now closely read the procedure.** By closely reading the procedure, you should have determined that a patrol supervisor could authorize a trooper to front cuff a prisoner. Also the procedure very clearly states that under no circumstances should a prisoner who has been front cuffed be left unattended.

4. **Use a mental picture.** Imagine yourself in the situation that the procedure and the question are describing. In the example given, think of a situation where you are a trooper who has arrested and rear cuffed a wanted felon. Then imagine a situation where you are given permission to front cuff such a prisoner. Who, according to the procedure, is allowed to give you such permission? All the while you should remember that you are not permitted to leave a prisoner who has been front cuffed unattended. Put yourself into the situation that is being described to develop a mental image of what is occurring.

5. **Select your answer.** Selecting your answer involves a process of elimination. For example, in the example question, choice A is inappropriate because a patrol supervisor is not the only officer who may front cuff a prisoner. A trooper could also do it with the permission of the patrol supervisor. Therefore, you should place an X through choice A and choice B, which is inappropriate for the same reason. Choice C is inappropriate, and you should put an X through it because a prisoner who has been front cuffed may never be left unattended. Choice D is the most appropriate choice because a trooper could front cuff a prisoner under certain circumstances. Choice D is, therefore, the answer.

APPLYING PROCEDURES TO SITUATIONS

In this type of question, the candidate is given a typical state trooper or highway patrol officer procedure. The candidate is given a story or narrative describing an incident or situation that an officer could be expected to encounter. In some instances, the candidate is then asked to identify the most appropriate (or inappropriate) course of action for the officer to take in the situation described based on the procedure provided. Procedures may be referred to by the candidates if necessary to answer the question. In other instances, the candidate must identify what action the officer should take next based on the procedure provided and the facts of the narrative or situation described. Both variations of this type of question are designed to test if a candidate can apply procedures to situations.

EXAMPLE OF AN APPLYING PROCEDURES TO SITUATIONS QUESTION

A trooper is required to prepare the form ACCIDENT REPORT when, as an operator of an official vehicle, the trooper is involved in a motor vehicle accident. A motor vehicle accident is defined as one that occurs on a public highway or on a public street between building lines. Regarding accidents involving official vehicles that occur on private property or on property to which the public does not have access, the form ACCIDENT REPORT shall not be prepared by the operator of the official vehicle because such incidents shall not be considered motor vehicle accidents. Instead, the operator of the official vehicle shall notify the patrol supervisor.

On July 12, 19xx, Highway Patrol Officer Bill Roe is driving a highway patrol car during routine highway patrol. Also assigned to the same vehicle as the recorder of messages directed to the vehicle is Highway Patrol Officer Frank Long. The officers are directed to respond to the Highway Patrol motor pool. While entering the private parking lot of the Highway Patrol motor pool, which is not accessible to the public, Officer Roe accidently hits a chain link fence causing some damage to the patrol car.

> Q2. Based solely on the preceding information, it would be most appropriate for
> (A) Officer Roe to prepare the form ACCIDENT REPORT.
> (B) Officer Long to prepare the form ACCIDENT REPORT.
> (C) Officer Long to notify the patrol supervisor.
> (D) Officer Roe to notify the patrol supervisor.

STRATEGIES FOR ANSWERING APPLYING PROCEDURES TO SITUATIONS QUESTIONS

1. **Scan the procedure.** Get a quick idea of what the procedure is about. What is the intent of the procedure? What is it describing? To whom does it apply? When should it be used?

   The intent of the procedure given in this example is to identify who is responsible for preparing a certain form and when that form should be prepared and what should be done when the form is not prepared. The important parts of the procedure should be highlighted or underlined. This includes the names of the forms involved, the circumstances under which they should be prepared, the persons charged with the responsibility of preparing them, and what should be done if the form is not required.

2. **Scan the narrative.** Quickly looking over the narrative in this example reveals that a highway patrol car is damaged in a parking lot not accessible to the public. The incident occurs while the operator and another officer are responding to the Highway Patrol motor pool.

3. **Scan the question.** By looking at the stem of the question and the choices, it should be clear that the question asks whether or not a form should be prepared, and if not, what should be done by whom. This should sensitize you as to what to focus on when performing the next step of the strategy.

4. **Closely reread the procedure.** This part of the strategy should not be time-consuming because you already underlined and highlighted the procedure when you previously scanned it. Now that you know what part of the procedure is being asked about, it is an easy task to focus on the relevant part(s) of the procedure.

5. **Closely reread the narrative.** While reading the narrative closely, we recommend that you put yourself into the narrative. Pretend, as in the example, that you are the driver of the vehicle and that the damage to the vehicle occurred while you were driving. Should this be considered a motor vehicle accident? If it should, what must you do? If it's not, what should you do?

6. **Pick your answer.** You must consider all choices. For example, in the example question, choice A is inappropriate because the form AC-CIDENT REPORT is not required because the incident did not occur on a public highway or on a public street between building lines. By definition, a motor vehicle accident has not occurred. The incident occurred on property to which the public does not have access. Choice B is inappropriate because, whenever it is appropriate for the form ACCIDENT REPORT to be prepared, it is the job of the operator of the vehicle to prepare the necessary form. Officer Long is not the

operator. Thus for the same reason, choice C is inappropriate because it is again the job of the operator to notify the patrol supervisor when an accident involving an official vehicle occurs on private property. The answer is choice D. Choice D, which calls for Officer Roe to notify the patrol supervisor, is correct because the incident is not considered a motor vehicle accident, and, in such instances, the operator of the vehicle is required to notify the patrol supervisor.

Practice Exercises

GROUP ONE

10 Questions—Time Allowed 20 Minutes

INSTRUCTIONS: Answer questions 1–10 based solely on the following information.

GENERAL PROCEDURES FOR HANDLING PRISONERS

A trooper upon making an arrest shall

1. request the Prisoner Detention Unit to assign cell space and determine the method of transportation to an activated detention facility.

2. comply with the instructions given by the Prisoner Detention Unit.

3. permit the prisoner to be interviewed by the following properly identified persons when they are on official business:

    a. a supervisory officer of the State Police

    b. a member of the State Police Detective Bureau

    c. the State Attorney General or a representative

    d. the Chief Medical Examiner or a representative

    e. the prisoner's legal representative (but only if the interview is conducted in a detective interview room)

    f. an official of a state agency if the prisoner is an employee of that agency

    g. a federal law enforcement officer

    h. a clergyman (but only upon request by the prisoner)

    i. a State Division of Parole officer (but only to serve parole violation papers)

---

4. prepare an ARREST REPORT.

5. prepare an ARREST REPORT SUPPLEMENT when an attorney interviews a prisoner while the prisoner is still in the trooper's custody.

6. permit parents or legal guardian to visit a prisoner between the ages of 16 and 21, for not longer than 20 minutes in the presence of the trooper. However, the prisoner must have been in custody more than four (4) hours.

7. advise the prisoner of telephone privileges and permit the prisoner to make use of telephone privileges. Only three local calls are permitted. Long distance calls may be made in place of local calls if the party receiving the call will accept the charges for the call. No one call shall be longer than 5 minutes.

8. not confine in a cell a female prisoner with a nursing baby.

1. When a trooper makes an arrest, the trooper shall request which of the following units to assign cell space?
   (A) Detective Bureau
   (B) State Attorney General
   (C) Prisoner Detention Unit
   (D) State Division of Parole

   A B C D
   1 ||||||||

2. A prisoner has been arrested by a trooper. The prisoner may be interviewed by a parole officer from the State Division of Parole on official business
   (A) only if the prisoner consents.
   (B) anytime the parole officer deems it necessary.
   (C) only to serve parole violation papers.
   (D) only with permission of a member of the State Police Detective Bureau.

   A B C D
   2 ||||||||

3. The preparation of an ARREST REPORT is the job of
   (A) the trooper making the arrest.
   (B) the State Attorney General or a representative.
   (C) a member of the State Police Detective Bureau.
   (D) a federal law enforcement officer who interviews the prisoner.

   A B C D
   3 ||||||||

4. When a prisoner's legal representative interviews a prisoner who has been arrested by a trooper, the interview
   (A) must be overheard by a member of the State Police Detective Bureau.
   (B) can be no longer than 20 minutes.
   (C) must be conducted in the presence of the trooper who made the arrest.
   (D) must be conducted in a detective interview room.

5. If a youth who is 17 years old is arrested at 10:00 A.M., which of the following is the earliest time that his parents would be allowed to visit him?
   (A) 11:01 A.M.
   (B) 12:01 A.M.
   (C) 1:01 P.M.
   (D) 2:01 P.M.

6. If the parents of an 18 year old who has been arrested are appropriately permitted to visit with the prisoner and if the visit began at 11:00 A.M., then the latest the visit could last is
   (A) 11:10 A.M.
   (B) 11:20 A.M.
   (C) 1:00 P.M.
   (D) 3:00 P.M.

7. A clergyman appears at a location where a prisoner who has been arrested by a trooper is being detained and asks to interview the prisoner. In such an instance, it would be most correct if the trooper
   (A) immediately allowed the clergyman to interview the prisoner.
   (B) politely told the clergyman that it is against policy to allow prisoners to be interviewed before they are arraigned.
   (C) told the clergyman to obtain permission from the trooper's immediate supervisor.
   (D) asked the prisoner if he requested the clergyman to appear.

8. Regarding the use of telephones by a prisoner who has been arrested by a trooper, which of the following statements is least accurate?
   (A) The trooper shall advise the prisoner of telephone privileges.
   (B) The prisoner is allowed to make three local telephone calls.
   (C) The prisoner can talk as long as desired as long as the prisoner absorbs any additional costs.
   (D) If long distance calls are made, they shall be considered made in place of local calls.

   A B C D
   8 | | | | | | |

9. It would be most correct to prepare which of the following forms when an attorney interviews a prisoner while the prisoner is still in the trooper's custody?
   (A) ARREST REPORT
   (B) ARREST REPORT SUPPLEMENT
   (C) AIDED REPORT
   (D) COURT AFFIDAVIT

   A B C D
   9 | | | | | | |

10. Upon making an arrest, a trooper may permit the prisoner to be interviewed by all the following properly identified persons when they are on official business except
   (A) any member of the State Police.
   (B) the State Attorney General.
   (C) the Chief Medical Examiner.
   (D) an official of a state agency if the prisoner is an employee of that agency.

   A B C D
   10 | | | | | | |

GROUP TWO

10 Questions—Time Allowed 20 Minutes

INSTRUCTIONS: Answer questions 11–17 based solely on the following procedure.

The purpose of this procedure is to assist parents in determining if a substance found in the possession of their children is, in fact, a narcotic substance. Persons using this program shall remain anonymous, and no criminal charges or investigation will be instituted against them unless it is evident that the program is being used to circumvent the law.

When a person indicates to a trooper a desire to participate in the program, the field trooper shall

1. direct the person to call the trooper post and comply with the directions of the desk officer.

The trooper assigned as the desk officer shall

1. ascertain from the caller the amount of the suspected controlled substance involved.

2. give the caller a code phrase consisting of

    a. the post designation (such as 10 for Post 10) AND

    b. any letter of the alphabet randomly selected AND

    c. a four (4) digit number (e.g., 10 - T - 2356).

3. instruct the caller to record and carry the code phrase on his or her person while enroute to the trooper post. Note that the purpose of the code phrase is to protect the caller who may become the subject of a search while enroute to the trooper post.

4. inform the person that the code phrase will expire in one (1) hour.

5. immediately dispatch a patrol car to a location agreed upon by the caller and have the caller transported to the trooper post, if there is reason to believe that a felony amount of controlled substance is involved.

Note: The following forms will be prepared by the trooper who actually receives the suspected substance:

    a. ANONYMOUS NARCOTICS RECEIPT

    b. PROPERTY CLERK'S VOUCHER

    c. LABORATORY EXAMINATION REQUEST

The trooper acting as a desk officer shall instruct the person to retain the copy of the ANONYMOUS NARCOTICS RECEIPT and call the trooper post after five (5) business days to obtain the analysis results by identifying himself with the code.

The trooper receiving the phone call asking about the results will do the following in this order:

1. Give the results of the analysis (positive or negative reply only) when the person calls with the appropriate code phrase.

2. Advise the person to contact the family physician or treatment agencies for treatment referral if the results are positive.

3. Ask the person if he wishes to cooperate in investigating the source of the controlled substance while still maintaining anonymity.

4. Obtain as much information as possible, and if the person cooperates, prepare a NARCOTICS INTELLIGENCE REPORT.

11. Trooper June Lakes is assigned to field duty. One morning, Mrs. Teller, a mother of a 14-year-old girl, approaches Trooper Lakes and tells her that she has found a powdery substance she thinks is narcotics under her daughter's bed. Mrs. Teller asks the trooper if there is any way that she can find out what the substance really is. The trooper accompanies Mrs. Teller to her home and collects the powdery substance. In this instance, the actions of Trooper Lakes are

(A) appropriate, because the sooner the substance is collected, the sooner it can be determined what the substance is.

(B) inappropriate, because Trooper Lakes should have called for the lab to respond to collect the powdery substance properly.

(C) appropriate, because under no circumstances should a civilian carry narcotics on a public street.

(D) inappropriate, because Trooper Lakes should have directed the person to call the trooper post.

A B C D
11 |||||||

12. Trooper Watts gives a parent, who is concerned that a substance found in the possession of his child might be a narcotic substance, a code phrase. The purpose of the code phrase is to protect him if he becomes the subject of an unrelated police search. If the code phrase given is 16-X-2399, then the post designation is most likely

(A) X.
(B) 16.
(C) 2339.
(D) 16-2399.

A B C D
12 |||||||

13. The trooper assigned as the desk officer should tell a person receiving a code phrase that the code phrase will be honored for only

(A) 30 minutes.
(B) 1 hour.
(C) 2 hours.
(D) 3 hours.

A B C D
13 |||||||

14. Trooper Don Baker is assigned as the desk officer at the post command. He receives a call from a man who claims that he has found a substance that he feels is narcotics in the possession of one of his children. Trooper Baker would be most correct to send a patrol car if
    (A) the caller merely asks for one.
    (B) there is reason to believe that a felony amount of the suspicious substance is involved.
    (C) the caller lives a considerable distance from the trooper post.
    (D) there is reason to believe that the caller may become the subject of a police search.

    A B C D
    14 | | | | | | |

15. Trooper Butcher has just received a suspicious substance from a parent who claims that this suspicious substance was found in his son's dresser. The parent believes that it may be narcotics. When Trooper Butcher receives the suspected substance, the trooper should complete all the following forms except
    (A) a PROPERTY CLERK'S VOUCHER.
    (B) an ANONYMOUS NARCOTICS RECEIPT.
    (C) a LABORATORY EXAMINATION REQUEST.
    (D) a NARCOTICS INTELLIGENCE REPORT.

    A B C D
    15 | | | | | | |

16. Trooper Frank Marks is acting as a desk officer at the post command when a parent, who had called earlier and received a code phrase, now delivers a suspicious substance to the trooper. The parent found the substance in the jacket pocket of his 14-year-old daughter. It would be most appropriate for the trooper to instruct the person to call the post command after
    (A) 3 calendar days.
    (B) 3 business days.
    (C) 5 calendar days.
    (D) 5 business days.

    A B C D
    16 | | | | | | |

17. Trooper Rivers has just received a phone call from a father who some time ago turned over a suspicious substance to the state police. The father had found the substance in his son's possession and wanted to have the substance analyzed. The father is now inquiring about the results. If Trooper Rivers performs the following four actions, which of them would most appropriately be performed last?

(A) Ask the father if he wishes to cooperate in investigating the source of the controlled substance while still maintaining anonymity.

(B) Give the results of the analysis (positive or negative reply only) when the person calls with the appropriate code phrase.

(C) Obtain as much information as possible, and if the person cooperates, prepare a NARCOTICS INTELLIGENCE REPORT.

(D) Advise the father to contact the family physician or treatment agencies for treatment referral if the results are positive.

Answer questions 18–20 based solely on the following procedure.

To prevent persons from jumping from structures, a trooper shall do the following, in this order.

Upon arriving at a location where a person is threatening to jump from a structure, a trooper shall

1. notify the radio dispatcher and request a life net.

2. attempt to persuade or prevent the person from jumping.

3. seek assistance from the person's relatives, friends, and clergyman.

4. confine the person to the side of the building facing the street, if possible, so that life nets may be used more effectively.

5. rope off the area below and prevent persons from entering the area.

18. Trooper May Smart arrives at the scene where a distraught male is perched on the roof of a six story building threatening to jump. Trooper Smart's first action should be

(A) to attempt to persuade the male from jumping.
(B) to try to confine the male to the side of the building that faces the street so that rescue equipment may be used.
(C) to notify the radio dispatcher and request a life net.
(D) to seek the assistance of the male's relatives.

A B C D
18 |||||||

19. One of the actions taken by Trooper Smart is to attempt to confine the male threatening to jump to the side of the building that does not face the street. According to procedure the trooper acted

(A) properly, mainly because innocent bystanders could be injured if the male jumped and landed on them.
(B) improperly, mainly because the public has a right to see all the actions of the police as they are occurring.
(C) properly, mainly because the size of the crowd of onlookers will be reduced.
(D) improperly, mainly because it makes the use of a life net less effective.

A B C D
19 |||||||

20. If Trooper Smart correctly followed procedure at the scene where the male is threatening to jump from the building, then of the following actions the one that should be performed last is

(A) to confine the person to the side of the building facing the street, if possible, so that life nets may be used more effectively.
(B) to rope off the area below and prevent persons from entering the area.
(C) to attempt to persuade or prevent the male from jumping.
(D) to seek the assistance of the male's friends.

A B C D
20 |||||||

Answer Key and Explanations

ANSWER KEY

1. **C**	5. **D**	9. **B**	13. **B**	17. **C**
2. **C**	6. **B**	10. **A**	14. **B**	18. **C**
3. **A**	7. **D**	11. **D**	15. **D**	19. **D**
4. **D**	8. **C**	12. **B**	16. **D**	20. **B**

ANSWER EXPLANATIONS

GROUP ONE

1. **C** Scanning the question stem and the choices before closely reading the procedure would have helped you to answer this question quickly and accurately.

2. **C** The importance of words such as *only* and *anytime* can be seen here. A prisoner may be interviewed by a parole officer from the State Division of Parole on official business not anytime but only when serving parole violation papers.

3. **A** When reviewing procedures it is always important to determine to whom the tasks are assigned. In this instance, all the tasks are assigned to the trooper making the arrest.

4. **D** When examining procedures, give special attention to what are known as qualifiers. They are statements that change a previously made statement. As in this example, obviously a prisoner may be interviewed by his attorney but notice the qualifier—that is, the interview must be conducted in a detective interview room.

5. **D** A prisoner between the ages of 16 and 21 years must be in custody for more than 4 hours before the parents can visit with the prisoner.

6. **B** The time limit for the visit is no longer than 20 minutes. If you selected choice D, then possibly you confused the time limit for the visit with the 4-hour period required before a visit with such a prisoner can take place.

7. **D** This is a good example of having to base your answer on the procedure that has been provided. Whereas it might seem logical to

simply allow a clergyman to interview a prisoner, it is not to be done unless the prisoner requests the clergyman.

8. **C**   The maximum length of time for one phone call is 5 minutes.

9. **B**   Choice B is stated in number 5 of the procedure.

10. **A**   The prisoner cannot be interviewed by any member of the State Police, but by a supervisory officer of the State Police or a member of the State Police Detective Bureau. Remember to carefully review statements that have words such as *only* and *any*.

GROUP TWO

11. **D**   Choices A and C are incorrect because the actions suggested are not appropriate according to the procedure upon which the answers are to be based. Choice B is incorrect because nothing in the procedure contains directions to involve the lab in collecting such substances.

12. **B**   According to the procedure, the first numerical designation preceding the letter is that of the post designation.

13. **B**   It is the job of the desk officer who gives a person a code phrase to advise the person that the code phrase will expire in 1 hour.

14. **B**   The thinking behind such a procedure is that if the amount of the suspicious substance is considerable (that is, enough that someone possessing it would be committing a felony), it should find its way into police custody as soon as possible.

15. **D**   According to the procedure, a NARCOTICS INTELLIGENCE REPORT is prepared by the trooper receiving the phone call asking about the results of the lab examination. In this fact pattern, the suspicious substance has not yet been examined.

16. **D**   The procedure is very clear. The call should be made after 5 business days.

17. **C**   The correct order would be choice B, then D, then A, and lastly choice C. The order in which tasks are performed is often quite important for troopers and highway patrol officers. Therefore, it can be expected that examiners will test candidates in this area.

18. **C**   The procedure states that certain actions should be performed in a certain order. Here the action indicated in choice C should be done first, followed by choices A, D, and then B.

19. **D** According to the procedure, the trooper acted improperly. The procedure clearly states that the trooper should confine the person to the side of the building facing the street, if possible, and the reason given is so that life nets may be used more effectively. Choice B, the other choice that suggests that the trooper acted improperly, can be eliminated because of the use of the word *all*. Obviously the public does not have a right to see all the actions of the police as they are occurring.

20. **B** This question should not have posed a problem, especially because you can refer to the procedure in these question types. Also note that, when a procedure tells you that certain steps must be performed in a certain order, you can be fairly certain that you will see a question regarding the order of some steps taken.

CHAPTER 10

Judgment/
Reasoning
Questions

Judgment/reasoning questions require test takers to exercise their judgment or reasoning skills to correctly answer them. There are two basic ways these questions are asked.

Direct Rule Interpretation Questions

In the first way of asking judgment/reasoning questions, the test taker is given a rule and then asked questions about that rule. This is what we call direct rule interpretation. This question type is very similar to some reading comprehension questions involving rules. The difference is that rule interpretation questions sometimes require test takers to arrive at the answers by using information or knowledge not contained in the rule.

EXAMPLE OF A DIRECT RULE INTERPRETATION QUESTION

Q1. A trooper must not be either over friendly nor overly strict with prisoners. This means that a trooper's attitude toward prisoners should be
(A) hostile.   (B) neutral.
(C) patronizing.   (D) scornful.

Please note that the rule is stated in that part of the question that comes before the choices, the part that we call the stem of the question. It informs the test taker that a trooper can't be overly friendly toward prisoners nor can a trooper be overly strict. In other words, the trooper's attitude toward prisoners should be neutral, as indicated in Choice B, which is the answer.

Also note that in some jurisdictions the test writers ask this type of question in the absence of the rule. In that case the preceding question would be asked in the following way.

Q2. A trooper's attitude toward prisoners should be
(A) hostile.   (B) neutral.
(C) patronizing.   (D) scornful.

Although we do not think that this type of question (where the rule is not given) is entirely appropriate for use on an entrance test, the matter is not fully resolved. It is still in use in some jurisdictions. Therefore, we include this type of question in our practice exercises at the end of this chapter and also on our full-length practice tests.

Rule Application Questions

In this second way of asking judgment/reasoning questions, the test taker is given a rule and then asked which of four actions is in accordance with the rule or which of four actions is not in accordance with the rule. In other words, to answer the question correctly, the test taker is required to apply the rule.

EXAMPLE OF A RULE APPLICATION QUESTION

Answer the following question based on the following rule.

Q3. Troopers are required to report all hazardous conditions immediately. Which one of the following should a trooper report immediately?
(A) Children are playing touch football on a quiet street.
(B) Cars are double-parked in the street.
(C) People have been waiting a long time to take the bus.
(D) A large amount of oil is spilled on a busy street.

Most of the time there are two choices that simply do not apply, such as choices A and C in this example. Then there is usually one choice that could arguably apply, such as choice B. But, the correct answer always clearly applies, as choice D. For this reason it is essential that you read all choices before choosing an answer.

Strategies for Taking Judgment/Reasoning Questions

1. If a rule is given, as is the case most of the time, you must spend a little time making sure that you understand the rule before you look at the question.

2. Before reading the choices, you must know whether you are looking for an example of the rule or an example of an exception to the rule. In other words, sometimes there are three good statements that support the rule and one bad statement in conflict with the rule. You must find the bad one. This kind of question might have a stem that reads something like this:

   > Q4. All the following actions are in accordance with the given rule except . . .

In this case, the choices would contain three good actions and one bad one. Your job is to select the bad one.

Other times there are three bad statements and one good one. This kind of question might have a stem that reads something like this:

   > Q5. Which one of the following actions are in accordance with the given rule?

In this case, the choices would contain three bad actions and one good one. This time your job is to select the good one.

3. Evaluate each choice as being good or bad. Do this by writing *good* or *bad* in the test booklet next to each choice. If you are not sure, put a question mark next to that choice. After you have evaluated each choice, if you have three goods and one bad, or three bads and one good, the answer is obvious. If, however, you have either three goods or three bads and a question mark, the question mark is probably the choice to select as the answer.

Practice Exercises

GROUP ONE

10 Questions—Time Allowed 20 Minutes

1. Trooper Smith is told to notify his supervisor immediately when he observes a dangerous condition. For which one of the following should Officer Smith notify his supervisor immediately?
   (A) A motorist is stalled in the street and is causing a traffic jam.
   (B) A parking sign has been painted over.
   (C) A car alarm has gone off.
   (D) Smoke is coming out of the first floor window of a neighborhood building.

2. When searching visitors to a state police jail facility, troopers must seize legally carried items that could very easily be used as a dangerous weapon. Which one of the following objects could most easily be used as a dangerous weapon?
   (A) a newspaper   (B) a nail file
   (C) lipstick   (D) tissues

3. A trooper's first action at the scene of a vehicle accident is to determine if anyone requires medical assistance. The main reason for this rule is that
   (A) ambulances often take a long time to arrive at the scene.
   (B) the protection of life is a trooper's first and most important responsibility.
   (C) a trooper receives special training in the administration of first aid.
   (D) the prevention of accidents is a very important responsibility of a trooper.

4. When questioning many witnesses to the same occurrence, a trooper must always separate them and question them individually. The most important reason for this rule is that
   (A) many witnesses tend to be improperly influenced by what they hear other witnesses say.
   (B) one of the witnesses may be the guilty party.
   (C) it guarantees that each witness will tell the truth.
   (D) it makes the trooper look more professional.

5. When questioning witnesses, a trooper should not ask leading questions. Questions should be framed in a manner that does not suggest the answers to them. Which of the following questions is most appropriate to ask a witness who is giving a description of a suspect?
   (A) Was he about 6 feet tall?
   (B) Did he walk with a limp?
   (C) What was his approximate weight?
   (D) Did he have blue eyes?

A B C D
5 ||||||||

6. While on patrol, a trooper observes what he believes to be a robbery in progress taking place in a liquor store. It seems to the trooper that there is only one robber. The trooper's first action should be to
   (A) enter the liquor store and confront the robber.
   (B) make an immediate call for assistance.
   (C) take cover and wait for the robber to exit the store.
   (D) fire a warning shot.

A B C D
6 ||||||||

7. When issuing a traffic citation to a motorist, a trooper should inform the motorist of the reason for the citation
   (A) only if the motorist asks for the reason.
   (B) only if the motorist is a resident of another state.
   (C) only if the motorist seems confused.
   (D) in every case.

A B C D
7 ||||||||

8. A state trooper should know when something unusual occurs on his post. In order for a trooper to recognize an unusual occurrence, he must first
   (A) know what is usual.
   (B) know everything about his post.
   (C) know the law.
   (D) know all the people who reside or do business on his post.

A B C D
8 ||||||||

9. When working at night in a business or residential area, a state trooper should give special attention to slowly moving cars that are apparently circling. The most probable reason for this rule is to
   (A) prevent traffic accidents.
   (B) prevent the commission of crimes.
   (C) recover stolen automobiles.
   (D) enforce traffic regulations.

A B C D
9 ||||||||

10. A trooper who is assigned to a local high school where drug sales are suspected has been instructed to monitor closely any suspicious activities. Which of the following situations should the trooper monitor closely?
    (A) Almost every school day, the principal of the school arrives 2 hours prior to the start of classes.
    (B) In the morning of every school day, a number of teachers double-park in front of the school.
    (C) The same two students are picked up at the school entrance immediately after classes every day.
    (D) A food vendor arrives at the school 10 minutes before the end of the lunch period every school day.

A B C D
10 | | | | | | |

GROUP TWO

10 Questions—Time Allowed 20 Minutes

11. It would be most appropriate for an armed trooper to shoot at a prisoner
    (A) who is trying to commit any crime.
    (B) who has just punched another trooper.
    (C) who is committing a serious violation of the rules governing the conduct of prisoners.
    (D) who is using or about to use deadly physical force against the trooper.

A B C D
11 | | | | | | |

12. A frisk of an arrested person must be made at the scene of the arrest. If possible, the frisk should be made by a trooper of the same sex as the arrested person. A thorough search of all arrested persons shall be made at Troop Headquarters. The primary purpose of this rule is most likely to
    (A) collect evidence.
    (B) promote personal safety.
    (C) ensure gender-based frisks and searches.
    (D) protect the constitutional rights of prisoners.

A B C D
12 | | | | | | |

13. A trooper should be open minded. This means that troopers should
    (A) consider both sides of a story.
    (B) impose their will on others.
    (C) never exercise discretion.
    (D) never believe a prisoner.

A B C D
13 | | | | | | |

14. A trooper is required to immediately report all dangerous conditions to a supervisor. Which of the following would require such an immediate report?
   (A) a crack in the sidewalk
   (B) a window that is broken
   (C) a traffic light signal that is defective
   (D) a billboard that is damaged

   A B C D
   14 || || ||||

15 To be effective, a trooper must be
   (A) an extremely physically strong person.
   (B) a thinking person.
   (C) a very emotional person.
   (D) an inflexible person.

   A B C D
   15 || || ||||

16. Troopers should not view their firearms as offensive weapons. This means that firearms would best be used
   (A) to prevent escapes.
   (B) to maintain order.
   (C) to promote compliance.
   (D) to defend against a threat to life.

   A B C D
   16 || || ||||

17. Troopers who investigate vehicle accidents must, in all cases, prepare detailed reports of the accidents. The primary reason for this rule is that the details contained in these reports are needed to
   (A) prevent future accidents.
   (B) prosecute offenders.
   (C) redesign roads.
   (D) support civil litigation.

   A B C D
   17 || || ||||

18. A trooper is preparing a wanted poster for an escaped prisoner. Of the following information, which would most likely lead to that prisoner's capture?
   (A) At the time of his escape, the prisoner was wearing prison clothing.
   (B) The escaped prisoner is about 5 feet 10 inches tall.
   (C) The escaped prisoner has long black hair.
   (D) The escaped prisoner has a 5-inch scar underneath his left eye.

   A B C D
   18 || || ||||

19. In certain situations, such as when a vehicle accident, an explosion, or a fire occurs, state troopers may have to close public streets to traffic. When would it be most appropriate for a trooper to close a public street to traffic?

    (A) An empty truck traveling down a dead-end street hits a tree late at night, and the truck's front lights are damaged.
    (B) An airplane skids off the runway while attempting to take off, and some passengers receive minor injuries.
    (C) A manhole cover explodes on a street during the morning rush hour and damages nearby buildings.
    (D) A fire breaks out on a yacht that is moored in the middle of the river.

    A B C D
    19 ‖‖‖‖

20. State troopers are required to give special attention to locations where criminal activities may be going on. Which of the following locations is one that most likely requires special attention?

    (A) a fast food restaurant that has become a meeting place for teenagers
    (B) an abandoned building that people enter and quickly leave, especially at night
    (C) a 24-hour store that is quite often frequented by residents of the area
    (D) an office building complex where numerous middle-aged women are seen entering in the evening and leaving around ten o'clock

    A B C D
    20 ‖‖‖‖

GROUP THREE

10 Questions—Time Allowed 20 Minutes

21. A trooper should treat all arrested persons
    (A) in a fair and consistent manner.
    (B) in a manner that is comfortable to the trooper.
    (C) in the same manner.
    (D) in the same manner that the prisoners treat them.

    A B C D
    21 ‖‖‖‖

22. Report writing is an essential part of the job of a trooper. The most important characteristic of a good report is
(A) brevity.
(B) accuracy.
(C) subjectivity.
(D) good grammar.

A B C D
22 |||||||

23. On occasion, troopers may require backup assistance from other officers. In which of the following situations would it be most appropriate for a trooper to request backup assistance?
(A) An argument between two senior citizens about a parking space is taking place in the street.
(B) A fight between two large groups of teenagers is taking place in a school yard.
(C) A prisoner is making a grievance about the treatment he received when he was arrested.
(D) A prisoner is quite upset about a recent decision of a judge who is trying his case.

A B C D
23 |||||||

24. State troopers at the scene of a fire are trained to be on the lookout for persons who seem to be spellbound by the fire. The primary reason for this training is so that troopers may
(A) identify the person who started the fire.
(B) find a person who can help to extinguish the fire.
(C) discover friends and relatives of injured persons.
(D) prevent people from interfering with the fire-fighting operation.

A B C D
24 |||||||

25. According to law, prior to making an arrest a state trooper must have reasonable cause to believe that the person to be arrested committed an illegal act. The primary purpose of this law is to
(A) eliminate lawsuits for false arrest.
(B) ensure convictions of those who are arrested.
(C) protect the constitutional rights of the general population.
(D) make sure that innocent persons are not arrested.

A B C D
25 |||||||

26. A trooper is sometimes authorized to exercise discretion when enforcing traffic rules and regulations. This means that

(A) a trooper can sometimes choose the best way to deal with an apparent violation.

(B) a trooper must always handle traffic violations in the same manner.

(C) a trooper should always consult with a supervisor when engaged in traffic enforcement.

(D) an officer is always free to handle traffic violations any way she sees fit.

A B C D
26 ||||||||

27. At the start of a tour of duty, a state trooper who is assigned to a patrol post must proceed immediately to that post. The primary reason for this rule is to

(A) make supervision of troopers more efficient.

(B) eliminate all crime on the posts involved.

(C) provide maximum protection of life and property on the posts involved.

(D) provide equal protection to all patrol posts.

A B C D
27 ||||||||

28. Troopers are required to maintain a neat and clean appearance. The primary justification for this rule is that

(A) a neat and clean appearance tends to win the respect and cooperation of the public.

(B) officers can be disciplined for presenting an unkempt appearance.

(C) the directions of sloppy officers are never followed.

(D) troopers are paid to be neat and clean.

A B C D
28 ||||||||

29. State troopers are trained to concentrate their traffic enforcement efforts on traffic violations that have the greatest potential for causing life-threatening accidents. Of the following, the traffic violation that should receive the greatest attention is

(A) obstructing traffic.

(B) speeding.

(C) failure to signal.

(D) following too closely.

A B C D
29 ||||||||

30. State troopers are required to keep a daily record of their activities. Which of the following is an important reason for this rule?
   (A) It provides supervisors with an excellent supervisory tool.
   (B) It acts to ensure accurate courtroom testimony.
   (C) It provides useful information for planning purposes.
   (D) All the above are important reasons for this rule.

_{A B C D}
30 |||||||

Answer Key and Explanations

ANSWER KEY

1. D	7. D	13. A	19. C	25. C
2. B	8. A	14. C	20. B	26. A
3. B	9. B	15. B	21. A	27. C
4. A	10. D	16. D	22. B	28. A
5. C	11. D	17. A	23. B	29. B
6. B	12. B	18. D	24. A	30. D

ANSWER EXPLANATIONS

GROUP ONE

1. **D** The possibility of fire is always to be considered as an extremely dangerous situation. Fire in a building can injure or kill many people.

2. **B** A nail file is a relatively sharp metal instrument that could be used as a weapon.

3. **B** The protection of life is always more important than the protection of property. Choice D is an excellent example of a valid statement that does not respond to the question.

4. **A** More aggressive and outspoken witnesses almost always influence other witnesses and tend to make them feel that what they have to say might be incorrect.

5. **C** The questions posed in choices A, B, and D all suggest an answer. Only choice C contains a question that allows the responder to give a free response.

6. **B** Don't let the fact that there seems to be only one robber lead you to believe that assistance is not needed. When coming upon a robbery in progress, a trooper should always call for assistance.

7. **D** Choice D is the professional course of action to follow. A trooper should never issue a citation without giving the offender the reason why the citation is being issued.

8. **A** It is a well-established concept that one must know what is usual before one can recognize what is unusual.

9. **B** This is a question type that should be answered by a process of elimination. Choices A, C, and D are too narrow. Choice B, which is broader, has to be the answer.

10. **D** The fact that the food vendor arrives when the lunch period is almost over is what makes choice D the answer.

GROUP TWO

11. **D** Shooting a firearm is employing deadly force. The use of deadly force can be justified to prevent someone from unlawfully using deadly force on another. With respect to choice C, punching someone is not the same as using deadly force.

12. **B** The field frisk of an arrested person is made to promote personal safety. Its purpose is to find and remove weapons. The fact that thorough searches of all prisoners are made upon arrival at Troop Headquarters should have tipped you off to the answer to this question.

13. **A** A person with an open mind is flexible and not rigid. Such a person considers all the facts, including both sides of a story.

14. **C** Remember that the protection of life is more important than anything else. A defective traffic light signal could very easily result in vehicle accidents that could cause death or serious bodily injury.

15. **B** Even though a trooper must be sound in mind and body, the word *extremely* makes choice A incorrect. The ability to think on one's feet is, however, an essential attribute of a trooper.

16. **D**   The firearm is not an offensive weapon. It is for defensive purposes. Remember that, even when used to protect lives, firearms should be used only as a last resort.

17. **A**   Traffic analysts use the information contained in accident reports to make recommendations to prevent future accidents.

18. **D**   Clothing can be changed, many people are 5 feet 10 inches tall, and hair can be cut, but a facial scar is quite difficult to conceal.

19. **C**   Only the situations described in choices A and C occurred on a public street, and the situation described in choice A occurred on a dead-end street.

20. **B**   The fact that the location is an abandoned building that is quite often visited for short periods of time most probably means that drug transactions are taking place at that location.

GROUP THREE

21. **A**   Fair and consistent treatment of people is the hallmark of a professional trooper. Remember that fair treatment is synonymous with equitable treatment. With respect to choice C, it is wrong because consistent treatment alone is inappropriate if it involves unfair treatment.

22. **B**   A report loses its value if it is not accurate. Concerning choice C, subjectivity is another word for bias and should be viewed as having negative connotations. On the other hand, objectivity connotes fairness and should be viewed as having positive connotations.

23. **B**   Choice B describes an ongoing situation of physical violence between two groups. It is clearly a situation that would require backup assistance.

24. **A**   A certain breed of arsonists are enthralled with the results of their deeds. They often return to the scene of their crime and become mesmerized or spellbound by the fire.

25. **C**   Choices A, B, and D are all absolute. Note the use of the words *eliminate, ensure,* and *make sure.* Choice C is the primary reason for this law. Even though this law doesn't guarantee that all arrests will be good ones, it does require that there be good cause present before any arrest can be made.

26. **A** To have the authority to exercise discretion is the same as being able to choose for yourself. Note, however, the use of the word *sometimes* in the rule. On the other hand, choice D is incorrect because of the word *always*.

27. **C** Good judgment dictates that the more quickly a trooper can arrive on post, the greater the protection that will be afforded.

28. **A** Study after study has confirmed the fact that a professional appearance increases the possibility of obtaining respect and cooperation. Choice C is incorrect because of the use of the word *never*.

29. **B** The faster a car is going when an accident occurs, the greater is the potential for death or other serious physical injury. Speed kills.

30. **D** Once again we point out the vital importance of careful reading. The question did not ask for the most important reason for the rule. Choice A, B, and C all present important reasons. The answer is choice D.

CHAPTER 11

Understanding Legal Definitions

State troopers are often called upon to make split-second decisions regarding whether or not they should take legal action. In order to perform such actions properly, two things are required. First, the trooper must know what the law defines as illegal, and then the trooper must be able to measure an existing situation against what the law defines as illegal. So much of what a trooper does calls for determining whether a violation of law has occurred. This requires knowledge of the law and analysis of the existing situation.

This chapter is designed to assist a candidate to deal with questions that determine whether the candidate can understand and apply legal definitions. The definitions found in this chapter are of the type that men and women working as state troopers and highway patrol officers would use while performing their duties. Sometimes the definitions that appear in this chapter are exactly as they are written in the law. At other times they are not. This is to make you aware that often on civil service examinations the definitions have been slightly changed by exam writers to make it easier for them to ask questions about the law. This is important to understand since most legal definitions type questions ask the candidate to answer such questions based solely on the basis of the information provided by the examination question. Therefore, a candidate answering legal definition questions in an entry-level state trooper examination should not rely on anything that the candidate might already know about the law. If the question directions clearly tell the candidate to answer the legal definition questions based solely on the basis of the information given, prior knowledge of the law is not needed.

The Three Signals

When a candidate examines a legal definition question, there are three specific signals that should be seen as sending a message alerting the candidate as to what the examiner will specifically ask about the legal definition.

First, are there any numbers such as distances, weights, ages, or other numerical amounts mentioned in the legal definition? If there are, then the candidate should pay specific attention to them because they usually will be the focus of questions.

EXAMPLE: Definition

Q1. It is first degree rape if someone who is at least 16 years of age has sexual intercourse with someone who is less than 10 years old. Based solely on the preceding information, of the following persons, who would be most likely to be charged with rape first degree?
   (A) Don who is 16 years of age has sexual intercourse with April who is 12 years of age.
   (B) Mark who is 15 years of age has sexual intercourse with June who is 8 years of age.
   (C) Tom who is 17 years of age forcibly has sexual intercourse with May who is 10 years of age.
   (D) Frank who is 16 years of age has sexual intercourse with Sherry who is 9 years of age.

The answer is choice D. Note that there were two numbers mentioned in the definition, and you should make note of them when reviewing the definition. They were the age requirements to be met for a charge of rape first degree, namely the perpetrator of the rape had to be at least 16 years of age and the victim had to be less than 10 years of age. Also note that although in most jurisdictions a use of force as described in choice C would result in a charge of rape first degree, such a situation was not mentioned in the given definition. The question indicated that the answer was to be based solely on the preceding information. Therefore, any prior knowledge of the law should not have been used in answering the question.

The second signal that sends a message to a candidate answering legal definition questions is the use of the word *and*. Lawmakers use the word *and* to indicate that more than one circumstance is required before a violation of a particular law has occurred. This means that when the word *and* is used, before a person is considered to have violated a certain law, more than one element must be present to turn a person's conduct into a criminal act.

The third signal is the use of the word *or.* At times one of two or more situations can turn someone's conduct into a criminal act. Unlike the situation when the use of the word *and* is used, where one element is needed in conjunction with another element for the crime to have been committed, the use of the word *or* indicates that only one of two or more elements is all that is needed for the crime to have been committed.

EXAMPLE

The crime of criminal mischief is committed when a person intentionally damages the property of another *OR*
when a person recklessly damages the property of another *and* the resulting damage is more than $250 dollars.

Q2. Based solely on the preceding information, which of the following statements is most correct?
   (A) Criminal mischief can be committed only when a person intentionally damages the property of another.
   (B) Criminal mischief can be committed only when someone recklessly damages the property of another.
   (C) Criminal mischief is committed whenever a person recklessly damages the property of another.
   (D) Criminal mischief occurs when someone acts recklessly and causes more than $250 in damages to the property of another.

The correct answer is choice D. Note that the use of the word *OR* indicates that criminal mischief can be committed by a person damaging property either intentionally or recklessly. Therefore, choices A and B are incorrect. Also note that choice C is incorrect because of the use of the word *and* in the part of the definition describing what is required for a criminal mischief to occur when a person recklessly damages the property of another. Specifically, a person must recklessly damage the property of another, *and* the resulting damage must be more than $250 dollars.

You must make sure you understand how the words *and* and *or* can change a legal definition. Use caution and stay particularly alert when you see any of these three signals used in legal definition questions:

- numbers

- the word *or*

- the word *and*

Two Types of Legal Definition Questions

DIRECT LEGAL DEFINITION QUESTIONS

This type of legal definition question is known as a direct legal definition question because, in this type of legal definition question, a candidate is presented with one or several legal definitions to review and then *directly* asked a question or questions about the legal definition(s). No additional information is given nor required to answer the question. For example, the candidate is required to select accurate or inaccurate statements about the legal definition(s) or to select which of several incidents offered by the choices is the best example of criminal conduct according to the legal definition(s). The instructions usually tell the candidate to answer questions based *solely* on the information contained in the legal definitions provided. While answering the questions, the candidate is permitted to go back and review the legal definitions.

STRATEGIES FOR ANSWERING DIRECT LEGAL DEFINITION QUESTIONS

1. **Quickly read and scan the legal definition(s) with your pencil.** This is done to understand what crimes or situations are being described by the legal definition(s). Is this the definition of a robbery or an assault? Or is this the definition of what is considered driving while intoxicated? While scanning, you should be identifying important parts of the definition(s) and key words such as *and* and *or* by underlining them. In addition, numerical amounts such as ages, dollar amounts, weights, and times should be noted because they are favorite areas for test writers. Look at the following examples of how to underline while scanning:

   A person is guilty of robbery in the third degree when such person <u>forcibly steals</u> the <u>property</u> of <u>another.</u> A person is guilty of grand larceny when <u>he steals</u> the <u>property of another</u> <u>and</u> the <u>property</u> is taken <u>directly from</u> the <u>person</u> of the <u>owner</u> who is <u>less than 21</u> years of age.

2. **Read the stem and choices quickly.** The stem is that part of a multiple-choice question that comes before the choices. By reading the stem quickly, you can determine what part or parts of the legal definitions will be asked about. Also take a quick look at the choices for the same reason. The stem of the question and its choices indicate what part of the definition will be asked about. The test writer will not ask you about all the parts of the legal definition. Time prohibits

this. Therefore, it's a waste of effort for you as the candidate to try to remember all the parts of a legal definition. It is much better to focus mainly on what the test writer might ask you about. You can do this by quickly reading the stem of the questions and their choices. You do this to get an idea about what parts of the legal definition the exam writer intends to test.

3. **Fully read the legal definition(s).** As you now carefully read the definitions, you should be focusing on those parts of the definitions that the test writer will ask you about, which you have already discovered by your previous quick reading of the stems and the choices of the questions. Now when you recognize those parts of the definitions that you will probably be asked about, you should be circling them.

4. **Reread and answer the questions.** As you again read the questions along with their choices, you should go back to those parts of the definitions that you circled and underlined based on your previous scanning efforts. Finally, select the correct answer to each question.

EXAMPLE

The crime of assault occurs when a person causes a physical injury to another person. A physical injury occurs when a victim experiences substantial pain.

Q3. Based solely on the preceding information, which of the following is the most correct statement concerning the crime of assault?
(A) If Tom kicks Pat an assault occurs.
(B) If May punches Ray an assault occurs.
(C) If Don intends to punch Frank but misses and strikes June causing substantial pain, an assault occurs.
(D) If Don becomes frustrated and pounds his fist on a table and substantially hurts his own hand, an assault has occurred.

Here you were given a legal definition and then *directly* asked a question about the legal definition with no additional information offered or required to answer the question. If you followed our strategy of

● quickly reading and scanning the legal definition with your pencil,

● reading the stem quickly and taking a quick look at the choices,

● fully reading the legal definition, and

- rereading and answering the questions,

you should have arrived at choice C as an answer. Don caused substantial pain, a physical injury, to another person, namely June. Choices A and B are incorrect because no substantial pain occurred. Choice D is incorrect because for a physical injury to occur, substantial pain to another, not oneself, must result.

INDIRECT LEGAL DEFINITION QUESTIONS

This type of legal definition question presents one or more legal definitions similar to the direct legal definition question type. However, in addition, a brief story or narrative, which usually describes some type of criminal conduct, is added. The candidate is then asked to answer questions that require him or her to apply the details of the narrative to the legal definitions that have been provided. Thus you are asked indirect questions about the legal definition(s).

STRATEGIES FOR ANSWERING INDIRECT LEGAL DEFINITION QUESTIONS

1. **Quickly scan the legal definition(s).** Look for and underline the elements that make up the law being described. Actually visualize what is being described and underline key words.

2. **Quickly scan the narrative** to see how the narrative relates to the legal definition(s).

3. **Scan the stem and the choices of the question(s).** In this way, when you take another look at the definition(s) and the narrative, you will be able to focus mainly on what is pertinent. You'll know what parts of the narrative the question(s) are asking about.

4. **Closely read the definitions.** Zero in on those parts that you previously underlined and circle those parts that you now recognize as relating to the narrative and the questions.

5. **Closely read the narrative,** especially those important parts of the narrative that you now recognize as relating to the definition(s) and the question(s).

6. **Answer the question(s).** Remember that, in this type of legal definition question, you are permitted to refer back to both the definition(s) and the narrative.

EXAMPLE

The crime of robbery occurs when a person takes permanent possession of the physical property of another by the use of force or the threat of force against another. The force used must be more than that needed merely to wrench or pull the property away from its owner.

One night while walking home, May is approached by Pat who forcefully pulls May's purse from under her arm and runs away with May's purse. Trooper North sees the incident and gives chase. A few blocks away, Pat is apprehended by the trooper. A search of Pat reveals that he is carrying an unloaded pistol concealed in his jacket. May arrives on the scene and tells the trooper that her purse was just purchased at a department store and is completely empty of any contents.

Q4. Based solely on the preceding information, Pat
   (A) has committed a robbery mainly because he was carrying a concealed pistol.
   (B) has committed no crime mainly because the purse was empty.
   (C) has committed a robbery mainly because he used some degree of force to remove the purse from May.
   (D) has possibly committed some crime but not robbery mainly because the kind of force required for a robbery was not used.

Here you were given a legal definition plus a narrative. You were then indirectly asked a question about the legal definition by asking you to apply the narrative to the legal definition. If you followed our strategy you should have

- quickly scanned and underlined the legal definition(s),

- quickly scanned the narrative to see how the narrative relates to the legal definition(s),

- scanned the stem and the choices of each question,

- closely read the underlined definitions and circled those parts now known to be important,

- closely read those parts of the narrative that relate to the definition(s) and the question(s), and

- answered the question(s).

In this case you should have arrived at choice D as the answer. The kind of force used was to merely pull the purse away from the victim. As indicated in the legal definition, that is not the force that is required for a robbery.

Practice Exercises

GROUP ONE

10 Questions—Time Allowed 20 Minutes

INSTRUCTIONS: Answer questions 1–6 based solely on the content of the legal definitions given. Do not use any other knowledge of the law that you might have. You may refer to the definitions when answering the questions.

The Law of Arrest—Without an Arrest Warrant

1. An offense is either a felony, a misdemeanor, or a violation. A traffic infraction is not an offense. Felonies are punished most severely, followed by misdemeanors and then violations.

2. A crime is either a felony or a misdemeanor.

3. A petty offense is either a violation or a traffic infraction.

4. A state trooper may arrest a person without a warrant of arrest:

   a. For any offense when the state trooper has reasonable cause to believe that such person has committed such offense in the trooper's presence; and

   b. For a crime when the state trooper has reasonable cause to believe that such person has committed such crime, whether in the trooper's presence or otherwise.

   c. Close Pursuit allows a state trooper to arrest a person for the commission of a crime committed within the state, outside of the state, if the apprehension is made as a result of close pursuit of the perpetrator by the arresting trooper.

5. A state trooper acting without a warrant, when legally arresting a person for an offense may do so at any hour of any day or night.

6. An arresting trooper must inform a person being arrested without an arrest warrant of the trooper's authority and purpose and of the reason for such arrest, unless the trooper meets physical resistance or flight.

7. If a person flees into his residence to avoid arrest, the arresting trooper may follow in close pursuit.

1. Which of the following is least likely to be considered an offense?
   (A) a felony
   (B) a misdemeanor
   (C) a violation
   (D) a traffic infraction

   A B C D
   1 | | | | | | |

2. Petty offenses include which of the following?
   (A) all crimes
   (B) a felony
   (C) a violation
   (D) a misdemeanor

   A B C D
   2 | | | | | | |

3. A state trooper can legally effect the arrest of a person without an arrest warrant when the trooper has reasonable cause to believe that such person has committed which of the following in the presence of the trooper?
   (A) only a felony
   (B) only a misdemeanor
   (C) only a violation
   (D) any offense

   A B C D
   3 | | | | | | |

4. Don is an experienced and knowledgeable state trooper. He is approached by Pat who is a newly hired state trooper. Pat asks Don to explain when an arrest can be made without a warrant. Don would be most correct if he responded,
   (A) "Only on weekdays but at any hour of the day."
   (B) "On weekdays but only between the hours of 6 A.M. and 12 midnight."
   (C) "On any day of the week but only between the hours of 6 A.M. and 12 midnight."
   (D) "At any hour of any day or night."

   A B C D
   4 | | | | | | |

5. In which of the following situations is it necessary according to the law of arrest to notify the person being arrested of the reason for the arrest?
   (A) an arrest for manslaughter where the defendant is found hiding under a car after a high-speed chase
   (B) an arrest for rape where the defendant has just fled the scene
   (C) an arrest for disorderly conduct, where the level of the charge is only a violation
   (D) an arrest for robbery, where the defendant fought with the arresting trooper

   A B C D
   5 | | | | | | |

6. Ray who is being arrested without an arrest warrant, suddenly runs into his own home to avoid arrest. In such an instance, the arresting trooper
   (A) may follow in close pursuit.
   (B) must wait until Ray comes out.
   (C) must arrest all occupants of the house.
   (D) may enter only if the charge is a felony.

A B C D
6 ||||||||

DIRECTIONS: Answer questions 7–10 based solely on the content of the legal definitions given. Do not use any other knowledge of the law that you might have. You may refer to the definitions when answering the questions.

The Law of Arrest—With an Arrest Warrant

When and how Warrants of Arrest are executed:

a. A Warrant of Arrest may be executed on any day of the week and at any hour of the day or night.

b. Unless encountering physical resistance or flight, the arresting trooper must inform the defendant that a warrant for his or her arrest for the offense designated therein has been issued.

c. If requested by the defendant, the arresting trooper must show the defendant the warrant if the trooper has possession of it. The trooper need not have possession of it, and, if he or she does not have possession, the trooper must show it to the defendant upon request as soon after the arrest as possible.

d. To effect the arrest of a person pursuant to the authority of an arrest warrant, the arresting trooper may enter any premises if the trooper reasonably believes the defendant is present in the premises. However, if the premises is the dwelling of a third party, said trooper must obtain a search warrant for said premises in addition to the currently held arrest warrant.

e. Before entering a premises to make the arrest with a warrant, the trooper must make a reasonable effort to give notice of his or her authority and purpose to an occupant of the premises, unless the trooper reasonably believes that giving such notice will

   i. result in the defendant escaping or attempting to escape;

   ii. endanger the life or safety of the trooper or another person;

   iii. result in the destruction, damage, or secretion of evidence.

f. If the trooper is authorized to enter the premises without giving notice of his or her authority and purpose, or if after giving such notice he or she is not admitted, the trooper may enter such premises, and by a breaking if necessary.

7. Trooper Frank executes a warrant of arrest on a Sunday at 5 A.M. In this instance Trooper Frank's action was
   (A) proper, mainly because a warrant of arrest may be executed on any day of the week and at any hour of the day or night.
   (B) improper, mainly because a warrant of arrest may not be executed on a weekend.
   (C) proper, as long as the Sunday is not the Sabbath of the person arrested.
   (D) improper, mainly because a warrant of arrest may not be executed before 6 A.M. regardless of the day of the week.

   A B C D
   7| | | | | | |

8. Trooper Frank has a valid warrant of arrest for Ray. Frank reasonably believes that Ray is present in a certain premises, which happens to be the dwelling of another person named Tom. Frank rings the bell of the premises, and the door is answered by Tom who tells Frank that he does not want to let Frank enter his dwelling. In such an instance, it would be most appropriate for Trooper Frank to
   (A) arrest Tom for interfering with a legal arrest.
   (B) obtain a search warrant for the premises.
   (C) obtain an arrest warrant for Tom.
   (D) push Tom aside and forcibly enter the premises.

   A B C D
   8| | | | | | |

9. If a state trooper has an arrest warrant for a person and such person is inside a premises, the trooper should announce his or her purpose and authority to an occupant of the premises. However, in certain instances the trooper is not required to make such an announcement if the trooper reasonably believes certain circumstances exist. Which of the following least accurately describes such an instance?
   (A) if it might result in the defendant attempting to escape
   (B) if it might result in the hiding of evidence
   (C) if the person sought is wanted for a serious felony
   (D) if someone's life in the premises could be endangered

   A B C D
   9| | | | | | |

10. Trooper Hoops arrives at a location to arrest Booker on the authority of a warrant of arrest. When the trooper arrives, she discovers that she does not have the warrant of arrest for Booker with her. Under these circumstances Trooper Hoops would be most correct if she

A B C D
10 ||||||||

(A) immediately ceases any arrest action until she physically possessed the warrant of arrest.

(B) arrested Booker but realized that if Booker asks to see the warrant she must release him.

(C) detained Booker until she obtained a copy of the warrant and then arrested Booker.

(D) arrested Booker since the trooper need not have the warrant in her possession.

GROUP TWO

10 Questions—Time Allowed 20 Minutes

INSTRUCTIONS: Answer questions 11–20 based solely on the content of the legal definitions given.

Do not use any other knowledge of the law that you might have. You may refer to the definitions when answering the questions.

Petit larceny—A person commits petit larceny when that person takes the property of another without such person's consent and intends to permanently keep the property for himself or another and the property is worth $1000 or less. Petit larceny is a misdemeanor.

Criminal impersonation—A person commits criminal impersonation when, with intent to have another submit to his or her authority, that person pretends to be a public servant such as a state trooper. Criminal impersonation is a misdemeanor.

Arson—A person commits arson when that person intentionally burns a building or a motor vehicle by causing an explosion or starting a fire. If the damage to a building is more than $50,000, or the damage to a motor vehicle is more than $15,000 it is second degree arson. If someone is injured as a result of the arson, it is arson first degree. All other arsons are third degree. All arsons are felonies.

Robbery—A person commits robbery when that person forcibly takes the property of another. Forcibly taking includes the use or threatened use of force against the owner of the property or another. The force exhibited in robbery must be to prevent or overcome resistance to the taking of the property. Robbery is always a felony.

Bribe giving—A person commits bribe giving when, with intent to influence the future action of a public servant, that person gives, offers to give, or agrees to give a benefit to some other person. Bribe giving is a felony.

Bribe receiving—A person commits bribe receiving when, with intent that his or her future official action will be influenced, that person asks for, receives, or agrees to receive a benefit. Bribe receiving is a felony.

Burglary—A person commits burglary in the third degree when that person knowingly enters or remains unlawfully in a building and intends to commit a crime in such building. Burglary becomes second degree when he or she injures a nonparticipant in the burglary either during the burglary or during immediate flight therefrom. A person commits burglary in the first degree when the building is a private dwelling.

Simple assault—A person commits simple assault when that person intentionally causes a physical injury to another. It is a misdemeanor. If a person intentionally causes a serious physical injury to another, or intentionally causes any injury to another by means of a deadly weapon, or the assault is carried out through the efforts of more than one person, it is felonious assault which is a Class C felony. A person, however, causing injury to another while in an act of self-defense is not considered to have committed assault.

11. Which of the following statements concerning petit larceny is most accurate?
    (A) If the property stolen is $1000, it is not petit larceny.
    (B) If Don borrows Tom's motor scooter worth $800 without Tom's permission, it is petit larceny.
    (C) Petit larceny is a misdemeanor.
    (D) Petit larceny is a felony.

    A B C D
    11 ||||||||

12. Don is in a bar and strikes up a conversation with several female patrons. Seeking to impress them, Don tells them he is a famous detective investigator with the state police. In reality, Don is an unemployed shoe salesman. In this instance, Don
    (A) has committed criminal impersonation, mainly because he intended to impress them.
    (B) has not committed criminal impersonation, mainly because he did not intend to have them submit to his authority.
    (C) has committed criminal impersonation, mainly because he did pretend to be a state trooper.
    (D) has not committed criminal impersonation, mainly because he never showed false identification.

    A B C D
    12 ||||||||

13. Ray intentionally burns down a building he owns. The building is worth less than $50,000. Ray did not want to collect any insurance but rather he wanted to put up a new building. However, unknown to Ray, a homeless person was sleeping in the building and was injured as a result of the fire. Ray has committed
    (A) arson third degree.
    (B) arson second degree.
    (C) arson first degree.
    (D) no arson since Ray owned the building.

    A B C D
    13 ||||||||

14. Frank is seated in his auto with his girlfriend waiting for a signal light to change. Suddenly Jay approaches the car and demands that Frank turn the auto over to him. Frank refuses, but Jay motions to his pocket where what appears to be the outline of a pistol is easily seen by Frank. Jay tells Frank that if Frank does not do as Jay wants, he will shoot Frank's girlfriend. Frank and his girlfriend exit the auto and Jay drives off with the auto. Jay has committed
    (A) robbery, mainly because he forcibly took the property of another.
    (B) larceny, mainly because no weapon was actually displayed.
    (C) assault, mainly because he threatened injury to another person.
    (D) some crime but not robbery, mainly because the owner of the property was not directly threatened.

    A B C D
    14 ||||||||

15. Jack damages a car worth $15,000 by setting fire to it. Jack has committed
    (A) arson first degree.
    (B) arson second degree.
    (C) arson third degree.
    (D) no arson because no building was damaged.

    A B C D
    15 ||||||||

16. Waters is a public servant working as a state building inspector. One day after inspecting a building he finds that no violations are present and that everything has been built properly according to building code regulations. As he is about to leave, Mark, the building contractor, approaches Waters and hands him $50 and tells Waters that he appreciates the fine job Waters has done. Mark has committed

    (A) bribe giving because money was offered.
    (B) bribe giving because Waters is a public servant.
    (C) bribe giving, but only a misdemeanor, because only $50 was offered.
    (D) possibly some crime but not bribe giving because the offering was not given to influence Waters' future official actions.

    A B C D
    16 ||||||||

17. Ray and Jay burglarize a factory. While inside the factory, Ray argues with Jay about the value of some tools in the factory. During the argument Ray strikes Jay and causes an injury to Jay. Ray has committed

    (A) burglary third degree.
    (B) burglary second degree.
    (C) burglary first degree.
    (D) only assault.

    A B C D
    17 ||||||||

18. May strikes Tab over the head with a deadly weapon causing an injury to Tab. May has committed

    (A) felonious assault.
    (B) either felonious or simple assault depending on whether a serious physical injury or merely a physical injury has resulted.
    (C) simple assault.
    (D) simple assault but only if it can be shown that it was an act of self-defense.

    A B C D
    18 ||||||||

19. Trooper Mack observes Hank stealing a late-model auto. The trooper takes no action. The next day Mack sees Hank and tells him that he could have arrested him but chose not to and thinks that he should be rewarded by Hank for what he did yesterday. Hank agrees and offers the trooper $500. Based on these circumstances which of the following statements is most correct?
    (A) Trooper Mack should be charged with bribe receiving.
    (B) Hank should be charged with bribe giving.
    (C) They should both be charged with both bribe receiving and bribe giving.
    (D) Trooper Mack should not be charged with bribe receiving and Hank should not be charged with bribe giving.

    A B C D
    19 |||||||

20. Jay enters a sports arena building after legitimately purchasing a ticket to see a basketball game. After the game Jay hides in the rest room awaiting an opportunity to steal some professional sports equipment located in the building. Jay has committed
    (A) burglary third degree.
    (B) burglary second degree.
    (C) burglary first degree.
    (D) no burglary since he legally entered the stadium.

    A B C D
    20 |||||||

Answer Key and Explanations

ANSWER KEY

1. **D**	5. **C**	9. **C**	13. **C**	17. **A**
2. **C**	6. **A**	10. **D**	14. **A**	18. **A**
3. **D**	7. **A**	11. **C**	15. **C**	19. **D**
4. **D**	8. **B**	12. **B**	16. **D**	20. **A**

ANSWER EXPLANATIONS

GROUP ONE

1. **D** The term *offense* includes felonies, misdemeanors, and violations.

2. **C** Petty offenses include violations and traffic infractions.

3. **D** A state trooper who has reasonable cause to believe that a person has committed an offense in the trooper's presence can arrest such person. Because an offense is either a felony, a misdemeanor, or a violation, choice D is correct.

4. **D** There are no time restrictions on arrests made without arrest warrants.

5. **C** An arresting trooper must inform a person being arrested of the reason for such arrest unless the trooper meets physical resistance or flight. All choices except choice C, the correct choice, indicate either physical resistance or flight.

6. **A** An arresting trooper may follow in close pursuit if a person flees into his residence to avoid arrest.

7. **A** A warrant of arrest may be executed anytime on any day of the week.

8. **B** Because the premises is the dwelling of a third party, namely Tom, Frank must obtain a search warrant for the premises in addition to the currently held arrest warrant for Ray.

9. **C** Choices A, B, and D are all valid reasons for a trooper to not announce his or her purpose and authority to an occupant of the premises. Choice C is not a valid reason.

10. **D** Although the trooper need not have a warrant of arrest in her possession, the trooper must show it to the defendant upon request as soon after the arrest as possible.

GROUP TWO

11. **C** Petit larceny is a misdemeanor. Choice A is incorrect because stealing property worth $1000 or less is petit larceny. Also choice B is incorrect because borrowing property means that there is no intent to permanently keep another's property; therefore, it is not a petit larceny.

12. **B** To commit criminal impersonation, you do not need to show the identification of a public servant but rather to intend to have someone submit to your authority.

13. **C** Regardless of who owns the building, damaging a building by a fire is arson and becomes first-degree arson if a person is injured as a result of the arson.

14. **A** Forcibly taking the property of another includes using or threatening to use force against the owner of the property or another, in this instance Frank's girlfriend. According to the information provided, there is no requirement for a weapon to be shown for a robbery to occur. Also, it cannot be an assault because no one suffered any injury. It is a robbery as suggested in choice A.

15. **C** A building or a motor vehicle may be the object of an arson. To become second-degree arson, the damage to the motor vehicle must be more than $15,000. Remember the importance of numbers when answering legal definition questions.

16. **D** Although it is true that Waters is a public servant, bribe giving has not taken place because the benefit is not being offered to influence the future actions of the public servant. It is offered to recognize proper work done in the past. This may be some crime, as choice D suggests, but it is not bribery.

17. **A** It is not a private dwelling so choice C is incorrect. It is third-degree burglary. The fact that one participant injured another participant does not raise the degree of the burglary to second degree.

18. **A** A person who intentionally causes any injury to another by means of a deadly weapon commits felonious assault. Thus choices B and C are incorrect. In addition, a person causing injury to another while in an act of self defense is not considered to have committed assault. This eliminates choice D, leaving choice A as the answer.

19. **D** The intent in both bribe receiving and bribe giving is to influence the future actions of a public servant. In this situation a benefit ($500) was being offered for the past improper action of the trooper. Possibly some other crime was committed but not bribe receiving nor bribe giving.

20. **A** Burglary can be committed both by entering or remaining unlawfully. In this instance, Jay remained unlawfully in a building with the intent to commit a crime in such building.

CHAPTER 12 ━━━━━━
Matching Sketches

In the matching sketches question type you are usually given a sketch of one face (called the model face) and then asked to pick out the same or matching face from among three or four other faces. In some instances you might be asked to pick out the one of several sketches that is different from the model face.

The Importance of the Instructions

As you will see, you can learn much from a close study of the instructions or directions that are typically given prior to a series of matching sketches questions. An example of such instructions follows:

DIRECTIONS: Answer questions 1–5 on the basis of the following sketches. The model face, the one appearing above the dotted line, is a sketch of a person who is wanted. Of the four comparison faces, the ones appearing below the dotted line, one of them is the way the model face looked after changing appearance. You are to assume that no surgical alteration of the wanted person's face has occurred. You are to select the face that is most likely that of the wanted person.

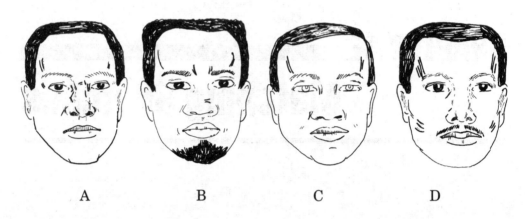

A   B   C   D

Let's discuss these directions in conjunction with a sample question. Assume that you looked at question 1 after you read these instructions. It would look something like what follows.

A review of the directions tells us the following. The person in the sketch is wanted and consequently has changed his/her appearance. The wanted person now looks like one, and only one, of the comparison faces shown in choices A, B, C, and D. Your job is to choose which of the four comparison faces is also the face of the wanted person. In so doing, you are to assume that no surgery has taken place.

Strategies for Taking Matching Sketches Questions

1. **Read the directions, which are sometimes called instructions, very carefully.** Also note that this strategy of reading the directions/instructions carefully applies to every type of question that has specific directions/instructions. You will not arrive at the right answer consistently if you do not know the ground rules established by the examiner. Some students believe that, after they understand a set of instructions for a certain question type, they do not have to ever read directions/instructions carefully again. This is an erroneous belief. You must understand that directions/instructions can, and often do, change from test to test.

2. **Don't select an answer based on a general overall impression.** The right answer to most matching sketches questions is quite often the face that, at a glance, looks the least like the wanted person depicted in the model face. Look, for example at our sample sketch. As will be explained later, the person shown in choice B is the same person as the model. Yet, based on general impressions, you would probably eliminate choice B first.

3. **According to the instructions, you are to assume that no surgery has been performed on the wanted person.** Therefore, limit yourself to using the eyes, ears, mouth, nose, shape of the chin, and facial lines such as moles and scars as the basis for comparison because these are the things in the sketch that can be changed only by surgery. Conversely, do not use such things as eyeglasses (which can be replaced by contact lenses), hair (which can be grown or cut), or items of clothing as a basis for comparison because these things are easily changed without surgery.

4. **Make one comparison at a time.** Start with what you judge to be the most significant feature of the model face. Then compare this feature with the same feature of each of the four choices and retain the choice if it is basically the same and reject it if it is markedly different. Notice that we said reject it if it is markedly different. Slight differences should not be a reason for rejection. After you reject one of the choices, do not consider it any longer.

   For example, referring back to the sample sketch, you might decide to start with the nose. When you compare the nose of the person in choice A with that of the model (the wanted person), it should be obvious to you that they are different. Therefore, put an X through choice A after circling the nose. The X through the sketch means that it is not the answer and the circle around the nose indicates that choice A was eliminated because of the nose. This is helpful information should you have time at the end of the test to review your work. You then compare the nose of the model face with the nose of the person in choice B and decide that it is similar so you leave choice B in as a possible answer. Similar nose comparisons would lead you to retain choice C and eliminate choice D.

   You now have narrowed the answer down to choices B and C. If the next item of comparison was the eyes, you would retain choice B and reject choice C with very little difficulty. After you have only one comparison face left, you need not go any further because you have found your answer. In this case, you would select choice B as your answer and move on to the next question.

5. **Always keep the following tips in mind:**

   a. Sometimes the test writer will try to confuse you by showing you a sketch of a person with a scar, mole, or some other facial line and then show you a sketch of a person with hair or clothing covering the area where the scar, mole, or facial line should be located. This does not mean that it is not there. For example, look again at our sample sketch. Notice that the model face has a scar or facial line on his chin. Then look at the face we selected as the answer, choice B, and notice that the chin is covered by facial hair. In these cases, you must make decisions based on other features.

b. Remember that, even though faces can become a little fatter, thinner, or older, the bone structure does not change.

c. For the sake of answering these questions, assume that facial lines do not change without surgery. Therefore, the face you choose as the matching face (the answer) must have the same facial lines as the model face or else there must be hair or clothing covering the area where the facial lines are located.

d. Remember to compare one feature at a time (e.g., the eyes, the nose). That is the real secret to doing well with matching sketches questions.

Practice Exercises

GROUP ONE

10 Questions—Time Allowed 20 Minutes

DIRECTIONS: Answer questions 1–10 on the basis of the following sketches. The model face, the one above the dotted line, is a sketch of a wanted person. One of the four sketches below the dotted line is the way the suspect looked after changing appearance. Assume that no surgery has been done on the wanted person. Select the face that is most likely that of the wanted person.

1.

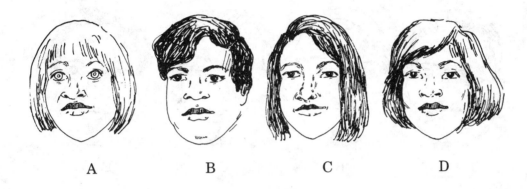

| A | B | C | D |

2.

| A | B | C | D |

3.

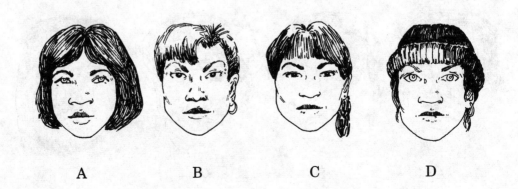

A   B   C   D

4.

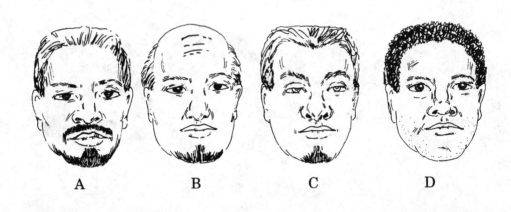

A   B   C   D

5.

    A   B   C   D

6.

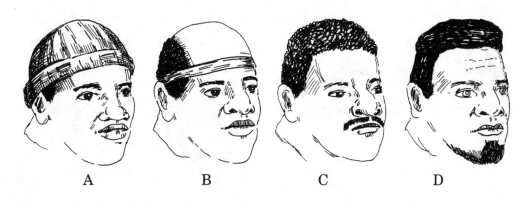

    A   B   C   D

7.

A   B   C   D

8.

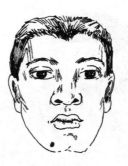

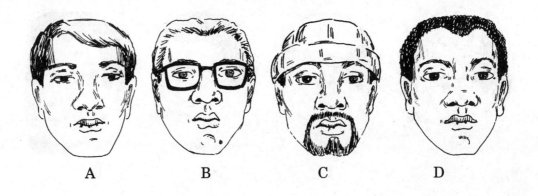

A   B   C   D

9.

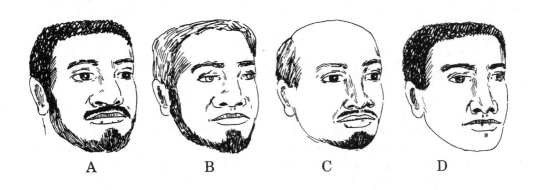

A   B   C   D

10.

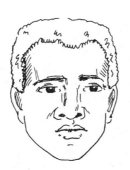

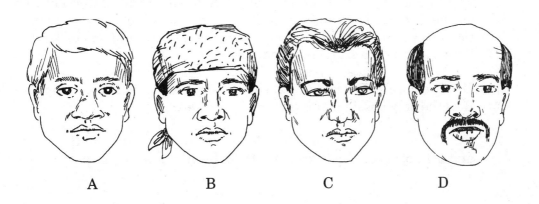

A   B   C   D

Answer Key and Explanations

ANSWER KEY

1. **D**	5. **C**	9. **A**
2. **C**	6. **B**	10. **B**
3. **A**	7. **D**	
4. **D**	8. **C**	

ANSWER EXPLANATIONS

1. **D** The eyes in choice A, the shape of the chin and the facial line on the chin in choice B, and the nose in choice C are the reasons for eliminating those three choices. Note that the answers to these matching sketches questions are not determined by a process of selection but by a process of elimination. Keep eliminating choices until there is only one left, and you have found the answer.

2. **C** The nose of choice A and the eyes and nose of choices B and D leave choice C as the only possible answer.

3. **A** The nose of choice B, the eyes of choice C, and the nose of choice D leave choice A as the only possible answer.

4. **D** If you started with the eyes you didn't have to go to any other feature. Eyes eliminate choices A, B, and C and leave D as the only possible answer.

5. **C** The mole on the forehead and the nose eliminate choice A. The eyes, the nose, and the lines on the forehead eliminate choice B. The eyes and the nose eliminate choice D. Remember that difference in one key feature is enough to eliminate a choice. We sometimes mention more than one eliminator because different candidates pick different features to start their comparisons.

6. **B** The nose of choice A and the lips of choices C and D leave choice B as the only possible answer.

7. **D** The eyes and nose of choice A, the nose of choice B, and the eyes and nose of choice C leave choice D as the only possible answer.

8. **C** The eyes and nose of choice A, the mole on choice B's chin, and the nose of choice D leave choice C as the only possible answer. Note that the model has a mole on his chin, and you cannot be sure whether choice C also has one but it doesn't matter because of the facial hair covering that area of choice C's face.

9. **A** The eyes of choice B and the nose of choices C and D are good reasons for selecting choice A as the answer.

10. **B** The eyes and nose of choices A and C and the lips and facial line on the chin of choice D leaves choice B as the only possible answer.

CHAPTER 13

Traffic Direction Questions

State troopers and highway patrol officers are often called upon by the radio dispatcher to respond in their patrol cars to scenes of emergencies and other calls for service. In responding to such calls, troopers must travel safely and quickly. This calls for these officers to be able to follow directions, read and understand maps, and develop a sense of direction while traveling in their patrol cars. Traffic direction questions are designed to test these abilities. Even though there can be many variations of this type of question, they all have the same central theme. The candidates are given a map and then asked either to select a route that they may quickly and safely follow while traveling in a patrol car from one point on the map to another or to answer a question about the map, which usually requires the candidates to illustrate an accurate sense of direction.

Identifying a Traffic Direction Question

Identifying a traffic direction question is simple. In this type of question, you are given a map containing either named streets or state and interstate roads. Typically, the map also has the following features:

- A compass symbol indicating the main directional points of north, east, south, and west. At times only north is indicated so you the candidate should fill in the other three main directional points.

- A legend that identifies buildings and points of interest on the map or that indicates which streets contain only one-way traffic and which contain two-way traffic.

- Accompanying instructions that state that the flow of traffic is indicated by arrows and that, if there is only one arrow shown, the traffic is permitted to flow only in the direction indicated by the arrow. If there are two arrows, then traffic is permitted to flow in both directions.

- Accompanying questions that are based solely on the map. Usually the questions insist that the flow of traffic must be followed in identifying the most direct route to follow in a patrol car when traveling from one point on the map to another. At times the questions will ask where one point or position on the map is in relation to another position on the map.

Strategies for Taking Traffic Direction Questions

1. **Carefully read all directions.** Know exactly what you are being required to do. Be particularly aware of the part of the directions that tells you to base your answers *solely* on the basis of the map.

2. **Examine any legends, codes, and compass points that appear on the map.** Now is when you should be taking the time to fully understand what they represent. Do not wait until you begin to answer the questions. If only one of the compass points, such as north, is given, immediately fill in the remaining main compass directional points. These points remain the same for all the questions based on that map. Therefore, it is important that you establish them prior to answering any questions.

3. **Walk through the map.** Using your index finger, quickly move through every part of the map, traveling through each street and thoroughfare. Become acquainted with those streets that are only one way and those that are two way. Identify which streets are dead ends or have detours, excavations, and other blockages to traffic.

4. **Eliminate the incorrect choices.** Unfortunately in traffic direction questions, when the candidate is asked to find the most direct route from one point on the map to another while obeying all traffic

directions, each choice must be examined. This is time-consuming and calls for concentration on the part of the candidate.

5. **Use the trace and erase method.** When following the directions offered by each choice, lightly trace the route suggested by the choice. Then, after evaluating the choice, erase the route suggested by that choice and begin tracing the route suggested by the next choice.

6. **Circle the part of the directions that makes the choice incorrect.** For example, a choice may be incorrect because it calls for traveling against traffic regulations (e.g., east on Smith Street which is a westbound-only street). In this way, later on when you are checking your work, you will be able to quickly determine why the choice was incorrect. Also circling the part of a choice that makes it incorrect will assist you in quickly identifying the same inappropriate directions if they should appear in another question. For example, after you determine that traveling east on Smith Street, which is a westbound-only street, is obviously incorrect, then whenever such directions appear in another choice in another question, you can quickly eliminate such choice.

7. **Always put yourself in the driver's seat.** When answering traffic direction questions, pretend that you are actually driving the vehicle facing in the actual direction the vehicle is heading. In this way, when you are directed by one of the choices to make a right or a left, you will be doing it from the actual perspective of the vehicle's operator.

Common Distractors Used By Examiners

1. Suggesting going against the flow of traffic. By far the most common distractor (i.e., inappropriate choice) used by examiners in traffic direction questions is directing the candidate to go against the flow of traffic, such as going the wrong way on a one-way street.

2. Suggesting going off the map. Following the directions given by one of the choices can cause the driver of the vehicle to go off the map. For example, a choice might require that the driver of the vehicle make a right turn and head east for six blocks. However, by following these directions, after making a right turn, only five blocks are available on the map to continue east. Thus following the directions would cause the driver to go off the map.

3. Suggesting going around in circles. Here the directions offered by the choice do get the driver to the location required by the question but it is not the most direct route. Usually following such directions

requires circling the same block more than once. Using our trace-and-erase strategy is very effective in identifying such an inappropriate choice.

Practice Exercises

GROUP ONE

5 Questions—Time Allowed 15 Minutes

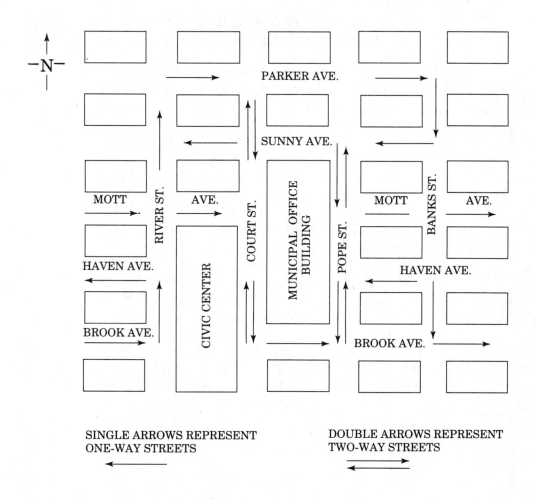

SINGLE ARROWS REPRESENT
ONE-WAY STREETS

DOUBLE ARROWS REPRESENT
TWO-WAY STREETS

INSTRUCTIONS: Answer questions 1–5 solely on the basis of the preceding map. The flow of traffic is as shown by the arrows. Where there is only one arrow, then the traffic flows only in the direction indicated by the arrow. You must follow the flow of traffic when moving from one location to another.

1. While parked in your patrol car in front of the Civic Center at the intersection of Brook Avenue and Court Street, you receive a call to respond to a vehicle accident at the intersection of Parker Avenue and Banks Street. Which of the following is the most direct route for you to take in your patrol car, making sure to obey all the traffic regulations?

   (A) Go east on Brook Avenue to Banks Street and then head north on Banks Street to Parker Avenue.
   (B) Head west on Brook Avenue to River Street. Make a right onto River Street and continue to Parker Avenue where you then head east to Banks Street.
   (C) Proceed east on Brook Avenue to Pope Street. Make a left on Pope Street and proceed to Sunny Avenue. Make a left at Sunny Avenue and continue to Court Street. Go north on Court Street to Parker Avenue. Make a right onto Parker Avenue and continue east to Banks Street.
   (D) Go east on Brook Avenue to Pope Street. Head north on Pope Street to Parker Avenue. Make a right onto Parker Avenue and proceed to Banks Avenue.

   A B C D
   1 || || || ||

2. From the accident at Parker Avenue and Banks Street, your present location, it would be most correct to state that the Civic Center is in which of the following directions?

   (A) due west
   (B) due south
   (C) southwest
   (D) northeast

   A B C D
   2 || || || ||

3. Two suspicious-looking males have been seen peering into parked cars on Brook Avenue between Pope Street and Banks Street. If Officer Carter is proceeding south on Court Street at Sunny Avenue in his patrol car and Officer Weeks is proceeding in her patrol car south on Banks Street at Mott Avenue, then when each officer reaches Brook Avenue, the suspicious-looking males would most likely be

    (A) to the right of Officer Carter and to the left of Officer Weeks.
    (B) to the left of Officer Carter and to the right of Officer Weeks.
    (C) to the right of both officers.
    (D) to the left of both officers.

    A B C D
    3 ||||||||

4. You are in your patrol car traveling north on River Street at the intersection of Mott Avenue. The dispatcher directs you to respond to a robbery at Banks Street between Haven and Brook Avenues. Which of the following is the most direct route for you to take in your patrol car, making sure to obey all of the traffic regulations?

    (A) Continue north on River Street to Sunny Avenue. Head east on Sunny Avenue to Banks Street. Head south on Banks Street to the scene of the robbery.
    (B) Proceed north to Parker Avenue. Make a right onto Parker Avenue to Banks Street. Turn south on Banks Street to the location of the robbery.
    (C) Go north to Sunny Avenue. Make a right onto Sunny Avenue and proceed to Banks Street. Head south on Banks Street to the scene of the robbery.
    (D) Make a right onto Mott Avenue and head east on Mott Avenue to Banks Street. Head south on Banks Street to the location of the robbery.

    A B C D
    4 ||||||||

5. While in your patrol car, you come upon a large disorderly group located on the thoroughfare between the Civic Center and the Municipal Office Building. You call the dispatcher for assistance. In describing the location, it would be most accurate if you described the thoroughfare as

    (A) a two-way street.
    (B) a street heading only south.
    (C) a street heading only east.
    (D) a street heading only north.

    A B C D
    5 ||||||||

GROUP TWO

5 Questions—Time Allowed 15 Minutes

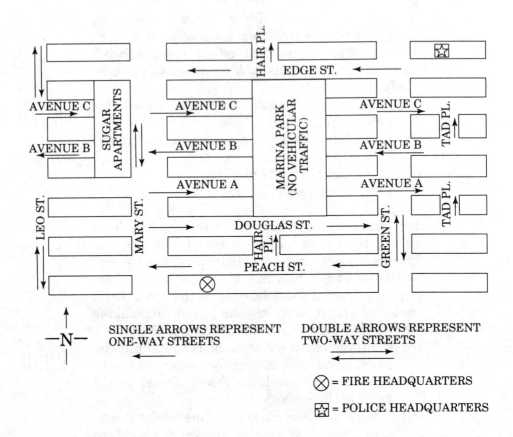

SINGLE ARROWS REPRESENT
ONE-WAY STREETS

DOUBLE ARROWS REPRESENT
TWO-WAY STREETS

—N—

⊗ = FIRE HEADQUARTERS

☆ = POLICE HEADQUARTERS

DIRECTIONS: Answer questions 6–10 solely on the basis of the preceding map. The flow of traffic is as shown by the arrows. Where there is only one arrow, the traffic flows only in the direction indicated by the arrow. You must follow the flow of traffic when moving from one location to another.

6. Trooper Marks has just entered his patrol car, which is parked in front of Police Headquarters. He is directed by the radio dispatcher to respond to a past burglary at the Sugar Apartments at Avenue B and Mary Street. Which of the following is the most direct route for him to take in his patrol car, making sure to obey all the traffic regulations?
   (A) Head west on Edge Street to Green Street and then make a left onto Green Street. Proceed to Avenue B and then make a left onto Avenue B and proceed to Mary Street, the location of the burglary.
   (B) Head west on Edge Street to Green Street and then make a right onto Green Street. Proceed to Avenue B and then make a left onto Avenue B and proceed to Mary Street, the location of the burglary.
   (C) Head west on Edge Street to Green Street. Make a left and head south on Green Street to Peach Street. Then head west on Peach Street to Mary Street and head north on Mary Street to the location of the burglary.
   (D) Head west on Edge Street to Mary Street. Make a left and head south on Mary Street to Avenue B, the location of the burglary.

7. If the flow of traffic were to be strictly followed then a vehicle leaving Fire Headquarters would be
   (A) making a right.
   (B) heading east.
   (C) heading west.
   (D) heading south.

8. Trooper June Flowers is directed to respond to a vehicle accident on Tad Place and Avenue A. She is presently parked on Avenue B at Leo Street. Which of the following is the most direct route for her to take in her patrol car, making sure to obey all the traffic regulations?

(A) Make a left onto Leo Street, turn left on Avenue A, and proceed to Tad Place.

(B) Make a left onto Leo Street and proceed to Douglas Street. Then head east on Douglas Street to Tad Place and head north one block to Avenue A.

(C) Make a right onto Leo Street and proceed to Avenue C. Head east on Avenue C to Green Street, turn south on Green Street to Avenue A, and then head east on Avenue A to Tad Place.

(D) Make a right onto Leo Street and proceed to Edge Street. Turn right onto Edge Street and head east to Green Street. Turn south on Green Street to Avenue A. Make a left on Avenue A to Tad Place.

A B C D
8 | | | | | | |

9. Trooper Marks is standing in the intersection of Green Street and Peach Street. He calls for assistance over his portable radio. Trooper Flowers informs him that she is heading east on Avenue C approaching Green Street. To reach Trooper Marks, Trooper Flowers should make a right onto Green Street and proceed

(A) north four blocks.
(B) south four blocks.
(C) north three blocks.
(D) south three blocks.

A B C D
9 | | | | | | |

10. Trooper Day is in an unmarked car at the intersection of Avenue B and Green Street following a suspected narcotics dealer. The suspect goes three blocks south, turns right, and travels west to the next two way street. The suspect then makes another right turn. In what direction is the suspect now heading?

(A) north
(B) east
(C) south
(D) west

A B C D
10 | | | | | | |

Answer Key and Explanations

ANSWER KEY

1. **D**	5. **A**	9. **B**
2. **C**	6. **D**	10. **A**
3. **B**	7. **C**	
4. **B**	8. **B**	

ANSWER EXPLANATIONS

GROUP ONE

1. **D** Remember that in this type of traffic direction question each choice must be examined because you must select which of the choices is the most direct route for you to take in your patrol car while obeying all the traffic directions. Therefore, you actually eliminate choices that are inappropriate. Here, choice A is incorrect because you are directed to head north on Banks Street. Choice B is incorrect because it requires you to head west on Brook Avenue, which is an eastbound street. Choice C would allow you to arrive at the location of Banks Street and Parker Avenue, but it is not as direct as Choice D, which is the most direct route.

2. **C** In traffic direction questions it is extremely important to immediately locate the part of the legend information that identifies the four points of the compass, namely north, east, south, and west. If you had done that here, you would have quickly selected choice C as the answer.

3. **B** If you incorrectly selected choice A, it was probably because you did not put yourself in the "driver's seat." Remember to always imagine that you are actually seated in the patrol car mentioned in a traffic direction question. This will give you a clearer understanding of left and right from the perspective of the driver of the patrol car.

4. **B** Choice A is incorrect because it requires you to head east on Sunny Avenue, which is a westbound-only street. Choice C is incorrect because it requires you to make a right on Sunny Avenue, which would cause you to head east on Sunny Avenue, a westbound-

only street. Examiners often offer the same incorrect directions in more than one choice. Choice D is incorrect because it would require driving through the Municipal Office Building, which is clearly not open to through traffic.

5. **A** The thoroughfare is that portion of Court Street from Mott Avenue to Brook Avenue, and it is a two-way street. This type of traffic direction question points up the need to examine the map quickly before answering any questions to become familiar with any structures and places of interest it might contain.

GROUP TWO

6. **D** Choice A is incorrect because making a left on Avenue B would not follow the flow of traffic, and also leads away from the required destination. Choice B is incorrect because making a right on Avenue B would cause the trooper to run into Marina Park through which vehicular traffic is not permitted. Following choice C will lead to the required destination, but it is not as direct as choice D. Because the directions tell you to select the most direct route, you must examine each choice.

7. **C** Because Fire Headquarters is located on Peach Street, which is a westbound street, vehicles leaving Fire Headquarters would be heading west as stated in choice C. Remember that in traffic direction questions part of the strategy calls for examining the map and any legends prior to answering the questions. In this instance being familiar with the location of Fire Headquarters prior to answering the question would have saved valuable time. Traffic direction questions are as much time-consuming as they are difficult. Therefore, any strategy that can save you time should be followed.

8. **B** Choices A and C are incorrect because both routes would be blocked by either the Sugar Apartments or Marina Park, which allows no vehicular traffic. Choice D is incorrect because heading east on Edge Street would be against the westbound flow of traffic.

9. **B** The best way to count blocks when dealing with traffic direction questions is to count from one intersection to another. For example, from the intersection of Avenue C and Green Street to Avenue B and Green Street is one block south, to Avenue A is two, to Douglas Street is three, and to Peach Street is four.

10. **A** Going three blocks south from the intersection of Avenue B and Green Street and then turning right would have the suspect traveling west on Peach Street. Heading west to the next two-way street and then making a right would have the suspect traveling north on Mary Street.

TEST YOURSELF

CHAPTER 14 ━━━━━━━━━━

Practice Examination One

This chapter contains the first practice examination for you to take. In the chapters that immediately follow you will find four more practice examinations.

Be sure to take each practice examination in one sitting. Each exam contains 100 questions, which you must answer in 3½ hours. It is imperative that you become accustomed to concentrating for the length of time required to complete an entire official examination. Also be sure to review the test-taking strategies outlined in Chapter 2 before taking this practice examination, to use that strategy when doing this examination, to record your answers on the following answer sheet, and to complete the diagnostic chart that appears at the end of this chapter after you score this practice examination.

Answer Sheet
Practice Examination One

Follow the instructions given in the test. Mark only your answers in the circles below.

WARNING: Be sure that the circle you fill is in the same row as the question you are answering. Use a No. 2 pencil (soft pencil).

BE SURE YOUR PENCIL MARKS ARE HEAVY AND BLACK. ERASE COMPLETELY ANY ANSWER YOU WISH TO CHANGE.

DO NOT make stray pencil dots, dashes or marks.

1. Ⓐ Ⓑ Ⓒ Ⓓ	2. Ⓐ Ⓑ Ⓒ Ⓓ	3. Ⓐ Ⓑ Ⓒ Ⓓ	4. Ⓐ Ⓑ Ⓒ Ⓓ
5. Ⓐ Ⓑ Ⓒ Ⓓ	6. Ⓐ Ⓑ Ⓒ Ⓓ	7. Ⓐ Ⓑ Ⓒ Ⓓ	8. Ⓐ Ⓑ Ⓒ Ⓓ
9. Ⓐ Ⓑ Ⓒ Ⓓ	10. Ⓐ Ⓑ Ⓒ Ⓓ	11. Ⓐ Ⓑ Ⓒ Ⓓ	12. Ⓐ Ⓑ Ⓒ Ⓓ
13. Ⓐ Ⓑ Ⓒ Ⓓ	14. Ⓐ Ⓑ Ⓒ Ⓓ	15. Ⓐ Ⓑ Ⓒ Ⓓ	16. Ⓐ Ⓑ Ⓒ Ⓓ
17. Ⓐ Ⓑ Ⓒ Ⓓ	18. Ⓐ Ⓑ Ⓒ Ⓓ	19. Ⓐ Ⓑ Ⓒ Ⓓ	20. Ⓐ Ⓑ Ⓒ Ⓓ
21. Ⓐ Ⓑ Ⓒ Ⓓ	22. Ⓐ Ⓑ Ⓒ Ⓓ	23. Ⓐ Ⓑ Ⓒ Ⓓ	24. Ⓐ Ⓑ Ⓒ Ⓓ
25. Ⓐ Ⓑ Ⓒ Ⓓ	26. Ⓐ Ⓑ Ⓒ Ⓓ	27. Ⓐ Ⓑ Ⓒ Ⓓ	28. Ⓐ Ⓑ Ⓒ Ⓓ
29. Ⓐ Ⓑ Ⓒ Ⓓ	30. Ⓐ Ⓑ Ⓒ Ⓓ	31. Ⓐ Ⓑ Ⓒ Ⓓ	32. Ⓐ Ⓑ Ⓒ Ⓓ
33. Ⓐ Ⓑ Ⓒ Ⓓ	34. Ⓐ Ⓑ Ⓒ Ⓓ	35. Ⓐ Ⓑ Ⓒ Ⓓ	36. Ⓐ Ⓑ Ⓒ Ⓓ
37. Ⓐ Ⓑ Ⓒ Ⓓ	38. Ⓐ Ⓑ Ⓒ Ⓓ	39. Ⓐ Ⓑ Ⓒ Ⓓ	40. Ⓐ Ⓑ Ⓒ Ⓓ
41. Ⓐ Ⓑ Ⓒ Ⓓ	42. Ⓐ Ⓑ Ⓒ Ⓓ	43. Ⓐ Ⓑ Ⓒ Ⓓ	44. Ⓐ Ⓑ Ⓒ Ⓓ
45. Ⓐ Ⓑ Ⓒ Ⓓ	46. Ⓐ Ⓑ Ⓒ Ⓓ	47. Ⓐ Ⓑ Ⓒ Ⓓ	48. Ⓐ Ⓑ Ⓒ Ⓓ
49. Ⓐ Ⓑ Ⓒ Ⓓ	50. Ⓐ Ⓑ Ⓒ Ⓓ	51. Ⓐ Ⓑ Ⓒ Ⓓ	52. Ⓐ Ⓑ Ⓒ Ⓓ
53. Ⓐ Ⓑ Ⓒ Ⓓ	54. Ⓐ Ⓑ Ⓒ Ⓓ	55. Ⓐ Ⓑ Ⓒ Ⓓ	56. Ⓐ Ⓑ Ⓒ Ⓓ
57. Ⓐ Ⓑ Ⓒ Ⓓ	58. Ⓐ Ⓑ Ⓒ Ⓓ	59. Ⓐ Ⓑ Ⓒ Ⓓ	60. Ⓐ Ⓑ Ⓒ Ⓓ
61. Ⓐ Ⓑ Ⓒ Ⓓ	62. Ⓐ Ⓑ Ⓒ Ⓓ	63. Ⓐ Ⓑ Ⓒ Ⓓ	64. Ⓐ Ⓑ Ⓒ Ⓓ
65. Ⓐ Ⓑ Ⓒ Ⓓ	66. Ⓐ Ⓑ Ⓒ Ⓓ	67. Ⓐ Ⓑ Ⓒ Ⓓ	68. Ⓐ Ⓑ Ⓒ Ⓓ
69. Ⓐ Ⓑ Ⓒ Ⓓ	70. Ⓐ Ⓑ Ⓒ Ⓓ	71. Ⓐ Ⓑ Ⓒ Ⓓ	72. Ⓐ Ⓑ Ⓒ Ⓓ
73. Ⓐ Ⓑ Ⓒ Ⓓ	74. Ⓐ Ⓑ Ⓒ Ⓓ	75. Ⓐ Ⓑ Ⓒ Ⓓ	76. Ⓐ Ⓑ Ⓒ Ⓓ
77. Ⓐ Ⓑ Ⓒ Ⓓ	78. Ⓐ Ⓑ Ⓒ Ⓓ	79. Ⓐ Ⓑ Ⓒ Ⓓ	80. Ⓐ Ⓑ Ⓒ Ⓓ
81. Ⓐ Ⓑ Ⓒ Ⓓ	82. Ⓐ Ⓑ Ⓒ Ⓓ	83. Ⓐ Ⓑ Ⓒ Ⓓ	84. Ⓐ Ⓑ Ⓒ Ⓓ
85. Ⓐ Ⓑ Ⓒ Ⓓ	86. Ⓐ Ⓑ Ⓒ Ⓓ	87. Ⓐ Ⓑ Ⓒ Ⓓ	88. Ⓐ Ⓑ Ⓒ Ⓓ
89. Ⓐ Ⓑ Ⓒ Ⓓ	90. Ⓐ Ⓑ Ⓒ Ⓓ	91. Ⓐ Ⓑ Ⓒ Ⓓ	92. Ⓐ Ⓑ Ⓒ Ⓓ
93. Ⓐ Ⓑ Ⓒ Ⓓ	94. Ⓐ Ⓑ Ⓒ Ⓓ	95. Ⓐ Ⓑ Ⓒ Ⓓ	96. Ⓐ Ⓑ Ⓒ Ⓓ
97. Ⓐ Ⓑ Ⓒ Ⓓ	98. Ⓐ Ⓑ Ⓒ Ⓓ	99. Ⓐ Ⓑ Ⓒ Ⓓ	100. Ⓐ Ⓑ Ⓒ Ⓓ

The Test

DIRECTIONS FOR QUESTIONS 1–8: Study for 5 minutes the following illustration, which depicts items taken from two prisoners immediately after they were arrested. Try to remember as many details as possible. Do not make written notes of any kind during this 5-minute period. After the 5 minutes are up, answer questions 1–8. When answering the questions, do not refer back to the illustration.

DO NOT PROCEED UNTIL 5 MINUTES HAVE PASSED.

DIRECTIONS: Answer questions 1–8 solely on the basis of the illustration on the preceding page. Do not refer back to it when answering these questions.

1. What is Alicia Smart's address?
   (A) 1362 64th Road
   (B) 1362 64th Avenue
   (C) 1632 46th Avenue
   (D) 1632 64th Road

2. Which prisoner probably has a daughter named Cathy?
   (A) Alicia Smart
   (B) Charles Adams
   (C) neither Alicia Smart nor Charles Adams
   (B) both Alicia Smart and Charles Adams

3. Which prisoner most likely rides the subway?
   (A) Alicia Smart
   (B) Charles Adams
   (C) neither Alicia Smart nor Charles Adams
   (D) both Alicia Smart and Charles Adams

4. How much money was taken from Charles Adams.
   (A) $10.30
   (B) $5.30
   (C) $10.25
   (D) No money was taken from Charles Adams.

5. Which prisoner was carrying two keys?
   (A) Alicia Smart
   (B) Charles Adams
   (C) neither Alicia Smart nor Charles Adams
   (D) both Alicia Smart and Charles Adams

6. Alicia smart owns a
   (A) 1996 Honda, plate CA 221.
   (B) 1996 Buick, plate HR 442.
   (C) 1996 Buick, plate CA 221.
   (D) 1996 Honda, plate HR 442.

7. Which prisoner was in possession of a writing implement?
   (A) Alicia Smart
   (B) Charles Adams
   (C) neither Alicia Smart nor Charles Adams
   (D) both Alicia Smart and Charles Adams

8. Which of the following is the most accurate statement about property taken from the two prisoners?
   (A) Smart had an address book, and Adams has an appointment book.
   (B) Smart has an appointment book, and Adams has an address book.
   (C) Smart had both an address book, and an appointment book.
   (D) Adams had both an address book and an appointment book.

Answer questions 9–11 based solely on the information contained in the following passage.

When a defendant in a criminal action has been found guilty, the courts have a number of sentencing options. The most commonly used sentencing option is probation. Over half of convicted felons are given a sentence of probation. Probation is defined as a sentence not involving confinement that imposes certain conditions on the convicted criminal. When a person is sentenced to probation, the courts retain the authority to resentence the offender if these certain conditions are violated. Probation has many advantages for offenders. It allows them to work, keep their families together, and avoid the stigma of going to prison. It must be remembered, however, that people on probation are not completely free to do as they choose. They remain under the supervision of a probation officer for their entire probation period. Although probation has many critics and people on probation often create serious crime problems, it is indispensable. Society could not afford the financial cost of sending all convicted persons to prison.

9. Probation is
   (A) the most frequently used sentencing option.
   (B) not an effective way to rehabilitate repeat offenders.
   (C) very expensive.
   (D) unfair to convicted felons.

10. People on probation
    (A) must spend some time in confinement.
    (B) find it difficult to keep their families together.
    (C) sometimes create serious crime problems.
    (D) are completely free to do as they choose.

11. Probation is a necessary sentencing option because it
    (A) allows offenders to work.
    (B) reduces the level of crime.
    (C) usually rehabilitates the offender.
    (D) is not as expensive as incarceration.

Answer questions 12–17 solely on the basis of the following passage.

State Trooper Ginty, shield 24758, assigned to the visitors arrival station at the state convention center and working a 4 P.M. to 12 P.M. tour on August 17th, is told by a visitor at 5:10 P.M. that an elderly woman who came to the center on a chartered bus is still outside on the bus and is in need of medical assistance.

Trooper Ginty notifies the dispatcher that she is responding to the charter bus parking area on the corner of Capital Avenue and 10th Street.

Trooper Ginty arrives at the charter bus parking area at 5:15 P.M. and finds three buses parked at that location. The trooper asks the driver of Bus Number 2356 if he has any knowledge of an elderly woman in need of medical assistance. The driver directs the trooper to Bus Number 2365, which is parked at the southeast corner of Capital Avenue and 10th Street. At 5:20 P.M., the trooper locates Bus Number 2365 and inside she finds the sick woman, the sick woman's niece, and two paramedics. The paramedics arrived 5 minutes before the trooper, having been called to the scene by the driver of the bus, Jack Hunt. Paramedics Green #7890 and Brown #1630 state to the trooper that the woman, identified as Pat White, age 66, date of birth 4/12/30, was in need of medical treatment, but she was refusing medical assistance.

Trooper Ginty tries but fails to convince the woman to go to the hospital. Mrs. Mary Martin, age 36, niece of Mrs. White, who resides at 1492 Columbus Avenue, apartment 12F, is also present, and she is able to convince her aunt to go to the hospital.

Mrs. White is removed from the bus at 6:00 P.M. and put in ambulance #1889 and taken to State Hospital. The ambulance arrives at the hospital at 6:15 P.M. and Mrs. White receives the medical attention she needs so urgently.

12. Trooper Ginty was initially informed about the sick woman on the bus by
(A) the radio dispatcher.
(B) a bus driver.
(C) a visitor.
(D) the sick woman's niece.

13. Which of the following is the correct time that Trooper Ginty arrived on Bus Number 2356?
(A) 5:15 P.M.   (B) 5:20 P.M.
(C) 6:00 P.M.   (D) 6:10 P.M.

14. At what time did the paramedics arrive on Bus Number 2365?
(A) 5:15 P.M.   (B) 5:20 P.M.
(C) 6:00 P.M.   (D) 6:10 P.M.

15. Which of the following is the correct name of the sick woman's niece?
    (A) Pat White   (B) Pat Martin
    (C) Mary Martin   (D) Mary White

16. Which of the following is the correct date of birth of Mrs. Pat White?
    (A) 4/12/30   (B) 4/22/30
    (C) 12/4/30   (D) 1/12/30

17. The paramedics were called to the scene by
    (A) Trooper Ginty.   (B) Jack Hunt.
    (C) Mary Martin.   (D) a visitor.

Answer question 18 based solely on the following rule.

Unless such action interferes with their prescribed duties, state troopers in uniform must stand at attention and render a hand salute before speaking to a supervisor or when spoken to by a supervisor.

18. State troopers
    (A) must always salute their supervisors before talking to them.
    (B) must always stand at attention when speaking with their supervisors.
    (C) who are not in uniform are not required to salute their supervisors.
    (D) who are in uniform must always salute their supervisors before speaking with them.

Answer question 19 based solely on the following rule.

State troopers shall not behave with disrespect toward a supervising officer.

19. For a state trooper to behave in a disrespectful way when dealing with a supervisor
    (A) is never permissible.
    (B) is sometimes allowed.
    (C) is always tolerated.
    (D) may or may not be permissible.

Answer questions 20–22 based solely on the following rule.

State troopers are responsible for the proper care and maintenance as well as the serviceable condition of agency equipment and/or property issued for their use. If at any time, equipment is properly passed from one trooper to another, the last trooper to receive the equipment shall be responsible for it. Whenever file cabinets are made available to state troopers, all official documents and records must be placed therein overnight. The last trooper leaving an office is responsible for turning off all lights, electrical appliances, and personal computers. Windows must be closed overnight in all offices that are not used at night.

20. State troopers
    (A) can be held responsible for the maintenance of all agency equipment.
    (B) are responsible for the serviceable condition of all agency property.
    (C) must take care of agency equipment that has been issued for their use.
    (D) are not responsible for the maintenance of any agency equipment.

21. When equipment is properly passed from one trooper to another,
    (A) responsibility for that equipment belongs to everyone who used it.
    (B) the first trooper who used it is responsible for it.
    (C) the last trooper who had the equipment is responsible for it.
    (D) no trooper can be held responsible for it.

22. The last trooper leaving an office
    (A) must always turn off all lights.
    (B) must always turn off all electrical appliances.
    (C) must always turn off all personal computers.
    (D) must always close all windows.

Answer question 23 based solely on the following rule.

Except in the line of duty, state troopers shall not carry packages into or from any state police facility without the prior authorization of the Commanding Officer of that facility.

23. State troopers
    (A) always need permission to take packages out of a state police facility.
    (B) must always get permission ahead of time to carry a package into a state police facility.
    (C) can sometimes carry packages into or out of a state police facility without anyone's permission.
    (D) can never carry packages into or out of a state police facility.

Answer question 24 based solely on the following rule.

Disciplinary charges may be made against any state trooper who fails to pay his or her just debts.

24. State troopers
    (A) may or may not be disciplined for failing to pay their debts.
    (B) are required to pay all their debts.
    (C) do not have to pay any of their debts.
    (D) must be punished for nonpayment of debts.

Answer question 25 based solely on the following rule.

State troopers shall not accept an award or gift for departmental services without the written consent of their respective commanding officers.

25. Gifts given to state troopers
    (A) must sometimes be refused.
    (B) can be accepted only with written permission of a commanding officer.
    (C) are all subject to the preceding rule.
    (D) are treated differently than awards.

Answer question 26 based solely on the following rule.

State troopers shall not intercede with any court for the discharge of or change of sentence for any accused person.

26. State troopers
    (A) need permission to intercede with a court concerning the discharge of an accused person.
    (B) are prohibited from asking a court to modify the sentence of a defendant.
    (C) can sometimes petition the courts to have a defendant's sentence reduced.
    (D) can sometimes petition the courts to have a defendant's sentence increased.

Answer questions 27 and 28 based solely on the following information.

Most experts agree that, although visible traffic enforcement is one of the most effective ways of deterring violations of the traffic laws, "hidden enforcement" has very little general deterrent effect. Hidden enforcement occurs when a trooper virtually hides from the motoring public in a secluded position until he/she observes a violation. Many subjects of hidden enforcement go away with a distinct feeling of being victimized and with a strong belief in the existence of a quota system. Hidden enforcement does have some limited usefulness, but only in areas with high accident rates.

27. Hidden enforcement of traffic laws
    (A) cuts down significantly on speeding violations.
    (B) does very little to prevent most traffic violations.
    (C) is widely accepted by the motoring public.
    (D) dispels the belief in a traffic ticket quota system.

28. Hidden enforcement can be useful at areas
    (A) where there is significant traffic congestion.
    (B) where teenagers drag race.
    (C) where there is heavy pedestrian traffic.
    (D) where there are many traffic accidents.

Answer questions 29–35 solely on the basis of the following information.

Upon responding to a crime that may require safeguarding evidence and detaining witnesses for further investigation, the responding highway patrol officer shall perform the following steps in this order.

1. Request response, through the communications dispatcher, of
   a. the patrol supervisor and then
   b. the detectives.

2. Remove unauthorized persons from the area and secure the crime scene.

    a. Evidence found at the scene shall not be disturbed.

3. Detain witnesses and persons with information pertinent to the crime.

4. Make appropriate entries in memo book of

    a. observations made,

    b. identity of suspects/witnesses with addresses and telephone numbers, and

    c. any relevant statements made whether casually or as a formal statement by a witness.

5. Advise the patrol supervisor and detectives of

    a. identity of witnesses detained and

    b. other information regarding the case.

6. Assess the crime scene.

7. Determine if the services of the Crime Lab Unit are required.

NOTE: The Crime Lab Unit will be requested for the following incidents:

    a. any homicide,

    b. any forcible rape,

    c. a robbery or a hijacking with injury caused by a firearm,

    d. an aggravated assault with dangerous instrument and the victim is likely to die, and

    e. any burglaries involving forced safes, or circumvented alarms,

    f. a criminal mischief where property damage is more than $1000.

8. Request Crime Lab Unit directly by telephone; if telephone is not available, then make the request through the communications dispatcher by portable radio. Include the following information in the request:

    a. exact location,

    b. time and date of occurrence,

    c. type of crime committed and type of weapons if used,

    d. number of victims involved, and

    e. name of the hospital treating persons removed from the scene.

9. Notify the desk officer of details and request additional assistance, if required.

10. Post crime scene signs.

29. According to procedure, the person required to post crime scene signs is
(A) the patrol supervisor.
(B) a detective.
(C) the crime lab technician who responds to the scene.
(D) the responding highway patrol officer.

30. After responding to a crime that requires safeguarding evidence and detaining witnesses for further investigation, Highway Patrol Officer Rivers properly requests the patrol supervisor. The officer's next step should be to
(A) detain witnesses.
(B) request the response of the detectives through the communications dispatcher.
(C) notify the desk officer.
(D) telephone the Crime Lab Unit.

31. According to procedure which of the following individuals has the responsibility to determine if the services of the Crime Lab Unit are required?
(A) the desk officer
(B) the detectives
(C) the patrol supervisor
(D) the responding highway patrol officer

32. In connection with a certain crime incident, the decision has properly been made to use the services of the Crime Lab Unit. In requesting the response of the Crime Lab Unit, certain information is required to be transmitted to the Crime Lab Unit. Which of the following choices is not required to be communicated to the Crime Lab Unit?
    (A) exact location and time and date of occurrence
    (B) name of the hospital treating persons at the scene
    (C) type of crime committed and type of weapons if used
    (D) number of victims involved

33. The first attempt to request the response of the Crime Lab Unit should be made
    (A) through the communication dispatcher.
    (B) by telephone direct.
    (C) through the desk officer.
    (D) through the patrol supervisor's portable radio.

34. According to procedure, it would be least correct to request the services of the Crime Lab Unit for
    (A) any rape.
    (B) any homicide.
    (C) a hijacking where someone has been shot by a firearm.
    (D) any burglary involving a circumvented alarm.

35. Highway Patrol Officer June Tiller would not be following procedure if she requested the services of the Crime Lab Unit for
    (A) a robbery where the victim was stabbed with a knife.
    (B) a burglary where a safe had been forcibly cracked open.
    (C) an aggravated assault where the perpetrator had very badly beaten the victim with his fists.
    (D) a criminal mischief where property damage exceeded $1200.

Answer questions 36–45 solely on the basis of the following information.

Upon making observations or receiving information regarding highway conditions requiring correction, a highway patrol officer shall perform the following actions in the following order.

1. Take corrective action, if possible, and then make a memo book entry of the condition and its location.

2. If the condition cannot be corrected by the highway patrol officer, notify the telephone switchboard operator at the post command who will make entries concerning the condition on the form HIGHWAY RECORD.

3. Notify the agency concerned as outlined below and sign the HIGHWAY RECORD upon completion of the shift.

4. Submit a signed and completed copy of the HIGHWAY RECORD to the post command desk officer upon completion of the shift.

The highway patrol officer who discovers the condition shall make the following notifications.

Condition	Agency Concerned
Inoperative/damaged signal light	Department of Traffic
Inoperative/damaged road light	Department of General Services
Defective/damaged roadway surface	Department of Transportation
Recently vacated/unsecured hazardous building	Department of Buildings
Obstruction of traffic control device (e.g., tree or bushes blocking visibility)	Department of Public Works
Obstruction on roadway	Department of Sanitation
Dead animal in road	Department of Sanitation
Flooding on roadways	Department of Environmental Protection
Clogged sewer drains	Department of Public Works
Missing/damaged traffic control devices (other than signal lights)	Private contractor concerned

Highway Patrol Officers observing conditions that may adversely affect the public, and for which no specific referral is available, will make a memo book entry describing the condition and notify the patrol supervisor immediately. It is incumbent upon the patrol supervisor to determine who should be notified to deal with the situation.

36. A highway patrol officer is notified regarding a highway condition by a passing motorist. If possible, the highway patrol officer's first action should be
(A) make a memo book entry of the condition.
(B) make a memo book entry of the location of the condition.
(C) correct the condition.
(D) notify the post command telephone switchboard operator.

37. According to procedure, the first person to make entries on the form HIGHWAY RECORD is
(A) the highway patrol officer discovering the highway condition.
(B) the post command telephone switchboard operator.
(C) the post command desk officer.
(D) the patrol supervisor.

38. Which of the following agencies should be notified if the highway condition is a dead animal?
(A) Department of Traffic
(B) Department of General Services
(C) Department of Sanitation
(D) Department of Public Works

39. To report a damaged signal light which of the following agencies should be notified?
(A) Department of Public Works
(B) private contractor concerned
(C) Department of Traffic
(D) Department of General Services

40. The form HIGHWAY RECORD has been appropriately completed according to procedure by Highway Patrol Officer Tom Drake. After examining the form, Highway Patrol Officer Drake signs the form and delivers it to the post command desk officer. Officer Drake then returns to his post and completes the remaining 3 hours of his shift. In this instance, Officer Drake has acted
    (A) properly, mainly because his signature is required on the form.
    (B) improperly, mainly because he was supposed to sign the form and hand it in at the completion of his shift.
    (C) properly, mainly because the safest place for the form to be kept is at the post command.
    (D) improperly, mainly because he was not supposed to sign the form at all.

41. While on patrol, Highway Patrol Officer Duke observes a recently vacated gas station that contains an unlocked hazardous building, which poses a potential danger to passersby. The agency that should be notified regarding the condition is
    (A) the Department of Traffic.
    (B) the Department of General Services.
    (C) the Department of Buildings.
    (D) the Department of Sanitation.

42. Highway Patrol Officer Melon, while on routine patrol, observes that a traffic control device, namely a stop sign, is missing. It has apparently been removed by vandals. In this instance, which of the following should be notified?
    (A) the private contractor concerned
    (B) Department of Public Works
    (C) Department of Traffic
    (D) Department of General Services

43. Highway Patrol Officer Baker discovers a highway condition for which there is no specific referral. In this instance which of the following should be notified?
    (A) the desk officer at the post command
    (B) the patrol supervisor
    (C) the telephone switchboard operator
    (D) Department of Public Works

44. An elderly male approaches Highway Patrol Officer Days and tells the officer that some hedges are blocking a yield sign at the intersection of Routes 12 and 24. The elderly male asks the officer the name of the agency that will be notified about the condition. In this instance the officer would be most correct if he indicated which of the following agencies should be notified?
(A) Department of General Services
(B) Department of Transportation
(C) Department of Public Works
(D) Department of Environmental Protection

45. As Highway Patrol Officer June Knight is patrolling her post, she notices that several sewer drains are clogged. Even though no flooding has occurred on the roadway she is inspecting, there may be in the near future if the condition is not corrected. The agency that should be notified is
(A) the Department of Traffic.
(B) the Department of Environmental Protection.
(C) the Department of Sanitation.
(D) the Department of Public Works.

Answer questions 46–48 solely on the basis of the following information.

When making entries in a memo book regarding information relating to assignments and actions taken, a trooper shall make entries in ink, beginning on the first line at the top of each page and continuing thereafter accounting for each scheduled tour of duty:

a. The blank side of each page shall be used for notes, diagrams, and sketches, when necessary.

b. The memo book shall be carried in a regulation leather binder.

c. Errors shall be corrected by drawing a single line through the incorrect entry and initialing it; no erasures are permitted.

d. Begin the tour's entries on the next open line, following the previous tour of duty's closing entry. No lines or pages are to be skipped.

e. Write or print legibly; abbreviations may be used.

f. Do not remove pages for any reason or use the memo book as scrap or for note pads.

g. Store active and completed ACTIVITY LOGS in the individually assigned department locker, available for inspection at all times.

46. Trooper Iris Mason is making entries in her memo book. She inadvertently makes an error. In this instance she should
   (A) erase the entry and make the correct entry.
   (B) circle the entry and initial the error.
   (C) draw a single line through the incorrect entry, and initial it.
   (D) remove the entire page and rewrite the entire entry.

47. When Trooper Don Walls completes a memo book, the trooper should
   (A) deliver the memo book to the post command desk officer.
   (B) store the memo book in his department locker.
   (C) keep the memo book for 5 years before destroying it.
   (D) store them at home in a safe place.

48. According to procedure, which of the following is least correct?
   (A) A trooper shall make entries in ink.
   (B) The memo book shall be carried in a regulation leather binder.
   (C) Abbreviations may not be used.
   (D) The blank side of each page of the memo book may be used for notes and diagrams.

DIRECTIONS: In each of questions 49–53, you will be given four choices. Three of the choices, A, B, and C, contain a written statement. You are to evaluate the statement in each choice and select the statement that is most accurately and clearly written. If all or none of the three written statements is accurately and clearly written, you are to select choice D.

49. According to the instructions, evaluate the following statements.
   (A) The principle of the training academy disciplined the recruits.
   (B) The post commander adapted the new procedure from last year's procedure.
   (C) She is the suspect whom I think did it.
   (D) All or none of the choices is accurate.

50. According to the instructions, evaluate the following statements.
    (A) The trooper went in his car to call the dispatcher.
    (B) I was already, but you never called.
    (C) Job stress can effect job performance.
    (D) All or none of the choices is accurate.

51. According to the instructions, evaluate the following statements.
    (A) The post commander decided to see the union delegates about there complaints.
    (B) I have never been their.
    (C) They're hiding behind the house.
    (D) All or none of the choices is accurate.

52. According to the instructions, evaluate the following statements.
    (A) The principle reason for crime is lack of parental care.
    (B) The principle of fair play demands such action.
    (C) The suspect was to tired to keep on running.
    (D) All or none of the choices is accurate.

53. According to the instructions, evaluate the following statements.
    (A) Whose shoes are on the table?
    (B) Whose going to cover the back?
    (C) The trooper whose the first to arrive will call headquarter.
    (D) All or none of the choices is accurate.

54. At the beginning of a shift the gas tank in a certain patrol car is five eighths full. During the shift two thirds of the fuel in the fuel tank was used. How much fuel was used if the total capacity of the fuel tank is 24 gallons?
    (A) 5 gallons
    (B) 10 gallons
    (C) 15 gallons
    (D) 18 gallons

55. A highway patrol officer recovers 6 pounds of heroin in the trunk of an abandoned vehicle. If 1 ounce of heroin is enough to make 375 bags of heroin selling for $5 apiece, what is the street value of the heroin?
(A) $100,000
(B) $150,000
(C) $180,000
(D) $200,000

56. While at the training academy, Trooper April Singer has to date received the following scores on her final examinations.

Law 95

Forensics 92

Police Science 88

Community Understanding 85

The only final examination left for her to take is the ethics examination.

    If Trooper Singer wishes to obtain exactly a final average of 90, she must receive which of the following marks for Ethics?
(A) 90
(B) 92
(C) 95
(D) 97

57. To discourage speeding on a certain turnpike, the highway patrol officers patrolling the turnpike are being requested by the local elected representatives in the area to increase the number of speeding summonses given to violators. Officer Pens increases the number of summonses given in a month from 125 to 155. In this instance, the officer has increased the number of summons given by him by
(A) 19.35%.
(B) 24%.
(C) 25%.
(D) 30%.

DIRECTIONS: Answer questions 58–65 solely on the basis of the information recorded on the following "Weekly Activities Report."

(FRONT)							
WEEKLY ACTIVITY REPORT–TROOP C **WEEK OF AUGUST 6–12**							
Trooper	**Sun**	**Mon**	**Tues**	**Wed**	**Thur**	**Fri**	**Sat**
	8/6	8/7	8/8	8/9	8/10	8/11	8/12
Wills	3	2/2	4/6	3/8	RDO	RDO	10
Hale	6	6	RDO	88	5	2	RDO
Akin	RDO	9	9	10	4/1	88	RDO
Ringer	1	3	4/1	RDO	RDO	2	88
Cory	10/9	RDO	88	6	2/3	2	RDO
Torino	1	1	10	9	RDO	RDO	4
Pinty	9/8	2	1	RDO	RDO	4	1
Baylor	9/8	1	2	RDO	RDO	2	1
Keflon	10/9	RDO	88	6	2/3	2	RDO
(REAR)							

When describing assignment activities use the Job Reference Number given below:

Job Reference Number	Assignment Activity Description
1	General Highway Patrol
2	Desk Officer Duties
3	Arrest Processing
4	Driving While Intox Road Checks
5	Roadblocks
6	Radar Speed Enforcement

7	General Traffic Enforcement
8	Narcotic Enforcement
9	Detention Cell Duty
10	In-service Training

(Each of the above assignment activities shall be assigned to a trooper for at least a 3-hour block of time. More than one reference number per day means that the trooper received more than one assignment that day.)

88	Off sick for entire tour of duty
RDO	Excusal—Regular day off
VAC	Vacation—Excused for entire day

| Date | Post Supervisor |
| August 14, 19xx | Sergeant—Ron Hats/Shield #749 |

58. Which of the following statements would be most correct regarding Trooper Keflon's weekly activities for the week of August 6–12?
    (A) Keflon is currently studying for promotion.
    (B) An activity done on 2 days by Keflon was desk officer duties.
    (C) Keflon did not report sick.
    (D) No other trooper had the exact same work activities as Keflon.

59. Of the following troopers, who was the only one to participate in a roadblock?
    (A) Wills
    (B) Hale
    (C) Pinty
    (D) Baylor

60. The minimum number of hours spent by all the troopers engaged in arrest processing was
    (A) 9 hours.
    (B) 12 hours.
    (C) 15 hours.
    (D) 18 hours.

61. On Tuesday, August 8th, Trooper Akin performed which of the following activities?
    (A) General Highway Patrol
    (B) Driving While Intox Road Checks
    (C) Training
    (D) Detention Cell Duty

62. Which of the following activities was performed most frequently by the troopers during the period indicated by the form?
    (A) General Highway Patrol
    (B) Radar Speed Enforcement
    (C) Driving While Intox Road Checks
    (D) In-service Training

63. Which of the following activities was not performed on Thursday?
    (A) Desk Officer Duties
    (B) Arrest Processing
    (C) Driving While Intox Road Checks
    (D) Narcotic Enforcement

64. Of the following troopers, who is the one that was off sick the most during the period indicated on the form?
    (A) Keflon
    (B) Baylor
    (C) Torino
    (D) Wills

65. Which of the following statements would be least correct regarding Trooper Torino's assigned activities during the period indicated by the form?
    (A) Only Torino had detention cell duty on Wednesday.
    (B) Torino performed general highway patrol.
    (C) Only Torino attended in-service training.
    (D) Torino conducted driving while intox road checks during the week.

Answer questions 66–73 based on the following data.

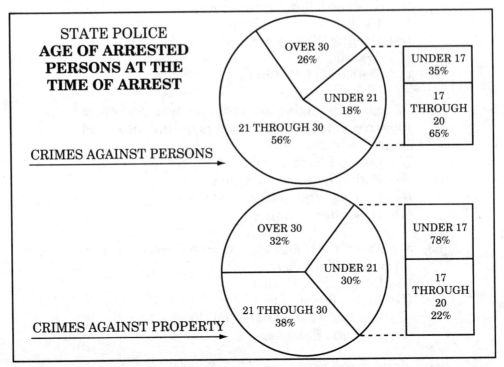

STATE POLICE
**AGE OF ARRESTED
PERSONS AT THE
TIME OF ARREST**

OVER 30
26%

UNDER 17
35%

UNDER 21
18%

17
THROUGH
20
65%

21 THROUGH 30
56%

CRIMES AGAINST PERSONS →

OVER 30
32%

UNDER 17
78%

UNDER 21
30%

17
THROUGH
20
22%

21 THROUGH 30
38%

CRIMES AGAINST PROPERTY →

Answer questions 66–73 based on the preceding data.

66. Most of the persons who are arrested by the state police and charged with robbery are
   (A) under 21.
   (B) between 21 and 30.
   (C) over 30.
   (D) of an age that cannot be determined from the data.

67. Of all the persons who have been arrested for committing crimes against persons, the majority of them are
   (A) under 21.
   (B) between 21 and 30.
   (C) over 30.
   (D) of an age that cannot be determined from the data.

68. Of all the persons under 21 who are arrested for committing a crime against a person, most of them are
   (A) under 17.
   (B) 17 through 20 years of age.
   (C) 18 years old.
   (D) of an age that cannot be determined from the data.

69. Of all the persons under 21 who enter the prison after being arrested for committing a crime against property, most of them are
    (A) under 17.
    (B) 17 through 20 years of age.
    (C) 16 years old.
    (D) of an age that cannot be determined from the data.

70. If 1000 new arrests were made of persons who committed a crime against property, then about
    (A) 320 of them would be over 30 years of age.
    (B) 560 of them would be between 21 and 30 years old.
    (C) 180 of them would be under 21 years of age.
    (D) 63 of them would be under 17 years of age.

71. Assume that in the coming year the percentage by age of persons arrested remains the same. If in that year 1000 persons are arrested for committing a crime against a person, approximately how many of them would be between 17 and 20 years old?
    (A) 180 persons
    (B) 300 persons
    (C) 117 persons
    (D) 63 persons

72. What percentage of all persons arrested for committing a crime against a person are over 21 years of age?
    (A) 56%
    (B) 26%
    (C) 82%
    (D) It cannot be determined.

73. Which of the following is the most accurate statement concerning the age of persons arrested by the state police?
    (A) Most are over 30.
    (B) Most get convicted.
    (C) Most are being arrested for the first time.
    (D) Most are over 21.

74. Mandatory lineups involving recently arrested persons shall be held upon the written request of a state police supervisor, but an attorney must be present when the lineup is conducted in order to protect the interests of the prisoner. Which of the following is not a correct interpretation of this rule?
    (A) Sometimes a prisoner lineup can be held in the absence of an attorney.
    (B) Prisoner lineups must be requested in writing.
    (C) Prisoner lineups must be requested by a police supervisor.
    (D) A prisoner cannot refuse to stand in a lineup.

75. During a street disorder, it is essential that the leaders of the disorder be dealt with immediately for the purpose of negating their influence on other participants. In accordance with this rule, when a disorder occurs, leaders of the disorder must be, as a first step,
    (A) disciplined immediately and publicly.
    (B) arrested and charged with inciting a riot.
    (C) handcuffed and removed from the scene.
    (D) identified as quickly as possible.

76. Troopers are required to unload their firearms prior to entering an area in the psychiatric ward of any hospital. Such a rule is necessitated primarily by
    (A) the need not to disturb patients in the ward.
    (B) the unpredictable mental state of many of the patients in such a ward.
    (C) the importance of maintaining good public relations.
    (D) the need to protect the rights of hospitalized persons.

77. Freedom of speech allows citizens to say rude and vulgar things to state troopers, but state police policy prohibits troopers from responding in kind. The primary reason for this policy is that
(A) troopers are not protected by the First Amendment.
(B) troopers must adhere to a Code of Ethics that demands that they behave in a professional manner.
(C) rude and vulgar language can create civil liability.
(D) rude and vulgar language always leads to violence.

78. A trooper believes she knows a better way of accomplishing a certain task than the way that task is now being officially accomplished. That trooper should
(A) experiment with her way of doing the task.
(B) submit her recommendation for change along with her reasons through the agency's employee suggestion system.
(C) wait until she assumes a position of greater responsibility and then implement the change.
(D) make an unofficial attempt at convincing other troopers that she has a good idea.

79. Public relations is a very important matter. When dealing with members of the public, a trooper should act
(A) in an aloof manner.
(B) in a courteous and tactful manner.
(C) in a somewhat friendly yet very stern manner.
(D) in a dignified but unfriendly manner.

80. Assume that you are a trooper assigned to handle a newsworthy incident. A reporter approaches you at the scene and asks you to comment on the incident. Under these circumstances, you should
(A) make only off-the-record statements.
(B) ask the reporter to contact you when you are off duty.
(C) refer the reporter to the person in the chain of command whose job it is to deal with the media.
(D) simply say, "No comment."

81. You are the trooper in charge of the troop's arsenal. During a routine inspection you discover a firearm that you are sure has been recently fired. You check the appropriate records and determine that there has been no official report of a firearms discharge. You should
(A) immediately inform your supervisor.
(B) take no action.
(C) make an unofficial inquiry whenever you get a chance.
(D) make an immediate notification to the office of the State Police Superintendent.

Answer questions 82–89 solely on the basis of the following legal definitions. Do not base your answers on any other knowledge of the law you may have. You may refer to the definitions when answering the questions.

NOTE: The perpetrators in the following definitions are referred to as *he,* but they actually refer to either gender. However, when the male and/or female gender is a factor in defining an offense or legal action, such distinction shall be made by the specific use of both pronouns *he* and *she.*

Culpable Mental State—refers to the mind-set of a criminal when committing a criminal offense and means to act intentionally, knowingly, recklessly, or with criminal negligence.

Intentionally—A person acts intentionally when his objective is to cause a certain specific conduct or to engage in certain specific conduct.

Knowingly—A person acts knowingly when he is exactly aware of his conduct even though he is not necessarily aware of the results of his conduct.

Recklessly—A person acts recklessly when he perceives a risk associated with his actions and disregards such risk.

Criminal Negligence—A person acts with criminal negligence when he fails to perceive a risk associated with his actions and the majority of persons under such circumstances would have perceived such a risk.

Deadly Physical Force—means physical force that, under the circumstances in which it is used, is readily capable of causing death or other serious physical injury.

Possess—means to have physical possession or otherwise exercise control over tangible property.

Benefit—means any gain or advantage to the beneficiary and includes any gain or advantage to a third person pursuant to the desire or consent of the beneficiary.

Public Officer—means any employee of the government or state and includes a person who has been elected or designated to become a public servant.

Conduct—means an act or omission and its accompanying mental state.

Infancy—means that a person less than 16 years old is not criminally responsible for conduct. But a person who is 7 but not yet 16 years old and commits an act, which if committed by an adult would be a crime, is considered a juvenile delinquent.

82. Tom, a foreman of a road construction crew, is told by State Trooper Green not to leave any cranes unsecured overnight. At the end of the work day, Tom notices that a crane that has been used during the day has not been tied down and secured. Tom realizes that it is risky to leave the crane in such condition but decides to do nothing about it. Overnight strong winds cause the crane to be overturned resulting in numerous injuries to motorists. In such an instance, Tom has acted
(A) intentionally.
(B) knowingly.
(C) recklessly.
(D) with criminal negligence.

83. May is a newly hired highway patrol officer. Her commanding officer tells her that she is not entitled to receive benefits from the public for official actions. In connection with such benefits, May would be least correct if she believed that
(A) a benefit may be money.
(B) a benefit could be tangible property other than money.
(C) a benefit must be given directly to her.
(D) a benefit does not have to be money or tangible property.

84. Which of the following statements is least accurate regarding the meaning of possess under the law?
    (A) If a gun is found in the pocket of a person, such person is considered to possess such gun.
    (B) If a packet of heroin is found on the desk of a person who is seated in a room by himself, such person is considered to possess the packet of heroin.
    (C) Only tangible property can be possessed.
    (D) When someone has control over his emotions, such person is considered to possess these emotions.

85. Pat is a gardener who is planting several bushes for a client. At the end of the work day, Pat leaves a large hole uncovered. Most people would have associated a risk with leaving such a large hole uncovered. Pat does not recognize any such risk. During the night a child falls into the hole and is injured. In this instance, Pat has acted
    (A) intentionally.
    (B) knowingly.
    (C) recklessly.
    (D) with criminal negligence.

86. Which of the following statements concerning deadly physical force is least accurate?
    (A) It must result in death.
    (B) It may include a slap.
    (C) It must include physical force.
    (D) It may include a blow struck by a child.

87. During a raid by some state troopers of an apartment occupied solely by Frank, a large quantity of cocaine is found in a locked safe in Frank's bedroom. When questioned Frank admits he was aware that the cocaine was in the safe but that he never thought about what the cocaine might do to those who use it. Regarding the cocaine, which Frank is not legally entitled to possess, Frank is acting with which of the following culpable mental states?
    (A) intentionally
    (B) knowingly
    (C) recklessly
    (D) with criminal negligence

88. Conduct occurs
    (A) only when a person performs an act.
    (B) only when a person fails to perform an act.
    (C) whether or not a mental state is present.
    (D) both when a person performs or fails to perform an act.

89. Which of the following persons under the appropriate circumstances is most likely to be considered a juvenile delinquent?
    (A) A 17 year old
    (B) A 16 year old
    (C) A 9 year old
    (D) A 6 year old

DIRECTIONS: Answer questions 90–94 solely on the basis of the following map.

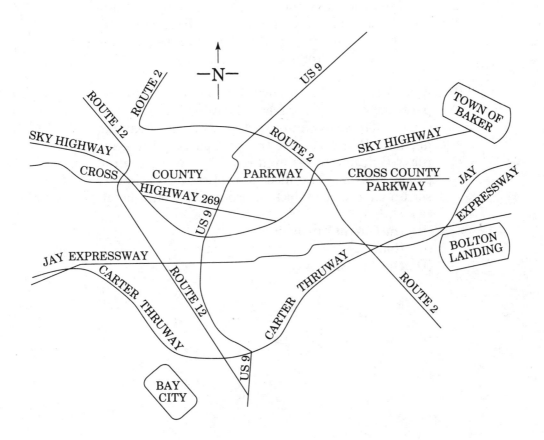

90. Trooper Dillon is in his patrol car on U.S. 9 at the intersection of Highway 269. The trooper is directed by the dispatcher to investigate a past robbery in the town of Baker. The most direct route for Trooper Dillon to follow in this instance is
    (A) to head south on U.S. 9 to the Carter Thruway and then head east on the Carter Thruway to the scene of the robbery.
    (B) to head west on Highway 269 to the Sky Highway and then head west on the Sky Highway to the Cross County Parkway and then head east on the Cross County Parkway to the scene of the robbery.
    (C) to head east on Highway 269 to the Cross County Parkway and then head east on the Cross County Parkway to the scene of the robbery.
    (D) to head north on U.S. 9 to the Cross County Parkway and then head east on the Cross County Parkway to the Sky Highway and then head east on the Sky Highway to the scene of the robbery.

91. A bank robbery has occurred in Bay City, and the perpetrator has just passed the interchange of the Carter Thruway and Route 12 while heading north on Route 12. The troopers assigned to Barracks B decide to set up a roadblock at an appropriate location. The most appropriate location to set up such a roadblock on Route 12 would be at
    (A) U.S. 9.
    (B) the Carter Thruway.
    (C) Route 2.
    (D) the Jay Expressway.

92. Highway Patrol Officer Christopher is notified to pick up some evidence from the scene of a fatal vehicle accident, which has just occurred on the Cross County Parkway west of U.S. 9 and east of Route 12. If Officer Christopher is presently traveling west on the Carter Thruway approaching the Jay Expressway at Bolton Landing, which of the following would be the most direct route for Officer Christopher to follow to arrive at the scene of the accident?
   (A) Head east on the Jay Expressway and then west on the Cross County Parkway to the scene of the accident.
   (B) Head west on the Carter Thruway to Route 2 and then head north on Route 2 to the scene of the accident.
   (C) Head west on the Carter Thruway to Route 2 and then head north on Route 2 to the Cross County Parkway and then head west on the Cross County Parkway to the scene of the accident.
   (D) Head west on the Carter Thruway to Route 12 and then head north on Route 12 to the scene of the accident.

93. Which of the following statements concerning Route 2 is most correct?
   (A) It is intersected by five other roads.
   (B) It is a four-lane road.
   (C) It is farther west than Route 12.
   (D) It is east of Bolton Landing.

94. Highway Patrol Officer Christopher requests Trooper Dillon to meet him in his patrol car where the Carter Thruway intersects with the Jay Expressway. In response, Trooper Dillon would be most correct if he told Highway Patrol Officer Christopher that his proposed meeting place
   (A) requires no further directions.
   (B) could be one of two different locations.
   (C) could be one of three different locations.
   (D) does not exist.

DIRECTIONS: Answer questions 95–100 on the basis of the following sketches. The model face, the one appearing above the dotted line, is a sketch of a person who is wanted. Of the four comparison faces, the ones appearing below the dotted line, one of them is the way the model face looked after changing appearance. You are to assume that no surgical alteration of the wanted person's face has occurred. You are to select the face that is most likely that of the wanted person.

95.

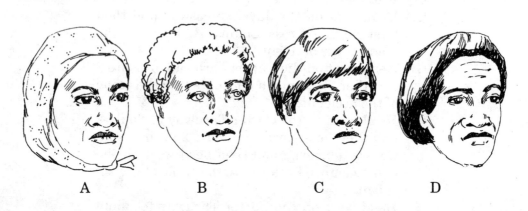

A   B   C   D

96.

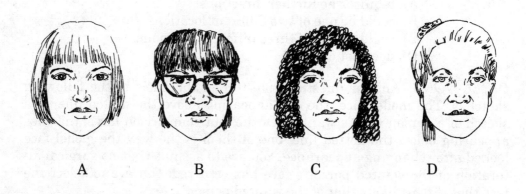

A   B   C   D

97.

A   B   C   D

98.

A   B   C   D

99.

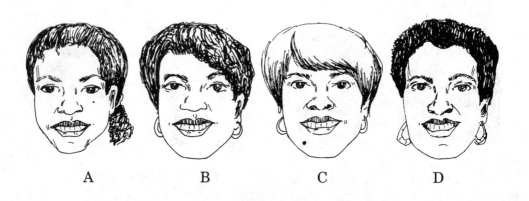

A   B   C   D

100.

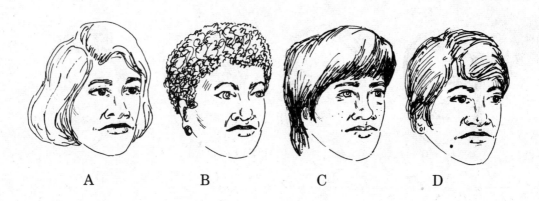

A   B   C   D

Answer Key

1. **D**	21. **C**	41. **C**	61. **D**	81. **A**
2. **B**	22. **D**	42. **A**	62. **A**	82. **C**
3. **B**	23. **C**	43. **B**	63. **D**	83. **C**
4. **D**	24. **A**	44. **C**	64. **A**	84. **D**
5. **B**	25. **A**	45. **D**	65. **C**	85. **D**
6. **C**	26. **B**	46. **C**	66. **D**	86. **A**
7. **A**	27. **B**	47. **B**	67. **B**	87. **B**
8. **C**	28. **D**	48. **C**	68. **B**	88. **D**
9. **A**	29. **D**	49. **B**	69. **A**	89. **C**
10. **C**	30. **B**	50. **D**	70. **A**	90. **D**
11. **D**	31. **D**	51. **C**	71. **C**	91. **D**
12. **C**	32. **B**	52. **B**	72. **C**	92. **C**
13. **A**	33. **B**	53. **A**	73. **D**	93. **A**
14. **A**	34. **A**	54. **B**	74. **A**	94. **C**
15. **C**	35. **C**	55. **C**	75. **D**	95. **A**
16. **A**	36. **C**	56. **A**	76. **B**	96. **B**
17. **B**	37. **B**	57. **B**	77. **B**	97. **C**
18. **C**	38. **C**	58. **B**	78. **B**	98. **C**
19. **A**	39. **C**	59. **B**	79. **B**	99. **B**
20. **C**	40. **B**	60. **C**	80. **C**	100. **A**

Diagnostic Chart

INSTRUCTIONS: After you score your test, complete the following chart by inserting in the column captioned "Your Number Correct" the number of questions you answered correctly in each of the ten sections of the test. Then compare your score in each section with the ratings in the column captioned "Scale." Finally, to correct your weaknesses follow the instructions found after the chart.

SECTION	QUESTION NUMBER	AREA	YOUR NUMBER CORRECT	SCALE
1	1–8	Memory (8 questions)		8 Right—Excellent 6–7 Right—Good 5 Right—Fair Under 5 Right—Poor
2	9–28	Reading Comprehension (20 questions)		20 Right—Excellent 18–19 Right—Good 16–17 Right—Fair Under 16 Right—Poor
3	29–48	Applying State Police Procedures (20 questions)		20 Right—Excellent 18–19 Right—Good 16–17 Right—Fair Under 16 Right—Poor

4	49–57	Verbal and Math (9 questions)	9 Right—Excellent 7–8 Right—Good 6 Right—Fair Under 6 Right—Poor
5	58–65	State Police Forms (8 questions)	8 Right—Excellent 6–7 Right—Good 5 Right—Fair Under 5 Right—Poor
6	66–73	Interpreting Data (8 questions)	8 Right—Excellent 6–7 Right—Good 5 Right—Fair Under 5 Right—Poor
7	74–81	Judgment and Reasoning (8 questions)	8 Right—Excellent 6–7 Right—Good 5 Right—Fair Under 5 Right—Poor
8	82–89	Legal Definitions (8 questions)	8 Right—Excellent 6–7 Right—Good 5 Right—Fair Under 5 Right—Poor
9	90–94	Traffic Directions (5 questions)	5 Right—Excellent 4 Right—Good 3 Right—Fair Under 3 Right—Poor
10	95–100	Matching Sketches (6 questions)	6 Right—Excellent 5 Right—Good 4 Right—Fair Under 4 Right—Poor

How to correct weaknesses:

1. If you are weak in Section 1, concentrate on Chapter 6.
2. If you are weak in Section 2, concentrate on Chapter 4.
3. If you are weak in Section 3, concentrate on Chapter 9.
4. If you are weak in Section 4, concentrate on Chapter 5.
5. If you are weak in Section 5, concentrate on Chapter 7.
6. If you are weak in Section 6, concentrate on Chapter 8.
7. If you are weak in Section 7, concentrate on Chapter 10.
8. If you are weak in Section 8, concentrate on Chapter 11.
9. If you are weak in Section 9, concentrate on Chapter 13.
10. If you are weak in Section 10, concentrate on Chapter 12.

Note: Consider yourself weak in a section if you receive other than an excellent rating in it.

Answer Explanations

1. **D** Notice the similarity among the four choices. If you noticed that her address is in multiples of 16 (16 (times 2) 32 (times 2) 64th Road), you would have had very little difficulty with this question.

2. **B** Because Charles Adams was carrying a letter addressed to Dad and signed by Cathy, it is probable that he has a daughter named Cathy. <u>C</u>harles has a daughter named <u>C</u>athy. Remember that you can make assumptions if they are based on facts depicted in the illustration.

3. **B** Because Charles Adams was carrying a subway token, it is likely that he rides the subway.

4. **D** If there is money in the picture, then you will almost certainly be asked a question about money. In this case, Alicia Smart was carrying $10.30 (choice A), but Charles Adams did not have any money taken from him.

5. **B** Alicia Smart had one key, and Charles Adams had two keys. Remember that, when there are similar items in the scene, you should count them.

6. **C** Notice how all the choices are some form of the two plate numbers in the illustration. You must develop associations to remember such things as plate numbers.

7. **A** Perhaps Alicia got so smart by writing things down.

8. **C** <u>A</u>licia had an <u>a</u>ddress book and an <u>a</u>ppointment book.

9. **A** Probation is the most commonly used sentencing option.

10. **C** People on probation often create serious crime problems.

11. **D** Society could not afford the cost of sending all convicted persons to prison. For this reason, probation is indispensable.

12. **C** It was a visitor who was the first to inform the trooper about the sick woman on the bus.

13. **A** Bus Number 2356 was the first bus the trooper found, and that was at 5:15 P.M.

14. **A** Trooper Ginty arrived on bus number 2365 at 5:20 P.M., and the paramedics had arrived 5 minutes earlier.

15. **C** The sick woman's niece was Mary Martin.

16. **A** Answering this question is nothing more than an exercise in paying attention to details.

17. **B** It was the driver of the bus, Jack Hunt, who called the paramedics to the scene.

18. **C** The entire rule is aimed only at state troopers who are in uniform. And, even those in uniform are not covered by the rule if saluting and standing at attention would interfere with their duties, such as during an emergency.

19. **A** This is what we call an absolute rule. It has no exceptions. Note the similarity between choices B and D. When you see such similarity between two choices, you must recognize that neither one can be the answer.

20. **C** The key to this question is the words *issued for their use*. These were the limiting words that established the answer.

21. **C** If, at any time, equipment is properly passed from one trooper to another, the last trooper to receive the equipment shall be responsible for it.

22. **D** The paragraph specifically states that the last trooper leaving an office is responsible for turning off all lights, personal computers, and electrical appliances.

23. **C** Permission is not required in "line-of-duty" situations. Whenever you see the word *except* in a rule, you can expect the answer to revolve around that word. Also, be aware that "line of duty" is the same as saying, "when doing your job."

24. **A** The key word in the rule is *may*. This is a flexible rule. It would be inflexible if the word *must* or *shall* was used in place of *may*. Also, the rule has to do with just debts, and not all debts.

25. **A** If the gift is one that is given for departmental services, and the commanding officer of the trooper involved does not give his written consent, then that gift cannot be accepted and, therefore, must be refused. The rule applies only to gifts given for departmental services. But, the rule is the same for gifts as it is for awards, and that is why choice D is wrong.

26. **B** This is an absolute rule. It has no exceptions. A state trooper cannot intercede with a court for the discharge of or change (modification) of sentence for any defendant (person formally accused of a crime).

27. **B** Hidden enforcement has very little general deterrent effect. To deter is to prevent things from happening at a given time and/or place.

28. **D** According to the passage, hidden enforcement does have some limited usefulness, but only in areas with high accident rates.

29. **D** The actions described in the procedure are to be performed by the responding highway patrol officer.

30. **B** Whenever you see that "in this order" or similar such words are used in a procedure to indicate that the steps in the procedure are sequential, you can expect a question asking about the sequence of the steps to be taken. In this instance, after the patrol supervisor is requested by the highway patrol officer, the highway patrol officer shall request the response of the detectives.

31. **D** It is the duty of the responding highway patrol officer to determine if the services of the Crime Lab Unit are required after assessing the crime scene.

32. **B** The name of the hospital treating persons removed from the scene, not at the scene, is required. The information contained in the remaining choices is required to be communicated to the Crime Lab Unit.

33. **B** The first attempt to request the response of the Crime Lab Unit should be made directly by telephone. If a telephone is not available, the request is then made through the communications dispatcher by portable radio.

34. **A** The services of the Crime Lab Unit are to be requested for any forcible rape, not any rape. An act that, because of the age of the victim, amounts to rape could occur without force being used. The situations described in the remaining choices are examples of when the services of the Crime Lab Unit are to be requested.

35. **C** For the services of the Crime Lab Unit to be requested, the assault should be an aggravated assault involving a dangerous instrument with the victim likely to die.

36. **C** The other actions will be done after the officer attempts to correct the condition.

37. **B** The switchboard operator at the post command will make entries concerning the condition on the form HIGHWAY RECORD before anyone else.

38. **C** If you scanned the stems of the questions before answering

them, then you were alerted as to what information in the procedure will serve as the basis of questions. Practicing such a strategy in this instance would have quickly led you to choice C, which indicates that the Department of Sanitation should be notified.

39. **C** The private contractor concerned is to be notified if a traffic control device, other than a signal light, is damaged; when a signal light is damaged, the Department of Traffic is to be notified.

40. **B** Choices A and C are incorrect because Officer Drake acted improperly; the form must be signed by him but at the end of the shift when it should be submitted to the post command desk officer. This reason would also eliminate choice D.

41. **C** For recently vacated and unsecured hazardous buildings, the Department of Buildings must be notified.

42. **A** The procedure specifically indicates that when traffic control devices, other than signal lights, are missing or damaged, the private contractor concerned shall be notified.

43. **B** When the procedure does not provide a specific agency to be notified regarding a certain condition, the highway patrol officer concerned shall notify the patrol supervisor.

44. **C** As stated in the procedure, the Department of Public Works should be notified.

45. **D** The procedure clearly states that the agency to be notified regarding clogged sewer drains is the Department of Public Works. If the condition was actual flooding, then choice B, which indicates the Department of Environmental Protection, would have been correct.

46. **C** Choice D is incorrect because pages are not to be removed. Choice A is incorrect because no erasures are permitted. The correct procedure is to draw a single line through the incorrect entry and initial it.

47. **B** According to the procedure, a trooper shall store both active and completed memo books in the trooper's department locker, available for inspection at all times. Note that the procedure makes no mention of time limits. This obviously seems unreasonable. However, remember that, according to the directions, your answers are to be based solely on the information provided.

48. **C** Statements A, B, and D are all found in the procedure and are, therefore, correct statements. However, choice C is incorrect because abbreviations may be used.

49. **B** Choice A is incorrect because the word *principal* should be used to express the head of a school or institution such as a training academy. Choice C is incorrect because it should state, ". . . who I think did it." Words such as *I think, I believe,* and *I feel,* do not affect the pronouns to be used such as *who.* In this question the statement is more easily analyzed by mentally eliminating the words *I think* and changing it to read, "She is the suspect whom did it." This should make it obvious that the use of the pronoun *whom* is incorrect. Choice B is correct because *adapt* means to adjust as needed, which is what the post commander did to the procedure.

50. **D** Choice A is incorrect because *into* should have been used to indicate movement toward a place. Choice B is incorrect because *all ready* should have been used to show being prepared. Choice C is incorrect because *affect* should have been used to show being influenced.

51. **C** Choice A is incorrect because *their* should have been used to show possession. Choice B is incorrect because *there* should have been used to show a location. *They're* means they are, which would be proper in this instance.

52. **B** Choice A is incorrect because to indicate a main idea or purpose requires the use of the word *principal.* Choice C is incorrect because the use of the word *too* should be used to indicate more than. The word *principle,* which means a basic rule or truth, was correctly used in choice B.

53. **A** Choices B and C are incorrect because *who's* should have been used to indicate who is. Choice A is correct because possession, which is intended in choice A, is expressed by the word *whose.*

54. **B** By computing ⅝ × 24 gallons, you can determine that 15 gallons of fuel were contained in the fuel tank at the beginning of the shift. This is arrived at as follows:

$$\frac{5}{8} \times \frac{24}{1} =$$

Multiply all the numerators, the numbers on the top of the fractions, or $5 \times 24 = 120$, and then multiply all the denominators, the numbers on the bottom of the fractions, or $8 \times 1 = 8$. This yields the fraction

$$\frac{120}{8} = 15$$

To arrive at how much fuel was used, remember that two thirds of what was in the tank at the beginning of the tour was used. Therefore, multiply ⅔ × 15 gallons, which equals 10 gallons.

55. **C** The first step is to convert the pounds of heroin to ounces of heroin or 6 pounds × 16 ounces (there are 16 ounces to a pound), which equals 96 ounces. Each ounce is enough to make 375 bags of heroin. Therefore, 96 ounces would yield 36,000 bags (96 × 375 = 36,000). The street value would be computed by multiplying $5 per bag × 36,000 bags = $180,000.

56. **A** Averages are computed by finding the sum of all the items in the group and then dividing by the number of items in the group. In this case, to arrive at a 90 average, the five items in the group would have to add up to a certain total and when that total is divided by 5 (the number of items in the group), the result should be 90. Expressed arithmetically, ?/5 = 90 or what number divided by 5 equals 90. The answer is 450 divided by 5 equals 90. However, the total of the four given items given is 360.

$$
\begin{array}{r}
95 \\
92 \\
88 \\
\underline{85} \\
360
\end{array}
$$

To bring the sum to 450, 90 must be added, which is what she must score on her ethics examination.

57. **B** When dealing with percentage increases or decreases, take the change between the two numbers given, (155 − 125 = 30) and then divide by the older number or the number that previously existed. Expressed arithmetically, 30/125 = 0.24 or 24%. If you selected A, you probably divided 30 by the more recent number 155 or 30/155 = 0.1935 or 19.35%.

58. **B** Keflon attended in-service training on Sunday, not promotion courses. Also Keflon was sick on Tuesday and had the exact same activities as Cory.

59. **B** Trooper Hale participated in a roadblock on Thursday, August 10th.

60. **C** Wills performed it twice, and Ringer, Cory, and Keflon each did it once, for a total of five occasions. Remember that, according to the information on the rear of the form, each activity is to be assigned for at least, or a minimum of, a 3-hour block of time. Therefore, five occasions multiplied by at least a 3-hour block of time for each occasion equals a total of at least, or a minimum of, 15 hours.

61. **D** Reference 9 on Tuesday August 8th represents Detention Cell Duty.

62. **A** To answer this question you should examine only the choices offered by the question. Our strategy, which recommends first scanning the choices and then examining the form, would have proven useful in answering this question. Of the choices offered by the question, the most frequently performed activity was General Highway Patrol.

63. **D** Only the activities listed on Thursday should be examined in answering this question, and Narcotic Enforcement which is number 8 is not listed.

64. **A** Keflon was the only trooper among those mentioned in the choices who was sick during the period covered by the form.

65. **C** Other troopers, for example Akin, also attended training. Also read carefully. The question asked for the least correct statement.

66. **D** Whenever there is a choice in data interpretation questions that suggests that the answer cannot be determined, you must give that choice serious consideration. In this case, there is no specific data about the crime of robbery.

67. **B** Of those arrested for committing crimes against persons, 56% are between 21 and 30 years of age. A majority is more than half. Choice B is the answer.

68. **B** Of those under 21 who enter the prison after being convicted of a crime against a person, 65% are between 17 and 20 years of age. Because *most* means more than half, choice B is the answer. Concerning choice C, there is no way of determining from the data any specific information about persons who are 18 years of age. 18-year-old arrested persons are included in the overall category of 17–20.

69. **A** Of those persons under 17 who are arrested for committing a crime against property, 78% are under 17.

70. **A** Choices B, C, and D would all be correct if the category involved were crimes against persons. However, the category was crimes against property. In the over-30 age group for the category crimes against property, 32% of arrested persons are over 30. Multiply 1000 new arrests by 0.32 (32% in decimal form), which equals 320, as indicated in choice A.

71. **C** This is a difficult question because it involves making two calculations. You must first determine the approximate number of persons arrested for committing crimes against persons who are under

21. This is accomplished by multiplying 1000 (the total number of new arrests) by 0.18 (the decimal equivalent of 18%). By doing this you determine that the number of newly arrested persons under 21 charged with committing a crime against a person is 180. Of that number, 65% of them are between 17 and 20 years old. This means that 117 of them are between 17 and 20 years old (180 multiplied by 0.65, the decimal equivalent of 65%).

72. **C** To determine the answer to this question, all you had to do was to pick the answer off the graph. Over 21 includes two categories, 21–30 and over 30. Because, in the category of crimes against persons, 56% are between 21 and 30 and 26% are over 30, simply add the two percentages to arrive at the answer, which is 82%, as indicated in choice C.

73. **D** 82% of those arrested for committing crimes against persons and 70% of those arrested for committing crimes against property are over 21.

74. **A** The rule clearly states that an attorney must be present to protect the interests of the prisoner whenever a prisoner stands in a mandatory lineup.

75. **D** Choices A, B, and C all involve instant judgment and punishment, which is *never* a recommended approach in our democratic society. As a first step, the action described in choice D is in accordance with the stated rule.

76. **B** Patients in psychiatric wards are often not responsible for their actions, and some may tend to be inclined toward violence.

77. **B** The rights contained in the First Amendment apply as well to state troopers as to anyone. However, a basic tenet of a Code of Ethics is to remain professional at all times. Regarding choice D, the word *always* is much too strong for this choice to be the answer.

78. **B** In official matters, troopers must follow the chain of command to implement change. If there were no employee suggestion system, the trooper would properly present her idea to her supervisor. But, until official change is made, the existing procedure must be followed. Unofficial experimentation or unofficial attempts at convincing others is never appropriate.

79. **B** Acting with courtesy and tact is a mark of a true professional.

80. **C** Off-the-record statements are always inappropriate. Only with prior permission should a trooper make detailed work-related statements to the media. Saying "No comment" is often misconstrued. The correct course of action is as stated in choice C.

81. **A** It is a definite responsibility of troopers to keep their supervisors informed of all important developments. Choice C is incorrect because such a serious situation warrants official and immediate action. Choice D is wrong because the chain of command must be maintained.

82. **C** To perceive a risk and then disregard it is an example of acting recklessly.

83. **C** A benefit may be any gain or advantage that therefore includes different kinds of tangible property as well as intangible things such as an advantage when applying for a mortgage. In addition, a benefit may be given to a third person other than a beneficiary pursuant to the wishes of the beneficiary, who in this case is the highway patrol officer. Thus choice C is incorrect. A benefit could be given to someone other than the officer pursuant to the wishes of the officer.

84. **D** Since *possess* means to have physical possession or otherwise exercise control over tangible property, choices A, B, and C are correct. Choice D is incorrect because, under the law as stated in the definitions provided, only tangible property can be possessed, and emotions are not tangible property.

85. **D** Pat failed to perceive a risk that the majority of persons would have perceived.

86. **A** Choices B, C, and D are accurate statements because deadly physical force is physical force that, under the circumstances in which it is used, can produce death or other serious physical injury. Thus even a slap or a blow struck by a child could under certain circumstances turn out to be deadly physical force.

87. **B** Frank acted knowingly because he was aware of his conduct, even though he was not necessarily aware of the results of his conduct.

88. **D** Conduct means to do something or fail to do something. However in both instances there must be an accompanying mental state.

89. **C** A person must be at least 7 but not yet 16 years old to be considered a juvenile delinquent. Only choice C indicates such a person.

90. **D** Choice A is incorrect because the Carter Thruway does not go directly into the Town of Baker. Choice C is incorrect because the Cross County Parkway cannot be accessed by heading east on Highway 269. Choice B is incorrect because, although the directions will lead you toward the Town of Baker, it is not the most direct route.

91. **D** Because the perpetrator was last seen heading north on Route 12 beyond where the Carter Thruway intersects Route 12, U.S. 9 and the Carter Thruway would be inappropriate locations for a roadblock. Thus choices A and B are incorrect. Because Route 2 never intersects with Route 12, the roadblock as suggested by Choice C would not be appropriate. Thus choice C is incorrect.

92. **C** Choice A is incorrect because the Jay Expressway does not interconnect with the Cross County Parkway. Choice B is incorrect because Route 2 does not lead to the scene of the accident. Choice D is incorrect because heading north on Route 12 does not lead to the scene of the accident.

93. **A** Choice B is incorrect because there is nothing on the map that indicates how many lanes exist on any of the roads. Choices C and D can be determined to be incorrect based on an examination of the map. Choice A is correct because Route 2 is intersected by U.S. 9, the Sky Highway, the Cross County Parkway, the Carter Thruway, and the Jay Expressway.

94. **C** The two roads intersect with each other in three locations.

95. **A** The eyes of choice B, the nose of choice C, and the facial lines of the forehead of choice D leave choice A as the only possible answer.

96. **B** The noses of choices A and C and the eyes of choice D leave choice B as the only possible answer.

97. **C** The nose of choice A, the eyes of choice B, and the nose of choice D leave choice C as the only possible answer.

98. **C** The eyes and lips of choice A, the eyes and nose of choice B, and the eyes of choice D leave choice C as the only possible answer.

99. **B** The chin line of choice A and the noses of choices C and D leave choice B as the only possible answer.

100. **A** The eyes of choices B and C and the mole on the chin of choice D leave choice A as the only possible answer.

CHAPTER 15

Practice Examination Two

This chapter contains the second of five practice examinations that you will be taking. Don't forget to:

1. Take the test in one sitting. You have 3½ hours to answer all 100 questions.

2. Use the test-taking strategies outlined in Chapter 2.

3. Use the answer sheet we have provided to record your answers.

4. Complete the diagnostic chart that appears at the end of this chapter after you score this practice examination.

Answer Sheet
Practice Examination Two

Follow the instructions given in the test. Mark only your answers in the circles below.

WARNING: Be sure that the circle you fill is in the same row as the question you are answering. Use a No. 2 pencil (soft pencil).

BE SURE YOUR PENCIL MARKS ARE HEAVY AND BLACK. ERASE COMPLETELY ANY ANSWER YOU WISH TO CHANGE.

DO NOT make stray pencil dots, dashes or marks.

1. Ⓐ Ⓑ Ⓒ Ⓓ   2. Ⓐ Ⓑ Ⓒ Ⓓ   3. Ⓐ Ⓑ Ⓒ Ⓓ   4. Ⓐ Ⓑ Ⓒ Ⓓ
5. Ⓐ Ⓑ Ⓒ Ⓓ   6. Ⓐ Ⓑ Ⓒ Ⓓ   7. Ⓐ Ⓑ Ⓒ Ⓓ   8. Ⓐ Ⓑ Ⓒ Ⓓ
9. Ⓐ Ⓑ Ⓒ Ⓓ   10. Ⓐ Ⓑ Ⓒ Ⓓ   11. Ⓐ Ⓑ Ⓒ Ⓓ   12. Ⓐ Ⓑ Ⓒ Ⓓ
13. Ⓐ Ⓑ Ⓒ Ⓓ   14. Ⓐ Ⓑ Ⓒ Ⓓ   15. Ⓐ Ⓑ Ⓒ Ⓓ   16. Ⓐ Ⓑ Ⓒ Ⓓ
17. Ⓐ Ⓑ Ⓒ Ⓓ   18. Ⓐ Ⓑ Ⓒ Ⓓ   19. Ⓐ Ⓑ Ⓒ Ⓓ   20. Ⓐ Ⓑ Ⓒ Ⓓ
21. Ⓐ Ⓑ Ⓒ Ⓓ   22. Ⓐ Ⓑ Ⓒ Ⓓ   23. Ⓐ Ⓑ Ⓒ Ⓓ   24. Ⓐ Ⓑ Ⓒ Ⓓ
25. Ⓐ Ⓑ Ⓒ Ⓓ   26. Ⓐ Ⓑ Ⓒ Ⓓ   27. Ⓐ Ⓑ Ⓒ Ⓓ   28. Ⓐ Ⓑ Ⓒ Ⓓ
29. Ⓐ Ⓑ Ⓒ Ⓓ   30. Ⓐ Ⓑ Ⓒ Ⓓ   31. Ⓐ Ⓑ Ⓒ Ⓓ   32. Ⓐ Ⓑ Ⓒ Ⓓ
33. Ⓐ Ⓑ Ⓒ Ⓓ   34. Ⓐ Ⓑ Ⓒ Ⓓ   35. Ⓐ Ⓑ Ⓒ Ⓓ   36. Ⓐ Ⓑ Ⓒ Ⓓ
37. Ⓐ Ⓑ Ⓒ Ⓓ   38. Ⓐ Ⓑ Ⓒ Ⓓ   39. Ⓐ Ⓑ Ⓒ Ⓓ   40. Ⓐ Ⓑ Ⓒ Ⓓ
41. Ⓐ Ⓑ Ⓒ Ⓓ   42. Ⓐ Ⓑ Ⓒ Ⓓ   43. Ⓐ Ⓑ Ⓒ Ⓓ   44. Ⓐ Ⓑ Ⓒ Ⓓ
45. Ⓐ Ⓑ Ⓒ Ⓓ   46. Ⓐ Ⓑ Ⓒ Ⓓ   47. Ⓐ Ⓑ Ⓒ Ⓓ   48. Ⓐ Ⓑ Ⓒ Ⓓ
49. Ⓐ Ⓑ Ⓒ Ⓓ   50. Ⓐ Ⓑ Ⓒ Ⓓ   51. Ⓐ Ⓑ Ⓒ Ⓓ   52. Ⓐ Ⓑ Ⓒ Ⓓ
53. Ⓐ Ⓑ Ⓒ Ⓓ   54. Ⓐ Ⓑ Ⓒ Ⓓ   55. Ⓐ Ⓑ Ⓒ Ⓓ   56. Ⓐ Ⓑ Ⓒ Ⓓ
57. Ⓐ Ⓑ Ⓒ Ⓓ   58. Ⓐ Ⓑ Ⓒ Ⓓ   59. Ⓐ Ⓑ Ⓒ Ⓓ   60. Ⓐ Ⓑ Ⓒ Ⓓ
61. Ⓐ Ⓑ Ⓒ Ⓓ   62. Ⓐ Ⓑ Ⓒ Ⓓ   63. Ⓐ Ⓑ Ⓒ Ⓓ   64. Ⓐ Ⓑ Ⓒ Ⓓ
65. Ⓐ Ⓑ Ⓒ Ⓓ   66. Ⓐ Ⓑ Ⓒ Ⓓ   67. Ⓐ Ⓑ Ⓒ Ⓓ   68. Ⓐ Ⓑ Ⓒ Ⓓ
69. Ⓐ Ⓑ Ⓒ Ⓓ   70. Ⓐ Ⓑ Ⓒ Ⓓ   71. Ⓐ Ⓑ Ⓒ Ⓓ   72. Ⓐ Ⓑ Ⓒ Ⓓ
73. Ⓐ Ⓑ Ⓒ Ⓓ   74. Ⓐ Ⓑ Ⓒ Ⓓ   75. Ⓐ Ⓑ Ⓒ Ⓓ   76. Ⓐ Ⓑ Ⓒ Ⓓ
77. Ⓐ Ⓑ Ⓒ Ⓓ   78. Ⓐ Ⓑ Ⓒ Ⓓ   79. Ⓐ Ⓑ Ⓒ Ⓓ   80. Ⓐ Ⓑ Ⓒ Ⓓ
81. Ⓐ Ⓑ Ⓒ Ⓓ   82. Ⓐ Ⓑ Ⓒ Ⓓ   83. Ⓐ Ⓑ Ⓒ Ⓓ   84. Ⓐ Ⓑ Ⓒ Ⓓ
85. Ⓐ Ⓑ Ⓒ Ⓓ   86. Ⓐ Ⓑ Ⓒ Ⓓ   87. Ⓐ Ⓑ Ⓒ Ⓓ   88. Ⓐ Ⓑ Ⓒ Ⓓ
89. Ⓐ Ⓑ Ⓒ Ⓓ   90. Ⓐ Ⓑ Ⓒ Ⓓ   91. Ⓐ Ⓑ Ⓒ Ⓓ   92. Ⓐ Ⓑ Ⓒ Ⓓ
93. Ⓐ Ⓑ Ⓒ Ⓓ   94. Ⓐ Ⓑ Ⓒ Ⓓ   95. Ⓐ Ⓑ Ⓒ Ⓓ   96. Ⓐ Ⓑ Ⓒ Ⓓ
97. Ⓐ Ⓑ Ⓒ Ⓓ   98. Ⓐ Ⓑ Ⓒ Ⓓ   99. Ⓐ Ⓑ Ⓒ Ⓓ   100. Ⓐ Ⓑ Ⓒ Ⓓ

The Test

DIRECTIONS FOR QUESTIONS 1–8: Before answering questions 1–8, take 5 minutes to examine the following four wanted posters with the information that accompanies each poster.

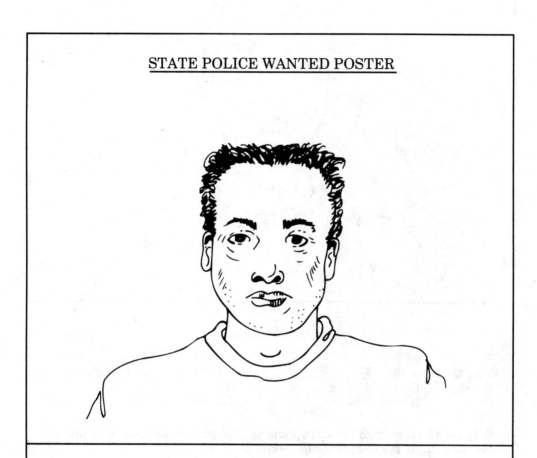

STATE POLICE WANTED POSTER

Samuel Youngblood

Age:	32	Race:	White
Height:	5' 9"	Weight:	200 pounds
Eyes:	Brown	Hair:	Bald
Scars:	None	Tattoos:	None

Subject, who escaped from State Prison where he was serving a life sentence for rape and child abuse, often wears a hairpiece as shown in above poster. Often loiters in the vicinity of schools in search of victims.

STATE POLICE WANTED POSTER

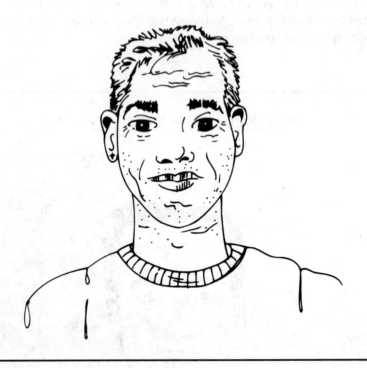

Jack Hunt

Age:	62		Race:	White
Height:	5' 10"		Weight:	210 pounds
Eyes:	Blue		Hair:	Brown
Scars:	None		Tattoos:	None

Subject, who is wanted for kidnapping and robbery, often uses the alias
Ben Hogan. He is a chronic drug user.

James Short

Age:	45		Race:	White
Height:	5' 9"		Weight:	160 pounds
Eyes:	Brown		Hair:	Brown
Scars:	None		Tattoos:	None

Subject, who is wanted for armed robbery, is considered to be armed and dangerous. His weapon of preference is a sawed-off shotgun, which he almost always carries on his person.

Chuckie Gifford

Age:	28	Race:	White
Height:	5' 9"	Weight:	225 pounds
Eyes:	Blue	Hair:	Brown
Scars:	None	Tattoos:	None

Subject, who is a lifelong con artist who preys on older women,
is wanted to answer an indictment, which charges five counts of larceny
by extortion. Often represents himself as a law enforcement officer.

DO NOT PROCEED UNTIL 5 MINUTES HAVE PASSED.

TURN TO NEXT PAGE

DIRECTIONS: Answer questions 1–8 solely on the basis of the wanted posters on the preceding pages.

1. Which of the wanted persons illustrated in the following posters wears a hairpiece?

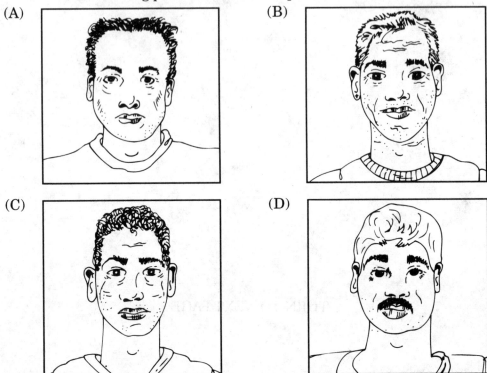

(A)

(B)

(C)

(D)

2. Which of the wanted persons illustrated in the
   following posters uses the alias Ben Hogan?

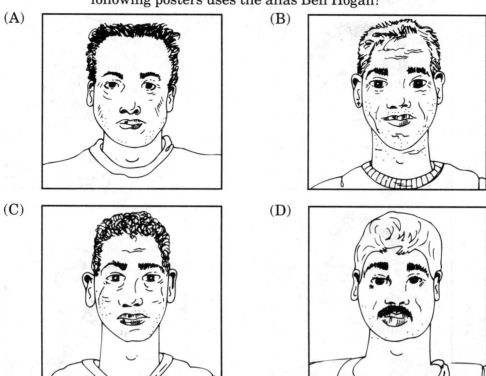

3. Which of the wanted persons illustrated in the
   following posters is a chronic drug user?

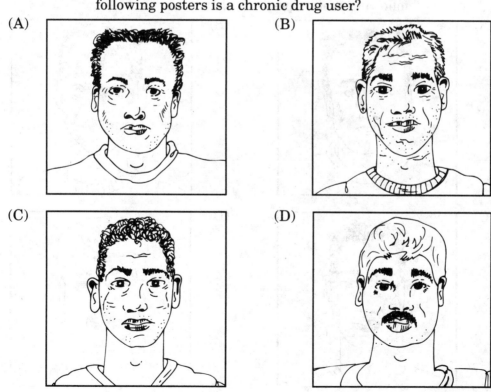

4. Which of the wanted persons illustrated in the
   following posters is the oldest?

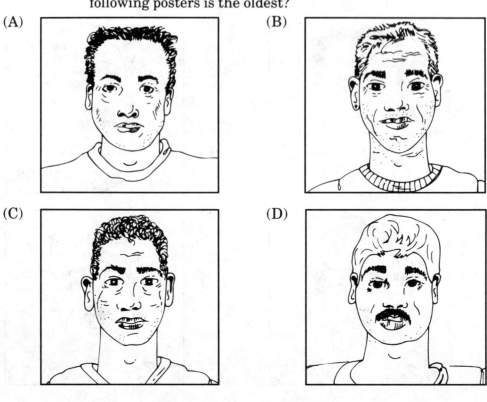

5. Which of the wanted persons illustrated in the
   following posters preys on older women?

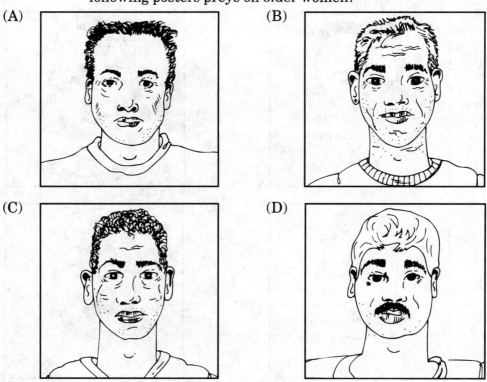

6. The subject illustrated in the wanted poster directly above
   (A) is almost always armed with a shotgun.
   (B) often loiters in the vicinity of schools.
   (C) is a chronic drug user.
   (D) often poses as a police officer.

7. The subject illustrated in the wanted poster directly above
   (A) often wears a hairpiece.
   (B) often loiters in the vicinity of schools.
   (C) is a chronic drug user.
   (D) often poses as a police officer.

8. The subject illustrated in the wanted poster directly above
   (A) is wanted for armed robbery.
   (B) often loiters in the vicinity of schools.
   (C) is a chronic drug user.
   (D) often poses as a police officer.

Answer questions 9–13 based solely on the following passage.

The main obstacle to a successful traffic stop is conflict. State troopers stopping motorists must remember that there will always be a certain amount of conflict involved in every traffic stop. The trick is to keep that conflict to a minimum. Conflict can be avoided by adhering to the following traffic stop guidelines.

   a. After greeting the driver, tell him/her why you made the stop and what action you intend to take.

   b. Allow a driver, especially one who is apparently accompanied by family or close friends, to save face.

   c. Don't be oversensitive.

   d. Don't be overtalkative.

   e. Don't be abrupt or impolite.

   f. Don't preach or be judgmental.

   g. Don't demean a driver's ability.

   h. Don't use the driver's first name.

   i. Never accept a billfold or wallet; instead, make the motorist take their documents out themselves and hand them to you.

   j. After the stop is over, assist the motorist to reenter the flow of traffic.

9. State troopers making traffic stops
   (A) should be able to eliminate conflict.
   (B) should strive to minimize conflict.
   (C) should not be concerned with conflict.
   (D) should arrest those who create conflict.

10. The primary barrier to a successful traffic stop is
    (A) quota systems.
    (B) inappropriate attitudes.
    (C) unlicensed operators.
    (D) conflict.

11. Which of the following is not a recommended guideline for a state trooper to follow when making a traffic stop?
    (A) Be polite.
    (B) Be more sensitive than necessary.
    (C) Allow a driver to save face.
    (D) Don't talk too much.

12. When making traffic stops, a state trooper should not
    (A) assist motorists to reenter the flow of traffic.
    (B) be sensitive.
    (C) accept a billfold or wallet.
    (D) forget to be judgmental.

13. A state trooper making a traffic stop should decide what action she intends to take
    (A) after hearing the motorist's story.
    (B) after checking the driver's credentials.
    (C) after inspecting the vehicle's equipment.
    (D) after greeting the driver.

Answer questions 14–16 based solely on the following passage.

State troopers should be familiar with the process used to incarcerate the prisoners they arrest. This process begins in local institutions. Jails, holding pens, and workhouses are the main types of local institutions. Jails have the authority to detain suspects for periods of 24 hours to 14 days; they also hold convicted inmates who are serving short-term sentences of 1 year or less. Jails are usually administered by the county marshall, but they are sometimes managed by the state police. Holding pens are generally found in city police stations or state police headquarters, and they hold suspects for periods of less than 24 hours. The primary function of workhouses—which are operated by cities and counties—is to hold convicted inmates sentenced to short terms of less than 3 months.

14. Which of the following is NOT a local institution?
    (A) a prison   (B) a jail
    (C) a holding pen   (D) a workhouse

15. The state police
    (A) do not get involved in local institutions.
    (B) sometimes manage jails.
    (C) sometimes manage holding pens.
    (D) sometimes manage workhouses.

16. A person who is convicted of a crime and who is
    serving a sentence of 9 months would be confined
    in a
    (A) jail.   (B) holding pen.
    (C) workhouse.   (D) prison.

Answer question 17 based solely on the following information.

State troopers are often responsible for the care and custody of recently arrested persons. They should, therefore, be aware of court rulings in this area. For example, most federal and state court decisions have rejected the claim that incarcerated prisoners should be able to freely express their personal views. The courts have refused to grant prisoners the First Amendment right of free speech because such a right could easily create demonstrations and riots in places used for the detention of prisoners.

17. The courts have not granted the right of free
    speech to prisoners because
    (A) citizens lose this right when they are con-
        victed of a crime.
    (B) of the potential for demonstrations and riots
        that free speech would create.
    (C) of the feeling that prisoners are not entitled
        to constitutional protection.
    (D) of existing laws.

Answer questions 18–23 based solely on the following passage.

The first concern of a state trooper investigating a traffic accident should be the safety of all concerned. Medical attention must be immediately requested for injured parties, and the normal flow of traffic should be restored as soon as possible, consistent with the investigation that must always take place. The investigating trooper must form an opinion of the cause of every accident he/she investigates. A very important point to emphasize to all troopers investigating a vehicle accident is to separate the motorists involved, as well as the witnesses, and keep them separated. They are to be interviewed separately.

Following are the recommended steps for a trooper to follow when conducting an accident investigation.

a. Arrive safely at the scene. Sometimes worse accidents are caused by troopers who are overanxious to get to the scene.

b. Perform first aid and request necessary medical assistance. Make a point to ask everyone involved if they require medical assistance. Examine the credentials of anyone who volunteers to render medical assistance before any such assistance is rendered.

c. Protect the accident scene. Put out cones, flares, and other such signals to prevent further accidents. The first cone placed should be the one that is going to be the greatest distance away from the accident scene.

d. Separate the motorists and obtain their credentials. Holding on to their credentials, such as drivers licenses and vehicle registrations, is good insurance against their leaving prematurely.

e. Locate witnesses and obtain their statements. Don't make general requests to a crowd for witnesses. Ask the drivers whom they saw on the scene when the accident occurred or immediately after and personally approach anyone so identified.

f. Check the highway and the vehicles involved. Especially check the vehicles against the story told by the drivers.

g. Care for the property of the injured. Remember that the police are responsible for the property of those removed to the hospital.

h. Gather evidence and determine the cause of the accident. Even though the trooper did not witness the accident, he/she must determine its cause. Sources to be used in making this determination are physical evidence, such as damage to the vehicles and skid marks, statements of the participants and witnesses, location of traffic control devices, and knowledge of the rules of the road.

18. A state trooper investigating a traffic accident should be most concerned with
   (A) restoring the normal flow of traffic.
   (B) discovering the cause of the accident.
   (C) the safety of all concerned.
   (D) completing the required forms and reports.

19. A state trooper
   (A) must form an opinion of the cause of every traffic accident he/she investigates.
   (B) should only form an opinion about the cause of the accident for those accidents he/she personally witnessed.
   (C) should rely exclusively on witnesses when determining the cause of a traffic accident.
   (D) should not be concerned about physical evidence when investigating a traffic accident.

20. Which of the following must be done right away at the scene of a traffic accident?
    (A) restore the normal flow of traffic
    (B) determine the cause of the accident
    (C) locate witnesses
    (D) request medical attention for the injured

21. What should be done prior to a trooper allowing someone to render medical assistance at the scene of a traffic accident?
    (A) The injured party must consent.
    (B) The credentials of the volunteer must be examined.
    (C) Hold harmless agreements have to be signed.
    (D) Clearance must be obtained via the radio dispatcher.

22. When protecting an accident scene via the placement of cones, the first cone to be placed should be
    (A) as close as possible to the accident scene.
    (B) the one that is going to be the greatest distance away from the scene.
    (C) either as close as possible to the scene or as far away as possible, depending on the location of the accident.
    (D) placed according to the best judgment of the trooper investigating the accident.

23. A good way to prevent motorists from leaving the accident scene while they are still needed is to
    (A) simply tell them not to leave.
    (B) obtain and hold their credentials.
    (C) keep them under constant observation.
    (D) threaten them with a citation if they attempt to leave.

Answer question 24 based on the following information.

The courts have ruled that in general the use of deadly force is permissible to prevent the infliction of serious injury or death. Therefore, the use of deadly force to prevent an arrested person from inflicting serious injury or death on another is lawful but only if such use of such force is a last resort.

24. A state trooper may use deadly force against an arrested person
    (A) anytime such a person attempts to escape.
    (B) anytime such a person attempts to kill another person.
    (C) only if the arrested person is committing some form of a felony.
    (D) only as a last resort to prevent an arrested person from seriously injuring or killing another person.

Answer question 25 based solely on the following information.

The typical chronic criminal is neither a hero nor a villain. He is a person who has lost in the game of life. He is an unsuccessful person who has failed in one venture after another. And, he is usually no better at committing crimes than he is at anything else.

25. The typical chronic criminal
    (A) is like everyone else.
    (B) usually fails in his criminal endeavors.
    (C) usually avoids detection.
    (D) is very often successful.

Answer questions 26–28 based solely on the following information.

It has long been recognized that the police cannot enforce all traffic laws. A policy of full enforcement would drain the resources of the entire criminal justice system. Instead, the police engage in a policy of selective enforcement of the traffic laws. Selective enforcement means the enforcement of certain specific accident-causing violations at times and locations in which a high number of vehicle accidents occur. The principle of selective enforcement also applies to the enforcement of criminal offenses. Although it is not practical for regular patrol units to engage in selective enforcement of the traffic laws, it is a good strategy to use specially designated selective enforcement units. It should be noted that it is never a good idea to "throw the book at a violator." When multiple violations are committed, only the violations that are more serious and provable should be cited.

26. A policy of full enforcement of traffic laws
    (A) is recommended, primarily because it would save lives.
    (B) is not recommended, primarily because the public would not stand for it.
    (C) is recommended, primarily because it would result in voluntary compliance.
    (D) is not recommended, primarily because it drains the resources of the criminal justice system.

27. For regular patrol units to engage in selective enforcement
    (A) is highly recommended.
    (B) is recommended in most cases.
    (C) is only recommended in rural areas.
    (D) is impractical.

28. When a motorist commits a number of violations, which ones to cite should depend on
    (A) only the seriousness of the various violations.
    (B) only which violations are easily provable.
    (C) both the seriousness and the provability of the violations involved.
    (D) neither the seriousness nor the provability of the violations involved.

Answer questions 29–36 solely on the basis of the following information.

To protect troopers from injury while conducting investigations involving stop-and-question situations, the following procedure will be followed by troopers.

To stop means to temporarily detain a person for questioning.

A frisk is a running of the hands over the clothing, feeling for a weapon.

To search means to place hands inside a pocket or other interior parts of clothing to determine if an object felt during a frisk is a weapon.

When a trooper reasonably suspects a person has committed, is committing, or is about to commit a felony or misdemeanor as defined in the State Penal Code, the trooper

1. Shall stop the person and request identification and an explanation of the person's conduct.

    a. Shall identify himself/herself as a police officer, if not in uniform.

2. May frisk the suspect, if the trooper reasonably suspects he/she is in danger of physical injury.

3. May search the suspect, if the frisk reveals an object that may be a weapon.

NOTE: Only that portion of the suspect's clothing where an object is felt may be searched.

4. Shall detain the suspect while conducting the investigation to determine whether there is probable cause to believe an offense has been committed by the suspect.

    a. A suspect may be detained for a period of time reasonably related to the facts that initially justified the stop or that are discovered during the stop.

    b. The trooper shall complete the investigation as expeditiously as possible.

5. Shall release the suspect immediately after completing the investigation if probable cause to arrest does not exist.

6. Shall prepare a STOP AND FRISK CARD for each person stopped, if:

    a. Person is stopped by use of force.

    b. Person stopped is frisked or frisked and searched.

    c. Person stopped is arrested.

    d. Person stopped refused to identify himself.

NOTE: If person stopped refuses to identify himself/herself (and there is no reason to take further action), enter "REFUSED" in the appropriate space on the STOP AND FRISK CARD and allow the suspect to depart only after completing the investigation and only if the investigation does not establish probable cause to believe the suspect has committed an offense. Request the patrol supervisor to respond and confirm the refusal, review STOP AND FRISK CARD, and action taken. Do not detain the suspect while awaiting the arrival of the patrol supervisor if the investigation is completed and no probable cause to arrest the suspect exists.

7. Enter the details in the trooper memo book.

8. Inform the post command desk officer of the facts.

9. Submit STOP AND FRISK CARD(S), if prepared, to the post command desk officer who shall review the STOP AND FRISK CARD(S).

A suspect should not be moved or transported from the location where he is stopped for questioning unless he voluntarily consents or there is an exigency (e.g., hostile crowd gathers and officer must move suspect from area for safety purposes, victim/witness is injured and cannot be brought to the location where the suspect is being detained, and so officer transports the suspect to injured party.)

Some factors that would create a reasonable suspicion include:

    a. The demeanor of the suspect.

    b. The gait and manner of the suspect.

    c. Any knowledge the officer may have of the suspect's background and character.

    d. Whether the suspect is carrying anything and what he is carrying.

e. Manner of dress of suspect including bulges in clothing.

f. Time of day or night.

g. Any overheard conversations of the suspect.

h. The particular streets and areas involved.

i. Any information received from third parties.

j. Proximity to scene of crime.

29. Concerning stop-and-question situations, which of the following is the most correct statement?
    (A) A frisk has the exact same meaning as a search.
    (B) A search usually precedes a frisk.
    (C) A frisk involves going inside a suspect's pockets.
    (D) A search is often preceded by a frisk.

30. The minimum level of proof required for a trooper to legally stop a person and request identification and an explanation of such person's conduct is
    (A) reasonable suspicion.
    (B) a hunch.
    (C) absolute certainty that something has occurred.
    (D) an educated guess.

31. Trooper June Downs is conducting a frisk of a suspect she has stopped when she feels something hard in the suspect's coat pocket. The trooper then searches the suspect's jacket pocket and then pants pocket. In the suspect's pants pocket the trooper finds a knife. In this instance the trooper acted
    (A) properly, mainly because she was able to find a weapon that could be used to injure someone.
    (B) improperly, mainly because she was legally allowed to search only the suspect's coat pocket.
    (C) properly, mainly because she was following up on what her frisk revealed.
    (D) improperly, mainly because searching inside pockets should only be made after an arrest is made.

32. The amount of time a trooper may legally detain a person who has been stopped for questioning is
   (A) 5 minutes.
   (B) 15 minutes.
   (C) 1 hour.
   (D) not a fixed period.

33. If, as a result of a stop-and-question incident, the trooper concerned finds no probable cause to arrest the suspect, the trooper should
   (A) bring the suspect to the post command.
   (B) release the suspect immediately after completing the investigation.
   (C) give the suspect a summons.
   (D) take a photo of the suspect.

34. In which of the following situations would it be least appropriate for a STOP AND FRISK CARD to be prepared by a trooper?
   (A) whenever a person is stopped
   (B) whenever a person is frisked
   (C) whenever a person who was frisked is arrested
   (D) whenever a person who is stopped refuses to identify himself

35. According to procedure, STOP AND FRISK CARD(S) are reviewed by
   (A) only the patrol supervisor.
   (B) only the desk officer.
   (C) by neither the patrol supervisor nor the desk officer.
   (D) by both the patrol supervisor and the desk officer.

36. Trooper Rays observes a person on a hot, dry August afternoon, wearing a long raincoat under which the trooper observes what looks like a rifle bulging out. The trooper decides to stop the person and request identification and an explanation of the person's conduct. In this instance, the trooper acted
   (A) properly, mainly because at this point enough proof exists to immediately arrest the person.
   (B) improperly, mainly because the trooper has no further information about the person.
   (C) properly, mainly because at this point the trooper has enough proof to create a reasonable suspicion.
   (D) improperly, mainly because a person can wear whatever that person wants.

Answer questions 37 and 38 solely on the basis of the following information.

When counterfeit money is detected by a trooper and it is determined that the passer is an innocent victim or there is no indication who passed it:

1. The trooper shall have the person last in possession write his name and date across the face of the bill or scratch his initials on a coin.

2. The trooper shall sign his/her rank, name, badge number and date on the bill or scratch his/her initials on the coin.

3. The trooper shall prepare four copies of a report describing in detail how the money came into the possession of the trooper, including the amount and serial numbers of all bills.

4. The post command desk officer shall assign a messenger to deliver the report and the money to the Special Agent-In-Charge of the local office of the United States Secret Service.

37. Trooper Barns is called to a gas station where a gas attendant states that he received from an unknown motorist what has turned out to be a counterfeit $10 bill. In this instance the trooper should
    (A) initial the bill.
    (B) have the attendant initial the bill.
    (C) have only the attendant sign the bill.
    (D) sign the bill along with the attendant.

38. After coming into possession of a counterfeit bill, Trooper Doe takes possession of the bill and immediately delivers it to a local office of the Secret Service. In this instance, the trooper acted
    (A) properly, mainly because the Secret Service stores counterfeit bills.
    (B) improperly, mainly because the Secret Service should respond to the post command to take possession of the counterfeit bill.
    (C) properly, mainly because the quicker an investigation can be commenced by the Secret Service, the quicker arrests can be made.
    (D) improperly, mainly because the post command desk officer will have the money delivered to the Secret Service.

Answer questions 39–41 solely on the basis of the following information.

TROOPER GUIDELINES AT ILLICIT DRUG LABORATORIES

When a trooper has cause to investigate a suspected illicit drug laboratory, an immediate notification will be made to the post command desk officer. The desk officer will notify the Forensic Laboratory, without delay, requesting a chemist be dispatched to the scene immediately. Certain substances in a laboratory are highly volatile, therefore, all troopers will follow these safety guidelines:

a. Ventilate the laboratory by opening doors and windows.

b. Do not turn on lights or use flashlights until the area is well ventilated. If necessary to enter prior to the room being ventilated, a flashlight may be used if it is turned on before entering the area.

c. Do not smoke at the scene.

d. If vapors are very strong or there is any odor of bitter almonds, remain outside and await arrival of the laboratory chemist.

e. Do not use portable radios while inside the laboratory.

f. Do not disturb flasks or containers that are being heated or cooled. Direct the attention of the chemist to such items.

g. Do not allow acid and cyanide to be mixed or come together. The fumes from this mixture can cause death.

When a search warrant has been obtained for a suspected illicit drug laboratory, the commanding officer of the forensic laboratory will be notified and a chemist will accompany the unit executing the warrant.

39. The radio dispatcher directs Trooper Drake to respond to an abandoned barn to investigate suspicious odors. Upon arriving the trooper quickly determines that the location is the site of an illicit drug lab. The trooper's first action should be
(A) to ventilate the area.
(B) to notify the post command desk officer.
(C) to determine if certain odors are present.
(D) apply for a search warrant.

40. While instructing a newly assigned trooper at the scene of a suspected illicit drug laboratory, Trooper King makes the following statements.

    1. Never use a flashlight inside such a place.

    2. Never use a portable radio while inside such a place.

Which of the following is most accurate concerning the preceding statements?
(A) Only statement 1 is correct.
(B) Only statement 2 is correct.
(C) Both statements 1 and 2 are correct.
(D) Neither statement 1 nor 2 is correct.

41. At the scene of a suspected illicit drug lab, Trooper Hills detects the odor of bitter almonds. The trooper would be most correct if the trooper
(A) turned off the lights.
(B) removed any flasks being heated from their heat source.
(C) remained outside the premises and waited for a chemist.
(D) had all flashlights turned off.

Answer questions 42–48 solely on the basis of the following information.

Upon notification or observation of a vehicle accident, the trooper concerned shall comply with the following procedure:

1. Park the patrol car behind the vehicles involved, so that traffic will not be impeded.

2. Ascertain if there are any injuries and request ambulance if needed.

    a. Place an IDENTIFICATION TAG on an unconscious person who is removed to the hospital.

3. Divert traffic if necessary.

    a. Use traffic cones, turret lights, and danger signs.

    b. Place the first cone at least 200 feet from the accident on high-speed highways.

4. Obtain the driver's license, vehicle registration, and insurance identification card from driver(s) involved.

    a. Record required information and return credentials to driver(s).

NOTE: The following vehicles do not require insurance identification cards:

    a. Taxis, buses, and other rented vehicles.

    b. Vehicles operating under the authority of the Public Service Commission.

    c. Government-owned vehicles.

    d. Certain farm vehicles.

5. Have the vehicles removed from the roadway as soon as practical.

6. Determine the cause of the accident by inquiry and observation.

7. If necessary, make arrests and give summonses.

8. Prepare the first line of the form INFORMATION EXCHANGE and give it to the drivers.

    a. Advise a driver if incapacitated, that another participant in the accident or the owner of the vehicle must complete the INFORMATION EXCHANGE.

9. Prepare one copy of TROOPER ACCIDENT REPORT.

10. Check appropriate "Duplicate Copy Required For" captions on rear of form and in addition, check box "Other Agency" and enter:

    a. Department of Consumer Affairs—if tow truck licensed by Department of Consumer Affairs is involved in accident

    b. Department of Transportation—if accident involved collision with a "crash cushion" or "highway impact attenuator"

    c. Department of Parks—if a person is killed or injured on a roadway under the jurisdiction of the Department of Parks

    d. Missing Persons Squad and the Accident Investigation Squad—if a person is killed in the accident

    e. Board of Education—if the vehicle accident involved a school bus

11. Sign and deliver the reports to the post command desk officer.

12. Make a complete memo book entry.

13. Prepare a TROOPER ACCIDENT REPORT for any accident case when an animal is killed or injured due to a vehicle accident.

14. Allow a sick/injured person to be treated by a doctor, emergency medical technician, or paramedic, pending arrival of an ambulance, if such person volunteers his/her services, and the trooper reasonably believes the volunteer is a professional.

a. Such medical attention should take place, if possible, under the observation of the trooper concerned.

b. When the emergency situation is under control, the trooper concerned shall request identification from the volunteer, including name and address.

c. The trooper concerned shall record this information in his/her memo book and under "Details" in a TROOPER ACCIDENT REPORT.

NOTE: The volunteer's role is limited to providing medical assistance ONLY. Determination regarding removal procedures via ambulance will be determined by Emergency Medical Service personnel.

15. Advise members of the public who seek information about a past accident they have been involved in to prepare a REQUEST FOR COPY OF ACCIDENT RECORD. These forms are available at any post command and at the Public Inquiry Section of headquarters.

42. A vehicle traffic accident on a high-speed highway is being handled by a trooper. In this instance, the trooper should place
   (A) the last cone at least 200 feet from the accident.
   (B) the first cone at least 300 feet from the accident.
   (C) the last cone at least 300 feet from the accident.
   (D) the first cone at least 200 feet from the accident.

43. Each of the following categories of vehicles do not require insurance cards except
   (A) all farm vehicles.
   (B) taxis.
   (C) buses.
   (D) government-owned vehicles.

44. Which of the following statements concerning the procedure dealing with vehicle accidents is most correct?
   (A) IDENTIFICATION TAGS are to be put only on persons who have died as a result of a vehicle accident.
   (B) Traffic should always be diverted at the scene of a vehicle accident.
   (C) No determination as to the cause of the accident should be made by the trooper concerned.
   (D) An INFORMATION EXCHANGE may be completed at times by other than a driver of one of the involved vehicles.

45. If an accident occurred on a roadway under the jurisdiction of the Department of Parks where, although no one was injured, a crash cushion was heavily damaged, then which of the following most accurately indicates who should receive a copy of the TROOPER ACCIDENT REPORT?
    (A) Department of Parks but not Department of Transportation
    (B) Department of Transportation but not Department of Parks
    (C) both Department of Parks and Department of Transportation
    (D) neither Department of Parks nor Department of Transportation

46. According to procedure, after a trooper prepares a TROOPER ACCIDENT REPORT, the trooper shall deliver the report to the
    (A) post command commanding officer.
    (B) post command desk officer.
    (C) patrol supervisor.
    (D) drivers of any vehicles involved.

47. While awaiting an ambulance at the scene of a vehicle accident where someone has been injured, a female approaches the trooper handling the accident and informs the trooper that she is a physician and would like to volunteer her services. The trooper reasonably believes that she is in fact a professional and allows her to begin immediate treatment. In this instance, the trooper acted
    (A) properly, mainly because the trooper reasonably believes that the female is a professional.
    (B) improperly, mainly because the trooper should have insisted on receiving documentation that the female is a physician.
    (C) properly, mainly because volunteered help, including determinations involving removal procedures of injured persons, is welcomed at the scene of an accident.
    (D) improperly, mainly because volunteers are not allowed to assist at vehicle accident scenes.

48. Trooper Drakes is approached by Joe Rays, a private citizen, who indicates that last week he was involved in an accident in the area. Mr. Rays would like some information about the accident. Trooper Drakes refers Mr. Rays to headquarters to obtain a form needed to acquire such information. In this instance the trooper acted
   (A) properly, mainly because the necessary forms to retrieve such information can be acquired at headquarters.
   (B) improperly, mainly because the trooper should have immediately given the citizen the information.
   (C) properly, mainly because headquarters is the only place where the necessary forms can be obtained to acquire such information.
   (D) improperly, mainly because such information is available only at the time of the accident.

DIRECTIONS: In each of questions 49–53 you will be given four choices. Three of the choices, A, B, and C, contain a written statement. You are to evaluate the statement in each choice and select the statement that is most accurately and clearly written. If all or none of the three written statements is accurately and clearly written, you are to select choice D.

49. According to the instructions, evaluate the following statements.
   (A) I can except how the courts treat felons.
   (B) That was such a good procedure that I would like to adopt it for my own use.
   (C) His idea is all together too silly.
   (D) All or none of the choices is accurate.

50. According to the instructions, evaluate the following statements.
   (A) Besides being an athlete, she is also a scholar.
   (B) The dog sat beside the patrol car.
   (C) I am all ready for the early morning raid.
   (D) All or none of the choices is accurate.

51. According to the instructions, evaluate the following statements.
   (A) After being arrested, the highway patrol officer searched the motorist.
   (B) After he was fingerprinted, the prisoner went in the cell.
   (C) The too of us should be troopers.
   (D) All or none of the choices is accurate.

52. According to the instructions, evaluate the following statements.
    (A) I could tell it was from the post command because of the officious letterhead.
    (B) You're right on target.
    (C) Because it was the captain, I had to act respectively.
    (D) All or none of the choices is accurate.

53. According to the instructions, evaluate the following statements.
    (A) Everyone liked the chief because he was a notorious author.
    (B) Everyone knew the prisoner as a noted killer.
    (C) It is easy to hit a stationary target.
    (D) All or none of the choices is accurate.

54. Jane Walker is an investigator with the state troopers. She is directed to fly to a neighboring state to interview a witness. Her airfare is $189.75 each way. If she also spends $55.00 per day for meals and $79.00 for each day's hotel lodging, what will be the cost of her trip if she is required to stay 3 days and then return?
    (A) $591.75
    (B) $623.50
    (C) $671.50
    (D) $781.50

55. The cost of a new trooper barracks was estimated at $1.5 million. However, due to increased material costs and pay raises, the cost of the barracks has increased by 8%. The new cost of the barracks is most nearly
    (A) $1.7 million.
    (B) $1,620,000.
    (C) $1.6 million.
    (D) $1,720,000.

Answer questions 56 and 57 based solely on the following partial calendar of the month of a certain September.

MON	TUES	WED	THURS	FRI	SAT	SUN
6	7	8	9	10	11	12

56. Trooper June Best has regular days off on Thursday and Friday. On which of the following dates could she not attend court due to a conflict with her scheduled regular days off?
   (A) September 21
   (B) September 22
   (C) September 23
   (D) September 28

57. If Trooper June Best works 8½ hours per shift per day, and assuming the trooper takes no additional days off other than those regularly scheduled days off, how many hours will the trooper work in the month of September?
   (A) 160.5 hours
   (B) 178 hours and 30 minutes
   (C) 187 hours and 30 minutes
   (D) 197.5 hours

DIRECTIONS: Answer questions 58–65 *solely* on the basis of the form STATE PATROL DAILY DUTY ROSTER.

STATE PATROL DAILY DUTY ROSTER

| POST # 9 | LOCATION: Townville | DAY: Tues. | TIME: 8 am–4 pm | DATE: August 10 |

TROOPERS	CAR	MEAL HOUR	ROUTE	ORDERS OTHER THAN REGULAR PATROL
BAILES	1930	10 am	US 9 from Rt 1–6	11:30–12 Noon Radar Enf.
ASKEW	2219	12 noon	US 9 from Rt 6–9	1 pm Desk Officer Relief
SEPE	3212	11:30 am	Rt 9 from US 9–10	9:30–11:30 am DWI Checks
RIDDLE	2837	12 noon	Rt 9 from US 8–9	12 noon–3 pm Narcotic Enf.
FORD	1227	11:30 am	Hwy 87	10 am–11 am Mail Run
CAMPLI	8218	1 pm	Rt 17 to City Limits	Special Attention to Speeders
ALBANESE	2318	1 pm	Rt 12 to City Limits	Special Attention to Drag Racing
CLARK	4649	11:30 am	Rt 8 Cloverleaf	8 am–10 am Commuter Breakdowns
TURNER	1287	12:30 pm	US 12 to City Limits	3 pm–4 pm Conduct Training
REIS	1288	11:30 am	Rt 24 to City Limits	3 pm–4 pm Attend Training
HILLS	1926	12:30 pm	Carter Expressway	Special Attention to Truckers
BOOTS	1936	11:30 am	Main Boulevard	Special Attention Narcotics Locations

COURT: 9 am Baker case/ of DOE Best case/ of HARE Xavier case/ of RAY	SERGEANT ON DUTY Clay Noren	OFFICE DUTY Clerk Harris Clerk Most Officer Brent Assigned as Desk Officer in Post Barracks	MOTOR POOL CARS AVAILABLE 1999 4685 943 978 9237 921
DETACHED OFFICERS: Butcher Kent Temporarily Assigned CAR 950 With Detectives	SICK REPORT Lopez Wilson ANNUAL LEAVE Naples		8218 CARS OUT OF SERVICE

MEMORANDA:			
PAGE __1__ OF __1___		Lieutenant Freedson BY ORDER OF POST COMMANDER	

58. Which of the following officers has a scheduling conflict?
(A) Bailes
(B) Sepe
(C) Riddle
(D) Ford

59. Who is scheduled to relieve Officer Brent?
(A) Askew
(B) Ford
(C) Reis
(D) Boots

60. The officer who is most likely to experience some problem with his or her assigned vehicle is
(A) Officer Hills.
(B) Officer Turner.
(C) Officer Campli.
(D) Officer Ford.

61. The officer who would most likely be available to conduct a surveillance at 2 P.M. is
(A) Officer Naples.
(B) Officer Hills.
(C) Officer Lopez.
(D) Officer Wilson.

62. Of the following officers, the one who most probably has some teaching experience is
(A) Boots.
(B) Hills.
(C) Turner.
(D) Reis.

63. If the post commander decided to reassign personnel to create a two-person vehicle at 9 A.M., the post commander would be most likely to select which of the following officers?
(A) Butcher and Kent
(B) Baker and Xavier
(C) Best and Campli
(D) Hills and Boots

64. If one of the cars developed mechanical problems, it could be replaced by any of the following cars except
(A) 943.
(B) 921.
(C) 950.
(D) 978.

65. Which of the following officers because of their "orders other than regular patrol assignments" are most likely to perform similar duties.
   (A) Officers Askew and Riddle
   (B) Officers Ford and Clark
   (C) Officers Reis and Boots
   (D) Officers Bailes and Campli

Answer questions 66–73 based on the following information.

SELECTED CRIME STATISTICS FOR TROOP 15

Note: All reported crimes in Troop 15 are given a report number starting with the number 0001 each year. Those crimes which involved the use of a weapon by the perpetrator are marked by an asterisk.

Report	Date	Day	Crime	Time	Location
*0148	2/1	Wednesday	Burglary	12:02 A.M.	190 Crest Ave.
*0165	2/3	Friday	Robbery	2:00 A.M.	230 Crest Ave.
0170	2/6	Monday	Burglary	3:20 P.M.	265 Morris Ave.
0174	2/6	Monday	Assault	8:00 A.M.	202 Davis Ave.
*0177	2/8	Wednesday	Assault	11:00 A.M.	235 Crest Ave.
0188	2/10	Friday	Burglary	3:00 A.M.	250 Crest Ave.
0190	2/10	Friday	Robbery	5:00 P.M.	225 Morris Ave.
0194	2/10	Friday	Burglary	5:45 P.M.	242 Clark St.
0196	2/11	Saturday	Robbery	4:00 P.M.	265 Morris Ave.
0218	2/15	Wednesday	Robbery	7:00 P.M.	240 Morris Ave.
*0230	2/17	Friday	Burglary	1:15 A.M.	262 Crest Ave.
0244	2/20	Monday	Assault	7:00 A.M.	251 Davis Ave.
0248	2/21	Tuesday	Assault	11:45 A.M.	261 Crest Ave.
0253	2/21	Tuesday	Burglary	5:00 A.M.	223 Morris Ave.

*0270	2/24	Friday	Burglary	7:00 A.M.	271 Crest Ave.
0282	2/25	Saturday	Robbery	9:00 P.M.	248 Davis Ave.
0286	2/25	Saturday	Robbery	11:00 P.M.	235 Davis Ave.
0298	2/28	Tuesday	Burglary	10:30 P.M.	111 Clark St.

66. A trooper would be most likely to reduce the number of burglaries by patrolling
    (A) Crest Avenue between 7:00 A.M. and 3:00 P.M. on Mondays.
    (B) Morris Avenue between noon and 8:00 P.M. on Sundays.
    (C) Crest Avenue between midnight and 8:00 A.M. on Fridays.
    (D) Morris Avenue between midnight and 8:00 A.M. on Mondays.

67. A trooper would most likely be able to reduce the number of robberies by patrolling
    (A) Davis Avenue between 3:00 P.M. and 11:00 P.M., Tuesdays through Saturday.
    (B) Morris Avenue between 2:00 P.M. and 10:00 P.M., Monday through Friday.
    (C) Morris Avenue between 3:00 P.M. and 11:00 P.M., Tuesday through Saturday.
    (D) Davis Avenue between noon and 8:00 P.M., Monday through Friday.

68. Assume that the reported burglary at 190 Crest Avenue is the first crime reported in the month of February. How many crimes were reported in January?
    (A) 147 crimes   (B) 210 crimes
    (C) 18 crimes   (D) 151 crimes

69. A trooper working on Crest Avenue should be aware that
    (A) it is the scene of many homicides.
    (B) crimes committed there often involve the use of weapons.
    (C) it is a safe block.
    (D) it is a less dangerous block than Clark Street.

70. What day of the week accounts for the most reported robberies, burglaries, and assaults?
    (A) Saturday   (B) Tuesday
    (C) Monday   (D) Friday

71. Assume that the burglary reported at 190 Crest Avenue was the first crime reported in February and that the burglary reported at 111 Clark Street was the last crime reported in the month of February. How many total crimes were reported during the month of February?
    (A) 147 crimes   (B) 210 crimes
    (C) 18 crimes   (D) 151 crimes

72. On which block were there no reported burglaries?
    (A) Crest Avenue   (B) Morris Avenue
    (C) Davis Avenue   (D) Clark Street

73. On which block were there neither any reported robberies nor any reported assaults?
    (A) Crest Avenue   (B) Morris Avenue
    (C) Davis Avenue   (D) Clark Street

74. Carelessness on the part of an on- or off-duty trooper in the carrying or safekeeping of firearms shall be deemed neglect of duty and is subject to disciplinary action. The primary intent of such a rule is to
    (A) deter carelessness in the carrying or handling of firearms.
    (B) punish careless troopers.
    (C) fully protect the general public.
    (D) prevent civil suits.

75. There are times when troopers must give testimony at a criminal trial. Of the following steps you take to prepare for giving such testimony, by far the MOST important step for you to take is to
    (A) refresh your memory about the case by reviewing your personal notes and any other available information.
    (B) go over your testimony with the prosecutor assigned to the case.
    (C) make sure that your uniform is neat and clean so that you make a professional appearance on the witness stand.
    (D) anticipate questions that you might be asked and answers you might give.

76. Except in the line of duty, a state trooper is prohibited from carrying any packages while on duty in uniform. Of the following reasons for the existence of this rule, the most important one is that the carrying of packages
    (A) takes away a trooper's ability to quickly defend herself should the need arise.
    (B) creates the impression that gifts are being accepted.
    (C) creates a definite risk of damaging or soiling the trooper's uniform.
    (D) makes a trooper look unprofessional.

77. State troopers should try to achieve a close relationship with the people who live or work on their posts. The primary purpose of this rule is that this close relationship
    (A) fosters citizen involvement in police affairs.
    (B) allows troopers to make new friends.
    (C) guarantees a reduction of crime.
    (D) reduces the need for police protection.

78. The success of the patrol function depends heavily upon the observation skills of the patrol officer. Therefore, good patrol officers must
    (A) have above average eyesight.
    (B) have extremely keen hearing.
    (C) have a better than average sense of smell.
    (D) develop all their senses.

79. A trooper should expect
    (A) to be treated with respect by all persons.
    (B) to be the subject of occasional verbal attack.
    (C) to be able to reason with all persons.
    (D) to have all persons always yield to your authority.

80. The main obstacle to a successful traffic stop is conflict. Which of the following is not a recommended tactic to follow to minimize conflict during a traffic stop?
    (A) allow a driver to save face
    (B) talk as much as you can
    (C) explain why the stop was made
    (D) explain what action you intend to take

81. At a crime scene, a trooper must seal off the scene and allow entrance to only those officially involved in the investigation of the crime. The primary reason for this rule is to
(A) prevent the destruction or contamination of evidence.
(B) assist investigators to identify witnesses.
(C) guard against the commission of an additional crime.
(D) ensure the safety of the investigators.

Answer questions 82–89 *solely* on the basis of the following legal definitions. Do not base your answers on any other knowledge of the law you may have. You may refer to the definitions when answering the questions.

NOTE: The perpetrators in the following definitions are referred to as *he,* but they actually refer to either gender. However, when the male and/or female gender is a factor in defining an offense or legal action, such distinction shall be made by the specific use of both pronouns *he* and *she.*

Assault in the third degree

  A person is guilty of assault in the third degree when:

1. With intent to cause a physical injury to another person, he causes a physical injury to such person or a third person; or

2. He recklessly causes physical injury to another person; or

3. With criminal negligence, he causes physical injury to another person by means of a deadly weapon or a dangerous instrument.

Assault in the third degree is a misdemeanor.

Assault in the second degree

  A person is guilty of assault in the second degree when:

1. With intent to cause serious physical injury to another person, he causes a serious physical injury to such person or to a third person; or

2. With intent to cause physical injury to another person he causes a physical injury to such person or to a third person by means of a deadly weapon or a dangerous instrument; or

3. With intent to prevent a police officer from performing a lawful duty, he causes a physical injury to such police officer; or

4. He recklessly causes serious physical injury to another person by means of a deadly weapon or a dangerous instrument.

Assault in the second degree is a class D felony.

Assault in the first degree

A person is guilty of assault in the first degree when:

1. With intent to cause serious physical injury to another person, he causes a serious physical injury to such person or to a third person by means of a deadly weapon or a dangerous instrument; or

2. With intent to maim or scar another person, he causes injury to such person or a third person.

Assault in the first degree is a class C felony, which is more serious than a class D felony.

Aggravated assault upon a police officer

A person is guilty of aggravated assault upon a police officer when, with intent to cause serious physical injury to a person whom he knows or reasonably should know to be a police officer engaged in the course of performing his official duties he causes a serious physical injury by means of a deadly weapon or dangerous instrument. Aggravated assault upon a police officer is a class B felony, which is more serious than a class C or D felony.

82. Ray intends to injure May by giving her a black eye. Ray strikes May in the face, but the blow does not result in a black eye as intended. Instead May suffers a swollen lip, which is also a physical injury. Ray has committed
    (A) assault in the third degree.
    (B) assault in the second degree.
    (C) assault in the first degree.
    (D) no assault because Ray did not intend to give May a swollen lip, the physical injury that actually resulted.

83. Don has never gotten along with his cousin, Trooper Marks. During a family gathering, Don, who wants to seriously injure Trooper Marks, strikes him over the head with a dangerous instrument, a beer bottle. Marks suffers a serious physical injury in the form of a concussion. In this instance, Don has committed
    (A) assault in the third degree.
    (B) assault in the second degree.
    (C) assault in the first degree.
    (D) none of the above.

84. May is being given a traffic summons by Highway Patrol Officer Digest. Intending to prevent the officer from issuing her the summons, May kicks the officer in the shins causing the officer to wince due to the pain of the physical injury. May has committed
(A) assault in the third degree.
(B) assault in the second degree.
(C) assault in the first degree.
(D) aggravated assault upon a police officer.

85. A person acting with criminal negligence would be most likely to commit which of the following?
(A) only assault in the third degree
(B) only assault in the second degree
(C) only assault in the first degree
(D) all the above

86. Pat intends to seriously injure Jack. Pat attempts to shoot Jack with a rifle, which is a deadly weapon. However, the rifle jams, and Pat uses the rifle as a dangerous instrument to beat Jack over the head, seriously injuring him. In this instance, Pat has committed
(A) assault in the first degree.
(B) assault in the second degree.
(C) assault in the third degree.
(D) no assault because the rifle failed to fire properly.

87. Hank is still infatuated with Trooper June Flowers whom he had dated socially in the past. Hank follows her home one night and makes his feelings known to her. When the trooper rebuffs his advances, Hank strikes her with a blackjack, which is a deadly weapon, causing her serious injuries about the face and neck. In this instance, Hank has committed
(A) assault in the third degree.
(B) assault in the second degree.
(C) assault in the first degree.
(D) aggravated assault upon a police officer.

88. Regarding the various degrees of the crime of assault, which of the following statements is most correct?
    (A) All degrees of assault require some type of injury to result.
    (B) There is no way to commit an assault without the use of some type of deadly weapon or dangerous instrument.
    (C) Every type of assault must be committed intentionally.
    (D) All degrees of assault are felonies.

89. Tom intended to seriously injure Frank through the use of a deadly weapon but instead causes a serious physical injury to June through the use of the deadly weapon. Tom has committed
    (A) assault in the third degree.
    (B) assault in the second degree.
    (C) assault in the first degree.
    (D) no assault because the person intended to be injured was not injured.

DIRECTIONS: Answer questions 90–94 solely on the basis of the following map. The flow of traffic is as shown by the arrows. Where there is only one arrow, then the traffic flows only in the direction indicated by the arrow. You must follow the flow of traffic when moving from one location to another.

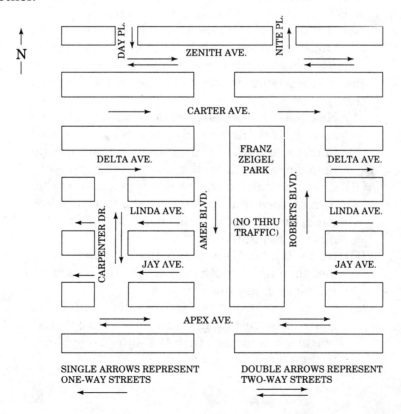

90. Assume you are in your patrol car on Jay Avenue at the intersection of Carpenter Drive. You receive a call on your radio to respond and investigate a past crime, which has occurred on Amee Boulevard and Linda Avenue. Which of the following is the most direct route for you to take in your patrol car, making sure to obey all the traffic regulations?

(A) Head east on Jay Avenue to Amee Boulevard and then head north on Amee Boulevard to the scene of the past crime.

(B) Turn onto Carpenter Drive and head north for one block; then make a right turn and head east for one block.

(C) Turn onto Carpenter Drive and head south for one block to Apex Avenue, make a left onto Apex Avenue and travel one block, and then head north for two blocks to the scene of the past crime.

(D) Turn onto Carpenter Drive and go north for two blocks, make a right turn and continue for one block, and then make a right and head south for one block to the scene of the past crime.

91. While heading east in your patrol car on Zenith Avenue at the intersection of Day Place, you are directed by the dispatcher to respond to Franz Zeigel Park at the intersection of Roberts Boulevard and Jay Avenue. Which of the following is the most direct route for you to take in your patrol car, making sure to obey all the traffic regulations?

(A) Head east on Zenith Avenue to the next intersection and then head south for one block. Make a left turn and proceed for one block; then head south to the place of assignment.

(B) Continue east to the next intersection, make a right turn and continue south to Linda Avenue, and then drive through the park to the place of assignment.

(C) Go to Zenith Avenue and Roberts Boulevard and then head south on Roberts Boulevard to the place of assignment.

(D) Go east to the next intersection and head south for five blocks, turn left and continue one block, and then turn left and go one block to the place of assignment.

92. While on Apex Avenue at the intersection of Roberts Boulevard, you are notified of an injured dog at Carpenter Drive and Jay Avenue. Which of the following is the most direct route for you to take in your patrol car, making sure to obey all the traffic regulations?

    (A) Head north on Roberts Boulevard for four blocks, make a left and head west for one block, head south for three blocks, and then head west for one block.

    (B) Head west on Apex Avenue for one block, make a right, head north for one block, and then head east for one block.

    (C) Proceed west on Apex Avenue for two blocks, make a right, and head north for one block.

    (D) Head west for one block and then head north for two blocks, make a left and proceed for one block, and then head south for one block.

93. If Officer Franks was traveling along the western border of Franz Zeigel Park and Officer Marks was traveling along the eastern border of the same park, assuming that both officers were following the legal flow of traffic, it would be most correct to state that

    (A) both officers would be heading north.

    (B) Officer Franks would be heading south, and Officer Marks would be heading north.

    (C) both officers would be heading south.

    (D) Officer Franks would be heading north, and Officer Marks would be heading south.

94. Officer Banks is proceeding south in her patrol car on Amee Boulevard. If the officer is currently between Zenith and Carter Avenue and continues to proceed only south in her patrol car, then the number of streets at which the officer may make a legal left turn is

    (A) 1.

    (B) 2.

    (C) 3.

    (D) 4.

DIRECTIONS: Answer questions 95–100 on the basis of the following sketches. The model face, the one appearing above the dotted line, is a sketch of a person who is wanted. Of the four comparison faces, the ones appearing below the dotted line, one of them is the way the model face looked after changing appearance. You are to assume that no surgical alteration of the wanted person's face has occurred. You are to select the face that is most likely that of the wanted person.

95.

A   B   C   D

96.

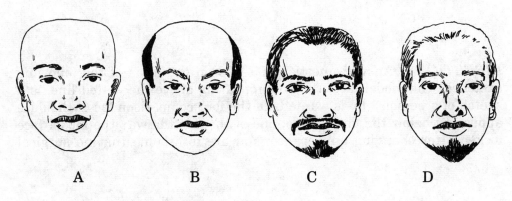

A   B   C   D

97.

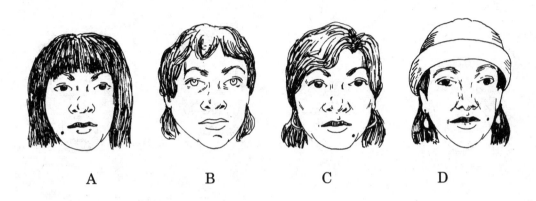

A   B   C   D

98.

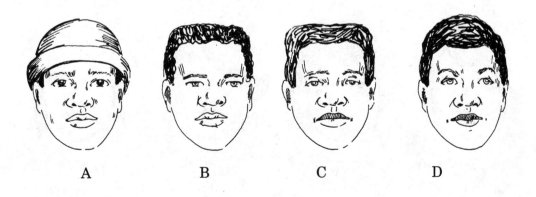

A   B   C   D

99.

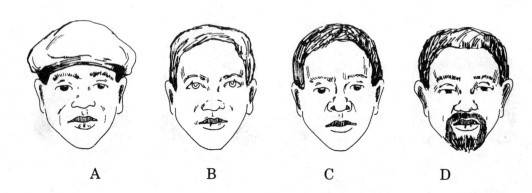

A   B   C   D

100.

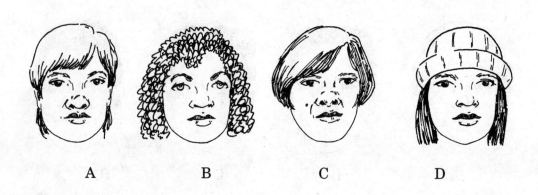

A   B   C   D

Answer Key

1. **A**	21. **B**	41. **C**	61. **B**	81. **A**
2. **B**	22. **B**	42. **D**	62. **C**	82. **A**
3. **B**	23. **B**	43. **A**	63. **D**	83. **C**
4. **B**	24. **D**	44. **D**	64. **C**	84. **B**
5. **D**	25. **B**	45. **B**	65. **D**	85. **A**
6. **A**	26. **D**	46. **B**	66. **C**	86. **A**
7. **D**	27. **D**	47. **A**	67. **C**	87. **C**
8. **B**	28. **C**	48. **A**	68. **A**	88. **A**
9. **B**	29. **D**	49. **B**	69. **B**	89. **C**
10. **D**	30. **A**	50. **D**	70. **D**	90. **D**
11. **B**	31. **B**	51. **D**	71. **D**	91. **D**
12. **C**	32. **D**	52. **B**	72. **C**	92. **C**
13. **D**	33. **B**	53. **C**	73. **D**	93. **B**
14. **A**	34. **A**	54. **D**	74. **A**	94. **B**
15. **B**	35. **D**	55. **B**	75. **A**	95. **B**
16. **A**	36. **C**	56. **C**	76. **A**	96. **A**
17. **B**	37. **D**	57. **B**	77. **A**	97. **C**
18. **C**	38. **D**	58. **C**	78. **D**	98. **A**
19. **A**	39. **B**	59. **A**	79. **B**	99. **A**
20. **D**	40. **B**	60. **C**	80. **B**	100. **D**

Diagnostic Chart

INSTRUCTIONS: After you score your test, complete the following chart by inserting in the column captioned "Your Number Correct" the number of questions you answered correctly in each of the ten sections of the test. Then compare your score in each section with the ratings in the column captioned "Scale." Finally, to correct your weaknesses follow the instructions found after the chart.

SECTION	QUESTION NUMBER	AREA	YOUR NUMBER CORRECT	SCALE
1	1–8	Memory (8 questions)		8 Right—Excellent 6–7 Right—Good 5 Right—Fair Under 5 Right—Poor
2	9–28	Reading Comprehension (20 questions)		20 Right—Excellent 18–19 Right—Good 16–17 Right—Fair Under 16 Right—Poor

3	29–48	Applying State Police Procedures (20 questions)	20 Right—Excellent 18–19 Right—Good 16–17 Right—Fair Under 16 Right—Poor
4	49–57	Verbal and Math (9 questions)	9 Right—Excellent 7–8 Right—Good 6 Right—Fair Under 6 Right—Poor
5	58–65	State Police Forms (8 questions)	8 Right—Excellent 6–7 Right—Good 5 Right—Fair Under 5 Right—Poor
6	66–73	Interpreting Data (8 questions)	8 Right—Excellent 6–7 Right—Good 5 Right—Fair Under 5 Right—Poor
7	74–81	Judgment and Reasoning (8 questions)	8 Right—Excellent 6–7 Right—Good 5 Right—Fair Under 5 Right—Poor
8	82–89	Legal Definitions (8 questions)	8 Right—Excellent 6–7 Right—Good 5 Right—Fair Under 5 Right—Poor
9	90–94	Traffic Directions (5 questions)	5 Right—Excellent 4 Right—Good 3 Right—Fair Under 3 Right—Poor
10	95–100	Matching Sketches (6 questions)	6 Right—Excellent 5 Right—Good 4 Right—Fair Under 4 Right—Poor

How to correct weaknesses:

1. If you are weak in Section 1, concentrate on Chapter 6.
2. If you are weak in Section 2, concentrate on Chapter 4.
3. If you are weak in Section 3, concentrate on Chapter 9.
4. If you are weak in Section 4, concentrate on Chapter 5.
5. If you are weak in Section 5, concentrate on Chapter 7.
6. If you are weak in Section 6, concentrate on Chapter 8.
7. If you are weak in Section 7, concentrate on Chapter 10.
8. If you are weak in Section 8, concentrate on Chapter 11.
9. If you are weak in Section 9, concentrate on Chapter 13.
10. If you are weak in Section 10, concentrate on Chapter 12.

Note: Consider yourself weak in a section if you receive other than an excellent rating in it.

Answer Explanations

1. **A** It might seem odd that a man named <u>Young</u>blood needs a hairpiece.

2. **B** Jack <u>Hunt</u> uses the alias Ben <u>Hogan</u>.

3. **B** Jack Hunt is a chronic drug user. He is always <u>hunt</u>ing for drugs.

4. **B** This is the third question in a row where Jack Hunt is the answer. Don't let that throw you. Never decide on an answer based on the frequency of previous answers. Hunt is 62 years old, and none of the other three wanted persons are even in their fifties.

5. **D** Chuckie Gifford is a lifelong con artist who preys on older women.

6. **A** James <u>S</u>hort's weapon of preference is a <u>s</u>awed off <u>s</u>hotgun, which he almost always carries on his person.

7. **D** Chuckie Gifford often represents himself as a law enforcement officer. This, of course, means that he often poses as a police officer. Don't expect to always see the exact words carried over from the poster to the question.

8. **B** Samuel <u>Young</u>blood often loiters in the vicinity of schools, and schools are where <u>young</u> people hang out.

9. **B** According to the passage, conflict is inevitable; that means it cannot be avoided. The trick is to keep it to a minimum.

10. **D** The question does not have to use the exact wording found in the passage. For example, to say the "primary barrier" is the same as saying the "main obstacle."

11. **B** To be more sensitive than necessary is to be oversensitive, and that is contrary to the recommended guidelines.

12. **C** Be careful with choice B. The guideline says, "don't be oversensitive." It doesn't say, "don't be sensitive."

13. **D** After greeting the driver, you are supposed to explain the purpose of the stop and the action you intend to take. Even though choice A seems the most logical, it is not supported in the passage.

14. **A** Prisons are not mentioned in the entire passage.

15. **B** Jails are usually administered by the county marshall, but they are sometimes managed by the state police.

16. **A** Jails have the authority to detain suspects for periods of 24 hours to 14 days; they also hold convicted inmates who are serving short-term sentences of 1 year or less.

17. **B** The right to free speech could easily create riots and demonstrations. That is the same as saying free speech creates the potential for riots and disorders.

18. **C** The passage begins by saying that the first concern of a trooper investigating a traffic accident should be the safety of all concerned.

19. **A** Even though the trooper did not witness the accident, he/she must determine its cause.

20. **D** Medical attention must be requested immediately.

21. **B** Although the passage is somewhat vague about what to look for, it specifically states that the trooper must examine the credentials of the volunteer before assistance is rendered.

22. **B** According to the passage, the first cone placed should be the one that is going to be the greatest distance away from the accident scene.

23. **B** Holding on to their credentials is good insurance against their leaving.

24. **D** The key to this answer is the statement from the passage that the use of deadly force to prevent an arrested person from inflicting serious injury or death on another is lawful but only if the use of such force is a last resort. The use of the word *anytime* in choice B makes that choice incorrect.

25. **B** He is an unsuccessful person who has failed in one venture after another. He is usually no better at committing crimes than he is at anything else.

26. **D** A policy of full enforcement would drain the resources of the entire criminal justice system.

27. **D** Although it is not practical for regular patrol units to engage in selective enforcement of the traffic laws, it is a good strategy to use specially designated selective enforcement units.

28. **C** When multiple violations are committed, only the violations that are more serious and provable should be cited.

29. **D** A search means to place hands inside a pocket or other interior parts of clothing to determine if an object felt during a frisk is a weapon. Thus it is clear that a search is often preceded by a frisk.

30. **A** If a trooper reasonably suspects a person has committed, is committing, or is about to commit a felony or misdemeanor as defined in the State Penal Code, the trooper may stop the person and request identification and an explanation of such person's conduct. Mere hunches and guesses are not enough to stop someone, and absolute certainty is much more than is required.

31. **B** Only that portion of the suspect's clothing where an object is felt as a result of a frisk may be searched. Since the trooper felt an object in the suspect's coat pocket, that would be the area that could be legally searched by the trooper, not the suspect's pants pocket.

32. **D** The amount of time is not a fixed period but is instead reasonably related to the facts that initially justified the stop or that are discovered during the stop.

33. **B** The procedure clearly states that the suspect under such circumstances must be immediately released.

34. **A** Choices B, C, and D are instances when a STOP AND FRISK CARD is to be prepared by a trooper. A trooper should prepare a STOP AND FRISK CARD when a person is stopped but only if the use of force was required.

35. **D** Both the patrol supervisor and the desk officer are required to review STOP AND FRISK CARD(S).

36. **C** A manner of dress of a suspect including bulges in clothing are enough to yield reasonable suspicion but not enough for an immediate arrest.

37. **D** Choices A and B are incorrect because counterfeit coins and not bills are to be initialed. Choice C is incorrect because, as stated in choice D, both the trooper and the attendant should sign the bill.

38. **D** The post command desk officer shall assign a messenger to deliver a report and the money to the Special Agent-In-Charge of the local office of the U.S. Secret Service.

39. **B** Choice A should be done by the trooper, but it is not the first action. Choices C and D describe actions that will occur, but choice B is what should be done first.

40. **B** Statement 1 indicates that a flashlight should never be used inside such a place. That is inaccurate because a trooper should not use a flashlight until the area is well ventilated. If necessary to enter prior to the room's being ventilated, a flashlight may be used if it is turned on before entering the area. The only correct statement here is statement 2.

41. **C** Choice C describes exactly what should be done under the circumstances when the odor of bitter almonds is detected. The actions described in choices A, B, and D are inappropriate because the procedure specifically states that they should not be done.

42. **D** As stated in the procedure, the first cone shall be placed 200 feet from the accident. Anytime you see numbers in a procedures pay attention to them. Examiners often ask questions about measurements.

43. **A** Choice A does not indicate a category of vehicles that does not require an insurance card because it is not all farm vehicles but only certain ones.

44. **D** Choice A is incorrect because an IDENTIFICATION TAG may be placed on an unconscious person who is removed to the hospital. Choice B is incorrect because traffic should be diverted if necessary. Choice C is incorrect because the trooper concerned should determine the cause of the accident by inquiry and observation. Choice D is correct because when a driver is incapacitated, then another participant in the accident or the owner of the vehicle must complete the INFORMATION EXCHANGE.

45. **B** The Department of Transportation receives a copy of a TROOPER ACCIDENT REPORT if an accident involved collision with a crash cushion or highway impact attenuator but the Department of Parks receives a copy only if a person is killed or injured on a roadway under the jurisdiction of the Department of Parks. Here no injuries took place.

46. **B** The trooper shall sign and deliver the reports to the post command desk officer.

47. **A** According to the procedure, volunteers can assist at a vehicle accident scene under certain circumstances. However, choice C is incorrect because volunteers are not permitted to assist in determinations involving the removal of injured persons. Choice A is as stated in the procedure.

48. **A** Choice C is incorrect because these forms are available at any post command and at the Public Inquiry Section of headquarters. A trooper is not able to give such information after an accident. It can be acquired, but a REQUEST FOR COPY OF ACCIDENT RECORD must be prepared. Therefore, choices B and D are incorrect.

49. **B** Choice A is incorrect because *except* means to exclude and the meaning intended in the choice would be more accurately expressed by the word *accept,* which means to take what is offered such as to accept how the courts treat felons. Choice C is incorrect because *all together* means in a group and the meaning intended in that choice is that the idea is totally or altogether too silly. Choice B is correct because *adopt* means to take for one's own use.

50. **D** All statements are accurately and clearly written.

51. **D** Choice A is unclear because it cannot be determined who was arrested, the motorist or the highway patrol officer. It should have stated, "After the motorist was arrested, ..." The use of the word *in,* which means location, instead of the word *into,* which means movement, makes choice B incorrect. Choice C is incorrect because the word *two* indicating a number should have been used instead of the word *too,* which means also.

52. **B** Choice A is incorrect because the word *official,* not *officious,* which means meddlesome, should have been used to indicate relating to a certain office. Choice C is incorrect because the word *respectfully,* not *respectively,* which means in the order given, should have been used to indicate a showing of respect or deference. *You're* means you are, the intended meaning of the correct choice, choice B.

53. **C** *Noted* means widely and favorably known, but *notorious* means widely and unfavorably known. Therefore, both choices A and B are incorrect because *noted* should have been used in choice A and *notorious* should have been used in choice B.

54. **D** The cost of this 3-day trip would be
Airfare $2 \times \$189.75 = \$379.50$
Meals $3 \times \$55.00 = 165.00$
Hotel lodging $3 \times \$79.00 = \underline{237.00}$
$\$781.50$

Choice A reflects only a one-way airfare. Choices B and C reflect that the meals and hotel lodging are for 1 day, not for 3 days.

55. **B** The original cost was \$1.5 million, which can be expressed as \$1,500,000. The cost has increased by 8%. To find a percentage of a number, convert the percent to a decimal by moving the decimal two places from the right to the left. In this instance, 8% is the same as 8.00%. (The decimal point is understood to be there.) Thus expressed as a decimal, 8% becomes 0.08. Therefore, multiplying
$0.08 \times \$1,500,000 = \$120,000.00$
The new cost would be

$\$1,500,000$
$\underline{+ 120,000}$
$\$1,620,000$

56. **C** If September 9 and 10 fall on a Thursday and Friday, respectively, then the remainder of Thursdays in this certain month of September are 16, 23, and 30, whereas the remainder of Fridays in this certain month of September are 17 and 24. And these days would be the trooper's regular days off and not available for court appearances. This question can be easily answered by adding 7 to the dates of the Thursdays and Fridays given in the partial calendar.

57. **B** The first action should be to fill out the partial calendar.

MON	TUES	WED	THURS	FRI	SAT	SUN
		1	2	3	4	5
6	7	8	9	10	11	12
13	14	15	16	17	18	19
20	21	22	23	24	25	26
27	28	29	30			

Next determine how many days the trooper will be excused due to regularly scheduled days off. A quick look at the filled in calendar indicates there are nine regularly scheduled days off. Subtracting 9 from 30 indicates that the trooper worked 21 days for 8½ hours. Multiplying $21 \times 8\frac{1}{2} = 178\frac{1}{2}$ hours or 178 hours and 30 minutes.

58. **C** Officer Riddle is scheduled to have a meal hour at 12 noon, the same time the officer is scheduled to begin narcotic enforcement.

59. **A** At 1 P.M. Officer Askew is to relieve Officer Brent as the desk officer.

60. **C** Officer Campli is, according to the duty roster, assigned to car 8218, which is out of service.

61. **B** Officers Lopez and Wilson are sick, and Officer Naples is on vacation.

62. **C** Officer Turner is the officer designated to conduct some training at 3 P.M.

63. **D** Choice A is incorrect because Officers Butcher and Kent are on a temporary assignment. Choices B and C are incorrect because Baker, Best, and Xavier are on sick report.

64. **C** Car 950 is detached or temporarily assigned to Officers Butcher and Kent who are working with the detectives.

65. **D** Officers Bailes and Campli are both directed by their "orders other than regular patrol assignments" to deal with speeding cars. Officer Bailes is on radar enforcement, and Officer Campli is to give special attention to speeders.

66. **C** Remember that, when doing this type of question, the trooper should be working when and where the crime to be prevented is being committed. Find out when and where most of the crimes to be prevented are being committed, and you have the answer. The table showed three burglaries committed on Crest Avenue on Fridays between midnight and 8:00 A.M.

67. **C** Of the six reported robberies, three were committed on Morris Avenue and two, on Davis Avenue. This eliminates choices A and D. Choice B is no good because one of the three robberies on Morris Avenue was committed on a Saturday.

68. **A** Remember that this question type tests your ability to read and interpret charts and tables. The table tells us that the first crime each year (the first one in January) is number 0001 for that year. If the first crime in February (the Burglary at 190 Crest Avenue) was number 0148, then 147 crimes were reported in January.

69. **B** There were five reported crimes on Crest Street that involved the use of weapons, as indicated by the asterisks in the table.

70. **D** Friday accounted for a total of six of these crimes.

71. **D** If you picked choice C, then you don't understand the table. It is not a listing of all crimes reported in February. It is a listing of selected crimes (e.g., burglaries, robberies, and assaults). The burglary at 111 Clark Street was number 0298. There were 147 reported crimes in January. This means that there were 151 reported crimes in February, (298 – 147). Remember that our strategy demands that you understand the chart or table before you begin answering questions about it.

72. **C** There were four reported burglaries on Crest Avenue, two on Morris Avenue, two on Clark Street, and none on Davis Avenue.

73. **D** Clark Street had only two reported burglaries. The other locations had either robberies and/or assaults.

74. **A** Troopers will be less apt to be careless with their firearms if they are certain that carelessness will not be accepted as an excuse for accidental discharge or loss of their firearms. Choice C is incorrect because of the word fully.

75. **A** It is absolutely essential to be as familiar as possible with the facts in the case when you take the stand. So, even though the actions described in choices B, C, and D are all beneficial, the most important step is as described in choice A.

76. **A** Safety and the protection of life are always a paramount concern and take precedence over such things as appearance and impressions.

77. **A** If people get to know the trooper assigned to the post where they live or work, they are more inclined to get involved in police affairs, especially in situations where the trooper needs assistance.

78. **D** Choices A, B, and C each deals with one facet of a person's observation skills. You must remember that good observation skills require the development of all of the senses.

79. **B** The most important thing to keep in mind is that a trooper must keep an even temper even in the face of insolent and rude verbal attack. Note the use of the limiting word *occasional* in the correct choice, and the use of the absolute words *all* and *always* in the incorrect choices.

80. **B** Being overtalkative during a traffic stop is a sure way to start a conflict.

81. **A** If evidence found at a crime scene is touched, examined, or otherwise altered by unauthorized persons, then the courts will not allow it to be introduced into any subsequent criminal trial.

82. **A** Ray intended to give another person a physical injury and that is what resulted. The charge is assault in the third degree.

83. **C** Intending to seriously injure someone and then seriously injuring someone with a dangerous instrument or a deadly weapon is assault in the first degree.

84. **B** May intended to prevent the police officer from performing a lawful duty and in so doing caused a physical injury to such police officer. May committed assault in the second degree. It is not aggravated assault upon a police officer because May did not intend to inflict a serious physical injury on the officer nor was a deadly weapon or dangerous instrument used.

85. **A** Only assault in the third degree can be committed while acting with criminal negligence.

86. **A** Pat intended to cause serious physical injury to another person and did cause a serious physical injury to such person by means of a dangerous instrument. That is one way of committing assault in the first degree.

87. **C** Choice D is incorrect because Trooper Flowers was not performing her official duties at the time of the attack. However, Jack intended to seriously injure another person with a deadly weapon and

actually did so. The charge would be as indicated in choice C, assault in the first degree.

88. **A** Choice B is incorrect because at times, such as in assault third degree, an assault can be committed merely by the use of one's hands without the use of a deadly weapon or dangerous instrument. Choice C is incorrect because some assaults may be committed recklessly as well as with criminal negligence. Choice D is incorrect because assault in the third degree is not a felony; it is a misdemeanor. As indicated in choice A, however, all assaults must result in some type of injury.

89. **C** When a person intends to seriously injure another person by the use of a deadly weapon, and such person or a third person is seriously injured by the use of the deadly weapon, the correct charge is assault in the first degree, as indicated in choice C.

90. **D** Choice A is incorrect because it requires you to go east on Jay Avenue, a westbound street. Choice B is incorrect because it requires you to head east on Linda Avenue, which is a westbound street. Choice C is incorrect because it requires you to travel north on Amee Boulevard, which is southbound.

91. **D** Choice A is incorrect because it requires you to head south on Roberts Boulevard, which is northbound. Choice B is incorrect because it requires you to drive through the park, which prohibits traffic. Choice C is incorrect because it requires heading south on Roberts Boulevard at a location where Roberts Boulevard is not accessible because it does not intersect with Zenith Avenue.

92. **C** Choice A requires you to head west on Carter Avenue, which is an eastbound street. Choices B and D both require you to head north on Amee Boulevard, which is a southbound street. Choice C offers the most direct route while complying with the traffic regulations.

93. **B** The importance of establishing the points of the compass as soon as you begin to examine the map in these type questions cannot be overstated.

94. **B** A left turn in such a situation would mean that the officer would be proceeding east. Under such circumstances the only two streets that permit travel in an easterly direction are Carter and Apex Avenues.

95. **B** The nose of choice A, the lips of choice C, and the nose and facial lines on the chin of choice D leave choice B as the only possible answer.

96. **A**   The eyes of choices B and C and the eyes and nose of choice D leave choice A as the only possible answer.

97. **C**   The mole on the right cheek of choice A, the facial line on the chin of choice B, and the nose of choice D leave choice C as the only possible choice.

98. **A**   The eyes of choices B, C, and D leave choice A as the only possible answer.

99. **A**   The eyes of choice B, the nose of choice C, and the ears and eyes of choice D leave choice A as the only possible answer.

100. **D**   The nose of choice A, the eyes of choice B, and the nose and mole of choice C leave choice D as the only possible answer.

CHAPTER 16

Practice Examination Three

This chapter contains the third of five practice examinations that you will be taking. Don't forget to:

1. Take the test in one sitting. You have 3½ hours to answer all 100 questions.

2. Use the test-taking strategies outlined in Chapter 2.

3. Use the answer sheet we have provided to record your answers.

4. Complete the diagnostic chart that appears at the end of this chapter after you score this practice examination.

Answer Sheet
Practice Examination Three

Follow the instructions given in the test. Mark only your answers in the circles below.

WARNING: Be sure that the circle you fill is in the same row as the question you are answering. Use a No. 2 pencil (soft pencil).

BE SURE YOUR PENCIL MARKS ARE HEAVY AND BLACK. ERASE COMPLETELY ANY ANSWER YOU WISH TO CHANGE.

DO NOT make stray pencil dots, dashes or marks.

1. Ⓐ Ⓑ Ⓒ Ⓓ   2. Ⓐ Ⓑ Ⓒ Ⓓ   3. Ⓐ Ⓑ Ⓒ Ⓓ   4. Ⓐ Ⓑ Ⓒ Ⓓ
5. Ⓐ Ⓑ Ⓒ Ⓓ   6. Ⓐ Ⓑ Ⓒ Ⓓ   7. Ⓐ Ⓑ Ⓒ Ⓓ   8. Ⓐ Ⓑ Ⓒ Ⓓ
9. Ⓐ Ⓑ Ⓒ Ⓓ   10. Ⓐ Ⓑ Ⓒ Ⓓ   11. Ⓐ Ⓑ Ⓒ Ⓓ   12. Ⓐ Ⓑ Ⓒ Ⓓ
13. Ⓐ Ⓑ Ⓒ Ⓓ   14. Ⓐ Ⓑ Ⓒ Ⓓ   15. Ⓐ Ⓑ Ⓒ Ⓓ   16. Ⓐ Ⓑ Ⓒ Ⓓ
17. Ⓐ Ⓑ Ⓒ Ⓓ   18. Ⓐ Ⓑ Ⓒ Ⓓ   19. Ⓐ Ⓑ Ⓒ Ⓓ   20. Ⓐ Ⓑ Ⓒ Ⓓ
21. Ⓐ Ⓑ Ⓒ Ⓓ   22. Ⓐ Ⓑ Ⓒ Ⓓ   23. Ⓐ Ⓑ Ⓒ Ⓓ   24. Ⓐ Ⓑ Ⓒ Ⓓ
25. Ⓐ Ⓑ Ⓒ Ⓓ   26. Ⓐ Ⓑ Ⓒ Ⓓ   27. Ⓐ Ⓑ Ⓒ Ⓓ   28. Ⓐ Ⓑ Ⓒ Ⓓ
29. Ⓐ Ⓑ Ⓒ Ⓓ   30. Ⓐ Ⓑ Ⓒ Ⓓ   31. Ⓐ Ⓑ Ⓒ Ⓓ   32. Ⓐ Ⓑ Ⓒ Ⓓ
33. Ⓐ Ⓑ Ⓒ Ⓓ   34. Ⓐ Ⓑ Ⓒ Ⓓ   35. Ⓐ Ⓑ Ⓒ Ⓓ   36. Ⓐ Ⓑ Ⓒ Ⓓ
37. Ⓐ Ⓑ Ⓒ Ⓓ   38. Ⓐ Ⓑ Ⓒ Ⓓ   39. Ⓐ Ⓑ Ⓒ Ⓓ   40. Ⓐ Ⓑ Ⓒ Ⓓ
41. Ⓐ Ⓑ Ⓒ Ⓓ   42. Ⓐ Ⓑ Ⓒ Ⓓ   43. Ⓐ Ⓑ Ⓒ Ⓓ   44. Ⓐ Ⓑ Ⓒ Ⓓ
45. Ⓐ Ⓑ Ⓒ Ⓓ   46. Ⓐ Ⓑ Ⓒ Ⓓ   47. Ⓐ Ⓑ Ⓒ Ⓓ   48. Ⓐ Ⓑ Ⓒ Ⓓ
49. Ⓐ Ⓑ Ⓒ Ⓓ   50. Ⓐ Ⓑ Ⓒ Ⓓ   51. Ⓐ Ⓑ Ⓒ Ⓓ   52. Ⓐ Ⓑ Ⓒ Ⓓ
53. Ⓐ Ⓑ Ⓒ Ⓓ   54. Ⓐ Ⓑ Ⓒ Ⓓ   55. Ⓐ Ⓑ Ⓒ Ⓓ   56. Ⓐ Ⓑ Ⓒ Ⓓ
57. Ⓐ Ⓑ Ⓒ Ⓓ   58. Ⓐ Ⓑ Ⓒ Ⓓ   59. Ⓐ Ⓑ Ⓒ Ⓓ   60. Ⓐ Ⓑ Ⓒ Ⓓ
61. Ⓐ Ⓑ Ⓒ Ⓓ   62. Ⓐ Ⓑ Ⓒ Ⓓ   63. Ⓐ Ⓑ Ⓒ Ⓓ   64. Ⓐ Ⓑ Ⓒ Ⓓ
65. Ⓐ Ⓑ Ⓒ Ⓓ   66. Ⓐ Ⓑ Ⓒ Ⓓ   67. Ⓐ Ⓑ Ⓒ Ⓓ   68. Ⓐ Ⓑ Ⓒ Ⓓ
69. Ⓐ Ⓑ Ⓒ Ⓓ   70. Ⓐ Ⓑ Ⓒ Ⓓ   71. Ⓐ Ⓑ Ⓒ Ⓓ   72. Ⓐ Ⓑ Ⓒ Ⓓ
73. Ⓐ Ⓑ Ⓒ Ⓓ   74. Ⓐ Ⓑ Ⓒ Ⓓ   75. Ⓐ Ⓑ Ⓒ Ⓓ   76. Ⓐ Ⓑ Ⓒ Ⓓ
77. Ⓐ Ⓑ Ⓒ Ⓓ   78. Ⓐ Ⓑ Ⓒ Ⓓ   79. Ⓐ Ⓑ Ⓒ Ⓓ   80. Ⓐ Ⓑ Ⓒ Ⓓ
81. Ⓐ Ⓑ Ⓒ Ⓓ   82. Ⓐ Ⓑ Ⓒ Ⓓ   83. Ⓐ Ⓑ Ⓒ Ⓓ   84. Ⓐ Ⓑ Ⓒ Ⓓ
85. Ⓐ Ⓑ Ⓒ Ⓓ   86. Ⓐ Ⓑ Ⓒ Ⓓ   87. Ⓐ Ⓑ Ⓒ Ⓓ   88. Ⓐ Ⓑ Ⓒ Ⓓ
89. Ⓐ Ⓑ Ⓒ Ⓓ   90. Ⓐ Ⓑ Ⓒ Ⓓ   91. Ⓐ Ⓑ Ⓒ Ⓓ   92. Ⓐ Ⓑ Ⓒ Ⓓ
93. Ⓐ Ⓑ Ⓒ Ⓓ   94. Ⓐ Ⓑ Ⓒ Ⓓ   95. Ⓐ Ⓑ Ⓒ Ⓓ   96. Ⓐ Ⓑ Ⓒ Ⓓ
97. Ⓐ Ⓑ Ⓒ Ⓓ   98. Ⓐ Ⓑ Ⓒ Ⓓ   99. Ⓐ Ⓑ Ⓒ Ⓓ   100. Ⓐ Ⓑ Ⓒ Ⓓ

The Test

DIRECTIONS FOR QUESTIONS 1–8: Study for 5 minutes the following illustration, which depicts items taken from two prisoners immediately after they were arrested. Try to remember as many details as possible. Do not make written notes of any kind during this 5-minute period. After the 5 minutes are up, answer questions 1–8. When answering the questions, do not refer back to the illustration.

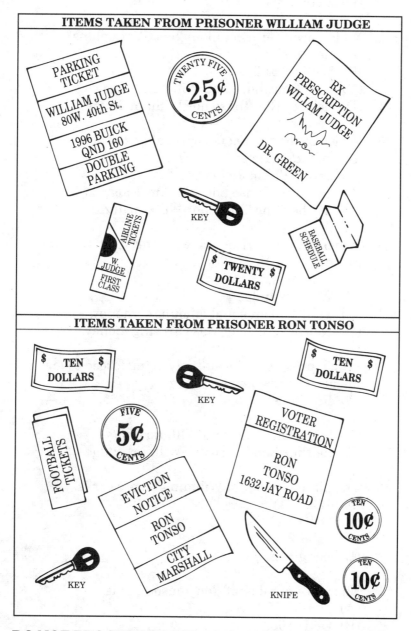

DO NOT PROCEED UNTIL 5 MINUTES HAVE PASSED.

DIRECTIONS: Answer questions 1–8 solely on the basis of the illustration on the preceding page. Do not refer back to it when answering these questions.

1. What is William Judge's address?
   (A) 80 W. 40th Street
   (B) 1632 Jay Road
   (C) 40 W. 80th Street
   (D) 3216 Jay Road

2. Which prisoner most likely has travel plans?
   (A) Ron Tonso
   (B) William Judge
   (C) both Ron Tonso and William Judge
   (D) neither Ron Tonso nor William Judge

3. Which of the prisoners is probably a sports fan?
   (A) only Ron Tonso
   (B) only William Judge
   (C) both Ron Tonso and William Judge
   (D) neither Ron Tonso nor William Judge

4. Which of the prisoners was carrying the most money?
   (A) Ron Tonso
   (B) William Judge
   (C) They had an equal amount of money.
   (D) Neither prisoner was carrying money.

5. Which prisoner is most likely being forced to leave his place of residence?
   (A) Ron Tonso
   (B) William Judge
   (C) both Ron Tonso and William Judge
   (D) neither Ron Tonso nor William Judge

6. The plate number of William Judge's car is
   (A) 1632 JAY.
   (B) QND 160.
   (C) 1996 BK.
   (D) not given.

7. The plate number of Ron Tonso's car is
   (A) 1632 JAY.
   (B) QND 160.
   (C) 1996 BK.
   (D) not given.

8. Which of the prisoners is most likely experiencing some sort of medical problem?
   (A) Ron Tonso
   (B) William Judge
   (C) both Ron Tonso and William Judge
   (D) neither Ron Tonso nor William Judge

Answer question 9 solely on the basis of the following information.

Crime is not a problem that can be easily solved by using the same strategies and methods that allowed man to split the atom or to put an astronaut on the moon. Nor can the problems created by crime be prevented by passing law after law. In fact, it is probably true that the crime problem in this country will never be truly solved.

9. The crime problem
   (A) is easily solved.
   (B) can be solved through technology.
   (C) can be solved through legislation.
   (D) is probably beyond solution.

Answer question 10 based solely on the following information.

The purpose of rehabilitation of criminals is to change their behavior. The supporters of rehabilitation as a basic goal of incarceration suggest that offenders can leave prisons as better people than when they entered. Those who argue against the concept of rehabilitation argue that it rarely occurs and that these people usually favor the concept of reparation. While the truth of the matter is unknown at this time, what is known is that reparation is being used more and more and rehabilitation is used less and less.

10. Rehabilitation
    (A) is definitely working.
    (B) is better than reparation.
    (C) rarely works.
    (D) is being used less and less.

Answer question 11 based solely on the following information.

There is perhaps no unresolved problem in the criminal field as complex as determining the ability of the death penalty to deter the commission of violent crimes.

11. The use of the death penalty
    (A) clearly prevents the commission of violent crimes.
    (B) is clearly favored by the majority of law-abiding people.
    (C) may or may not prevent the commission of violent crimes.
    (D) definitely does not prevent the commission of violent crimes.

Answer question 12 based solely on the following rule.

All state troopers will unload their revolvers or other firearms prior to entering any area in the psychiatric unit of any prison or hospital. Upon departure from such areas, they shall reload revolvers and other firearms.

12. While in a psychiatric unit of a hospital, a state trooper
    (A) can be armed if off duty.
    (B) can be armed if on duty.
    (C) can obtain special permission to be armed.
    (D) can never be armed.

Answer question 13 based solely on the following rule.

Carelessness by a state trooper in the carrying, handling or safekeeping of personal or department firearms, while on or off duty, shall be deemed neglect of duty.

13. An off-duty state trooper who carelessly handles his own handgun
    (A) does not violate any department rule.
    (B) may face disciplinary charges.
    (C) is guilty of neglect of duty.
    (D) might be considered negligent.

Answer questions 14–17 solely on the basis of the following information.

Relatives or friends over 16 may visit an inmate in a state police detention facility provided that the inmate consents to the visit. These visits must be held during normal visiting hours, which are from Monday to Friday, from 10:00 A.M. to 4:00 P.M. Children between the ages of 10 and 16 may visit inmates but only on those days that are specifically designated as family visiting days. At least three family visiting days per month will be held. Children under the age of 10 are not allowed on prison grounds.

Clergy persons are allowed to visit inmates on any day of the week at any hour between 8:00 A.M. and 11:00 P.M. Such visits require the consent of the inmate. Attorneys are allowed to visit inmates but require written authorization from the inmate. Attorney visits can be held on any day of the week between the hours of 10:00 A.M. and 10:00 P.M. Troopers investigating crimes may also visit prisoners on the same day and during the same times that attorneys are allowed to visit. Visits from the police require written authorization from the inmate or a court order.

14. A 9-year-old child
    (A) could visit a parent in prison on family visiting days.
    (B) is never allowed to visit an inmate in prison.
    (C) could visit a parent in prison on weekdays.
    (D) must be accompanied onto prison grounds by an adult.

15. Which of the following categories of visitors has the greatest number of possible visiting hours each week?
    (A) relatives
    (B) clergy persons
    (C) attorneys
    (D) friends

16. Which of the following categories of visitors could possibly visit an inmate without the inmate's consent?
    (A) relatives or friends
    (B) clergy persons
    (C) attorneys
    (D) police personnel

17. A 12-year-old boy whose father is serving a life sentence can visit his father
    (A) as often as he pleases.
    (B) once a week.
    (C) at least 36 times a year.
    (D) only four times a month.

Answer questions 18 and 19 based on the following legal rule.

State troopers are legally entitled to use physical force upon another person when and to the extent they reasonably believe to be necessary to defend themselves or a third person from what they reasonably believe to be the use or imminent use of unlawful physical force by such other person. State troopers may not use deadly physical force upon another person unless they reasonably believe that such other person is using or about to use deadly physical force against them or another.

18. State troopers
    (A) can use force only to defend themselves.
    (B) can always use an unlimited amount of force to defend themselves.
    (C) can sometimes use force to defend others.
    (D) are not entitled to use physical force upon another person.

19. The use of deadly physical force by state troopers
    (A) is only legally permitted in a prison setting.
    (B) is sometimes legally permissible.
    (C) is never legally authorized.
    (D) is always lawful to prevent escapes.

Answer question 20 based solely on the following information.

A state trooper may make an arrest of a person for a felony when the trooper has reasonable cause to believe such person has committed a felony. But, a state trooper may make an arrest of a person for a misdemeanor or for a violation only when the trooper has reasonable cause to believe such person has committed the misdemeanor or violation in that trooper's presence.

20. If a criminal offense is either a felony, a misdemeanor, or a violation, then a state trooper
    (A) can arrest for a felony even if the trooper was not present when the felony was committed.
    (B) can arrest for a misdemeanor even if the trooper was not present when the misdemeanor was committed.
    (C) can arrest for a violation even if the trooper was not present when the violation was committed.
    (D) is prohibited from making an arrest for any criminal offense unless the offense is committed in the presence of the trooper.

Answer questions 21 and 22 based solely on the following information.

The courts have ruled that a juvenile, someone under the age of 16, who has been accused of a crime, has the right to counsel. The counsel may be of the juvenile's own choosing or appointed by the court for financial or other reasons. Therefore, a state trooper who finds it necessary to arrest a juvenile must give notice of the juvenile's right to counsel. This notice must be clearly understood by both the juvenile and at least one of the juvenile's parents or legal guardians. In addition, such notice must be given both verbally and in writing. Although a waiver of the right to counsel may be made, it is not effective unless the waiver is made in writing by both the juvenile and at least one of the juvenile's parents or legal guardians.

21. A lawyer who represents a juvenile who has been accused of a crime
    (A) must be one who is chosen by the juvenile.
    (B) must be one who is chosen by the parents or legal guardians of the juvenile.
    (C) must be one who is appointed by the courts.
    (D) may be chosen by the juvenile or appointed by the court.

22. A juvenile who is accused of a crime
    (A) must be represented by a lawyer.
    (B) can decide on his/her own not to have a lawyer.
    (C) can state orally that he/she does not want a lawyer as long as one parent or guardian also agrees.
    (D) can waive the right to a lawyer if at least one of the juvenile's parents or legal guardians agrees provided that their waiver is put in writing.

Answer questions 23–26 based solely on the following passage.

State Troopers Green and Hill, working an 8:00 A.M. to 4:00 P.M. shift on general patrol in an area under the exclusive jurisdiction of the state police, received directions from the radio dispatcher to investigate a theft from an automobile at 780 Broom Street. Trooper Green told his partner, who is a newly hired state trooper, that it is not uncommon in this area to receive "theft from auto" calls at about 8:30 A.M. This happens because residents come out at that time to move their vehicles in order to comply with the 8:30 A.M. to noon alternate side parking regulations.

Turning into Broom Street, the troopers noticed that there were five automobiles parked on the south side of the street. Trooper Green took a parking spot in front of 781 Broom Street, which is behind the last of the five cars. As the troopers got out of their patrol vehicle, they were greeted by Mrs. Brown. She told the troopers that at 8:15 A.M. she discovered that the passenger side front window of her brand new blue Buick had been broken and that her compact disk player worth $600 had been stolen. She informed the troopers that the cars of two of her neighbors, Don Artist and Bob Short, were also broken into.

Mr. Artist, who lives at 780 Broom Street, then came out of his house and walked across the street to speak to the troopers. As Trooper Hill recorded Mrs. Brown's report, Trooper Green was told by Mr. Artist that at about 10:05 P.M. the previous night Artist discovered that his car was also broken into. In his case, it was the car's computer, valued at $400, that was stolen. Mr. Artist explained that he called the state police when he discovered the theft, but he was asked at that time to call again in the morning. Trooper Green then completed a report on Mr. Artist's car and rejoined his partner, who was in the process of completing a report on Bob Short's car. After being on the scene for 1 hour and 5 minutes the troopers, their assignment being completed, left Broom Street and resumed patrol at 9:50 A.M.

23. Trooper Hill completed reports on
    (A) Mrs. Brown and Mr. Artist.
    (B) Mr. Artist and Bob Short.
    (C) Mrs. Brown and Bob Short.
    (D) Mrs. Brown, Mr. Artist, and Mr. Short.

24. Which side of the street does Mr. Artist live on?
    (A) east   (B) west
    (C) north   (D) south

25. What was the approximate time of day when the troopers initially arrived at the scene?
    (A) 8:00 A.M.   (B) 8:30 A.M.
    (C) 8:45 A.M.   (D) 9:50 A.M.

26. The report for which person will contain a date of occurrence that will be different from the others?
    (A) Mrs. Brown   (B) Mr. Artist
    (C) Mr. Short   (D) Mrs. Short

Answer questions 27 and 28 solely on the basis of the following information.

There is nothing more valuable to a state trooper than information. Every working day a state trooper needs access to information about people, places, causative factors, and property. The amount of information a state trooper needs is staggering.

The information that state troopers need in the field comes primarily from information fed into the State Police Information System from other state troopers, although some of it also comes from private industry, governmental units, and nonprofit agencies.

The taking of notes in the field is unquestionably the most important step in the entire process by which the state police obtain information from their field personnel. After the field troopers take their notes, they complete official reports. These reports are then reviewed by supervisors for accuracy, they are forwarded to a central location, and they are then entered into the State Police Information System via computers that are specially designed to interpret the information.

27. Most of the information needed by state troopers in the field comes from
    (A) government agents.   (B) private agencies.
    (C) state troopers.   (D) nonprofit agencies.

28. Which of the following steps in the process by which the state police obtain information from their field personnel is the most vital?
    (A) the taking of notes in the field
    (B) the completion of official reports
    (C) the review by supervisors of official reports
    (D) the entry of data into computers

Answer questions 29–33 solely on the basis of the following information.

To process controlled substances/marijuana contraband and store it securely in the controlled substances locker in the post command, the following procedure will be followed.

Upon obtaining controlled substances/marijuana contraband, the trooper concerned shall, in this order:

1. Bring the contraband to the post command and notify the post command desk officer.

2. Prepare an INVOICE WORKSHEET.

The command clerk shall:

3. Prepare an INVOICE from the WORKSHEET.

4. Prepare a REQUEST FOR LABORATORY EXAMINATION.

The trooper concerned shall:

5. Request a serially numbered security lock-type envelope from the post command desk officer.

6. Complete the captions on the security envelope.

7. Mark the contraband for future identification.

   a. Consecutively number the glassine envelopes and note the total number of envelopes (e.g., 1/5, 2/5, 3/5) on each glassine envelope in addition to initialing the envelopes.

8. Place the contraband in the security envelope.

9. Moisten the flap, insert the metal clasp, seal and sign, and enter shield number, command and date across flap.

10. Attach the INVOICE and a copy of the REQUEST FOR LABORATORY EXAMINATION to the security envelope.

11. Deposit the sealed security envelope with forms attached into the controlled substances locker.

NOTE: Steps 7 through 11 will be supervised by and performed in the presence of the post command desk officer.

In addition, to prevent injury/infections when handling or forwarding hypodermic needles/syringes to the Forensic Laboratory, troopers shall

1. place such items in plastic tubes, needle end first. The plastic tube will be capped, if possible. However, if the syringe extends beyond the tube, it will be secured with tape.

Under no circumstances should a trooper attempt to remove or dislodge a needle from a hypodermic syringe.

29. Trooper Halls obtains some marijuana and brings it to the desk officer at the post command. According to procedure, which of the following should the trooper do next?
(A) Prepare an INVOICE WORKSHEET.
(B) Prepare an INVOICE.
(C) Prepare a REQUEST FOR LABORATORY EXAMINATION.
(D) Make a memo book entry.

30. According to procedure, a trooper processing a controlled substance that has come into the trooper's possession is required to request a serially numbered security lock-type envelope from
(A) the command clerk.
(B) the patrol supervisor.
(C) the post command desk officer.
(D) the post command commanding officer.

31. Which of the following actions is not required to be performed by the trooper concerned in the presence, and under the supervision, of the post command desk officer?
(A) Complete the captions on the security envelope.
(B) Mark the contraband for future identification.
(C) Attach the INVOICE and a copy of the REQUEST FOR LABORATORY EXAMINATION to the security envelope.
(D) Place the contraband in the security envelope.

32. Trooper Wilson has recovered a hypodermic needle during a drug raid. In preparing to send the hypodermic needle to the Forensic Laboratory, it would be least appropriate for the trooper
   (A) to place it in a plastic tube, needle end first.
   (B) to cap the plastic tube in which needles are placed, if possible.
   (C) to remove the needle from the hypodermic syringe
   (D) to secure the syringe with tape if it extends beyond the tube.

33. According to procedure, which of the following is responsible for placing marijuana contained in a sealed security envelope into the controlled substances locker in the post command?
   (A) the post command desk officer
   (B) the trooper who recovered the marijuana
   (C) the station house clerk
   (D) the preparer of the INVOICE

Answer questions 34–39 solely on the basis of the following information.

An aided case is an occurrence coming to the attention of a trooper that requires that a person, OTHER THAN A PRISONER, receive medical aid or assistance because such person is

a. sick or injured (except from a vehicle accident).

b. dead (except from a vehicle accident).

c. lost.

d. mentally ill.

e. an abandoned, destitute, abused, or neglected child.

Upon arrival at the scene of an aided case, the trooper concerned shall, in this order:

1. render reasonable aid to a sick or injured person.

2. request an ambulance or doctor, if necessary.

   a. If the aided person is wearing a Medic Alert emblem indicating diabetes, heart disease, etc., notify radio dispatcher and bring this to the attention of the ambulance attendant. A trooper shall not remove a Medic Alert emblem.

3. wait in view to direct the ambulance or have some responsible person do so.

4. make a second call in 20 minutes if ambulance does not arrive.

5. make a memo book entry.

   a. include the name of person notified regarding any Medic Alert emblem.

6. accompany an unconscious or unidentified aided to the hospital in the body of the ambulance.

7. obtain name, address, and telephone number of a relative or friend for notification.

8. prepare an AIDED REPORT form and deliver it to the post command clerk who shall have relatives/friends notified if the aided is admitted to a hospital or dies.

34. The first action that a trooper should take at the scene of an aided case is
(A) to request an ambulance.
(B) to render reasonable aid.
(C) to check for a Medic Alert emblem.
(D) make a memo book entry of the facts.

35. Trooper Mays arrives at the scene of an aided case and appropriately calls for an ambulance at about 10:05 A.M. According to procedure, which of the following is the earliest that a second call for the ambulance should be made?
(A) 10:40 A.M.
(B) 10:30 A.M.
(C) 10:25 A.M.
(D) 10:15 A.M.

36. According to procedure, which of the following is least likely to be considered an aided case?
(A) a lost person
(B) a missing person
(C) an abandoned child
(D) a mentally ill person

37. While handling an aided case, Trooper Lopez discovers a Medic Alert emblem on the aided person. In this instance the trooper should
(A) notify only the radio dispatcher.
(B) call the hospital and notify the medical staff.
(C) remove the emblem and turn it over to the ambulance attendant.
(D) make a memo book entry and include the name of the person notified about the Medic Alert emblem.

38. Which of the following incidents should be considered an aided case?
    (A) any injured person
    (B) any dead person
    (C) a destitute child
    (D) a delinquent child

39. A citizen while out alone has been injured and has been taken to the hospital where he is admitted. According to procedure, which of the following is responsible for notifying the relatives of the injured person?
    (A) the patrol supervisor
    (B) the post command desk officer
    (C) the post command clerk
    (D) the trooper who responded to the scene

Answer questions 40–48 solely on the basis of the following information.

To insure the safety of all concerned, a trooper shall adhere to the following when dealing with an emotionally disturbed person (EDP).

Maintain a Zone of Safety, which is the distance to be maintained between the EDP and the responding troopers. This distance may vary with each situation (e.g., type of weapon possessed, condition of EDP, surrounding area). A minimum distance of twenty (20) feet is recommended. An attempt will be made to maintain the "zone of safety" if the EDP does not remain stationary.

1. Upon arrival at the scene, assess the situation as to threat of immediate serious injury to the EDP, other persons present, or troopers.

    a. If the actions of an EDP constitute an immediate threat of serious physical injury or death to himself or others:

       1) Take reasonable action to terminate or prevent such behavior. Deadly physical force will be used only as a last resort to protect the life of persons present.

    b. If an EDP is unarmed, not violent, and willing to leave voluntarily:

       1) The EDP may be taken into custody without the specific direction of a patrol supervisor.

    c. In all other cases, if EDP's actions do not constitute an immediate threat of serious physical injury or death to himself or others:

       1) Attempt to isolate and contain the EDP while maintaining a zone of safety until arrival of the patrol supervisor.

       2) Do not, under these circumstances, attempt to take an EDP into custody without specific direction of the patrol supervisor.

2. Request an ambulance, if one has not already been dispatched.

    a. Ascertain if the patrol supervisor is responding, and, if not, request the patrol supervisor's response.

3. Establish police lines.

4. Take the EDP into custody if EDP is unarmed, not violent, and willing to leave voluntarily.

When an EDP is isolated/contained but will not leave voluntarily, the patrol supervisor shall

5. Establish firearms control.

6. Deploy protective devices such as shields.

    a. Employ nonlethal devices carried in the patrol supervisor's patrol car to insure the safety of all present.

7. Establish police lines, if not already done.

When the EDP has been restrained, the trooper concerned shall:

8. Remove property that is dangerous to life or will aid escape.

9. Have the EDP removed to the hospital in an ambulance.

    a. Restraining equipment including handcuffs may be used if the patient is violent, resists, or upon direction of a physician examiner.

    b. If unable to transport with reasonable restraint, ambulance attendant or doctor will request special ambulance.

    c. When possible, a female patient being transported should be accompanied by another female or by an adult member of her immediate family.

10. Ride in body of ambulance with the patient.

    a. At least two troopers will safeguard the EDPs if more than one patient is being transported.

NOTE: If an ambulance is not available and the situation warrants, transport the EDP to the hospital by patrol car, if able to do so with reasonable restraint. Under no circumstances will an EDP be transported to a police facility.

11. When applicable, inform the examining physician, upon arrival at the hospital of the use of nonlethal devices on an EDP.

12. Safeguard the patient at the hospital until examined by a psychiatrist.

13. Enter the details in the memo book and prepare an AIDED REPORT form.

14. Deliver an AIDED REPORT to the post command desk officer.

40. In connection with the handling of EDPs, which of the following is the most accurate statement concerning a zone of safety?
    (A) A maximum of 20 feet is recommended.
    (B) A minimum of 20 feet is recommended.
    (C) The zone of safety never varies.
    (D) It is really not necessary to maintain a zone of safety.

41. At the scene of an EDP, because the EDP, who refuses to leave voluntarily, is nonviolent and unarmed, the trooper on the scene takes the EDP into custody before the arrival of the patrol supervisor. In this instance, the trooper acted
    (A) properly, mainly because the sooner an EDP receives treatment, the better the prognosis for recovery.
    (B) improperly, mainly because the EDP refused to leave voluntarily.
    (C) properly, mainly because an unarmed EDP can never injure anyone.
    (D) improperly, mainly because a patrol supervisor must always be present before an EDP is taken into custody.

42. In handling an EDP, a trooper found it necessary to use nonlethal devices to take the EDP into custody. According to procedure, these devices would most likely be found
    (A) in the patrol supervisor's patrol car.
    (B) in the trooper's patrol car.
    (C) at the post command.
    (D) in the ambulance that responds to the scene.

43. At the scene of an EDP, the responsibility to establish police lines rests
    (A) only with the patrol supervisor.
    (B) initially with the trooper who responds to the scene.
    (C) with the desk officer.
    (D) with ambulance personnel.

44. According to procedure, if three EDPs are being transported in an ambulance, then the minimum number of troopers that could be assigned to safeguard the EDPs is
(A) one.
(B) two.
(C) three.
(D) four.

45. An ambulance has been called to the scene of an EDP; however, information is received that an ambulance is not available. The trooper at the scene places the EDP in the patrol car and transports the EDP to the post command. In this instance, the trooper acted
(A) properly, mainly because an EDP may be transported in a patrol car.
(B) improperly, mainly because an EDP should never be transported to a post command.
(C) properly, mainly because time is of the essence when dealing with an EDP.
(D) improperly, mainly because an EDP should always be transported in an ambulance.

46. An EDP is able to break loose from his restraints and bolts from the body of an ambulance. The assigned trooper who had been riding in the front of the ambulance with the ambulance driver was able to quickly apprehend the EDP and return him to the body of the ambulance in handcuffs. In this instance, the actions of the trooper were
(A) proper, mainly because the EDP was quickly recaptured.
(B) improper, mainly because the trooper should have been riding in the body of the ambulance with the EDP.
(C) proper, mainly because the EDP was again restrained and placed in the body of the ambulance.
(D) improper, mainly because the trooper should have placed the EDP in the front of the ambulance.

47. Trooper Regal uses a nonlethal device on an EDP. Upon arrival at the hospital, the trooper should advise which of the following regarding the use of the nonlethal device?
(A) the hospital administrator
(B) the examining physician
(C) the ambulance attendant
(D) the patrol supervisor

48. After completing an AIDED REPORT, the trooper should deliver the report to
(A) the examining physician.
(B) the ambulance attendant.
(C) the post command desk officer.
(D) the patrol supervisor.

DIRECTIONS: In each of questions 49–53 you will be given four choices. Three of the choices, A, B, and C, contain a written statement. You are to evaluate the statement in each choice and select the statement that is most accurately and clearly written. If all or none of the three written statements is accurately and clearly written, you are to select choice D.

49. According to the instructions, evaluate the following statements.
(A) Based on the clues found at the scene, the trooper should be able to infer what actually took place.
(B) Moral is very high in the barracks.
(C) People who use common sense are usually practicable.
(D) All or none of the choices is accurate.

50. According to the instructions, evaluate the following statements.
(A) The sergeant picked Ray and I.
(B) I wanted to have a party to formerly thank him.
(C) You should always appraise your boss of unusual occurrences.
(D) All or none of the choices is accurate.

51. According to the instructions, evaluate the following statements.
(A) Its time to meet the undercover officer.
(B) Ray and May are good troopers, but I prefer the later.
(C) Lay your radio on the hood of the car.
(D) All or none of the choices is accurate.

52. According to the instructions, evaluate the following statements.
    (A) I know it very good.
    (B) As the trooper approached Tom on the sidewalk, Tom ran into the house.
    (C) They haven't got a brain among the two of them.
    (D) All or none of the choices is accurate.

53. According to the instructions, evaluate the following statements.
    (A) I am faster than she.
    (B) He gives the allusion of being taller.
    (C) Beside being angry, he was violent.
    (D) All or none of the choices is accurate.

54. If robberies have increased by 20% over last year's total of 455 robberies, and burglaries have increased by 25% over last year's total of 292 burglaries, then the number of robberies and burglaries combined have increased this year over last year most nearly by
    (A) exactly 20%.
    (B) almost 22%.
    (C) exactly 25%.
    (D) almost 27%.

Answer questions 55 and 56 based solely on the following information.

Five trooper recruits have just been assigned to the Big River Post Command. The age of the recruits are 31, 24, 22, 28, and 25.

55. The average age of the recruits is
    (A) 25.
    (B) 26.
    (C) 27.
    (D) 28.

56. If the existing average age of the 110 troopers already assigned to the Big River Post Command was 35, what will be the average age of the troopers assigned to the Big River Post Command after the five new recruits are assigned?
    (A) exactly 28 years old
    (B) slightly less than 35 years old
    (C) slightly more than 35 years old
    (D) exactly 30.5 years old

57. The time is now 10:15 A.M. Trooper Tom Marks is to pack certain equipment needed for the execution of a search warrant. He takes exactly 53 minutes to accomplish this task. He then spends 23 minutes awaiting the arrival of his supervisor. Along with his supervisor, he then travels for three quarters of an hour to arrive at the location to be searched. After waiting one third of an hour for backup, the trooper finally executes the search warrant. The amount of time that elapsed from the beginning of the preparation of equipment to the actual execution of the warrant was most nearly

(A) 2 hours and 35 minutes.
(B) about 2⅓ hours.
(C) exactly 2.2 hours.
(D) about 2½ hours.

DIRECTIONS: Answer questions 58–65 based solely on the following narrative and the form STATE PATROL PERSONNEL COMPLAINT, which appears after the narrative. Some of the captions on the form may be numbered; some may not. The boxes are not necessarily consecutively numbered.

On September 5, 19xx, a personnel complaint was made by telephone by a civilian motorist against State Highway Patrol Officer Pat Mays, shield number 1706, assigned to the Bay River Post, Troop B of Division 9. The facts and circumstances are as follows.

On September 4, Mrs. June Tailor of 665 Morris Avenue, apartment 3E, Best City, telephone number 555-2222, was driving south on Route 7 while following her husband who was also driving south on Route 7. At about 9:30 A.M., Mrs. Tailor observed Officer Mays pull onto the highway with lights and sirens in use. Mrs. Tailor then observed Officer Mays signal to her husband to pull onto the shoulder of the highway. She also pulled onto the shoulder. Mrs. Tailor stopped and exited her vehicle and approached Officer Mays who was questioning Mrs. Tailor's husband, Bob Tailor of 996 Court Street, apartment E9, Best City, telephone number 555-1220. Mr. Tailor is informally separated from his wife.

Mrs. Tailor then alleges that Officer Mays told Mr. Tailor he was intoxicated and arrested him for driving under the influence of alcohol. Several empty and opened beer cans were found in Mr. Tailor's vehicle by Officer Mays. See voucher number 8879. Mrs. Tailor further alleges that when she attempted to ask the officer what was going on, Officer Mays responded by saying, "You better stay out of my way or else I can make you two closer than you have ever been. I'll handcuff you to him and lock you up too." At the time of the incident a line man from the county power authority was fixing downed power lines in the area and Mrs. Tailor claims that he witnessed the entire incident. He has been identified as Frank Homes of 310 Park Avenue, Best City, telephone number 555-1100.

Mrs. Tailor states she waited to make the complaint because she did not know how to make such a complaint. She decided to make the complaint after discussing the matter with her cousin who is a local deputy sheriff. He is identified as Deputy Sheriff Don Booth of the Best City Sheriff's Office, telephone number 555-1818. Mrs. Tailor made the complaint by telephone to State Highway Patrol Officer Tab Minks, shield number 1566, assigned to the Bay River Post, Troop B of Division 9. The call was logged in at 10:30 A.M. Post Commander Sergeant Tom Winked was immediately notified at that time.

The investigation is continuing under Department Complaint number 1919.

STATE HIGHWAY PATROL
PERSONNEL COMPLAINT
DATE RECEIVED (4)

COMPLAINANT'S NAME: (TYPE OR PRINT)

_____(1)_____
LAST   FIRST   MIDDLE

COMPLAINANT'S ADDRESS:
_____(2)_____

TELEPHONE NUMBER:

_____(3)_____

LOCATION WHERE INCIDENT OCCURRED:
_____(5)_____

APPROXIMATE TIME OF INCIDENT: (6) AM PM

_____(7)_____   _____(8)_____
DAY OF WEEK   MONTH–DAY–YEAR

NAME OF ARRESTED PERSON(S):
1. _____(9)_____
2. _____
3. _____

ADDRESS OF ARRESTED PERSON(S):
_____(10)_____
_____
_____

TELEPHONE NO:
_____(11)_____
_____
_____

INDICATE RELATIONSHIP OF ARRESTED PERSON TO COMPLAINANT:
_____(12)_____

DEPARTMENT USE ONLY:
COMPLAINT NUMBER: _____(13)_____

WITNESSES: (IF ANY)

NAME	ADDRESS	PHONE NUMBER
1. (14)	(15)	(16)
2.		
3.		
4.		

HAVE YOU DISCUSSED THIS COMPLAINT WITH ANY MEMBER OF THE STATE HIGHWAY PATROL? (17) ☐ NO ☐ YES

IF YES, WITH WHOM? _____(18)_____

NATURE OF COMPLAINT(S):

CLEARLY INDICATE THE NATURE OF YOUR COMPLAINT(S).
_____(19)_____
_____
_____
_____
_____

_____(20)_____
SIGNATURE OF TELEPHONE RECIPIENT

_____(21)_____
SIGNATURE OF COMPLAINANT
(OPTIONAL)

58. Which of the following entries would be most appropriately entered in caption 9.
    (A) June Tailor
    (B) Pat Minks
    (C) Bob Tailor
    (D) Frank Homes

59. The most correct entry for caption 18 is
    (A) Officer Pat Mays.
    (B) Officer Tab Minks.
    (C) Deputy Sheriff Don Booth.
    (D) none of the above.

60. Caption 21 will probably not be completed, mainly because
    (A) Mrs. Tailor made the complaint over the phone.
    (B) it is optional and the complainant chose not to make an entry.
    (C) Mrs. Tailor was angry.
    (D) Mr. Tailor is required to sign it, and presently he is under arrest.

61. The most appropriate entry for caption 10 is
    (A) 665 Morris Avenue.
    (B) 996 Court Street.
    (C) 310 Park Avenue.
    (D) Best City Sheriff's Office.

62. The most correct entry for caption 16 is
    (A) 555-2222.
    (B) 555-1220.
    (C) 555-1100.
    (D) 555-1818.

63. In this instance, the only signature on the form would be that of
    (A) Officer Mays.
    (B) Officer Minks.
    (C) Sergeant Tom Winked.
    (D) Mr. Bob Tailor.

64. The address 665 Morris Avenue should be entered in caption
    (A) 2.
    (B) 5.
    (C) 10.
    (D) 15.

65. The correct entry for caption 13 is
   (A) 1909.
   (B) 1919.
   (C) 1706.
   (D) not available.

Answer questions 66–73 based on the following data.

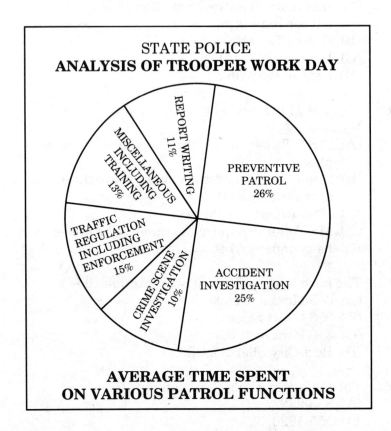

Answer questions 66–73 based on the preceding data.

66. If during the month of January troopers spent an average of 43 hours each investigating accidents, what was the average amount of total work hours performed on patrol by each trooper?
(A) 160 hours   (B) 172 hours
(C) 40 hours   (D) 180 hours

67. Which of the following patrol functions involves the least amount of time utilization by the average trooper?
(A) report writing
(B) crime scene investigation
(C) traffic regulation
(D) preventive patrol

68. According to the graph, it would be most correct to state that
(A) one fourth of the average trooper's patrol time involves the investigation of accidents.
(B) the average trooper spends the majority of his/her time investigating accidents.
(C) time spent in enforcement activities is included in the accident investigation function.
(D) accident investigation is the most time-consuming patrol function performed by the average trooper.

69. What is the exact percentage of training time spent by the average trooper?
(A) 13%
(B) 6%
(C) 15%
(D) It cannot be determined from the data given.

70. If the percentage of time spent writing reports and investigating crime scenes were combined, they would represent what percent of the overall time spent of patrol functions by the average trooper?
(A) 21%
(B) 11%
(C) 10%
(D) 24%

71. The total percentage of the average trooper's time spent on preventive patrol, accident investigation, crime scene investigation, traffic regulation, and report writing represents what percentage of his/her total time spent performing patrol functions?
    (A) 77%
    (B) 87%
    (C) 97%
    (D) 100%

72. For the average trooper, traffic enforcement
    (A) cannot account for more than 15% of time spent on patrol functions.
    (B) usually accounts for more than 15% of time spent on patrol functions.
    (C) always takes up 15% of time spent on patrol functions.
    (D) generally involves as much time as the investigation of accidents.

73. If the average amount of time spent on patrol functions in a given month was 200 hours, then what would be the average number of hours spent on preventive patrol?
    (A) 26 hours
    (B) 48 hours
    (C) 52 hours
    (D) It cannot be determined based on the data provided.

74. During a search for a suspected explosive device, a trooper discovers a suspicious package that might be a bomb. Under these circumstances the trooper should
    (A) examine the package closely to determine if it is in fact a bomb.
    (B) make note of the location of the suspected bomb and continue searching.
    (C) make an immediate request for a properly trained and equipped expert to examine the package.
    (D) order a complete evacuation of the area being searched.

75. While on foot patrol, a trooper observes an armed robbery taking place inside a liquor store. It appears as if there is only one robber. The trooper's first action should be to
(A) enter the store and confront the robber.
(B) make an immediate call for assistance.
(C) attempt to shoot the robber.
(D) call for the robber to surrender.

76. While searching for a suspect at the scene of a violent homicide, a trooper who is dressed in civilian clothes is confronted by a uniformed trooper who has her gun drawn and hears the uniformed trooper say, "Police, don't move." In this situation, the first action of the trooper in civilian clothes should be to
(A) reach for his official identification.
(B) explain that he too is a state trooper.
(C) cease all movement.
(D) ignore the warning and continue searching.

77. While on patrol, a state trooper is approached by an elderly woman who informs the trooper that she was just robbed by a single perpetrator who fled on foot immediately after the robbery. After supplying the trooper of a description of the perpetrator, the woman states that she was unharmed by the robber. The trooper's first action should be to
(A) pursue the robber.
(B) file an official report.
(C) call for medical assistance for the victim.
(D) broadcast the description of the robber.

78. While investigating a crime, a trooper receives anonymous information relating to her investigation. The trooper should
(A) follow up on the information.
(B) discount the information because its source is unknown.
(C) identify the source of the information before taking any other action.
(D) immediately accept the information as valid.

79. All arrested persons should be handcuffed immediately after their arrest. The primary purpose of this rule is to
    (A) promote safety.
    (B) follow procedures.
    (C) eliminate escape attempts.
    (D) protect the rights of arrested persons.

80. Assume that you are a newly hired state trooper. On your first day of work, your supervisor gives you instructions that you do not completely understand. You should
    (A) ask a veteran trooper for advice.
    (B) follow the instructions as best you can.
    (C) ask the supervisor for clarification.
    (D) contact your commanding officer.

81. While on patrol, you observe a man who has a firearm tucked into the waistband of his pants. You should
    (A) immediately arrest the man.
    (B) ignore the situation.
    (C) cautiously approach the man and question him.
    (D) refrain from taking action until he commits a crime.

Answer questions 82–89 solely on the basis of the following legal definitions. Do not base your answers on any other knowledge of the law you may have. You may refer to the definitions when answering the questions.

NOTE: The perpetrators in the following definitions are referred to as *he*, but they actually refer to either gender. However, when the male and/or female gender is a factor in defining an offense or legal action, such distinction shall be made by the specific use of both pronouns *he* and *she*.

Sexual intercourse has its ordinary meaning and occurs upon any penetration, however slight.

Deviate sexual intercourse means sexual conduct between persons not married to each other consisting of contact between the mouth and the penis, the penis and the anus, or the mouth and the vulva.

A person commits rape in the third degree when, being 21 years old or older, he or she engages in sexual intercourse with another person to whom the actor is not married and is less than 17 years old.

A person commits rape in the second degree when, being 18 years old or more, he or she engages in sexual intercourse with another person to whom the actor is not married and is less than 14 years old.

A person commits rape in the first degree when such person engages in sexual intercourse with another

  a. by forcible compulsion or

  b. who is unable to consent due to being physically helpless or

  c. who is less than 11 years old.

A person is guilty of sodomy in the third degree when, being 21 years old or more, he engages in deviate sexual intercourse with a person to whom the actor is not married and is less than 17 years old.

A person commits sodomy in the second degree when, being 18 years old or more, he or she engages in deviate sexual intercourse with another person to whom the actor is not married and is less than 14 years old.

A person commits sodomy in the first degree when such person engages in deviate sexual intercourse with another

  a. by forcible compulsion or

  b. who is unable to consent due to being physically helpless or

  c. who is less than 11 years old.

A person commits sexual abuse in the third degree when such person engages in sexual contact with another person without the latter's consent.

A person commits sexual abuse in the second degree when such person submits another person to whom the actor is not married to sexual contact and such other person is less than 14 years old.

A person commits sexual abuse in the first degree when such person submits another person to sexual contact

  a. by forcible compulsion or

  b. who is unable to consent due to being physically helpless or

  c. when such other person is less than 11 years old.

A person commits sexual misconduct when such person engages in sexual intercourse with an animal or a dead human body.

A person becomes legally responsible for his or her actions as an adult upon reaching the age of 16 years old.

First degree offenses are more serious offenses than second degree offenses, which in turn are more serious offenses than third degree offenses.

82. Mark is a 10th grade student at Manor High School. May is a student teacher. One afternoon Mark who is 13 years old tells May who is 21 years old and unmarried that he has a crush on her. May invites Mark to her van and engages in sexual intercourse with Mark. In this instance
    (A) both Mark and May are guilty of rape in the third degree.
    (B) only Mark is guilty of rape in the third degree.
    (C) both Mark and May are guilty of rape in the second degree.
    (D) only May is guilty of rape in the second degree.

83. Tom, who is 35 years old and is an orderly in a hospital, enters June's hospital room. Tom then has sexual intercourse with June who is 16 years old and is lying helpless in a coma. The most serious offense Tom has committed is
    (A) rape in the first degree.
    (B) rape in the second degree.
    (C) rape in the third degree.
    (D) sexual misconduct.

84. Don forces his way into the apartment of Joy. At gunpoint, Don, who is only 16 years old, forces Joy, who is 13, to perform oral sex on Don. Of the following, the most serious offense committed by Don is
    (A) sodomy in the third degree.
    (B) sodomy in the second degree.
    (C) sodomy in the first degree.
    (D) none of the above because of Don's age.

85. Tab, who is 22, is riding on a crowded train during evening rush hour. He positions himself next to Mark, who is 25 years old, and with his hand, Tab begins to engage in sexual conduct by rubbing Mark's genitals. Mark does not object. In this instance,
    (A) both have committed sexual misconduct.
    (B) both have committed sodomy.
    (C) Tab has committed sexual abuse.
    (D) neither have committed sexual abuse.

86. Digger works in a funeral parlor. A beautiful actress has been killed and is being prepared for her funeral by Digger who decides to, and does, have sexual intercourse with her. In this instance Digger has committed
    (A) no offenses since the female was dead.
    (B) sodomy in the first degree.
    (C) sexual misconduct.
    (D) sexual abuse in the third degree.

87. Ray, who is 17, and Jay, who is 21, force April into their van where they compel her to engage in anal intercourse with each of them. April is 12 years old. In this instance Ray and Jay both committed
    (A) sodomy in the first degree.
    (B) sodomy in the second degree.
    (C) sodomy in the third degree.
    (D) sexual misconduct.

88. May is less than 16 years old. Her aunt June is 34 years old. June invites May to the movies. After the movies on the way home while in her car, June begins to kiss May, and in turn May performs oral sex on June. May does so willingly. In this instance, which of the following indicates the most serious offense(s) committed?
    (A) Both have committed sexual misconduct.
    (B) Both have committed sexual abuse in the third degree.
    (C) May committed sodomy in the third degree.
    (D) June committed sodomy in the third degree.

89. After a prom, Tucker, who is 16, has sexual intercourse with his girlfriend May, who is 17. In this instance,
    (A) only Tucker has committed rape in the third degree.
    (B) only May has committed rape in the third degree.
    (C) both have committed rape in the third degree.
    (D) neither has committed rape in the third degree.

DIRECTIONS: Answer questions 90–94 solely on the basis of the following map. The flow of traffic is as shown by the arrows. Where there is only one arrow, then the traffic flows only in the direction indicated by the arrow. You must follow the flow of traffic when moving from one location to another.

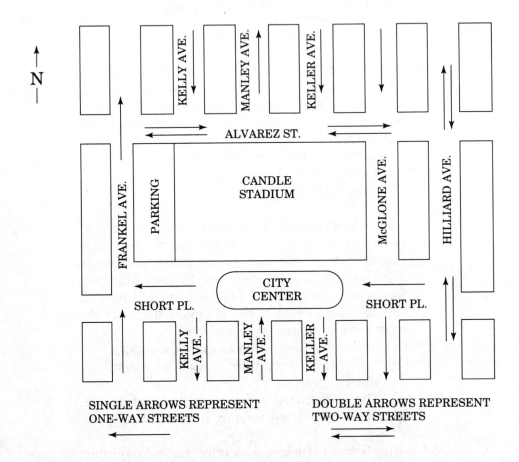

90. The radio dispatcher directs you to respond to the parking area adjacent to Candle Stadium. Presently you are in your patrol car at Alvarez Street and Hilliard Avenue. Which of the following is the most direct route for you to take in your patrol car, making sure to obey all the traffic regulations?
    (A) Proceed south on Hilliard Avenue to Short Place, make a left on Short Place, and continue on to Frankel Avenue where you should make a right turn.
    (B) Head west on Alvarez Street to Frankel Avenue and then head south on Frankel Avenue.
    (C) Proceed west on Alvarez Street for one block, turn left and continue south to Short Place, make a left and proceed west to Frankel Avenue, and make a left into Frankel Avenue.
    (D) Head south on Hilliard Avenue to Short Place, head west on Short Place to Frankel Avenue, and then head north on Frankel Avenue.

91. You are in your patrol car heading south on Kelly Avenue approaching Alvarez Street. The radio dispatcher directs you to handle a dispute at the City Center. Which of the following is the most direct route for you to take in your patrol car, making sure to obey all the traffic regulations?
    (A) Continue south on Kelly Street directly to the City Center.
    (B) Head west on Alvarez Street to Frankel Avenue, make a left onto Frankel Avenue and continue to Short Place, and then head east to the City Center.
    (C) Make a left onto Alvarez Street and proceed east for three blocks, head south for one block, and then make a right and proceed west to the City Center.
    (D) Head east on Alvarez Street to Keller Avenue and then head south on Keller Avenue directly to the City Center.

92. While in your patrol car at the City Center, you are requested to respond to Short Place and Hilliard Avenue. In order to comply with this request, you must first head in which of the following directions?
   (A) north
   (B) east
   (C) south
   (D) west

93. After a sports event, a disorderly group has gathered on McGlone Avenue between Alvarez Street and Short Place, adjacent to Candle Stadium. You have just completed handling a call on Short Place at Manley Avenue and are requested to respond to investigate the disorderly group. Which of the following is the most direct route for you to take in your patrol car, making sure to obey all the traffic regulations?
   (A) Head west on Short Place to Frankel Avenue, make a right turn and continue to Alvarez Street, make a right turn on Alvarez Street and continue to McGlone Avenue, and then head south on McGlone Avenue.
   (B) Head east on Short Place to McGlone Avenue and then head north on McGlone Avenue.
   (C) Head north on Manley Avenue to Alvarez Street, head east on Alvarez Street to McGlone Avenue, and then head south on McGlone Avenue.
   (D) Head east on Short Place to Hilliard Avenue, head north on Hilliard Avenue to Alvarez Street, head west on Alvarez Street, and then make a left onto McGlone Avenue and continue south on McGlone Avenue.

94. While in your patrol car and exiting the parking area of Candle Stadium onto Frankel Avenue, you are requested to respond to Keller Avenue and Alvarez Street. In order to comply with this request, you must first head in which of the following directions?
   (A) north
   (B) east
   (C) south
   (D) west

DIRECTIONS: Answer questions 95–100 on the basis of the following sketches. The model face, the one appearing above the dotted line, is a sketch of a person who is wanted. Of the four comparison faces, the ones appearing below the dotted line, one of them is the way the model face looked after changing appearance. You are to assume that no surgical alteration of the wanted person's face has occurred. You are to select the face that is most likely that of the wanted person.

95.

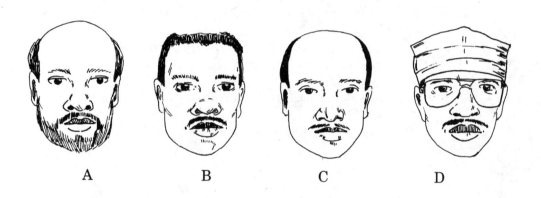

A   B   C   D

96.

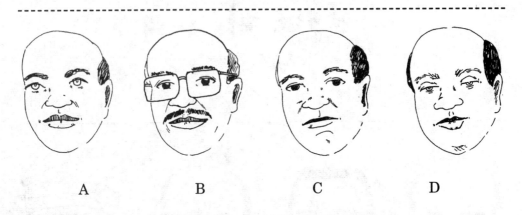

A   B   C   D

97.

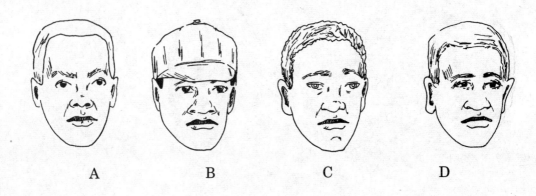

A   B   C   D

98.

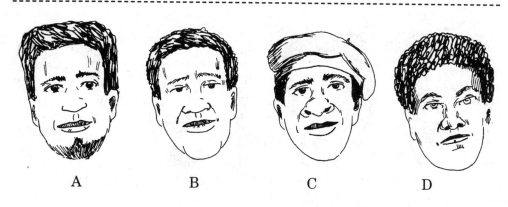

A   B   C   D

99.

A   B   C   D

100.

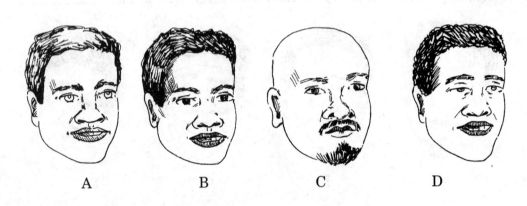

A   B   C   D

Answer Key

1. **A**	21. **D**	41. **B**	61. **B**	81. **C**
2. **B**	22. **D**	42. **A**	62. **C**	82. **D**
3. **C**	23. **C**	43. **B**	63. **B**	83. **A**
4. **C**	24. **C**	44. **B**	64. **A**	84. **C**
5. **A**	25. **C**	45. **B**	65. **B**	85. **D**
6. **B**	26. **B**	46. **B**	66. **B**	86. **C**
7. **D**	27. **C**	47. **B**	67. **B**	87. **A**
8. **B**	28. **A**	48. **C**	68. **A**	88. **D**
9. **D**	29. **A**	49. **A**	69. **D**	89. **D**
10. **D**	30. **C**	50. **D**	70. **A**	90. **D**
11. **C**	31. **A**	51. **C**	71. **B**	91. **C**
12. **D**	32. **C**	52. **B**	72. **A**	92. **D**
13. **C**	33. **B**	53. **A**	73. **C**	93. **A**
14. **B**	34. **B**	54. **B**	74. **C**	94. **A**
15. **B**	35. **C**	55. **B**	75. **B**	95. **A**
16. **D**	36. **B**	56. **B**	76. **C**	96. **B**
17. **C**	37. **D**	57. **C**	77. **D**	97. **B**
18. **C**	38. **C**	58. **C**	78. **A**	98. **A**
19. **B**	39. **C**	59. **D**	79. **A**	99. **B**
20. **A**	40. **B**	60. **A**	80. **C**	100. **B**

Diagnostic Chart

INSTRUCTIONS: After you score your test, complete the following chart by inserting in the column captioned "Your Number Correct" the number of questions you answered correctly in each of the ten sections of the test. Then compare your score in each section with the ratings in the column captioned "Scale." Finally, to correct your weaknesses follow the instructions found after the chart.

SECTION	QUESTION NUMBER	AREA	YOUR NUMBER CORRECT	SCALE
1	1–8	Memory (8 questions)		8 Right—Excellent 6–7 Right—Good 5 Right—Fair Under 5 Right—Poor
2	9–28	Reading Comprehension (20 questions)		20 Right—Excellent 18–19 Right—Good 16–17 Right—Fair Under 16 Right—Poor

3	29–48	Applying State Police Procedures (20 questions)	20 Right—Excellent 18–19 Right—Good 16–17 Right—Fair Under 16 Right—Poor
4	49–57	Verbal and Math (9 questions)	9 Right—Excellent 7–8 Right—Good 6 Right—Fair Under 6 Right—Poor
5	58–65	State Police Forms (8 questions)	8 Right—Excellent 6–7 Right—Good 5 Right—Fair Under 5 Right—Poor
6	66–73	Interpreting Data (8 questions)	8 Right—Excellent 6–7 Right—Good 5 Right—Fair Under 5 Right—Poor
7	74–81	Judgment and Reasoning (8 questions)	8 Right—Excellent 6–7 Right—Good 5 Right—Fair Under 5 Right—Poor
8	82–89	Legal Definitions (8 questions)	8 Right—Excellent 6–7 Right—Good 5 Right—Fair Under 5 Right—Poor
9	90–94	Traffic Directions (5 questions)	5 Right—Excellent 4 Right—Good 3 Right—Fair Under 3 Right—Poor
10	95–100	Matching Sketches (6 questions)	6 Right—Excellent 5 Right—Good 4 Right—Fair Under 4 Right—Poor

How to correct weaknesses:

1. If you are weak in Section 1, concentrate on Chapter 6.
2. If you are weak in Section 2, concentrate on Chapter 4.
3. If you are weak in Section 3, concentrate on Chapter 9.
4. If you are weak in Section 4, concentrate on Chapter 5.
5. If you are weak in Section 5, concentrate on Chapter 7.
6. If you are weak in Section 6, concentrate on Chapter 8.
7. If you are weak in Section 7, concentrate on Chapter 10.
8. If you are weak in Section 8, concentrate on Chapter 11.
9. If you are weak in Section 9, concentrate on Chapter 13.
10. If you are weak in Section 10, concentrate on Chapter 12.

Note: Consider yourself weak in a section if you receive other than an excellent rating in it.

Answer Explanations

1. **A** William Judge's street number, 80, is double his house number, 40.

2. **B** William Judge had a plane ticket. Ron Tonso was not carrying anything that would indicate travel plans.

3. **C** William Judge had a baseball schedule, and Ron Tonso had football tickets. This doesn't mean that they are definitely sports fans, but it raises the probability that they are and probability is what the question is asking about.

4. **C** William Judge had $20.25 on his person and so did Ron Tonso.

5. **A** Ron Tonso was in possession of an eviction notice.

6. **B** Plate numbers, when given, are very often the subject of questions.

7. **D** Asking for information that is not supplied is a common test writer's technique.

8. **B** William Judge was in possession of a prescription for medicine signed by a Dr. Green.

9. **D** It is probably true that the crime problem in this country will never be truly solved.

10. **D** Choices A, B, and C are opinions and not facts. D is factual.

11. **C** This question demonstrates quite clearly the danger of introducing personal knowledge into the answering of reading comprehension questions. It is common knowledge that choice B is in fact true, but it is not mentioned in the paragraph so it cannot be the answer. The instructions clearly state that the answer must be based solely on the information contained in the passage.

12. **D** This rule is absolute. There are no exceptions.

13. **C** The rule covers off-duty incidents and includes personal firearms.

14. **B** According to the passage, children under 10 are not even allowed on prison grounds.

15. **B** Clergy persons can visit 15 hours a day, 7 days a week.

16. **D** Police can visit if they have a court order.

17. **C** 12 year olds can visit only on family visiting days, which are held at least 3 times a month, or at least 36 times a year (12×3).

18. **C** State troopers are sometimes legally entitled to use force to defend themselves or a third party against unlawful force.

19. **B** State troopers may not use deadly physical force upon another person unless they reasonably believe that such other person is using or about to use deadly physical force against them or another.

20. **A** The restriction that arrests can be made only if the offense was committed in the presence of the trooper does not apply to felonies. It applies ONLY to misdemeanors and violations. This means that arrests can be made for felonies even if the arresting trooper was not present when they occurred.

21. **D** Having the right to counsel means having a right to a lawyer. The counsel (lawyer) may be of the juvenile's own choosing or may be appointed by the court for financial or other reasons.

22. **D** *To waive* means to give up or to relinquish. Even though a waiver (a giving up) of the right to counsel may be made, it is not effective unless the waiver is made in writing by both the juvenile and at least one of the parents or legal guardians.

23. **C** Trooper Green completed the report on Mr. Artist's car. This information rules out choices A, B, and D. The answer is choice C.

24. **C** The troopers parked their car behind the last of the five cars on the south side of Broom Street. When Mr. Artist came out of his house, he walked across the street to talk to the troopers. Therefore, Mr. Artist lives on the north side of the street (opposite the south side).

25. **C** The troopers left the scene at 9:50 A.M. after having spent 1 hour and 5 minutes there. This means that they initially arrived on the scene at 8:45 A.M. (9:50 A.M. minus 1 hour and 5 minutes).

26. **B** Mr. Artist's car was broken into on the previous night at 10:05 P. M.

27. **C** Information that state troopers need in the field comes primarily from information fed into the State Police Information System from other state troopers.

28. **A** The taking of notes in the field is unquestionably the most important step in the entire process by which the state police obtains information from their field personnel.

29. **A** The trooper's next step is to prepare an INVOICE WORK-SHEET. The forms described in choices B and C are not prepared by the trooper. They are prepared by the command clerk. There is no mention in the procedure of making a memo book entry.

30. **C** The trooper must request this envelope from the post command desk officer.

31. **A** The actions described in choices B, C, and D must be performed by the trooper concerned in the presence of and under the supervision of the post command desk officer. However, the action described in choice A, even though it is to be done by the trooper, does not have to be done under the supervision of the post command desk officer.

32. **C** Under no circumstances should a trooper attempt to remove or dislodge a needle from a hypodermic syringe.

33. **B** It is the responsibility of the trooper who obtained the marijuana to deposit the sealed security envelope containing it, along with the appropriate forms attached, into the controlled substances locker.

34. **B** Although the actions indicated by all the choices should be done by the trooper on the scene, the first thing a trooper should do at the scene of an aided case is to render reasonable aid to a sick or injured person.

35. **C** A second call for an ambulance should be made in 20 minutes if the ambulance does not arrive.

36. **B** A missing person is not mentioned in the definition of what an aided case is. The other persons are part of the definition of an aided case.

37. **D** If the aided person is wearing a Medic Alert emblem, the trooper shall notify radio dispatcher and ambulance attendant. A trooper shall not remove a Medic Alert emblem but shall make a memo book entry, including the name of the person notified regarding any Medic Alert emblem. Therefore, choices A, B, and C are incorrect, and choice D is correct.

38. **C** Choices A and B are incorrect because the use of the word *any* would include injured and dead persons as a result of a vehicle accident, which are not aided cases. Choice D is not found in the definition of an aided case. Choice C is the correct answer.

39. **C** The post command clerk shall have relatives/friends notified if the aided is admitted to a hospital or dies.

40. **B** Choice A is incorrect because a *minimum* distance of twenty (20) feet is recommended. Choice C is incorrect because this distance may vary with each situation. Choice D is incorrect because an attempt will be made to maintain the zone of safety if the EDP does not remain stationary.

41. **B** Before an EDP may be taken into custody without the specific direction of a patrol supervisor, the EDP must be not only unarmed and not violent but also willing to leave voluntarily.

42. **A** Nonlethal devices are carried in the patrol supervisor's patrol car.

43. **B** Choice A is incorrect because the patrol supervisor will establish police lines, if it has not already been done by the trooper who responds to the scene. Therefore, the responsibility to establish police lines does not rest only with the patrol supervisor.

44. **B** The procedure states that at least two troopers will safeguard the EDPs if more than one patient is being transported. This would certainly include three EDPs, which obviously is more than one EDP. Therefore, in safeguarding three EDPs, a minimum of only two troopers is required.

45. **B** Under no circumstances will an EDP be transported to a police facility. When you review a procedure, anytime you see absolute expressions such as *always, never, under no circumstances,* and so on, pay particular attention to them. The concepts tied to these expressions often become the basis of questions.

46. **B** According to the procedure, the trooper should have been riding in the body of the ambulance with the patient.

47. **B** The trooper concerned shall inform the examining physician, upon arrival at the hospital, of the use of nonlethal devices on an EDP.

48. **C** As stated in the procedure, the trooper concerned shall deliver an AIDED REPORT to the post command desk officer.

49. **A** Choice B is incorrect because *moral* means good conduct. The word *morale* should have been used to express the mood found in the barracks. Choice C is incorrect because *practicable* means feasible. The meaning intended in choice C is *sensible,* which should have been expressed by the use of the word *practical*. The word *infer,* which is used to conclude by logical reasoning, was properly used in the answer, choice A.

50. **D** Choice A is incorrect because the word *me* is to be used when receiving the action instead of the word *I.* Choice B is incorrect because *formally,* which means to act in a required way, should have been used instead of *formerly,* which means at an earlier time. Choice C is incorrect because you should *apprise,* which means to inform your boss, and not *appraise,* which means to evaluate.

51. **C** Choice A is incorrect because the word *it's* to indicate it is should have been used instead of *its,* which shows possession. Choice B is incorrect because the word *latter* to express the second of two persons that were mentioned should have been used in place of *later,* which indicates more late in time. *Lay* as used in choice C is correctly used to express placing something.

52. **B** Choice A is incorrect because the word *well* should be used instead of *good. Well* should be used when describing how something is done. Choice C is incorrect because *between* should be used instead of *among* when referring to two persons. Choice B is correct because into describes movement.

53. **A** Choice B is incorrect because *illusion* should have been used to express a misleading appearance. *Allusion* means a hint or casual reference. Choice C is incorrect because *besides,* which means in addition to, should have been used. *Beside* means next to a location. Choice A is correct because understood is, "I am faster than she (is)."

54. **B** First find the number of robberies that occurred this year by multiplying 20% × 455, the number of robberies last year. 20% = .2 as a decimal; therefore, 0.2 × 455 = 91, which represents the increase in the number of robberies. This means that this year there have been 455 + 91 = 546 robberies. Doing the same for burglaries 292 × 0.25 = 73. This means that this year there have been 292 + 73 = 365 burglaries. Thus the combined number of robberies and burglaries in this year are
$$546 + 365 = 911.$$

Robberies and burglaries in last year are
$$455 + 292 = 747.$$

To find the percentage increase, find the difference between the two numbers 911 − 747 = 164 and then divide by the number that previously existed, which is 747.
$$\frac{164}{747} = .219 = 21.9\%$$

(Move the decimal two places to the right to change a decimal to a percent.)

55. **B** Add up the items and divide by the number of items.
$$31 + 24 + 22 + 28 + 25 = \frac{130}{5} = 26.$$

56. **B** If an average is found by adding the items and dividing by the number of items, then the existing average age of 35 years was found by dividing a certain number by 110 (the number of troopers already assigned before the arrival of the five recruits). Or stated by example ?/110 = 35. We can find that number by multiplying $35 \times 110 = 3850$. The more recent average age, which includes the ages of the recruits, may be found by adding the combined ages of the five recruits (previously calculated to be 130) to 3850, the combined ages of the 110 already assigned troopers, and then dividing by the total number of items which including the five recruits is now 115 (110 + 5).

Thus
$$3850 + 130 = \frac{3980}{115} = 34.6.$$

You incorrectly selected choice D if you added the average age of the new recruits 26 to the average age of the already assigned troopers 35 and divided by 2,
$$30 + 26 = \frac{61}{2} = 30.5$$

57. **C** The starting time was 10:15 A.M. The amount of time used was:

To pack certain equipment	53 minutes
Awaiting the arrival of his supervisor	23 minutes
Traveling to the location ($\frac{3}{4} \times 60$ minutes)	45 minutes
Waiting for backup ($\frac{1}{3} \times 60$ minutes)	<u>20 minutes</u>
	141 minutes

and 141 minutes divided by 60 minutes, the number of minutes in an hour, equals 2 hours and 21 minutes, which is about 2⅓ hours.

58. **C** Caption 9 asks for the name of the person arrested, who was Bob Tailor.

59. **D** Caption 18 asks, "Have you discussed this matter with any member of the State Patrol and if yes, with whom?" The complainant, Mrs. June Tailor, discussed the matter with Deputy Sheriff Don Booth, who, although he is a law enforcement officer, is not a member of the State Highway Patrol.

60. **A** Caption 21 requires the signature of the complainant. Although it is true that such signature is optional, in this instance the complainant could not have signed the form because the complaint was made over the telephone.

61. **B** The person arrested is Bob Tailor, who is not currently living at the same address as his wife, but instead resides at 996 Court Street.

62. **C** The telephone number of the witness, Frank Homes should be entered in Caption 16.

63. **B** Officer Minks is the telephone recipient, and in caption 20 his signature is required. The importance of quickly reviewing the form before beginning to answer questions cannot be stressed enough. Familiarity with the form would have helped in quickly and accurately answering this question.

64. **A** Caption 2 asks for the address of the complainant who is Mrs. June Tailor, whose address is 665 Morris Avenue.

65. **B** The complaint number, which is 1919 should be entered in caption 13. Notice that choice A offered a number similar to the correct answer. Examiners often do this to determine if you are concentrating.

66. **B** If 43 hours, the time spent on accident investigation, represents 25% of the overall time in a month, that means 25% of some unknown quantity or X is equal to 43 hours. Or as an equation
$$0.25 \times X = 43 \text{ hours.}$$
Dividing both sides by 0.25, we get
$$\frac{0.25X}{0.25} = \frac{43}{0.25},$$
$$X = 172 \text{ hours}$$

67. **B** Crime scene investigation takes up only 10% of the average trooper patrol time.

68. **A** If you knew that one fourth is the same as 25%, then this question was easy for you. If not, you still could have eliminated choices B, C, and D because they are all inaccurate.

69. **D** The percentage of time spent in training is included in the miscellaneous category and cannot be exactly determined.

70. **A** Report writing represents 11% of the average trooper time spent on patrol functions, and investigating crimes represents 10% of that time. Combining them yields 21%.

71. **B** The importance of examining the chart and being familiar with it is evident in answering this question. If you recognized that the only patrol function not mentioned was the miscellaneous category, or 13% of the total patrol time, then that 13% could have been simply subtracted from 100% to give you the answer of 87%. This would be quicker than having to add up the five other percentages to arrive at 87%.

72. **A** Once again, being familiar with the chart enables you to quickly and easily answer this question. Traffic enforcement is included in the broader category of traffic regulation, which accounts for 15% of the average trooper's time spent on patrol functions. Even if the average trooper spent all of his/her traffic regulation time in enforcement, it would not exceed 15%.

73. **C** This question is the opposite of question 66. Here we are given the total number of hours spent on all patrol functions in a month and asked to find the monthly number for a specific function, preventive patrol. The answer is arrived at by multiplying the total number of hours, 200 hours, by the percentage of average time spent on preventive patrol, 26%. The answer is 52 hours.

74. **C** Suspected explosives and suspected hazardous materials should not be examined by anyone other than properly trained and equipped experts.

75. **B** In these situations good judgment demands that a trooper's first action be to call for assistance.

76. **C** To do other than cease all movement in such a situation could easily result in a tragedy.

77. **D** If you picked choice A, you overlooked the fact that police work is a team effort. The chances of capturing the robber is better once all troopers in the area are made aware of the description of the robber.

78. **A** Anonymous information is often quite valuable and should never be discounted simply because it comes from an unknown source. But, to immediately accept the information as being valid is inappropriate.

79. **A** The word *eliminate* in choice C is too strong. Even though it is true that the use of handcuffs minimizes escape attempts, it does not eliminate them. In any case, the primary purpose of handcuffs is to promote safety, as indicated in the answer, choice A.

80. **C** Never accept an assignment from a supervisor if you do not have complete understanding of the details of the assignment.

81. **C** When possible, a trooper should follow the adage, "facts before acts." Choice A is wrong for this reason. Perhaps the man is authorized to carry a gun. However, choice B is also wrong because the man might be in illegal possession of the firearm. Choice D is wrong because waiting could cause someone to be seriously injured. You

must obtain additional facts before deciding what to do. Test writers often frame questions to see if you are aware of the necessity to have all the facts that are available before you choose a course of action to follow.

82. **D** May is more than 18 years old and engages in sexual intercourse with Mark, who is less than 14 years old. They are not married to each other. That is rape in the second degree on the part of May but not Mark.

83. **A** Tom has had sexual intercourse with a person who is unable to consent due to being physically helpless. The most serious charge is rape in the first degree. Although it is true that Tom could be charged with rape in the third degree because of the ages involved, the most serious offense is as indicated in Choice A.

84. **C** Don engaged in deviate sexual intercourse with Joy by forcible compulsion. He committed, as indicated in choice C, sodomy in the first degree.

85. **D** Because of their ages, Tab and Mark more than sufficiently qualify as adults. Hence lack of consent cannot be attributed to them as a result of their ages. Also the sexual contact was not done with anyone's lack of consent, which is a key element of sexual abuse. Thus no sexual abuse took place.

86. **C** Sexual intercourse with a dead human body constitutes sexual misconduct.

87. **A** Ray is only 17 years old. For Ray to commit sodomy in the second degree, he would have to be 18 years or older. To commit sodomy in the third degree, he would have to be 21 years or older. Thus choices B and C may be eliminated. Because deviate sexual intercourse has occurred, choice D can be eliminated. This is sodomy in the first degree as indicated in Choice A because force was used to engage in deviate sexual intercourse.

88. **D** Choice A can be eliminated because deviate sexual intercourse has occurred. Choice B can be eliminated because there was no lack of consent as required in the definition of sexual abuse. Because June is 21 years old and May is less than 17, June, but not May, committed sodomy in the third degree. This eliminates choice C and leaves choice D as the most serious offense.

89. **D** For a charge of rape in the third degree one of the participants must be 21 or older and the other participant must be less than 17 years old.

90. **D** Choice A is incorrect because it directs you to make a left on Short Place, which would not only be against traffic but would also

direct you off the map. Choice B is incorrect because it directs you to head south on Frankel Avenue, which is a northbound street. Choice C is incorrect because it requires you to make a left turn into Frankel Avenue, which would send you against traffic and off the map.

91. **C**   Choices A and D are incorrect because they both direct you to drive through area that is blocked by Candle Stadium. Choice B is incorrect because it directs you to make a left onto Frankel Avenue, which would cause you to head south on a northbound street.

92. **D**   If you are at the City Center, then you are on Short Place in the vicinity of Keller, Manley, or Kelly Avenues. To proceed to Short Place and Hilliard Avenue requires that our first direction is to follow the traffic on Short Place, which is a westbound street.

93. **A**   Choices B and D are incorrect because they direct you to head east on Short Place, which is a westbound street. Remember that, to arrive at the correct answer in this type of question, you must examine all the choices and eliminate the incorrect ones. Also note that at times the examiner will give the same incorrect directions in more than one choice, as was seen in this question where choices B and D required that you head east on Short Place, a westbound street. Choice C is incorrect because following its directions would have you driving through the City Center and Candle Stadium.

94. **A**   The stem of the question places you on Frankel Avenue, and the only direction you may travel on Frankel Avenue is north.

95. **A**   The nose of choice B, the nose of choice C, and the lips of choice D leave choice A as the only possible answer.

96. **B**   The eyes of choice A, the lips of choice C, and the eyes and lips of choice D leave choice B as the only possible answer.

97. **B**   The eyes of choice A, the ears and eyes of choice C, and the ears and eyes of choice D leave choice B as the only possible answer.

98. **A**   The eyes of choice B, the nose of choice C, and the eyes, nose, and lips of choice D leave choice A as the only possible answer.

99. **B**   The eyes and chin line of choice A, the eyes and chin line of choice C, and the ears and eyes of choice D leave choice B as the only possible answer.

100. **B**   The eyes of choice A, the ears and lips of choice C, and the eyes of choice D leave choice B as the only possible answer.

CHAPTER 17

Practice Examination Four

This chapter contains the fourth of five practice examinations that you will be taking. Don't forget to:

1. Take the test in one sitting. You have 3½ hours to answer all 100 questions.

2. Use the test-taking strategies outlined in Chapter 2.

3. Use the answer sheet we have provided to record your answers.

4. Complete the diagnostic chart that appears at the end of this chapter after you score this practice examination.

Answer Sheet
Practice Examination Four

Follow the instructions given in the test. Mark only your answers in the circles below.

WARNING: Be sure that the circle you fill is in the same row as the question you are answering. Use a No. 2 pencil (soft pencil).

BE SURE YOUR PENCIL MARKS ARE HEAVY AND BLACK. ERASE COMPLETELY ANY ANSWER YOU WISH TO CHANGE.

DO NOT make stray pencil dots, dashes or marks.

1. Ⓐ Ⓑ Ⓒ Ⓓ   2. Ⓐ Ⓑ Ⓒ Ⓓ   3. Ⓐ Ⓑ Ⓒ Ⓓ   4. Ⓐ Ⓑ Ⓒ Ⓓ
5. Ⓐ Ⓑ Ⓒ Ⓓ   6. Ⓐ Ⓑ Ⓒ Ⓓ   7. Ⓐ Ⓑ Ⓒ Ⓓ   8. Ⓐ Ⓑ Ⓒ Ⓓ
9. Ⓐ Ⓑ Ⓒ Ⓓ   10. Ⓐ Ⓑ Ⓒ Ⓓ   11. Ⓐ Ⓑ Ⓒ Ⓓ   12. Ⓐ Ⓑ Ⓒ Ⓓ
13. Ⓐ Ⓑ Ⓒ Ⓓ   14. Ⓐ Ⓑ Ⓒ Ⓓ   15. Ⓐ Ⓑ Ⓒ Ⓓ   16. Ⓐ Ⓑ Ⓒ Ⓓ
17. Ⓐ Ⓑ Ⓒ Ⓓ   18. Ⓐ Ⓑ Ⓒ Ⓓ   19. Ⓐ Ⓑ Ⓒ Ⓓ   20. Ⓐ Ⓑ Ⓒ Ⓓ
21. Ⓐ Ⓑ Ⓒ Ⓓ   22. Ⓐ Ⓑ Ⓒ Ⓓ   23. Ⓐ Ⓑ Ⓒ Ⓓ   24. Ⓐ Ⓑ Ⓒ Ⓓ
25. Ⓐ Ⓑ Ⓒ Ⓓ   26. Ⓐ Ⓑ Ⓒ Ⓓ   27. Ⓐ Ⓑ Ⓒ Ⓓ   28. Ⓐ Ⓑ Ⓒ Ⓓ
29. Ⓐ Ⓑ Ⓒ Ⓓ   30. Ⓐ Ⓑ Ⓒ Ⓓ   31. Ⓐ Ⓑ Ⓒ Ⓓ   32. Ⓐ Ⓑ Ⓒ Ⓓ
33. Ⓐ Ⓑ Ⓒ Ⓓ   34. Ⓐ Ⓑ Ⓒ Ⓓ   35. Ⓐ Ⓑ Ⓒ Ⓓ   36. Ⓐ Ⓑ Ⓒ Ⓓ
37. Ⓐ Ⓑ Ⓒ Ⓓ   38. Ⓐ Ⓑ Ⓒ Ⓓ   39. Ⓐ Ⓑ Ⓒ Ⓓ   40. Ⓐ Ⓑ Ⓒ Ⓓ
41. Ⓐ Ⓑ Ⓒ Ⓓ   42. Ⓐ Ⓑ Ⓒ Ⓓ   43. Ⓐ Ⓑ Ⓒ Ⓓ   44. Ⓐ Ⓑ Ⓒ Ⓓ
45. Ⓐ Ⓑ Ⓒ Ⓓ   46. Ⓐ Ⓑ Ⓒ Ⓓ   47. Ⓐ Ⓑ Ⓒ Ⓓ   48. Ⓐ Ⓑ Ⓒ Ⓓ
49. Ⓐ Ⓑ Ⓒ Ⓓ   50. Ⓐ Ⓑ Ⓒ Ⓓ   51. Ⓐ Ⓑ Ⓒ Ⓓ   52. Ⓐ Ⓑ Ⓒ Ⓓ
53. Ⓐ Ⓑ Ⓒ Ⓓ   54. Ⓐ Ⓑ Ⓒ Ⓓ   55. Ⓐ Ⓑ Ⓒ Ⓓ   56. Ⓐ Ⓑ Ⓒ Ⓓ
57. Ⓐ Ⓑ Ⓒ Ⓓ   58. Ⓐ Ⓑ Ⓒ Ⓓ   59. Ⓐ Ⓑ Ⓒ Ⓓ   60. Ⓐ Ⓑ Ⓒ Ⓓ
61. Ⓐ Ⓑ Ⓒ Ⓓ   62. Ⓐ Ⓑ Ⓒ Ⓓ   63. Ⓐ Ⓑ Ⓒ Ⓓ   64. Ⓐ Ⓑ Ⓒ Ⓓ
65. Ⓐ Ⓑ Ⓒ Ⓓ   66. Ⓐ Ⓑ Ⓒ Ⓓ   67. Ⓐ Ⓑ Ⓒ Ⓓ   68. Ⓐ Ⓑ Ⓒ Ⓓ
69. Ⓐ Ⓑ Ⓒ Ⓓ   70. Ⓐ Ⓑ Ⓒ Ⓓ   71. Ⓐ Ⓑ Ⓒ Ⓓ   72. Ⓐ Ⓑ Ⓒ Ⓓ
73. Ⓐ Ⓑ Ⓒ Ⓓ   74. Ⓐ Ⓑ Ⓒ Ⓓ   75. Ⓐ Ⓑ Ⓒ Ⓓ   76. Ⓐ Ⓑ Ⓒ Ⓓ
77. Ⓐ Ⓑ Ⓒ Ⓓ   78. Ⓐ Ⓑ Ⓒ Ⓓ   79. Ⓐ Ⓑ Ⓒ Ⓓ   80. Ⓐ Ⓑ Ⓒ Ⓓ
81. Ⓐ Ⓑ Ⓒ Ⓓ   82. Ⓐ Ⓑ Ⓒ Ⓓ   83. Ⓐ Ⓑ Ⓒ Ⓓ   84. Ⓐ Ⓑ Ⓒ Ⓓ
85. Ⓐ Ⓑ Ⓒ Ⓓ   86. Ⓐ Ⓑ Ⓒ Ⓓ   87. Ⓐ Ⓑ Ⓒ Ⓓ   88. Ⓐ Ⓑ Ⓒ Ⓓ
89. Ⓐ Ⓑ Ⓒ Ⓓ   90. Ⓐ Ⓑ Ⓒ Ⓓ   91. Ⓐ Ⓑ Ⓒ Ⓓ   92. Ⓐ Ⓑ Ⓒ Ⓓ
93. Ⓐ Ⓑ Ⓒ Ⓓ   94. Ⓐ Ⓑ Ⓒ Ⓓ   95. Ⓐ Ⓑ Ⓒ Ⓓ   96. Ⓐ Ⓑ Ⓒ Ⓓ
97. Ⓐ Ⓑ Ⓒ Ⓓ   98. Ⓐ Ⓑ Ⓒ Ⓓ   99. Ⓐ Ⓑ Ⓒ Ⓓ   100. Ⓐ Ⓑ Ⓒ Ⓓ

The Test

DIRECTIONS FOR QUESTIONS 1–8: The following story is about an occurrence involving state troopers. You are allowed 10 minutes to read it and commit to memory as much about it as you can. You are not allowed to make any written notes during the time you are reading. At the end of 10 minutes, you are to stop reading the material and answer 8 questions about the story without referring back to it.

Memory Story—10-Minute Time Limit

On February 6th, at 9:30 A.M., Joan Larkin, a female, white, 36 years old, of 5556 Madison Avenue, opened the Togs Clothing Store, 6555 Madison Avenue, where she is employed as the manager. Shortly afterwards, the subject female saw an old station wagon pull up in front of the store and a male get out. The male, who is white and about 30 years old, entered the store.

Once inside, the male asked Ms. Larkin if she was alone. She immediately became concerned. The unknown male then showed her a gold-colored badge with the word *Detective* on it. He said he was investigating a narcotics complaint and that she might be of some help. He asked if they could talk in the rear of the store away from the front window so no one would spot them together. Ms. Larkin said there was an office in the rear of the store where they could talk. Once in the office area, the male, who identified himself as Detective John Kelly, shield 2346, and who spoke with a northern European/Irish accent, took out a silver handgun, forced Ms. Larkin to disrobe, and demanded that she have sexual intercourse with him. After consummating an act of rape, the male struck his female victim with his handgun and fled.

As soon as the rapist fled the store, Ms. Larkin called her fiancee, Don Wood, who then notified the state police. Ms. Larkin described the perpetrator to the police as follows:

> He was a male, white, about 30 years old. He was wearing a waist-length jacket, a ski cap, and loafer-type shoes. He had on designer jeans. His hair was brown and partly balding. He kind of looked like a cop because his hair was short. His eyes were blue and, if it were not for his mustache, his medium complexion would not make him particularly noticeable. He had an offensive body odor and a birthmark on his neck.

Trooper Richard Green, shield 2468, took Ms. Larkin's complaint and then said that there had been a rash of crimes where a male fitting the description she had given was impersonating a detective and raping females.

DO NOT PROCEED UNTIL 10 MINUTES HAVE PASSED.

DIRECTIONS: Answer questions 1–8 solely on the basis of the above story. Do not refer back to the story when answering these questions.

1. Ms. Larkin's first name is
   (A) Jane.
   (B) Joan.
   (C) Jean.
   (D) Jo Ann.

2. How old is Ms. Larkin?
   (A) 26 years old
   (B) 36 years old
   (C) 30 years old
   (D) Ms. Larkin's age was not given.

3. What is the address of the Togs Clothing Store?
   (A) 6555 Madison Street
   (B) 5556 Madison Street
   (C) 6555 Madison Avenue
   (D) 5556 Madison Street

4. What is Ms. Larkin's position at the Togs Clothing Store?
   (A) owner
   (B) salesperson
   (C) manager
   (D) cashier

5. According to the victim, the rapist kind of looked like a cop because
   (A) he was tall.
   (B) his hair was short.
   (C) he showed a detective's shield.
   (D) he had a mustache.

6. Trooper Green's shield number is
   (A) 2346.
   (B) 2468.
   (C) 2368.
   (D) 2446.

7. The rapist was armed with a
   (A) knife.
   (B) shotgun.
   (C) silver handgun.
   (D) stainless steel revolver.

8. The state police were notified by
   (A) the victim.
   (B) a witness.
   (C) the victim's fiancee.
   (D) a passerby.

Answer questions 9–11 based solely on the information contained in the following paragraph.

Most ordinary citizens believe that juvenile criminals are not any different from adult criminals. They reason that the only difference between the two groups is age. Nothing could be farther from the truth. Even though both groups of criminals can be held to know the difference between right and wrong, juvenile offenders often lack an appreciation of the effects of their crimes on the rest of the community.

To a lesser degree juveniles do not see the risks of punishment to themselves as a result of their actions. They see themselves as being eternal and indestructible. Even though juveniles see on television how criminals are punished and are also told about prison life by ex-convicts returning to the neighborhood, they remain unaware of the punishments able to be dealt out by the state mainly because of a lack of personally experiencing adult incarceration.

To try to bridge this gap of inexperience with the realities of prison life, programs such as "Scared Stiff" have been developed. These programs take juveniles identified by the local police as headed in the wrong direction and have them live a day in the life of an adult inmate in an adult correctional facility. The day is complete with the feeling of being locked away in a tiny cell and even limited supervised interaction with volunteer adult inmates who pull no punches and treat the juveniles as they would any new inmate. The hope is that by seeing what prison life is really like some change in attitude will occur in the juvenile. Although such programs are not seen as the cure-all for rising juvenile crime nor as a replacement for the role of parents or educational institutions, some progress has been realized.

9. Based on the passage which of the following statements is most correct?
   (A) The ordinary citizen sees great differences between an adult inmate and a juvenile inmate.
   (B) The only difference between an adult inmate and a juvenile inmate is age.
   (C) Juvenile criminals are not expected to know the difference between right and wrong.
   (D) Juvenile offenders often lack an understanding of the results of their criminal activity on the rest of the community.

10. Juveniles do not see the risks of punishment to themselves as a result of their actions mainly because
   (A) they see themselves as being eternal and indestructible.
   (B) they do not see on television how criminals are punished.
   (C) ex-convicts returning to the neighborhood do not talk about their prison life.
   (D) of a juvenile's lack of personally experiencing adult incarceration.

11. "Scared Stiff" programs
   (A) hope that a change in attitude will occur in certain juveniles.
   (B) are seen as the cure-all for rising juvenile crime.
   (C) can be a replacement for the role of parents.
   (D) are structured to take the place of educational institutions.

Answer questions 12–17 solely on the basis of the following passage.

Trooper Gabriella Ginty is off-duty. She is shopping in a local mall. At about 1:35 P.M. she observes two males she believes might be escaped prisoners. The two males are sitting on a bench watching shoppers as they pass. Trooper Ginty knows that she is authorized to make off-duty arrests even though the mall is not within the jurisdiction of the state police. She also knows that when she makes an off-duty arrest she is required to notify her commanding officer by telephone within 1 hour of the arrest. In this case, Trooper Ginty does not make immediate arrests because she is not really sure if the two males are indeed escaped prisoners.

At 1:40 P.M., the two males get up from the bench and start walking away. Trooper Ginty decides to follow the two males because they are acting suspiciously. The first suspect is a male, white, about 35–40 years old, wearing black pants and a black jacket. The second is a male, black, about 25–30 years old, wearing brown pants and a white coat. The two suspects stop in front of a bank, which is located right next to an exit from the mall into a parking lot. Trooper Ginty observes the two men as they watch people enter and leave the bank. At about 1:50 P.M., an elderly woman carrying her pocketbook in her hand leaves the bank. The two men follow her out of the mall into the parking lot. Thinking that the men were about to steal the woman's pocketbook, Trooper Ginty follows them out of the mall.

Sure enough, when the trooper spots the two men in the parking lot, they are holding up the old lady. The male with the black jacket has a gun, and the other male is removing cash from the lady's pocketbook. Fearing for the victim's safety, the trooper waits for the two robbers to finish their crime before she takes any action. At 1:55 P.M., when the robbers are fleeing the scene of the crime, the trooper, with gun drawn for her own safety, catches them by surprise and arrests them.

Trooper Ginty then notifies the local police about her arrests. When the police sergeant arrives on the scene and hears the story, he tells Trooper Ginty that she should have notified the local police sooner and that it was a mistake for her to take police action against armed perpetrators without sufficient backup.

12. Trooper Ginty did not arrest the two males at 1:35 P.M. because
    (A) she is not authorized to make off-duty arrests.
    (B) she is required to obtain the permission of her commanding officer before making an off-duty arrest.
    (C) she wasn't sure if they were escaped prisoners.
    (D) she wanted to wait to get backup assistance.

13. Why did Trooper Ginty decide to follow the two males at 1:40 P.M.?
    (A) They were escaped prisoners.
    (B) They were acting suspiciously.
    (C) They were going to steal an old lady's pocketbook.
    (D) They were armed.

14. The suspect who had the gun was
    (A) a white male.
    (B) about 25–30 years old.
    (C) a black male.
    (D) wearing brown pants.

15. The trooper waited for the crime in the parking lot to be completed before taking any action because
    (A) she was waiting for backup assistance.
    (B) she was concerned for the safety of the victim.
    (C) she wanted to gather evidence.
    (D) she wasn't sure what to do.

16. The police sergeant believed Trooper Ginty made a mistake by
    (A) making an off-duty arrest.
    (B) following the suspects.
    (C) acting alone.
    (D) unholstering her gun.

17. How long does Trooper Ginty have to notify her commanding officer about the arrests?
    (A) until 2:55 P.M.
    (B) until the next day
    (C) until 4:00 P.M.
    (D) until midnight

Answer questions 18–20 solely on the basis of the information contained in the following passage.

Most crimes fall into one of two categories, felonies or misdemeanors. Felonies are more serious than misdemeanors. They are considered serious enough to deserve severe punishment or even death. At one time the distinction between felonies and misdemeanors was based on the fact that all felonies were capital offenses punishable by death. The present-day distinction between a felony and misdemeanor in the United States is usually based on the length of the sentence imposed. Felony convictions require a sentence of more than 1 year in prison. Misdemeanors, however, account for a great majority of arrests made. There are almost 3 million misdemeanor arrests made each year. A misdemeanor conviction involves a sentence of 1 year or less. Convictions for either felonies or misdemeanors can result in the assessment of a fine.

18. Misdemeanors are
    (A) less serious than felonies.
    (B) punishable by more than 1 year in prison.
    (C) sometimes punishable by death.
    (D) capital offenses.

19. In the United States, the difference between felonies and misdemeanors is usually based
    (A) on the length of the sentence imposed.
    (B) on the location where confinement takes place.
    (C) on the intent of the criminal.
    (D) on the amount of fine that can be imposed.

20. Which of the following is the most accurate statement concerning fines?
    (A) They may be imposed only for misdemeanor convictions.
    (B) They may be imposed only for felony convictions.
    (C) They may be imposed for both felony and misdemeanor convictions.
    (D) They may not be imposed for felony convictions.

Answer questions 21–23 based only on the information contained in the following passage.

The criminal justice system is comprised of four separate components—police, prosecutor, courts, and corrections. Each of these four components has its own specific tasks. A major problem for the overall system is that each of the four components acts independently of one another. This is true despite the fact that what happens in one component definitely has an impact on what happens in the other three. For example, an increase in arrest activity by the police always results in an increased workload for the rest of the system. And, if corrections does not do their job properly, the police become overloaded with repeat offenders. The problem is made worse by the fact that the four components of the system compete with one another for funding. By far, the component that receives the most funding is the police, and the most underfunded component is corrections. This is a difficult fact to understand because it is corrections that has the most complex problems. Clearly, however, the most powerful component is the courts. The police, the prosecutor, and corrections are all responsible to and supervised by the courts.

21. The component of the criminal justice system that receives the most money to operate is the
(A) police.
(B) prosecutors.
(C) courts.
(D) corrections.

22. The courts
(A) have the most complex problems.
(B) receive less money than the other three components.
(C) exercise authority over the other three components.
(D) have fewer problems than the other three components.

23. A major problem of the criminal justice system is that
(A) there are insufficient funds available.
(B) there are many complex problems to solve.
(C) the amount of crime is increasing drastically.
(D) there is a lack of coordinated action.

Answer questions 24–26 based solely on the information contained in the following passage.

From state to state, and even from county to county, the definition of what exactly constitutes a missing person varies. In some states any unaccounted for person under the age of 21 is considered a missing person regardless of whether or not the absence is voluntary. In other jurisdictions a requirement still exists that, in order for a person to be classified as missing, a certain time period must elapse. Properly, however, more and more jurisdictions have come to realize that no time requirement should be a factor in determining if a person is to be considered a missing person. After all, a person missing 16 hours is no less missing than the same person will be in 24 hours. This is especially evident when the person missing might have been considering suicide.

What has really changed regarding missing persons is the perception of the public that the number of missing persons in our nation is growing at an epidemic rate. Adults, teenagers, and young children alike seem to be disappearing in alarming numbers. However, some experts feel that this perception on the part of the public is actually the result of a heightened sense of awareness on the part of the public of an already existing problem. These same experts maintain that what has raised the public sense of awareness of this problem is the attention to the problem given by the media and also federal law enforcement's realization that, in order to find such missing persons, law enforcement actions must be federally coordinated.

The media's attention to the problem has been seen in everything from missing persons posters appearing on milk containers to weekly investigative programs. The efforts of law enforcement range from technical assistance in conducting missing persons investigations to information storage at the National Crime Information Center.

24. Which of the following statements is most correct concerning the nation's missing person problem?
   (A) There is definitely no missing person problem.
   (B) What makes a missing person investigation easy is the total similarities in tactics among all law enforcement jurisdictions.
   (C) How long a person is missing should not determine whether a person should actually be considered a missing person.
   (D) Persons considering suicide should not be considered missing persons.

25. What has really changed regarding missing persons is
    (A) that only adults seem to be disappearing in large numbers.
    (B) the perception of the public that the number of missing persons in our nation is growing at an epidemic rate.
    (C) that only teenagers seem to be disappearing in large numbers.
    (D) that young children seem to be disappearing in alarming numbers faster than any other segment of our population.

26. Some experts maintain that the public's current feeling toward the state of the nation's missing persons problem is
    (A) that there really is no problem.
    (B) the same as it has always been.
    (C) is really the result of a heightened sense of awareness.
    (D) that the problem is less today than in years gone by due to the increased efforts of law enforcement.

Answer questions 27 and 28 based solely on the following rule.

A complaint is an allegation of an improper or unlawful act committed by a state trooper provided that the act relates to the business of the state police agency that employs the trooper. A complaint shall be thoroughly investigated by the supervisor to whom it is referred, and if the condition complained of actually exists, it shall be corrected and steps shall be taken to prevent its recurrence.

27. Complaints
    (A) must involve an unlawful act.
    (B) must relate to the business of a state police agency.
    (C) must be promptly made.
    (D) must be made in person.

28. Complaints
    (A) must be investigated by a supervisor.
    (B) cannot be anonymously made.
    (C) must all result in some form of corrective action.
    (D) do not all have to be investigated.

Answer questions 29–37 solely on the basis of the following information.

Whenever a firearm comes into possession of a trooper, the trooper shall:

1. Unload any ammunition from the chamber or magazine.

NOTE: Do not handle unnecessarily to prevent possible destruction of fingerprints or other evidentiary matter. If the firearm is difficult to unload, safeguard it in its original condition and notify the post command desk officer.

2. Scratch an identifying mark on the side of the cartridge case of any ammunition removed. A spent bullet shall be marked on its base.

3. Place the ammunition removed from the firearm in an envelope and seal.

4. Mark "Ammunition Removed From Firearm" across the face of the envelope, include the serial number of the firearm, or if there is no serial number, the number of the security lead seal placed on the firearm from which cartridges were removed.

5. Place additional ammunition, other than that removed from the firearm, in a separate envelope and cross-reference it to the firearm.

NOTE: Ammunition removed from a firearm and from other sources, such as that removed from clothing or a drawer, are not to be mixed.

6. Deliver firearm(s) and ammunition to the post command desk officer.

7. Prepare a CLERK'S INVOICE WORKSHEET.

   a. Describe the firearm(s) fully (calibre, make, model, type, and serial number).

   b. Affix a security lead seal if no serial number is distinguishable.

8. Mark initials on the flat surface of the firearm frame in evidence cases.

9. Prepare two copies of a PISTOL INDEX CARD for each handgun with serial number.

10. Notify the Stolen Property Section when a firearm, with a distinguishable serial number, is seized in connection with an arrest, or is obtained under circumstances requiring investigation.

11. Enter on CLERK'S INVOICE WORKSHEET:

a. Identity of the person notified at Stolen Property Section.

b. Information received, including:

    1) "NO HIT," if there is no record

    2) "HIT," if there is a record.

NOTE: A trooper recovering a firearm wanted on alarm will not cancel the alarm. Cancellation of alarms will be made only by the Stolen Property Section after examination of firearms by the Ballistic Unit.

12. Have the command clerk type:

a. CLERK'S INVOICE from the information on the trooper's completed CLERK'S INVOICE WORKSHEET.

b. COMPLAINT REPORT, if required.

c. REQUEST FOR LABORATORY EXAMINATION.

13. Obtain a Clerk's Envelope from the post command desk officer.

14. Place the firearm, bullets, and shells, if any, in the envelope and seal it, in the presence of the post command desk officer, to prevent loss of contents.

15. Present to the post command desk officer:

a. Clerk's Envelope containing firearm.

b. CLERK'S INVOICE.

c. REQUEST FOR LABORATORY EXAMINATION.

d. PISTOL INDEX CARDS, if prepared.

Requests for gun traces concerning contraband weapons will be made to the Alcohol, Tobacco, and Firearms Bureau through the Ballistics Unit. The Ballistics Unit will forward a report of the results to the requesting trooper and the Intelligence Division.

    29. According to the procedure, it would be most appropriate to make a request for a gun trace for a contraband weapon through
        (A) the Alcohol, Tobacco, and Firearms Bureau.
        (B) the Ballistics Unit.
        (C) the Intelligence Division.
        (D) the post command desk officer.

30. A firearm came into the possession of Trooper Days while the trooper was on patrol. In this instance, the trooper's first action should be
(A) to look for the serial number of the firearm.
(B) to verify the owner.
(C) to unload it.
(D) to call the patrol supervisor.

31. At the scene of a robbery, a spent bullet has been recovered by Trooper Eaves. In such a situation, the trooper should
(A) initial the side of the bullet.
(B) mark the base of the bullet.
(C) wrap a lead security seal around the bullet.
(D) wrap the bullet in tape.

32. Which of the following is responsible for preparing a CLERK'S INVOICE WORKSHEET?
(A) the trooper concerned
(B) the command clerk
(C) the detective assigned
(D) the post command desk officer

33. According to procedure, a trooper should affix a security lead seal to a firearm if the firearm
(A) has been modified.
(B) has no registered owner.
(C) has no serial number.
(D) has no firing pin.

34. According to procedure, alarms on wanted firearms may be cancelled only by
(A) the trooper who recovered the firearm.
(B) the Stolen Property Section.
(C) the Ballistics Unit.
(D) the post command desk officer.

35. A trooper seizes a firearm in connection with making an arrest. The firearm has no serial number. The trooper then notifies Stolen Property Section. In this instance, the actions of the trooper were
    (A) proper, mainly because the Stolen Property Section is to be notified of all firearms seized in connection with arrests.
    (B) improper, mainly because the Stolen Property Section is not required to be notified about recovered firearms that do not have a serial number.
    (C) proper, mainly because the Stolen Property Section examines recovered firearms.
    (D) improper, mainly because it is never necessary to notify the Stolen Property Section about firearms recovered in connection with an arrest.

36. Which of the following forms is not required in every instance to be submitted to the post command desk officer by the trooper recovering the firearm?
    (A) an envelope containing the firearm
    (B) CLERK'S INVOICE
    (C) REQUEST FOR LABORATORY EXAMINATION
    (D) PISTOL INDEX CARDS

37. Trooper Dawns has recovered a firearm and is attempting to unload it. The firearm is difficult to unload, so the trooper safeguards it in its original condition. In this instance, the trooper should notify
    (A) the Ballistics Unit.
    (B) the post command desk officer.
    (C) the patrol supervisor.
    (D) any detective on duty.

Answer questions 38–41 solely on the basis of the following information.

Upon being exposed to an infectious disease or suffering a human bite or hypodermic needle puncture wound, the affected trooper shall

1. Notify the post command desk officer who shall:

   a. Notify the Medical Unit and obtain an Exposure Report number.

b. Make a Post Command Log entry of the information including the Exposure Report number in the Log entry.

c. Notify the department physician of the facts involved.

d. Contact the trooper involved and advise of necessary treatment.

2. Comply with the directions of the department surgeon.

3. Make a memo book entry of the facts involved including the Exposure Report number.

ACCIDENTAL SPILLS OF BLOOD OR BODY FLUIDS:

A supply of household bleach will be maintained at all post commands. Accidental spills of blood or body fluids on floors, cells, patrol cars, or other surfaces, other than clothing or fabric, may be cleaned by applying a freshly mixed solution of one part household bleach with ten parts water. It is imperative that the preceding mixture be carefully followed. Household bleach is not to be mixed with any solution other than water, and it must be freshly mixed for each use.

Troopers are reminded that this mixture of bleach and water will cause damage if used to clean uniforms. Uniform items soiled with blood or body fluids can be effectively cleaned by routine laundering or dry cleaning procedures. Bleach should not be used to cleanse hands.

In addition, bleach mixed with any substance other than water may cause a toxic gas. Therefore, disposal of bleach or bleach dilutions should be performed only in a sink (not a urinal or toilet since they sometimes contain chemical deodorizers). When preparing a bleach dilution, the container used for the diluted solution must be cleaned with water and free of any other solution.

38. According to procedure, which of the following is least appropriate when dealing with accidental spills of blood and body fluids?
(A) Bleach must be freshly mixed for each use.
(B) Household bleach is not to be mixed with any solution other than water.
(C) When mixing household bleach with water, mix ten parts of household bleach with one part water.
(D) Bleach should not be used to cleanse hands.

39. According to procedure, which of the following is most appropriate when dealing with accidental spills of blood and body fluids?
    (A) The container used for a diluted solution of bleach must be cleaned with water and free of any other solution.
    (B) Bleach dilutions should be performed in a urinal or toilet.
    (C) Bleach dilutions should not be performed in a sink.
    (D) Mixtures of bleach should be used to clean uniforms.

40. Trooper Collars suffers a human bite wound while effecting an arrest. According to procedure, which of the following should the trooper notify first?
    (A) the department physician
    (B) the post command desk officer
    (C) the patrol supervisor
    (D) the Medical Unit

41. According to procedure the Exposure Report number is to be entered
    (A) only in the Post Command Log.
    (B) only in the memo book of the trooper involved.
    (C) in both the Post Command Log and the memo book of the trooper involved.
    (D) neither in the Post Command Log nor the memo book of the trooper involved.

Answer questions 42–48 solely on the basis of the following information.

When a trooper effects an arrest, the trooper shall in the following order:

1. Inform the prisoner of the authority for the arrest and the cause of the arrest, unless physical resistance or flight render such notification impractical.

2. Handcuff the prisoner with the prisoner's hands behind the prisoner's back.

3. Immediately field search the prisoner and search adjacent vicinity for weapons, evidence, and/or contraband.

4. Advise the prisoner of the prisoner's constitutional rights before questioning.

a. If a juvenile is taken into custody, the parents/guardian will be notified immediately.

b. When questioning a juvenile, both the juvenile and parent/guardian, if present, will be advised of the juvenile's constitutional rights.

5. Have vehicles or other conveyances not required as evidence safeguarded, if appropriate.

6. Remove the prisoner to the precinct of arrest and inform the desk officer of the charge(s).

7. Notify the post command desk officer if force was used to effect the arrest.

NOTE: If an arrest is made by an off-duty trooper, the post command desk officer is required to notify the duty captain who will respond to the post command to determine the validity of the arrest.

8. Make a thorough search of the prisoner in the presence of the command desk officer.

9. Remove the following property from the prisoner.

a. Property unlawfully carried.

b. Property required as evidence.

c. Property lawfully carried, but dangerous to life or that would facilitate escape.

d. Property that can be used to deface or damage property.

e. Personal property, except clothing, if prisoner is intoxicated or unconscious.

NOTE: A prisoner's funds should be counted and returned by the arresting trooper.

10. Advise the prisoner of the right to make three (3) telephone calls within the state without charge or to make collect calls, outside the state, if toll charges are accepted.

a. Make the telephone calls if the prisoner is incapacitated by alcohol or drugs.

11. Permit the prisoner to converse on telephone, except where the ends of justice may be defeated or a dangerous condition may be created.

12. Notify the prisoner's relatives or friends if the prisoner is under 19 years of age or is admitted to a hospital or is apparently of unsound mind.

13. Prepare a MISSING PERSON REPORT and notify the Missing Persons Squad if unable to make such notification.

14. Deliver all forms completed in connection with the arrest to the post command desk officer.

NOTE: Troopers at the scene of an incident at which a prisoner is acting in a deranged, erratic manner apparently caused by a drug overdose, i.e., cocaine psychosis, angel dust, heroin overdose, etc., will request the response of the patrol supervisor, if an ambulance is not immediately available. The supervisor will determine if the prisoner should be removed to the appropriate hospital by utilizing a patrol car or await the arrival of an ambulance. The prisoner is not to be brought to a state police facility.

42. Trooper Bob Carter has just arrested Don Frank for a robbery. After Trooper Carter informs the prisoner of his authority and the cause of the arrest, he properly handcuffs the prisoner. According to procedure, the trooper should now immediately
(A) advise the prisoner of his rights.
(B) field search the prisoner.
(C) notify the post command desk officer.
(D) request the response of the patrol supervisor.

43. While off duty, Trooper June White arrests a man who attempted to steal her car. She brings the suspect to the post command for booking purposes. While there, the validity of the arrest she has just made should be determined by
(A) the duty captain.
(B) the post command desk officer.
(C) the patrol supervisor.
(D) the detective on duty.

44. While effecting the arrest of a burglary suspect, Trooper Green uses force to subdue the suspect who is resisting arrest. According to procedure, Trooper Green should notify
(A) the duty captain.
(B) the post command desk officer.
(C) the patrol supervisor.
(D) the detective on duty.

45. According to procedure, which of the following would be least correct?
   (A) A prisoner's funds should be counted and returned by the arresting trooper.
   (B) Unlawfully carried property should always be removed from a prisoner.
   (C) Evidence should always be removed from a prisoner.
   (D) Personal property should never be removed from a prisoner.

46. Tom Banks has been arrested for the sale of narcotics. At the time of his arrest, Banks is under the influence of narcotics. He asks the arresting trooper if he can make a phone call. The arresting trooper would be most correct if he
   (A) told Banks that he could make the calls only when Banks becomes sober.
   (B) told the prisoner to give up his rights because he is incapacitated.
   (C) made the calls for Banks.
   (D) allowed him to make the call despite the fact he was incapacitated.

47. An 18-year-old suspect has been arrested by Trooper Hall. The trooper attempts to notify the prisoner's friends or relatives but is unsuccessful. In this situation, the trooper should notify
   (A) the duty captain.
   (B) the Missing Persons Squad.
   (C) the post command desk officer.
   (D) the patrol supervisor.

48. Pat Walker is arrested while acting in a deranged manner caused by a drug overdose. The arresting trooper is informed that an ambulance is not available. In this instance, the arresting trooper
   (A) should deliver the prisoner immediately to the hospital in a patrol car.
   (B) bring the prisoner to the post command.
   (C) request the response of the patrol supervisor.
   (D) make a second call for an ambulance.

DIRECTIONS: In each of questions 49–53 you will be given four choices. Three of the choices, A, B, and C, contain a written statement. You are to evaluate the statement in each choice and select the statement that is most accurately and clearly written. If all or none of the three written statements is accurately and clearly written, you are to select choice D.

49. According to the instructions, evaluate the following statements.
    (A) During roll call the sergeant made an illusion to yesterday's robbery.
    (B) We sat altogether at the convention.
    (C) He is the principle suspect.
    (D) All or none is accurate.

50. According to the instructions, evaluate the following statements.
    (A) Their tired and should not be questioned any more.
    (B) The officer never looked there.
    (C) Whose in charge here?
    (D) All or none is accurate.

51. According to the instructions, evaluate the following statements.
    (A) The highway patrol officers accepted Tom from the roster.
    (B) After a close vote the new amendment to their constitution was adapted by the members of the organization.
    (C) Because the hat was too loose, he looked sloppy.
    (D) All or none is accurate.

52. According to the instructions, evaluate the following statements.
    (A) Do you know who stole the jewels?
    (B) The court went too far this time.
    (C) This time you're not right.
    (D) All or none is accurate.

53. According to the instructions, evaluate the following statements.
    (A) She was found hiding in the attic between two boxes.
    (B) A number of suspects was questioned.
    (C) The number of troopers assigned are significant.
    (D) All or none is accurate.

Answer questions 54–57 based solely on the information that follows:

FELONY ARRESTS MADE BY TROOPERS ASSIGNED TO THE BALDWIN POST COMMAND

Trooper	Last Year	This Year
Marks	20	18
Baker	10	12
Rivers	26	14
Walls	17	15
Coils	18	20
Cuffs	19	14
Tock	24	15
Bell	16	12

54. Which of the following troopers had the largest percentage increase in felony arrests when comparing this year's to last year's arrest record?
(A) Marks
(B) Baker
(C) Coils
(D) Bell

55. Which of the following troopers had the largest percentage decrease in felony arrests when comparing this year to last year?
(A) Bell
(B) Tock
(C) Cuffs
(D) Walls

56. If all the felony arrests were added up and a comparison made between this year and last year, it would be most correct to state there has been
(A) a 20% decrease.
(B) a 25% decrease.
(C) a 30% decrease.
(D) less than a 10% decrease.

57. Which of the following troopers had the greatest number of felony arrests when considering this year and last year?
   (A) Marks
   (B) Baker
   (C) Walls
   (D) Cuffs

DIRECTIONS: Answer questions 58–65 based solely on the following narrative and the form STATE TROOPER INJURY REPORT, which is found after the narrative. Some of the captions on the form may be numbered; some may not. The boxes are not necessarily consecutively numbered.

On May 5, 19xx, at 1040 hours, State Trooper Tom Powers, shield number 957, of the Outer Ridge Post, Troop C, Division 10, was injured in the line of duty. The details are recorded under Department Injury Case Number 1812 and are as follows:

At about 1040 hours on May 5, 19xx, Trooper Powers, performing tour 0800x1600 hours and assigned to Sector Charlie covering the American Amateur Soccer Championship match, observed two males fighting. Trooper Powers approached the two males and observed one of the males, later identified as Don Kites, a male white, 35 years old of 102 Grand Avenue, kicking the other male, later identified as Jose Cruz, a male Hispanic, 30 years old of 156 High Street.

Officer Powers in attempting to separate them was struck several times in both eyes by both males, who were attempting to continue the dispute, which apparently stemmed from the results of the soccer match.

Trooper Frank Marks, shield number 493, responded to the scene as a result of a call over the portable radio of "Officer needs assistance" and aided in subduing both males and restoring order to the area by dispersing the large crowd that had gathered.

Officer Powers was removed to St. Helen's Hospital by ambulance 1906 and treated by Dr. Foot who diagnosed the injury as cuts and bruises of both eyes. Officer Powers returned to his post and remained on duty for the remainder of his tour. The incident was investigated by Officer Powers's supervisor, Sergeant May Short, shield number 1492, who was also the Post Commander. Sergeant Short interviewed a witness, Mr. Tom Cans, a soccer fan who was on his way home from the soccer match at the time of the incident. As a result of the interview of Mr. Cans and other investigative efforts, Sergeant Short determined that no misconduct existed on the part of any troopers. Mr. Kites and Mr. Cruz were arrested for assaulting an officer, arrest numbers 2001 and 2002, respectively, and will be arraigned on May 6.

TROOPER INJURY REPORT

Injured Employee Information

Rank_____(1)_____Name_____(4)_____

                                        (Last)   (First)

Shield#____(2)___ Soc/Sec #____ (3)___ Assignment____(5)__

Date of Birth___(6)___Ht.____(7)___Wt.____(8)____

Check One: [ ] On____(9)____ [ ] Off____(10)____Duty

- -

When Injury Occurred

Date:____(11)____ Time:____(12)____

- -

Where Injury Occurred

Post No.____(13)____ Address ____(14)____

Check One [ ] Indoors____(15)____ [ ] Outdoors____(15A)____

- -

Description Of Injury

Dept. Injury Case Number_____(16)_____

Member Remained On Duty? Circle One:____(17)___Yes / No___

Treated By_____(18)_____Diagnosis ____(19)____

Injury Was To: Check one_____(20)____

[ ] Head [ ] Arms [ ] Legs [ ] Torso [ ] Eyes [ ] Feet

[ ] Hands [ ] Other

Was Trooper Assaulted? Circle One:____(21)____Yes / No

Type Of Assault_____Circle One____(22)____

Cut / Stab / Shot / Bite / Kick / Struck by object / Other /

- -

Injured Employee's Account Of Incident:

_____(23)_____

_____

_____

- -

Witness (if any) Account Of Incident:

Name_____(24)_____

Address_____(24A)_____

- -

Details Of Supervisor's Investigation Of Incident:

_____(25)_____

_____

_____

Signature of:

Supervisor_____(26)_____ Shield #_____(27)_____

Injured Employee_____(28)_____

Post Commander_____(29)_____ Shield #_____(30)_____

58. Which of the following should be entered in caption number 1?
    (A) Sergeant
    (B) Doctor
    (C) Trooper
    (D) Post Commander

59. In which of the following captions should the name Foot be entered?
    (A) 4
    (B) 18
    (C) 28
    (D) 29

60. It would be most appropriate to enter information about being injured in both eyes in which of the following captions?
    (A) 20
    (B) 21
    (C) 22
    (D) 26

61. The entries in which of the following captions would be identical?
    (A) 26 and 30
    (B) 28 and 29
    (C) 27 and 28
    (D) 26 and 29

62. The fact that the employee who was injured remained on duty should be entered in which of the following captions?
    (A) 9
    (B) 10
    (C) 17
    (D) 19

63. There is enough information provided to complete which of the following captions accurately?
    (A) 3
    (B) 5
    (C) 6
    (D) 7

64. It would be most appropriate to enter the number 1812 in which of the following captions?
    (A) 2
    (B) 13
    (C) 16
    (D) 30

65. Which of the following entries would correctly appear twice on the form?
    (A) 957
    (B) 1492
    (C) 1906
    (D) 493

Answer questions 66–73 based solely on the following data.

INFORMATION FOR TROOPERS ON PATROL

Post	Location	Suspected Condition
Post 3	*229 Elm St.	Sale of narcotics
Post 5	*453 Elm St.	Sale of narcotics
Post 7	*125 Main St.	**Sale of narcotics
Post 9	*215 Park St.	Illegal gambling
Post 15	Elm St., 10–11 Aves.	***Prostitution
Post 19	110–118 Oak St.	Disorderly youths
Post 20	321–329 Main Ave.	**Sale of narcotics
Post 24	Oak St., 3–9 Aves.	Auto theft
Post 27	Pine St., 2–14 Aves.	+Drag racing
Post 29	Elm St. & 14 Ave.	++Carjacking
Post 33	Main St., 16–18 Aves.	**Sale of firearms
Post 35	*432 Main Ave.	Sale of narcotics
Post 38	Pine St., 3–5 Aves.	Prostitution
Post 40	919 Elm St.	Sale of narcotics
Post 42	545 Main St.	Sale

LEGEND

  * = Inside location.
 ** = Exercise caution, suspects may be armed.
*** = Arrests of prostitutes are to be made only after conferral
       with a supervisor.
  + = Notify Auto Squad before taking any action if condition is
       observed.
 ++ = Fixed Post, assigned trooper must notify supervisor before
       leaving post for any reason.

Answer questions 66–73 based on the preceding data.

66. It is suspected that street sales of narcotics are taking place on
    (A) Post 7.
    (B) Post 20.
    (C) Post 35.
    (D) Posts 7, 20, and 35.

67. Before leaving post, a trooper assigned to Post 29 must
    (A) notify a supervisor.
    (B) be properly relieved.
    (C) obtain permission from the desk officer.
    (D) notify the radio dispatcher.

68. Armed suspects would most likely be encountered
    (A) only on Post 7.
    (B) only on Post 20.
    (C) only on Post 33.
    (D) on Posts 7, 20, and 33.

69. A trooper assigned to Post 27 who observes drag racing must
    (A) notify a supervisor.
    (B) notify the Auto Squad.
    (C) arrest those responsible.
    (D) obtain immediate assistance.

70. Which of the following is the most accurate statement?
    (A) Street sales of narcotics is suspected on Post 3.
    (B) Street gambling is suspected on Post 9.
    (C) Street firearms sales is suspected on Post 33.
    (D) Street sales of narcotics is suspected on Post 35.

71. Most of the posts with suspected sale of narcotics conditions are located on
    (A) Main Street.
    (B) Elm Street.
    (C) Pine Street.
    (D) Oak Street.

72. The sale of firearms is suspected on
    (A) Post 3.
    (B) Post 20.
    (C) Post 33.
    (D) Post 40.

73. On which of the following posts is suspected sale of heroin taking place?
    (A) Post 3
    (B) Post 33
    (C) Post 40
    (D) It cannot be determined from the data.

74. The unauthorized use by a trooper of any firearm while on or off duty is prohibited and will result in disciplinary action being taken. Joe, who is a trooper, used his weapon while on duty. Mary, who is also a trooper, used her weapon while off duty. It is correct to say that
    (A) Joe will definitely receive disciplinary action.
    (B) Mary will definitely receive disciplinary action.
    (C) Neither Joe nor Mary could receive disciplinary action.
    (D) Both Joe and Mary may or may not receive disciplinary action.

75. While on patrol a trooper is informed by a reputable citizen of a fire that is burning in a nearby nursing home. The trooper's first action should be to
    (A) rush to the scene of the fire and begin evacuation of the residents.
    (B) insist that the citizen informant produce satisfactory identification.
    (C) notify the fire department.
    (D) verify the citizen's information.

76. Fingerprints have tremendous value as evidence chiefly because
    (A) no two people have the same fingerprints.
    (B) everyone has fingerprints.
    (C) criminals always leave their fingerprints behind.
    (D) fingerprint evidence is always admissible at a criminal trial.

77. When it is deemed necessary at any time to search the person of any on-duty state police employee, such search shall be made by a police supervisor. Refusal of any such employee to be searched shall constitute grounds for possible dismissal. This means that
    (A) state police employees can always be searched.
    (B) any state police employee can search another employee.
    (C) state police employees who refuse to be searched may be fired.
    (D) state police employees often bring contraband into troop headquarters.

78. A trooper may make an arrest of a person for a felony, such as an escape or an escape attempt, when he/she has reasonable cause to believe such person has committed a felony. But, a trooper may make an arrest of a person for a misdemeanor, such as a simple assault or petit larceny, or for a violation, such as harassment, only when he/she has reasonable cause to believe such person has committed the misdemeanor or violation in his/her presence. Of the following, which situation does not violate this rule?
    (A) A trooper arrests a prisoner for an escape attempt, even though the trooper was not present when the attempt was made.
    (B) A trooper arrests a prisoner for a simple assault, even though the trooper was not present when the assault occurred.
    (C) A trooper arrests a prisoner for a petit larceny, even though the trooper was not present when the larceny occurred.
    (D) A trooper arrests a prisoner for harassment, even though the trooper was not present when the harassment occurred.

79. The prevalence of drugs in our society is a major cause of our crime problem. Based on this statement, we could conclude that one of the main causes of crime is the
    (A) widespread availability of drugs.
    (B) cheap cost of drugs.
    (C) role of drugs in the commission of violent crime.
    (D) need for people to obtain money to purchase drugs.

80. Statistics indicate that persons who become career criminals have average intelligence but have a below average level of formal education. Based on this statement, it is most reasonable to conclude that
    (A) there seems to be a relationship between criminal careers and the level of formal education.
    (B) stupid people are responsible for most criminal acts.
    (C) criminals are actually smarter than the average citizen.
    (D) people with above average intelligence do not commit crimes.

81. One frequent and continuous argument against capital punishment is the disproportionate infliction of capital punishment against minorities. This means most nearly that
    (A) the death penalty represents cruel and unusual punishment.
    (B) the death penalty discriminates against minorities.
    (C) only minorities receive the death penalty.
    (D) the death penalty does not deter crime.

Answer questions 82–89 solely on the basis of the following legal definitions. Do not base your answers on any other knowledge of the law you may have. You may refer to the definitions when answering the questions.

NOTE: The perpetrators in the following definitions are referred to as *he,* but they actually refer to either gender. However, when the male and/or female gender is a factor in defining an offense or legal action, such distinction shall be made by the specific use of both pronouns *he* and *she.*

A person commits murder in the first degree when with intent to cause the death of another person, he causes the death of such person and

1. the victim is a police officer, or correctional employee, performing his official duties, and the perpetrator is more than 18 years of age at the time of the commission of the offense, or

2. the perpetrator is in prison serving a life sentence and the perpetrator is more than 18 years of age at the time of the commission of the offense.

A person commits murder in the second degree when he intends to cause the death of one person and causes the death of such person or another; or under circumstances evincing a depraved indifference to human life, he recklessly causes the death of another; or during the commission of a serious offense such as a robbery, rape, or kidnapping one of the participants in the offense causes the death of a person other than a participant.

A person commits manslaughter in the first degree when, with intent to cause serious physical injury to another person, he causes death to such person or a third person; or during the performance of an illegal abortional act on a pregnant female, a person causes the death of the pregnant female who is 24 weeks or more pregnant.

A person commits manslaughter in the second degree when a person intentionally aids another person to commit suicide.

An abortional act is any act that is done to cause the miscarriage of a female.

An abortional act is not considered legal unless it is done by a physician to a pregnant female before she is 24 weeks pregnant, or unless it is done by a physician anytime to a female to save her life.

A person commits abortion when he performs an illegal abortional act on a female who is 24 weeks or more pregnant and causes her miscarriage.

A female commits self-abortion when being pregnant for 24 weeks or more she submits to, or commits, an illegal abortional act on herself that causes her miscarriage.

82. For a proper charge of murder in the first degree
   (A) the victim must be a police officer.
   (B) the victim must be a correction officer.
   (C) the perpetrator must be over 18 years of age at the time of the offense.
   (D) the perpetrator must be serving a life sentence at the time of the offense.

83. Mr. Jay is 80 years old and is angry at Mr. Burns. Jay sees Burns who is 72 years old making a pass at Jay's wife who is 78 years old while they are all having coffee in Jay's home. Jay takes a gun from a desk drawer and aims it at Burns and fires intending to kill Burns. Jay however misses and strikes and kills his wife. In this instance, the most proper charge against Jay would be
   (A) murder in the first degree.
   (B) murder in the second degree.
   (C) manslaughter in the first degree.
   (D) manslaughter in the second degree.

84. Dr. Tubs gives Ms. Green, who is in excellent health and who is 30 weeks pregnant, a liquid to drink. The liquid is intended to cause Ms. Green to have a miscarriage. Ms. Green willingly drinks the liquid and as a result has a miscarriage. In this instance, Dr. Tubs has committed
    (A) no crime since Ms. Green willingly drank the liquid.
    (B) murder in the second degree.
    (C) manslaughter in the first degree.
    (D) abortion.

85. In the situation described in question 84, the actions of Ms. Green would properly be classified as
    (A) no crime since she followed Dr. Tubs' orders.
    (B) abortion.
    (C) self abortion.
    (D) manslaughter in the second degree.

86. In the situation described in question 84, if as a result of the actions of Dr. Tubs, Ms. Green were to die, then Dr. Tubs should be charged with
    (A) murder in the second degree.
    (B) manslaughter in the first degree.
    (C) manslaughter in the second degree.
    (D) self abortion.

87. Pat wrongly believes he is suffering from an incurable disease and will die in 1 week. Pat asks Don to lend him his pistol so that Pat can kill himself. Don complies with Pat's request and lends Pat his pistol. Pat kills himself. In this instance, Don has committed
    (A) no offense since Pat initiated the request for the pistol.
    (B) murder in the second degree.
    (C) manslaughter in the first degree.
    (D) manslaughter in the second degree.

88. Knuckles is an enforcer for an organized crime gang. The boss of the gang orders Knuckles to beat up Ray who has not paid money owed to the gang for gambling debts. Knuckles beats up Ray with a baseball bat. Although Knuckles intended only to cause Ray some serious physical injuries, he actually kills Ray. In this instance, Knuckles has committed
   (A) murder in the first degree.
   (B) murder in the second degree.
   (C) manslaughter in the first degree.
   (D) manslaughter in the second degree.

89. Ray is angry at Tab and follows Tab home. Ray takes a gun from his pocket and, intending to kill Tab, shoots at Tab. Instead of striking Tab, the bullet strikes and kills Police Officer Baker, who is on duty and directing traffic at the time. If Ray is 19 years old at the time of the incident, then the most serious charge against Ray is
   (A) murder in the first degree.
   (B) murder in the second degree.
   (C) manslaughter in the first degree.
   (D) manslaughter in the second degree.

DIRECTIONS: Answer questions 90–94 solely on the basis of the following map.

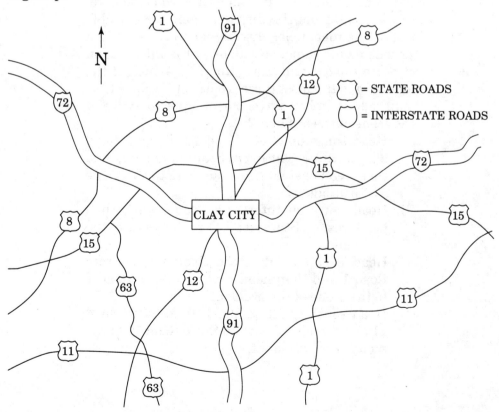

90. State Trooper Matthew and Highway Patrol Officer Patrick must meet to confer on a joint arrest they made last week. If State Trooper Matthew is heading in his patrol car north on State Road 12 approaching the intersection with State Road 63, and Highway Patrol Officer Patrick is heading in his patrol car north on State Road 1 approaching the intersection with Interstate Road 72, then the officers would be most likely to intersect if
    (A) State Trooper Matthew continued to head north and Highway Patrol Officer Patrick headed south.
    (B) both officers headed west.
    (C) State Trooper Matthew headed south and Highway Patrol Officer Patrick continued to head north.
    (D) both officers continue to head north.

91. Based on an examination of the map, which of the following statements is most correct?
    (A) State Roads 8 and 15 do not intersect.
    (B) State Roads 11 and 15 do not intersect.
    (C) State Roads 1 and 63 do not intersect.
    (D) State Roads 12 and 11 do not intersect.

92. State Trooper Virginia Herman is attending a community meeting in Clay City when she receives a call from the dispatcher on her portable radio. The dispatcher directs her to respond to a serious motor vehicle accident at the intersection of State Road 1 and State Road 11. Which of the following is the most direct route for Trooper Herman to take in her patrol car in order to arrive at the scene of the accident?
    (A) Head south on State Road 12 to State Road 63, continue south on State Road 63, and then head east on State Road 11 to the scene of the accident.
    (B) Head south on Interstate Road 91 and then head west on State Road 11 to the scene of the accident.
    (C) Head east on Interstate Road 72 to State Road 1 and then head south on State Road 1 to the scene of the accident.
    (D) Head south on State Road 91 to State Road 11 and then head east on State Road 11 to the scene of the accident.

93. State Trooper Jackie Bands is directly behind a stolen vehicle that she is pursuing. The vehicle is attempting to reach State Road 15 by heading west on State Road 8. As the stolen vehicle is approaching State Road 12, Trooper Bands calls for assistance and asks that other troopers in the area assist in setting up a roadblock. Which of the following troopers would be least likely to be able to assist Trooper Bands based on each individual trooper's present location?
   (A) Trooper Jason is currently heading north on State Road 1 after passing the intersection with State Road 12.
   (B) Trooper James is currently heading south on Interstate Road 91 approaching State Road 1.
   (C) Trooper Hanks is currently heading south on State Road 63 approaching State Road 12.
   (D) Trooper Nicole is currently heading west on Interstate Road 72 approaching State Road 15.

94. Based on an examination of the map, which of the following statements is least correct?
   (A) State Road 1 intersects with six other roads.
   (B) All roads intersect with at least one other road.
   (C) State Road 1 intersects at least three of the same roads that State Road 12 intersects.
   (D) State Road 8 intersects with more roads than State Road 11.

DIRECTIONS: Answer questions 95–100 on the basis of the following sketches. The model face, the one appearing above the dotted line, is a sketch of a person who is wanted. Of the four comparison faces, the ones appearing below the dotted line, one of them is the way the model face looked after changing appearance. You are to assume that no surgical alteration of the wanted person's face has occurred. You are to select the face that is most likely that of the wanted person.

95.

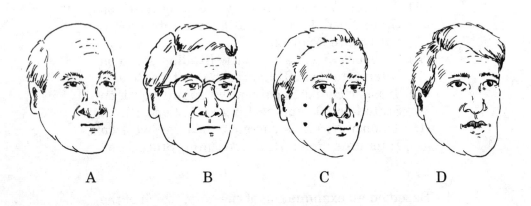

A   B   C   D

96.

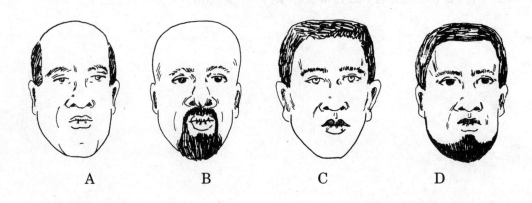

A   B   C   D

97.

A   B   C   D

98.

A   B   C   D

99.

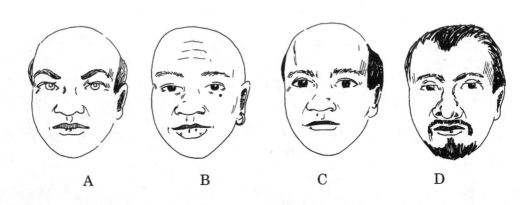

A   B   C   D

100.

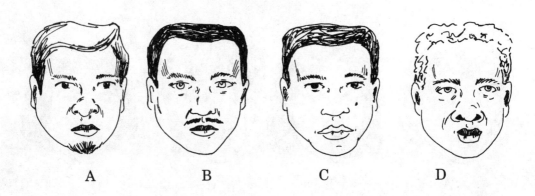

A   B   C   D

ANSWER KEY

1. **B**	21. **A**	41. **C**	61. **D**	81. **B**
2. **B**	22. **C**	42. **B**	62. **C**	82. **C**
3. **C**	23. **D**	43. **A**	63. **B**	83. **B**
4. **C**	24. **C**	44. **B**	64. **C**	84. **D**
5. **B**	25. **B**	45. **D**	65. **B**	85. **C**
6. **B**	26. **C**	46. **C**	66. **B**	86. **B**
7. **C**	27. **B**	47. **B**	67. **A**	87. **D**
8. **C**	28. **A**	48. **C**	68. **D**	88. **C**
9. **D**	29. **B**	49. **D**	69. **B**	89. **B**
10. **D**	30. **C**	50. **B**	70. **C**	90. **D**
11. **A**	31. **B**	51. **C**	71. **B**	91. **C**
12. **C**	32. **A**	52. **D**	72. **C**	92. **C**
13. **B**	33. **C**	53. **A**	73. **D**	93. **C**
14. **A**	34. **B**	54. **B**	74. **D**	94. **D**
15. **B**	35. **B**	55. **B**	75. **C**	95. **B**
16. **C**	36. **D**	56. **A**	76. **A**	96. **D**
17. **A**	37. **B**	57. **A**	77. **C**	97. **D**
18. **A**	38. **C**	58. **C**	78. **A**	98. **C**
19. **A**	39. **A**	59. **B**	79. **A**	99. **C**
20. **C**	40. **B**	60. **A**	80. **A**	100. **B**

Diagnostic Chart

INSTRUCTIONS: After you score your test, complete the following chart by inserting in the column captioned "Your Number Correct" the number of questions you answered correctly in each of the ten sections of the test. Then compare your score in each section with the ratings in the column captioned "Scale." Finally, to correct your weaknesses follow the instructions found after the chart.

SECTION	QUESTION NUMBER	AREA	YOUR NUMBER CORRECT	SCALE
1	1–8	Memory (8 questions)		8 Right—Excellent 6–7 Right—Good 5 Right—Fair Under 5 Right—Poor
2	9–28	Reading Comprehension (20 questions)		20 Right—Excellent 18–19 Right—Good 16–17 Right—Fair Under 16 Right—Poor

3	29–48	Applying State Police Procedures (20 questions)	20 Right—Excellent 18–19 Right—Good 16–17 Right—Fair Under 16 Right—Poor
4	49–57	Verbal and Math (9 questions)	9 Right—Excellent 7–8 Right—Good 6 Right—Fair Under 6 Right—Poor
5	58–65	State Police Forms (8 questions)	8 Right—Excellent 6–7 Right—Good 5 Right—Fair Under 5 Right—Poor
6	66–73	Interpreting Data (8 questions)	8 Right—Excellent 6–7 Right—Good 5 Right—Fair Under 5 Right—Poor
7	74–81	Judgment and Reasoning (8 questions)	8 Right—Excellent 6–7 Right—Good 5 Right—Fair Under 5 Right—Poor
8	82–89	Legal Definitions (8 questions)	8 Right—Excellent 6–7 Right—Good 5 Right—Fair Under 5 Right—Poor
9	90–94	Traffic Directions (5 questions)	5 Right—Excellent 4 Right—Good 3 Right—Fair Under 3 Right—Poor
10	95–100	Matching Sketches (6 questions)	6 Right—Excellent 5 Right—Good 4 Right—Fair Under 4 Right—Poor

How to correct weaknesses:

1. If you are weak in Section 1, concentrate on Chapter 6.
2. If you are weak in Section 2, concentrate on Chapter 4.
3. If you are weak in Section 3, concentrate on Chapter 9.
4. If you are weak in Section 4, concentrate on Chapter 5.
5. If you are weak in Section 5, concentrate on Chapter 7.
6. If you are weak in Section 6, concentrate on Chapter 8.
7. If you are weak in Section 7, concentrate on Chapter 10.
8. If you are weak in Section 8, concentrate on Chapter 11.
9. If you are weak in Section 9, concentrate on Chapter 13.
10. If you are weak in Section 10, concentrate on Chapter 12.

Note: Consider yourself weak in a section if you receive other than an excellent rating in it.

Answer Explanations

1. **B**   Ms. Larkin's first name, Joan, was used only once in the entire passage. Yet, names of victims are "who" questions that must be remembered.

2. **B**   Joan Larkin was described as being a female, white, who is 36 years old.

3. **C**   The Togs Clothing Store is located at 6555 Madison Avenue.

4. **C**   Ms. Larkin is the manager of the store.

5. **B**   Even though C may seem like a more logical choice, the passage very clearly stated that he kind of looked like a cop because his hair was short.

6. **B**   Choice A is the shield number of the bogus shield shown by the rapist. The other choices, though wrong, are very similar to the answer.

7. **C**   Once again, we remind you that, if a weapon is mentioned in a memory story or depicted in a memory illustration, that weapon will be the subject of at least one question.

8. **C**   As soon as the rapist fled the store, Ms. Larkin called her fiancee, Don Wood, who then notified the state police.

9. **D**   Most ordinary citizens believe that juvenile inmates are not any different from adult inmates and that the only difference is age. Nothing could be farther from the truth. While both groups of criminals can be held to know the difference between right and wrong, juvenile offenders often lack an appreciation (understanding) of the effects (results) of their crimes on the rest of the community. At times an examiner may change the words in an answer choice slightly, but the choice still reflects the meaning or intent of the passage.

10. **D**   Choices B and C are incorrect statements in that juveniles do see how criminals are treated in prison on television and are told some things about prison life by neighborhood ex-convicts. Choice A is mentioned in the passage, but the main reason that juveniles do not see the risks of punishment to themselves is as stated in choice D.

11. **A**   The hope of such programs is that, by seeing what prison life is really like, some change in attitude will occur in the juvenile. Although such programs are not seen as the cure-all for rising

juvenile crime nor as a replacement for the role of parents or educational institutions, progress is being made.

12. **C** At 1:35 P.M., although the trooper believed the two males might be escaped prisoners, she wasn't sure so she did not make an arrest.

13. **B** Don't let what you think or assume is going on influence your choice of answers. It clearly states in the passage that the trooper decided to follow the males in the first place because they were acting suspiciously.

14. **A** Test writers often make it necessary to relate information from one part of the passage to another. That is what happened here. The suspect with the gun had on a black jacket. Earlier in the passage it stated that the suspect with the black jacket was a white male.

15. **B** Fearing for the victim's safety, the trooper waited for the crime to be completed before taking any action.

16. **C** The police sergeant felt that the trooper should have called for backup assistance.

17. **A** The first paragraph states that commanding officers have to be notified of off-duty arrests within 1 hour of the arrest. The arrest was made at 1:55 P.M.

18. **A** Felonies are the most serious of the two categories of crime.

19. **A** The present-day distinction between a felony and misdemeanor in the United States is usually based on the length of the sentence imposed.

20. **C** Convictions for either felonies or misdemeanors can result in the assessment of a fine.

21. **A** By far, the component that receives the most funding is the police.

22. **C** The other three components are supervised by the courts.

23. **D** A major problem for the overall system is that each of the four components acts independently of one another.

24. **C** A person missing 16 hours is no less missing than the same person will be in 24 hours.

25. **B** Choice B is found in the second paragraph of the passage.

26. **C** The public's current feeling is, as stated in the passage, actually

the result of a heightened sense of awareness on the part of the public of an already existing problem.

27. **B** Complaints can involve either improper or unlawful acts. But, they must relate to the business of a state police agency. Choices C and D are not mentioned in the rule.

28. **A** A complaint shall be thoroughly investigated by the supervisor to whom it is referred. If the condition complained of actually exists, it shall be corrected, and steps shall be taken to prevent its recurrence.

29. **B** Requests for gun traces concerning contraband weapons will be made to the Alcohol, Tobacco, and Firearms Bureau through the Ballistics Unit. The Ballistics Unit will then forward a report of the results to the requesting trooper and the Intelligence Division.

30. **C** Safety is always important; hence, the first step is to unload the firearm.

31. **B** It would not be a good idea to mark a spent bullet on its side since there might be ballistic marking there from the firearm that discharged the bullet. As stated in the procedure, it should be marked on its base.

32. **A** As stated in the procedure, it is the job of the trooper concerned.

33. **C** The trooper shall affix a security lead seal if no serial number is distinguishable. Without a distinguishable serial number, its future identification while in police custody is made more difficult. The placing of a security lead seal helps in identifying it in the future.

34. **B** Choice A is incorrect because a trooper recovering a firearm wanted on alarm will not cancel the alarm. Cancellation of alarms will be made only by the Stolen Property Section after examination of firearms by the Ballistics Unit. Choice B is correct.

35. **B** Choice C is incorrect because the Ballistics Unit examines firearms. Choices A and D are incorrect because, although the Stolen Property Section will be notified, the trooper recovering the firearm will notify Stolen Property Section if the firearm is seized in connection with an arrest or an investigation is required, and in addition has a distinguishable serial number.

36. **D** The procedure directs that the trooper recovering a firearm prepare two copies of a PISTOL INDEX CARD for each handgun with serial number. Hence, if a firearm without a serial number is recovered, there would be no need for two copies of a PISTOL INDEX

CARD to be prepared. Therefore, they would not be required to be presented to the post command desk officer.

37. **B** The procedure requires that the post command desk officer be notified. It would seem somewhat logical that possibly the Ballistics Unit should be notified for its help in such a situation. However, in procedure-type questions, the answer must be selected based on what is contained in the procedure.

38. **C** The statements in choices A, B, and D are right out of the procedure. Choice C is incorrect because the proper mix is a solution of one part household bleach with ten parts water.

39. **A** Choices B and C are incorrect because bleach dilutions should be performed only in a sink, not a urinal or toilet, because they sometimes contain chemical deodorizers. Choice D is incorrect because a mixture of bleach and water will cause damage if used to clean uniforms.

40. **B** The first action for the trooper involved is to make a notification to the post command desk officer.

41. **C** According to the procedure, the Exposure Report number is to be entered in both the Post Command Log and the memo book of the trooper involved.

42. **B** After properly handcuffing the prisoner, the next step the trooper should take immediately is to field search the prisoner.

43. **A** According to procedure, when an off-duty trooper makes an arrest, a determination of the validity of the off-duty arrest should be made by the duty captain.

44. **B** The trooper should notify the post command desk officer if force was used to effect the arrest.

45. **D** Choices A, B, and C are as stated in the procedure. However, personal property, except clothing, may be removed if the prisoner is intoxicated or unconscious. Therefore, choice D is incorrect.

46. **C** After making an arrest, the arresting trooper should make the telephone calls a prisoner is entitled to make if the prisoner is incapacitated by alcohol or drugs.

47. **B** The arresting trooper is required to notify the prisoner's relatives or friends if the prisoner is under 19 years of age. If the trooper is unable to make this notification, the trooper shall notify the Missing Persons Squad.

48. **C** Under these circumstances the trooper is required to request the response of the patrol supervisor if an ambulance is not immediately available. It is the supervisor who will determine if the prisoner should be removed to the hospital by patrol car or await the arrival of an ambulance. The prisoner is not to be brought to a state police facility.

49. **D** Choice A is incorrect because the word *allusion* to indicate a casual mentioning should have been used instead of *illusion.* Choice B is incorrect because *all together,* which means in a group, should have been used instead of *altogether,* which means totally. Choice C is incorrect because *principal,* which means the main person, should have been used in place of *principle,* which means a basic truth.

50. **B** Choice A is incorrect because *they're* to indicate *they are* should have been used. Choice C is incorrect because *who's* to express *who is* should have been used. Choice B is accurately and clearly stated.

51. **C** Choice A is incorrect because *excepted* to indicate being excluded should have been used instead of *accepted.* Choice B is incorrect because *adopted,* which means to take as one's own, should have been used. Choice C is clearly and accurately stated.

52. **D** All the choices are clearly and accurately stated.

53. **A** *A number* indicates something plural, whereas *the number* indicates something singular. Therefore, *were* should have been used in choice B and *is* should have been used in choice C. Choice A is accurately and clearly stated.

54. **B** Choices A and D can be eliminated because the arrest activity of both troopers decreased. Percentage increase is found by finding the space (difference) between the two numbers being examined and the dividing by the older or previously existing number. Choice C represents about an 11% increase ($20 - 18 = \frac{2}{18} = 0.11 = 11\%$). Choice B or Trooper Baker's arrest activity increased 20% ($12 - 10 = \frac{2}{10} = 0.2$ or 20%).

55. **B**

	Last Year	This Year	Difference	% Decrease
Bell	16	12	4	$\frac{4}{16} = 25\%$
Tock	24	15	9	$\frac{9}{24} = 37.5\%$
Cuffs	19	14	5	$\frac{5}{19} = 26.3\%$
Walls	17	15	2	$\frac{2}{17} = 11.8\%$

56.	**A**	The number of felony arrests this year was 120 compared with 150 last year. A decrease obviously occurred and the percentage decrease was 20% ($150 - 120 = \frac{30}{150} = \frac{1}{5}$ or 0.20 or 20%). Choice B would mistakenly be selected if instead of dividing by the old or previously existing number, this year's number or more current number of 120 had been used to divide ($\frac{30}{120} = \frac{1}{4} = 0.25 = 25\%$).

57.	**A**

Marks had 20 + 18 = 38

Baker had 10 + 12 = 22

Walls had 17 + 15 = 32

Cuffs had 19 + 14 = 33

58.	**C**	The rank of the employee who was injured should be entered in caption 1. In this instance, a trooper was injured while breaking up a fight.

59.	**B**	Foot is the name of the doctor who treated the injury and should be entered in caption 18.

60.	**A**	Caption 20 records which part of the body was injured, which in this case was the eyes.

61.	**D**	Caption 26 asks for the signature of the supervisor, and caption 29 asks for the signature of the Post Commander. However, they are the same person, May Short. Thus the entries should be identical.

62.	**C**	Caption 17 requires that either *yes* or *no* be circled to indicate if the trooper (employee) remained on duty. Remember that when you are given questions that ask about "which of the following captions . . . ," it is not necessary to examine the entire form. You should focus on the captions suggested by the choices to make your selection. Choices A and B were a little tricky in that they referred to captions concerning whether the trooper was injured while on or off duty. However, the question dealt with whether the trooper remained on duty *after* being injured.

63.	**B**	From the narrative the assignment of Trooper Powers can be determined. This allows caption 5 to be accurately completed. But there is no information available concerning captions 3, 6, and 7, the officer's social security number (Soc/Sec #), date of birth, and height (Ht.), respectively.

64.	**C**	The number 1812 is the Department Injury Case Number, which should be entered in caption 16.

65. **B** The number 1492 is the shield number of the supervisor and also the Post Commander because they are the same person, Sergeant May Short. Therefore, 1492 would correctly appear in both captions 27 and 30.

66. **B** Posts 7 and 35 are sites of suspected inside drug sales (not in the street) as indicated by the single asterisk and as explained in the legend.

67. **A** As indicated by the double plus sign in the legend, a trooper assigned to Post 29 must notify the supervisor before leaving post for any reason.

68. **D** If you jumped on choice A as the answer, you probably made the mistake of not reading all the choices. Also, be careful of the word *only*. In this case, double asterisks indicate armed suspects on Posts 7, 20, and 33.

69. **B** The single plus sign next to the condition statement for Post 27, as explained in the Legend, means that the trooper must notify the Auto Squad before taking any action if drag racing is observed.

70. **C** The information about Posts 3, 9, and 35 all contain single asterisks indicating inside locations.

71. **B** If you missed this one, it was because you were careless. Posts 20 and 35 are on Main Avenue and not Main Street.

72. **C** Don't look for tricks when they are not there. And, don't make careless mistakes.

73. **D** Nothing in the data specifically mentions heroin. You cannot make assumptions when answering questions when the directions tell you to answer the questions solely on the basis of the information supplied.

74. **D** Not enough information is given to state definitely one way or the other whether Joe or Mary will receive disciplinary action. The missing information is whether they used their weapons in an authorized or unauthorized manner.

75. **C** In these situations time is of the essence. The fire department must be notified. If the trooper subsequently determines that the information is faulty, an appropriate follow-up notification can be made.

76. **A** Hopefully you ruled out choices C and D because of the word *always*. Fingerprints are valuable as evidence because everyone has a distinct fingerprint pattern.

77. **C** Only on-duty employees can be searched, and only supervisors can do the searching. Choice D may be true, but it cannot be assumed from the rule. Note the use of the limiting word *may* in the correct answer. There is a world of difference between saying employees must be fired and employees may be fired.

78. **A** According to the information given, an escape or an attempted escape is a felony. According to this rule, felonies represent the only crime where an arrest can be made even though the arresting trooper was not present at the time of the commission of the felony.

79. **A** *Prevalence* means widespread. Note that answering this question correctly depends on the extent of your vocabulary. This is why we stress the importance of increasing your vocabulary by using a dictionary to look up words you are unfamiliar with.

80. **A** People who become career criminals tend to have a below-average level of formal education. From these facts it is safe to say that there is probably a relationship between formal education and becoming a career criminal.

81. **B** Minorities receive the death penalty not in proportion to their numbers in the overall population. This is what disproportionate means. It is another way of saying that, with respect to the death penalty, minorities are discriminated against.

82. **C** An offense becomes murder in the first degree when someone causes the death of a victim who is either a police officer or a correctional employee performing official duties; or, regardless of who the victim is, the offense becomes murder in the first degree if the perpetrator is in prison serving a life sentence. However, regardless of any of these circumstances, the perpetrator must be more than 18 years old at the time of the commission of the offense. Therefore, choices A, B, and D may be eliminated, and choice C is the answer.

83. **B** If a person intends to cause the death of one person and causes the death of such person or another, the person commits murder in the second degree.

84. **D** When an illegal abortional act is done to a female and causes her miscarriage, the offense is abortion. In this instance, the abortional act is illegal because it was not done to save the female's life and was done to a female who is 24 weeks or more pregnant.

85. **C** Ms. Green committed self abortion because she submitted to an illegal abortional act that was not done to save her life while she was 24 or more weeks pregnant and that resulted in her miscarriage.

86. **B** If a person during the performance of an illegal abortional act on a pregnant female causes the death of the pregnant female who is 24 weeks or more pregnant, such person commits manslaughter in the first degree.

87. **D** By intentionally aiding another person to commit suicide, Don committed manslaughter in the second degree.

88. **C** Knuckles had the intent to cause serious physical injury to another person; instead, he caused death to such person. Knuckles committed manslaughter in the first degree.

89. **B** The charge cannot be murder in the first degree because the intent must be to kill the person actually killed. However, in murder in the second degree, the intent may be to kill another person and such other person or another may die as a result of the action taken. This is exactly what took place here. The person who was intended to be killed was not killed. However, another person died as a result of the action taken. The correct charge is murder in the second degree.

90. **D** If both officers headed north, their paths would intersect where State Road 12 intersects with State Road 1 in the area directly above State Road 15. The importance of quickly determining where north, south, east, and west are located on the map before beginning to answer any questions is made clear by this question. Although north is located on the top of the map, do not always assume this to be the case. Examine the map and locate the compass or other directional aid that establishes which direction is north.

91. **C** State Roads 8 and 15 intersect in the western portion of the map. So choice A is incorrect. Choice B is incorrect because State Roads 11 and 15 intersect in the eastern portion of the map. Choice D is incorrect because State Roads 12 and 11 intersect in the southern portion of the map.

92. **C** Choice B is incorrect because, if its directions were followed, Trooper Herman would be heading west, which is away from the scene of the accident. Choice D is incorrect because it directs Trooper Herman to head south on State Road 91. However, according to the legend on the map, the road bearing number 91 is an Interstate Road and not a State Road. Therefore, State Road 91 is not displayed by the map provided. The importance of examining legends and other material contained on the map before answering the questions is highlighted here. Following the instructions found in choice A will lead the trooper to the scene of the accident but not as directly as the instructions found in choice C.

93. **C**   Trooper Hanks is currently heading away from the area of the pursuit.

94. **D**   They intersect with an equal number of roads; each intersects with five other roads.

95. **B**   The nose of choice A, the moles of choice C, and the lips of choice D leave choice B as the only possible answer.

96. **D**   The chin line and eyes of choice A, the nose of choice B, and the ears of choice C leave choice D as the only possible answer.

97. **D**   The eyes of choice A and the eyes and noses of choices B and C leave choice D as the only possible answer.

98. **C**   The nose of choice A, the nose and lips of choice B, and the chin line and nose of choice D leave choice C as the only possible answer.

99. **C**   The eyes of choice A, the lips of choice B, and the eyes and nose of choice D leave choice C as the only possible answer.

100. **B**   The nose of choice A, the lips of choice C, and the nose and lips of choice D leave choice B as the only possible answer.

CHAPTER 18

Practice Examination Five

This chapter contains the fifth practice examination that you will be taking. Don't forget to:

1. Take the test in one sitting. You have 3½ hours to answer all 100 questions.

2. Use the test-taking strategies outlined in Chapter 2.

3. Use the answer sheet we have provided to record your answers.

4. Complete the diagnostic chart that appears at the end of this chapter after you score this practice examination.

Answer Sheet
Practice Examination Five

Follow the instructions given in the test. Mark only your answers in the circles below.

WARNING: Be sure that the circle you fill is in the same row as the question you are answering. Use a No. 2 pencil (soft pencil).

BE SURE YOUR PENCIL MARKS ARE HEAVY AND BLACK. ERASE COMPLETELY ANY ANSWER YOU WISH TO CHANGE.

DO NOT make stray pencil dots, dashes or marks.

1. Ⓐ Ⓑ Ⓒ Ⓓ   2. Ⓐ Ⓑ Ⓒ Ⓓ   3. Ⓐ Ⓑ Ⓒ Ⓓ   4. Ⓐ Ⓑ Ⓒ Ⓓ
5. Ⓐ Ⓑ Ⓒ Ⓓ   6. Ⓐ Ⓑ Ⓒ Ⓓ   7. Ⓐ Ⓑ Ⓒ Ⓓ   8. Ⓐ Ⓑ Ⓒ Ⓓ
9. Ⓐ Ⓑ Ⓒ Ⓓ   10. Ⓐ Ⓑ Ⓒ Ⓓ   11. Ⓐ Ⓑ Ⓒ Ⓓ   12. Ⓐ Ⓑ Ⓒ Ⓓ
13. Ⓐ Ⓑ Ⓒ Ⓓ   14. Ⓐ Ⓑ Ⓒ Ⓓ   15. Ⓐ Ⓑ Ⓒ Ⓓ   16. Ⓐ Ⓑ Ⓒ Ⓓ
17. Ⓐ Ⓑ Ⓒ Ⓓ   18. Ⓐ Ⓑ Ⓒ Ⓓ   19. Ⓐ Ⓑ Ⓒ Ⓓ   20. Ⓐ Ⓑ Ⓒ Ⓓ
21. Ⓐ Ⓑ Ⓒ Ⓓ   22. Ⓐ Ⓑ Ⓒ Ⓓ   23. Ⓐ Ⓑ Ⓒ Ⓓ   24. Ⓐ Ⓑ Ⓒ Ⓓ
25. Ⓐ Ⓑ Ⓒ Ⓓ   26. Ⓐ Ⓑ Ⓒ Ⓓ   27. Ⓐ Ⓑ Ⓒ Ⓓ   28. Ⓐ Ⓑ Ⓒ Ⓓ
29. Ⓐ Ⓑ Ⓒ Ⓓ   30. Ⓐ Ⓑ Ⓒ Ⓓ   31. Ⓐ Ⓑ Ⓒ Ⓓ   32. Ⓐ Ⓑ Ⓒ Ⓓ
33. Ⓐ Ⓑ Ⓒ Ⓓ   34. Ⓐ Ⓑ Ⓒ Ⓓ   35. Ⓐ Ⓑ Ⓒ Ⓓ   36. Ⓐ Ⓑ Ⓒ Ⓓ
37. Ⓐ Ⓑ Ⓒ Ⓓ   38. Ⓐ Ⓑ Ⓒ Ⓓ   39. Ⓐ Ⓑ Ⓒ Ⓓ   40. Ⓐ Ⓑ Ⓒ Ⓓ
41. Ⓐ Ⓑ Ⓒ Ⓓ   42. Ⓐ Ⓑ Ⓒ Ⓓ   43. Ⓐ Ⓑ Ⓒ Ⓓ   44. Ⓐ Ⓑ Ⓒ Ⓓ
45. Ⓐ Ⓑ Ⓒ Ⓓ   46. Ⓐ Ⓑ Ⓒ Ⓓ   47. Ⓐ Ⓑ Ⓒ Ⓓ   48. Ⓐ Ⓑ Ⓒ Ⓓ
49. Ⓐ Ⓑ Ⓒ Ⓓ   50. Ⓐ Ⓑ Ⓒ Ⓓ   51. Ⓐ Ⓑ Ⓒ Ⓓ   52. Ⓐ Ⓑ Ⓒ Ⓓ
53. Ⓐ Ⓑ Ⓒ Ⓓ   54. Ⓐ Ⓑ Ⓒ Ⓓ   55. Ⓐ Ⓑ Ⓒ Ⓓ   56. Ⓐ Ⓑ Ⓒ Ⓓ
57. Ⓐ Ⓑ Ⓒ Ⓓ   58. Ⓐ Ⓑ Ⓒ Ⓓ   59. Ⓐ Ⓑ Ⓒ Ⓓ   60. Ⓐ Ⓑ Ⓒ Ⓓ
61. Ⓐ Ⓑ Ⓒ Ⓓ   62. Ⓐ Ⓑ Ⓒ Ⓓ   63. Ⓐ Ⓑ Ⓒ Ⓓ   64. Ⓐ Ⓑ Ⓒ Ⓓ
65. Ⓐ Ⓑ Ⓒ Ⓓ   66. Ⓐ Ⓑ Ⓒ Ⓓ   67. Ⓐ Ⓑ Ⓒ Ⓓ   68. Ⓐ Ⓑ Ⓒ Ⓓ
69. Ⓐ Ⓑ Ⓒ Ⓓ   70. Ⓐ Ⓑ Ⓒ Ⓓ   71. Ⓐ Ⓑ Ⓒ Ⓓ   72. Ⓐ Ⓑ Ⓒ Ⓓ
73. Ⓐ Ⓑ Ⓒ Ⓓ   74. Ⓐ Ⓑ Ⓒ Ⓓ   75. Ⓐ Ⓑ Ⓒ Ⓓ   76. Ⓐ Ⓑ Ⓒ Ⓓ
77. Ⓐ Ⓑ Ⓒ Ⓓ   78. Ⓐ Ⓑ Ⓒ Ⓓ   79. Ⓐ Ⓑ Ⓒ Ⓓ   80. Ⓐ Ⓑ Ⓒ Ⓓ
81. Ⓐ Ⓑ Ⓒ Ⓓ   82. Ⓐ Ⓑ Ⓒ Ⓓ   83. Ⓐ Ⓑ Ⓒ Ⓓ   84. Ⓐ Ⓑ Ⓒ Ⓓ
85. Ⓐ Ⓑ Ⓒ Ⓓ   86. Ⓐ Ⓑ Ⓒ Ⓓ   87. Ⓐ Ⓑ Ⓒ Ⓓ   88. Ⓐ Ⓑ Ⓒ Ⓓ
89. Ⓐ Ⓑ Ⓒ Ⓓ   90. Ⓐ Ⓑ Ⓒ Ⓓ   91. Ⓐ Ⓑ Ⓒ Ⓓ   92. Ⓐ Ⓑ Ⓒ Ⓓ
93. Ⓐ Ⓑ Ⓒ Ⓓ   94. Ⓐ Ⓑ Ⓒ Ⓓ   95. Ⓐ Ⓑ Ⓒ Ⓓ   96. Ⓐ Ⓑ Ⓒ Ⓓ
97. Ⓐ Ⓑ Ⓒ Ⓓ   98. Ⓐ Ⓑ Ⓒ Ⓓ   99. Ⓐ Ⓑ Ⓒ Ⓓ   100. Ⓐ Ⓑ Ⓒ Ⓓ

The Test

DIRECTIONS FOR QUESTIONS 1–8: Study for 5 minutes the following illustration, which depicts items taken from two prisoners immediately after they were arrested. Try to remember as many details as possible. Do not make written notes of any kind during this 5-minute period. After the 5 minutes are up, answer questions 1–8. When answering the questions, do not refer back to the illustration.

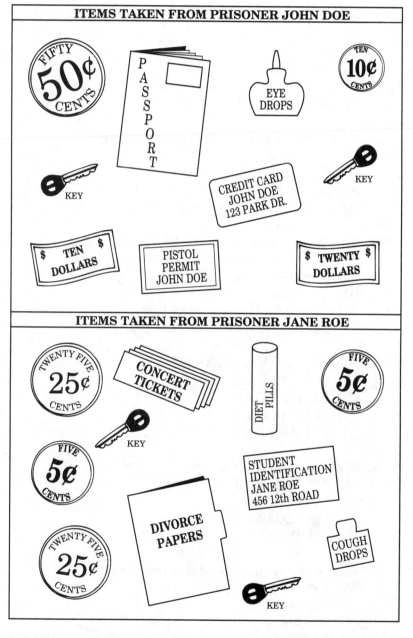

DO NOT PROCEED UNTIL 5 MINUTES HAVE PASSED.

DIRECTIONS: Answer questions 1–8 solely on the basis of the illustration on the preceding page. Do not refer back to it when answering these questions.

1. The prisoner who is most likely to be experiencing eye problems is
   (A) John Doe.
   (B) Jane Roe.
   (C) both John Doe and Jane Roe.
   (D) neither John Doe nor Jane Roe.

2. Which prisoner is most likely experiencing marital problems?
   (A) John Doe
   (B) Jane Roe
   (C) both John Doe and Jane Roe
   (D) neither John Doe nor Jane Roe

3. Which prisoner is authorized to carry a pistol?
   (A) John Doe
   (B) Jane Roe
   (C) both John Doe and Jane Roe
   (D) neither John Doe nor Jane Roe

4. Which prisoner is most likely experiencing a weight control problem?
   (A) John Doe
   (B) Jane Roe
   (C) both John Doe and Jane Roe
   (D) neither John Doe nor Jane Roe

5. What is Jane Roe's address?
   (A) 456 12th Road
   (B) 123 Park Drive
   (C) 123 12th Road
   (D) 456 Park Drive

6. What is John Doe's address?
   (A) 456 12th Road
   (B) 123 Park Drive
   (C) 123 12th Road
   (D) 456 Park Drive

7. How much money was John Doe carrying?
   (A) $.60
   (B) $30.60
   (C) $20.60
   (D) $10.60

8. Which of the prisoners is most likely to be attend-
ing school?
(A) John Doe
(B) Jane Roe
(C) both John Doe and Jane Roe
(D) neither John Doe nor Jane Roe

Answer questions 9–11 solely on the basis of the following information.

Because of its extreme importance, patrol is the one police function that
cannot be eliminated. The patrol division is the backbone of the police department. Most of the money in a police department's operating budget is
earmarked for salaries, and the greatest number of officers are assigned
to the patrol division. Therefore, most of the money in the budget is used
to support the patrol function. One very critical point about the patrol division is that its effectiveness has an impact on the effectiveness of all
other line units, including investigations, traffic, youth, and vice. The reason for this is that the police officer on patrol acts as the eyes and ears of
the rest of the department. So, if the effectiveness of the patrol division
decreases, as a general rule, so does the effectiveness of all line divisions.
There is a definite irony involved in this state of affairs. It is a fact that,
although it is unanimously agreed that patrol is vital to the success of the
entire department, the more experienced and qualified patrol officers are
often removed from patrol duties at the peak of their careers to become
specialists.

9. Patrol is
(A) an essential police function.
(B) a necessary evil.
(C) far too expensive.
(D) a very effective police function.

10. The success of the traffic division is influenced by
(A) the quality of training that traffic officers
receive.
(B) the amount of experience possessed by traffic
officers.
(C) the quality of its immediate supervisors.
(D) the effectiveness of the patrol division.

11. The most expensive police function is
(A) traffic.
(B) vice.
(C) patrol.
(D) investigations.

Answer questions 12–23 solely on the basis of the following passage.

State troopers Billy Collela and Joe Connors are dispatched to 93-77 Richards Avenue, Apartment 13F, at 7:53 P.M. on November 8th, in response to a burglary reported by a Mr. King. They arrive at the apartment at 7:58 P.M., ring the doorbell, and are greeted by Mr. and Mrs. King. Mr. King tells the troopers that he left for his foreman's job at the telephone company at 6:00 A.M. and that his wife left for her secretary's job 10 minutes later. After work, Mr. King picked up his wife, and they returned to their apartment at 7:40 P.M., having eaten dinner out. When Mrs. King entered the bedroom, she noticed her jewelry box on the floor. She told her husband, who then called the state police. While the Kings waited for the troopers to arrive, they discovered that all Mrs. King's jewelry and Mr. King's coin collection, as well as approximately $275 in cash, were missing.

While trooper Collela begins to fill out a crime report, Trooper Connors visits other apartments in the building to interview neighbors who might have additional information about the burglary.

Mrs. James, age 25, a salesperson, who lives in apartment 13C located directly opposite the elevator, reports to Trooper Connors that she heard voices in the hallway outside her apartment door at 3:30 P.M. She said she thought the voices were those of a neighbor's children who often play in the hallway. When she opened the door to chase them away, she saw two strangers standing by the elevator. They were both males, and they wore brown work clothes. She observed that the taller man was Hispanic, about 38 years old, 5'11", 155 pounds, with brown hair and was carrying a black leather case. He had a tattoo of an eagle on his left hand. The second male, who was carrying a flashlight, was white, about 31 years old, 5'8", 140 pounds, with black hair and a scar on the right side of his face.

Trooper Connors then contacts other residents at apartments 13D, 13E, and 13G. All of them tell the trooper that they did not see or hear anything unusual. Trooper Connors then goes back to the Kings' apartment to inform his partner about what he has learned. In the meantime, Officer Collela determined from Mr. King that his coin collection was in a round brown leather carrying case.

Trooper Collela was also informed that Mr. King is 32 years old. His telephone number at work is 555-3168, and his work address is 372 Western Avenue. Mrs. King's business telephone number is 555-2379, and her work address is 311 North Moore Street. The Kings' home phone number is 555-3714. Mrs. James' telephone number at home is 555-1427.

Troopers Collela and Connors then finish their assignment and complete the necessary burglary report, at which time they resume patrol.

12. At about what time were the two strange males seen in the hallway?
(A) 7:00 A.M.
(B) 7:40 A.M.
(C) 3:30 P.M.
(D) 7:53 P.M.

13. Which of the following apartments is directly opposite the elevator?
    (A) 13B
    (B) 13C
    (C) 13F
    (D) 13G

14. Which of the following items was not stolen during the burglary of the Kings' apartment?
    (A) $275
    (B) Mr. King's coin collection
    (C) Mrs. King's jewelry
    (D) credit cards

15. What is Mrs. King's business address?
    (A) 311 North Moore Street
    (B) 372 Western Avenue
    (C) 93-77 Richards Avenue
    (D) 311 South Moore Street

16. At what time did the Kings return to their apartment?
    (A) 7:40 P.M.
    (B) 7:45 P.M.
    (C) 7:53 P.M.
    (D) 7:58 P.M.

17. What is Mrs. King's occupation?
    (A) teacher
    (B) telephone operator
    (C) secretary
    (D) foreman

18. What is Mr. King's telephone number at work?
    (A) 555-2379
    (B) 555-1427
    (C) 555-3714
    (D) 555-3168

19. What is the reported age of the shorter of the two strangers seen standing near the elevator?
    (A) approximately 31 years old
    (B) approximately 38 years old
    (C) approximately 41 years old
    (D) approximately 48 years old

20. The male stranger who was seen near the elevator and who was carrying a flashlight was described as being
    (A) white, 5'11", 140 pounds, with a scar
    (B) Hispanic, 5'8", 130 pounds, with a scar
    (C) white, 5'8", 140 pounds, with a facial scar
    (D) Hispanic, 5'11", 130 pounds, with a facial scar

21. Which one of the following was reported about the taller man seen standing near the elevator?
    (A) He had a scar on his face.
    (B) He had a mole on his face.
    (C) He had a tattoo on his hand.
    (D) He had a birthmark on his neck.

22. Who employs Mr. King?
    (A) He is self-employed.
    (B) the telephone company
    (C) the gas company
    (D) the cable company

23. When did Mrs. King leave for work?
    (A) 6:00 A.M.
    (B) 6:10 A.M.
    (C) 6:30 A.M.
    (D) 7:40 A.M.

Answer questions 24–28 solely on the basis of the following information.

Troopers Jake Tom Random and Don Love were on patrol on the state thruway. The date was November 13th. At 9:15 A.M. they came upon a traffic accident on the northbound lane of the thruway, 300 feet south of Exit 28. They later determined that the accident occurred 5 minutes prior to their arrival on the scene.

Officer Love notified the state police radio dispatcher at 9:20 A.M. that he and his partner were handling an accident involving a van and a station wagon. He further reported to the dispatcher that there were no injuries involved in the accidents, although both cars involved had been damaged and, as a result, were both disabled and needed towing.

The troopers checked the driver's license of the operators of both vehicles, their vehicle insurance cards, and their registration certificates. The driver of the van was John Hood, age 26, of 1002 North Elm Avenue. Mr. Hood was driving a 2-year-old blue Dodge van, license plate #1234HG, owned by his employer, Acme Trucking Company, of 157 East 36th Street.

The driver of the station wagon was Mrs. Pat Crow, age 28, whose home address is 39 Fairway Drive. Mrs. Crow's vehicle was a brand new Chevrolet station wagon, license plate #4321GH. Her driver's license identification number is C876543, and its expiration date is May 31st, of next year.

Examination of the vehicles revealed that the station wagon was dented on its left side near the rear door and that the van had a dented front fender.

After completing Accident Report #SP-8743 and arranging for the vehicles to be towed, the troopers resumed patrol at about 9:45 A.M.

24. The accident occurred at
   (A) 9:15 A.M.
   (B) 9:10 A.M.
   (C) 9:45 A.M.
   (D) 10:00 A.M.

25. The accident occurred on the state thruway
   (A) in the southbound lane.
   (B) on the exit ramp.
   (C) near Exit 28.
   (D) 300 feet north of Exit 28.

26. How many people were injured in the accident?
   (A) none
   (B) one
   (C) two
   (D) three

27. How old is Mrs. Crow?
   (A) 26 years old
   (B) 28 years old
   (C) 36 years old
   (D) 38 years old

28. The van had
   (A) no damage.
   (B) a dented left rear panel.
   (C) a dented front fender.
   (D) a dented rear fender.

Answer questions 29–34 solely on the basis of the following information.

An identification lineup is the placing of a criminal suspect in a lineup (six persons) with at least five other persons for purpose of identification by a victim or a witness.

When a criminal suspect in police custody is to be placed in an identification lineup at a post command or other place of confinement, the trooper concerned shall:

1. Resolve any doubt concerning the need for, or legality of, conducting a lineup or showup by conferring first with the patrol supervisor. If the patrol supervisor is unavailable, the trooper shall confer with the post command desk officer.

NOTE: The suspect must be arrested before being forced to appear in a lineup. However, an arrest is not necessary if the suspect voluntarily consents to appear in a lineup. Identification procedures ordinarily are not necessary where the witness/victim and the perpetrator are known to each other, including relatives or other close acquaintances, or the perpetrator is apprehended by a police officer in the act of committing the crime.

2. Give the suspect Miranda warnings (i.e., alerting a suspect about the suspect's constitutional rights while being questioned), if the suspect is to be interrogated before, during, or after the lineup.

3. Inform the suspect that he/she will appear in a lineup for the purpose of identification in connection with a crime.

4. Do not advise the suspect that he/she has the right to an attorney.

5. Inform the suspect that he/she does not have a right to a lawyer only when he/she requests an attorney for the lineup.

NOTE: Prior to conducting the lineup, a detective supervisor will be consulted and will then personally supervise the entire procedure and then after the lineup actually prepare the form, LINEUP REPORT.

6. Permit an attorney who is present at the site of a lineup to observe the manner in which the lineup is conducted.

   a. The attorney may observe the lineup from any place where he/she cannot be observed.

7. Inform an attorney who contacts the police and states that he/she represents the suspect and that he/she wishes to be present when the lineup is conducted that the lineup will be delayed for a reasonable time to permit him/her to appear.

NOTE: When determining what is a reasonable delay, the trooper conducting the lineup should consider whether the delay would result in a significant inconvenience to the witness or would undermine the substantial advantages of a prompt identification confrontation.

8. Do not permit the attorney to talk to witnesses participating in the identification of the suspect.

9. Inform the attorney that suggestions concerning the lineup should be directed to the officer conducting the lineup.

10. Do not permit the attorney to interfere with the conduct of the lineup.

   a. The trooper conducting the lineup may consider suggestions of the attorney to improve the fairness of the lineup if suggestions are reasonable and practical.

29. Trooper Nelly Bailes is doubtful as to whether a lineup she intends to conduct involving a robbery suspect is actually needed. To resolve her doubt she should first confer with
   (A) the post command desk officer.
   (B) the suspect's attorney.
   (C) the patrol supervisor.
   (D) the state's attorney.

30. The minimum number of persons required in order to conduct an identification lineup is
   (A) four.
   (B) five.
   (C) six.
   (D) seven.

31. Which of the following is least accurate, according to the procedure dealing with identification lineups?
   (A) A suspect who has not yet been arrested could be part of a lineup.
   (B) If a victim and the perpetrator are related, a lineup is not usually required.
   (C) If a police officer catches a perpetrator in the act of committing a crime, a lineup is not needed.
   (D) Miranda warnings are not required to be given to a suspect who is interrogated during a lineup.

32. In connection with the conducting of a lineup, the form LINEUP REPORT is prepared by the arresting trooper after the lineup. According to procedure, in this instance the action of the arresting trooper should be considered
    (A) proper, mainly because it is the duty of the arresting trooper to prepare the form.
    (B) improper, mainly because it is the duty of the detective supervisor to prepare the form.
    (C) proper, mainly because the form may be prepared either before or after the lineup is conducted.
    (D) improper, mainly because the form should be prepared before the lineup is conducted.

33. Pat Tomes is an attorney. She telephones a post command where an identification lineup involving her client is to be conducted. She asks if it is possible to delay the lineup until she arrives at the post command. In this instance, she should be told that the lineup
    (A) could be delayed 1 hour.
    (B) could be delayed a reasonable time.
    (C) could be delayed 2 hours.
    (D) could not be delayed.

34. Concerning the procedure dealing with identification lineups, which of the following is least correct?
    (A) A suspect's attorney should not be permitted to talk with witnesses participating in the identification of the suspect.
    (B) Any suggestions that an attorney may have concerning the lineup should be directed to the officer conducting the lineup.
    (C) A suspect's attorney is not allowed to observe the conducting of the actual lineup.
    (D) Under certain circumstances, the recommendations of an attorney, concerning a lineup in which the attorney's client is participating, could be considered.

Answer questions 35–39 solely on the basis of the following information.

When a trooper issues a traffic summons, the following steps should be followed in sequential order by the trooper issuing the summons:

1. Inform the violator of the violation committed.

2. Request the violator to show proof of identity and residence.

   a. Examine driver's license, vehicle registration, further proof of identity, residence, and, when appropriate, insurance identification cards.

3. Bring the violator to the post command for investigation if any doubt concerning identity exists.

   a. If the identity is verified, serve the summons and immediately release the violator.

   b. The post command desk officer will make a post command log entry when a violator has been taken to the station house for identification, is served a summons, and immediately released. Entry will include the following:

      1) Name, address, and physical description of the violator.

      2) Location, time of incident, and reason for removal to the post command.

      3) Name, rank, and shield number of the trooper who brought the violator to the post command.

      4) Violation(s) charged and control number(s) of summons(es) served.

      5) Time violator entered and departed the post command.

4. Issue the summonses in numerical order.

5. Use a ballpoint pen to legibly print information in block letters.

6. Enter all available information required by the captions on the summons.

7. Enter only one violation on each summons.

8. Use a separate summons for each additional violation.

9. Give the violator the first part of the summons.

10. Enter complete details of the incident in the memo book.

11. Detach and retain the last copy of the summons.

12. When issuing a summons to a pedestrian for jaywalking, the part of

the summons requiring information about the type of vehicle will be left blank.

Any person who violates any applicable provisions of the Traffic Laws will be issued a summons, providing such individual is sober and 16 years of age or older; a Youth Report Card will be prepared for a violator who is at least 7 and less than 16 years of age. Traffic violators who are ineligible to receive a summons solely due to intoxication will not receive a summons. Such persons will be arrested.

35. Trooper Bud Spring pulls Mr. Don Bonds over while Mr. Bonds is driving a late-model sedan. The trooper had observed Mr. Bonds exceeding the highway speed limit. According to procedure, the first action the trooper should take is to
   (A) examine Mr. Bonds's license.
   (B) tell Mr. Bonds he was speeding.
   (C) ask for an insurance identification card.
   (D) ask for the registration for the sedan.

36. A certain traffic violator is brought to the post command due to some doubt concerning the violator's identity. The post command desk officer makes a log entry concerning this action. All the following are required to be entered in the log except
   (A) the name, rank, and shield number of the trooper who brought the violator to the post command.
   (B) the name, address, and physical description of the violator.
   (C) the license plate of the vehicle the violator was driving.
   (D) the time the violator entered and departed the post command.

37. While issuing a summons, Trooper Olive Baker engages in certain actions. Which of the following is not an appropriate action for the trooper to take according to the procedure for issuing summonses?
   (A) to use a ball point pen when preparing the summons
   (B) to enter no more than one violation on a summons
   (C) to include the complete details of the incident in her memo book
   (D) to give the last copy of the summons to the violator

38. Pat Younger has been caught by Trooper Tab More violating the Traffic Law by driving without a license. Pat's identity is able to be verified, and in addition Pat is found to be 15 years old. In this instance, the trooper should
    (A) issue a summons for driving without a license.
    (B) bring the youth to the post command.
    (C) prepare a Youth Report Card.
    (D) arrest the youth.

39. Frank Spirits is 17 years old and, while on foot and intoxicated, crosses a major roadway against the traffic signals. He also crosses at a location other than that allocated for pedestrian crossings. The violation is observed by Trooper Topper. In this instance the trooper should
    (A) arrest him.
    (B) issue him a summons for jaywalking.
    (C) bring him to the post command and issue him a summons when he sobers up.
    (D) prepare a Youth Report Card.

Answer questions 40–45 solely on the basis of the following information.

Upon arresting a person for operating a vehicle, while under the influence of alcohol,

1. The arresting trooper shall remove the prisoner to the post command

2. The post command desk officer shall verify the arrest and

    a. direct the arresting trooper to request the Communications Division to dispatch an Alcohol Test Unit Technician to the driver testing location.

        1) State time of arrest when making request.

NOTE: The chemical test of prisoners charged with operating a vehicle while under the influence of alcohol must be administered within 2 hours of the time of arrest.

3. The arresting trooper shall prepare an Arrest Report.

4. The post command desk officer shall

    a. direct the arresting trooper to remove the prisoner, in a patrol car, to the driver testing location.

b. make an entry in the post command log of the identity of the arresting trooper and the prisoner.

c. have the prisoner's vehicle removed to the post command for safeguarding. If it remains in police custody 48 hours after the time of arrest, the vehicle shall be removed to the Auto Pound.

5. The arresting trooper shall

a. report, with the prisoner, to the desk officer at the driver testing location.

b. conduct an examination of the prisoner.

6. The Alcohol Test Unit Technician shall

a. administer the chemical test to the prisoner.

b. conduct the "Coordination Test" of the prisoner, in the presence of the arresting trooper.

NOTE: In the event that the examination of the prisoner cannot be videotaped, the desk officer at the driver testing location will supervise the examination.

c. sign the INTOXICATED PRISONER form and have the arresting trooper sign the form. The desk officer, at the driver testing location, will also sign the form if the examination was not videotaped.

7. The arresting trooper must notify the prosecutor if the prisoner has any previous convictions for the same crime within the past ten years.

NOTE: If a prisoner requests to be tested for intoxication by his personal physician, the test will not be allowed until the department testing has been completed. If the prisoner refuses the administration of a chemical test by this department he shall not be allowed to have a test be administered by his personal physician.

40. After effecting the arrest of Bob Hall for driving under the influence of alcohol, Trooper Wells brings him to the post command. At the post command the arrest should be verified by the
(A) the patrol supervisor.
(B) the post command desk officer.
(C) the duty captain.
(D) the technician from the Alcohol Testing Unit.

41. An arrest is made by a certain trooper for driving under the influence of alcohol. The arrest is made at 8:30 A.M. The trooper brings the prisoner to the post command arriving at 8:45 A.M. The trooper departs 30 minutes later with the prisoner to a driver testing location where certain tests in connection with the arrest are to be conducted. At 9:45 A.M., the trooper arrives at the testing location. According to procedure, the latest the chemical test can be administered is
    (A) 10:30 A.M.
    (B) 10:45 A.M.
    (C) 11:30 A.M.
    (D) 11:45 A.M.

42. According to procedure, which of the following is responsible for conducting a coordination test of a prisoner who was arrested for driving while under the influence of alcohol?
    (A) the arresting trooper
    (B) the post command desk officer
    (C) the Alcohol Test Unit technician
    (D) the patrol supervisor

43. Concerning the procedure for processing the arrest of a prisoner who has been arrested for driving under the influence of alcohol, which of the following is least correct?
    (A) The desk officer of the testing location will always supervise the examination of the prisoner.
    (B) A prisoner's vehicle may be removed to the post command for safeguarding.
    (C) If a prisoner's vehicle is still in police possession after 48 hours, the vehicle will be removed to the Auto Pound facility.
    (D) The Alcohol Testing Unit technician and the arresting trooper will sign the INTOXICATED PRISONER form.

44. The arresting officer shall notify the prosecutor if the prisoner has
    (A) any previous arrests in the last 10 years.
    (B) any previous convictions in the last 10 years.
    (C) any previous arrests for the same crime in the last 10 years.
    (D) any previous convictions for the same crime in the last 10 years.

45. Ray Larks is arrested for driving under the influence of alcohol. During the arrest processing he refuses to be tested for intoxication unless he is first tested by his own physician. In this instance,
   (A) he should be allowed to be tested by his own physician before he is tested by department personnel.
   (B) he should not be allowed to be tested until the department testing is completed.
   (C) he should be allowed to be tested by his own physician at the same time as the test by department personnel.
   (D) he should not be allowed to be tested by his own physician under any circumstances.

Answer question 46 solely on the basis of the following information.

When attention is drawn to an apparently lost adult, the trooper concerned shall in the following order:

1. Interview the person and direct the person to the destination sought.

2. Deliver the person to the post command if unable to direct the person.

3. Inform the post command desk officer of the facts.

4. Prepare an AIDED REPORT and enter all details in the memo book.

5. Telephone the Missing Persons Squad and give a complete description of the lost adult.

6. Attempt to locate relatives or friends.

46. The radio dispatcher directs Trooper Barker to respond to a shopping center where a local merchant has discovered an elderly male who is apparently lost and seems confused about his whereabouts. When the trooper arrives in his patrol car, he immediately places the elderly male in the patrol car and brings him to the post command. In this instance according to procedure, the actions of the trooper were
   (A) proper, mainly because the post command desk officer needs to be notified of the facts.
   (B) improper, mainly because the trooper should first make a memo book entry.
   (C) proper, mainly because the Missing Person Squad needs to be notified.
   (D) improper, mainly because the trooper should have first interviewed the elderly male.

Answer questions 47 and 48 solely on the basis of the following information.

When a trooper comes in contact with an apparently lost child, the trooper shall:

1. Notify the post command desk officer and the radio dispatcher.

2. Make brief inquiry in the vicinity of the place where the child was found.

3. Bring the child to the post command if a relative is not located.

4. Prepare an AIDED REPORT.

5. Telephone the Missing Persons Squad and give a complete description.

6. Complete all captions on the AIDED REPORT.

   a. If the child is not reunited with relatives within a reasonable time, deliver the child to the nearest shelter.

   b. Inform the Missing Persons Squad if the child is moved from the post command to another location.

47. Trooper Mason has had a lost child in his custody at a certain post command for more than a reasonable period of time. The trooper properly decides to move the child from the post command to a nearby shelter. According to procedure, in this instance, the trooper should notify
(A) the patrol supervisor.
(B) the Missing Persons Squad.
(C) the post command desk officer.
(D) the radio dispatcher.

48. Upon finishing a meal break, Trooper Bolts comes upon a 3-year-old lost male wandering around a parking lot. The trooper is told by the child that he was shopping with his mother and somehow became separated from his mother. The trooper briefly makes some inquiries around the area but is unable to find the child's mother. The trooper then notifies the post command desk officer and the radio dispatcher. According to procedure, in this instance, the trooper acted
(A) properly, mainly because the child's mother might still be in the area.
(B) improperly, mainly because the trooper should have first notified the desk officer and the radio dispatcher.
(C) properly, mainly because someone in the area might recognize the child and be acquainted with his mother.
(D) improperly, mainly because the Missing Persons Squad should have been notified immediately.

DIRECTIONS: In each of questions 49–53 you will be given four choices. Three of the choices, A, B, and C, contain a written statement. You are to evaluate the statement in each choice and select the statement that is most accurately and clearly written. If all or none of the three written statements is accurately and clearly written, you are to select choice D.

49. According to the instructions, evaluate the following statements.
(A) It takes too long to question each employee.
(B) The captain was so direct his instructions were very implicit.
(C) The aim of the employee of the month award is to raise moral.
(D) All or none is accurate.

50. According to the instructions, evaluate the following statements.
    (A) The teller's very clever plan to steal from the bank was ingenuous.
    (B) The post commander is very flexible, but there is some conduct he simply will not accept.
    (C) The subject of the interview was considered ingenious because she answered the questions so openly and honestly.
    (D) All or none is accurate.

51. According to the instructions, evaluate the following statements.
    (A) The sergeant praised Wolf and myself.
    (B) The suspect who you know committed the murder was caught.
    (C) I am as good as her in fingerprint identification.
    (D) All or none is accurate.

52. According to the instructions, evaluate the following statements.
    (A) I found it easy to learn whenever the sergeant would teach the roll call lesson.
    (B) The barricaded robber has laid down his weapons.
    (C) I would like to counsel him.
    (D) All or none is accurate.

53. According to the instructions, evaluate the following statements.
    (A) She paid him a real complement.
    (B) Her mode of dress was very causal.
    (C) He was formerly the president of the club.
    (D) All or none is accurate.

Answer questions 54–57 based solely on the following information:

ROSTER OF HIGHWAY PATROL OFFICERS ASSIGNED TO SQUAD ONE NORTH CENTRAL COMMAND

Highway Patrol Officer	Age	Time with Highway Patrol
Banks	38	15
Dice	32	10
Bello	39	9
Dubs	25	2
Love	45	20
Ling	33	11
Roe	40	17
Barns	30	8

54. A highway patrol officer is eligible to retire from the department when the officer has at least 25 years of service and is at least 50 years old. Which of the following officers will be eligible for retirement first?
(A) Bello
(B) Dubs
(C) Love
(D) Ling

55. Based on the preceding information, which of the following statements would be most accurate?
(A) The combined ages of the two oldest officers is at least twice that of the two youngest officers.
(B) The combined time with the agency of the two oldest officers is four times that of the two youngest officers.
(C) The combined ages of the two oldest officers is at least 30 years more than that of the two youngest officers.
(D) The combined time with the agency of the two oldest officers is 40 years more than that of the two youngest officers.

56. The average age of the officers assigned to Squad
    One is between
    (A) 31 and 32 years of age.
    (B) 33 and 34 years of age.
    (C) 35 and 36 years of age.
    (D) 37 and 38 years of age.

57. The average length of time with the agency of the
    officers assigned to Squad One is between
    (A) 9 and 10 years.
    (B) 11 and 12 years.
    (C) 12 and 13 years.
    (D) 14 and 15 years.

DIRECTIONS: Answer questions 58–65 based solely on the following
narrative and the form PRIVATE PROPERTY ACCIDENT REPORT,
which appears after the narrative. Some of the captions on the form may
be numbered; some may not. The boxes are not necessarily consecutively
numbered.

On April 7, 19xx, at about 10:30 A.M., a motor vehicle accident occurred
in the private employee parking lot of Trailson Refrigeration Company.
The accident involved two vehicles and resulted in one personal injury
and also property damage. The occurrence was reported to State Trooper
Neil Bailes, shield number 6332, of the Kingate Post, of Troop A of the
Circle Division. In keeping with state police policy, the occurrence, which
occurred on private property, was recorded on department form PRIVATE
PROPERTY ACCIDENT REPORT. The details are as follows.

On the date of occurrence at 10:35 A.M., Trooper Bailes received a call
from the radio dispatcher requesting his response to a past signal 1020, a
motor vehicle accident resulting in injury. When Trooper Bailes arrived at
the scene at 10:40 A.M., he was greeted by Ms. Vivian Bianco, of 229 North
160 Street, telephone 555-7460, a female, white, 39 years. She informed
Trooper Bailes that her vehicle, known hereafter as vehicle one, while unattended and appropriately parked in her assigned parking space had
been struck in the rear by a black Ford Explorer, with current Florida
plates bearing the number ITAN 1. The owner and driver of the Ford Explorer, known hereafter as driver two and vehicle two, respectively, was
Mr. Sal Marini, a male, white, 55 years old, who is a traveling salesman
residing at 2239 Grant Avenue in Del Ray, Florida.

Investigation revealed that Ms. Bianco's vehicle is a white Pontiac
Trans-Am, registered to her and bearing current Ohio license plates
8567TJ. Investigation also revealed that the owner of the Ford Explorer
was backing out of a visitor's parking space when he became lightheaded
and lost control of the vehicle causing it to veer backwards thereby striking Ms. Bianco's vehicle and causing damage to her vehicle's radiator
and the rear passenger wheel of Mr. Marini's vehicle. Mr. Marini was removed to Shomrim Medical Center via ambulance 3344 with ambulance

attendant Michael Bayside. Mr. Marini was treated by Dr. Karen Binghamton and was held for overnight observation after complaining of neck and chest pains. Although the damage to both vehicles was moderate and both vehicles required towing services by Bilecki Towing Service, there was no other property damage. Both vehicle owners had valid driver's licenses. Ms. Bianco's license number from New York State was B4142889. Mr. Marini's license number from Florida was M4124888. Mr. Marini's insurance company is the Plaza Insurance Company; the policy number is DEA4459. Ms. Bianco's insurance company is the CPB Insurance Company; the policy number is DDT5637. Sergeant Collars responded and was informed of all actions taken. The case is recorded under case number 3356.

PRIVATE PROPERTY ACCIDENT REPORT
(THIS FORM TO BE USED FOR PRIVATE PROPERTY ONLY)
****

Case Number ____(2)____ Date ____(1)____ Time Officer Notified ____(3)____

County ____(4)____ City ____(5)____ Time Officer Arrived ____(6)____

Location of Accident ____(7)____

Driver #1 ____(8)____ Sex ____(9)____ Race ____(10)____ D.O.B. ____(11)____

Driver's License # ____(12)____ State ____(13)____ Class ____(14)____ Expiration Date ____(15)____

Vehicle Owner, Address and Phone # ____(16)____

____(16a)____

Vehicle # 1 Make ____(17)____ Model ____(18)____ Year ____(19)____ Tag # ____(20)____ Year ____(21)____ State ____(22)____

Insurance Company and Policy # ____(23)____

Damage to Vehicle: (24) None _____ Slight _____ Moderate _____ Extensive _____

****

Driver #2 ____(25)____ Sex ____(26)____ Race ____(27)____ D.O.B. ____(28)____

Driver's License # ____(29)____ State ____(30)____ Class ____(31)____ Expiration Date ____(32)____

Vehicle Owner, Address and Phone # ____(33)____

____(33a)____

Vehicle # 2 Make ____(34)____ Model ____(35)____ Year ____(36)____ Tag # ____(37)____ Year ____(38)____ State ____(39)____

Insurance Company and Policy # ____(40)____

Damage to Vehicle: (41) None _____ Slight _____ Moderate _____ Extensive _____

Other Property Damage ____(42)____

Injuries:

Name ____(43)____ Age ____(43a)____ Sex ____(43b)____ Vehicle # ____(43c)____

Name ____(44)____ Age ____(44a)____ Sex ____(44b)____ Vehicle # ____(44c)____

Name ____(45)____ Age ____(45a)____ Sex ____(45b)____ Vehicle # ____(45c)____

Name ____(46)____ Age ____(46a)____ Sex ____(46b)____ Vehicle # ____(46c)____

Vehicle #1 Towed by ____(47)____ Vehicle #2 Towed by ____(48)____

Officer ____(49)____ Badge # ____(50)____ Agency ____(51)____

Supervisor ____(52)____

58. The most correct entry for caption 2 is
    (A) April 7.
    (B) 10:30 A.M.
    (C) 3356.
    (D) 6332.

59. Regarding captions 47 and 48, it would be most correct to state that
    (A) a different entry should be made in each one.
    (B) the most appropriate entry for both captions is Bilecki Towing Service.
    (C) both captions should be left blank.
    (D) not enough information is provided to make an appropriate entry in either caption.

60. The name Mr. Sal Marini would most correctly be inserted in caption
    (A) 8.
    (B) 43.
    (C) 49.
    (D) 52.

61. The number 55 should appear in
    (A) caption 43A only.
    (B) caption 28 only.
    (C) caption 43A and caption 28.
    (D) neither caption 28 nor 43A.

62. The word Florida would most appropriately appear in caption
    (A) 43B.
    (B) 22.
    (C) 51.
    (D) 39.

63. The most appropriate entry for caption 43C is
    (A) 1.
    (B) 2.
    (C) 3.
    (D) 4.

64. It would be most correct to insert the word *male* in
    (A) captions 9 and 43B.
    (B) captions 26 and 43B.
    (C) captions 26 and 44B.
    (D) captions 9 and 44B.

65. The most correct entry for caption 3 is
    (A) 10:20 A.M.
    (B) 10:30 A.M.
    (C) 10:35 A.M.
    (D) 10:40 A.M.

Answer questions 66 through 73 based on the following data.

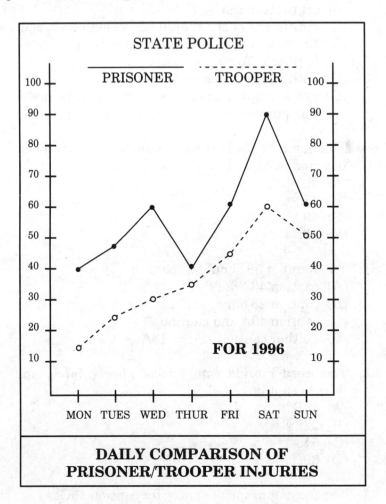

DAILY COMPARISON OF PRISONER/TROOPER INJURIES

Answer questions 66–73 based on the preceding data.

66. The day of the week in 1996 that accounted for the most injuries to prisoners
    (A) was Wednesday.
    (B) was Friday.
    (C) was Saturday.
    (D) cannot be determined from the data.

67. On the average, injuries to troopers
    (A) were lower than injuries to prisoners on every day of the week.
    (B) were higher than injuries to prisoners on Thursdays.
    (C) were higher than injuries to prisoners on Saturdays.
    (D) were higher than injuries to prisoners on Sundays.

68. The percentage of all injuries to prisoners that occurred on Saturday
    (A) was approximately 15%.
    (B) was approximately 23%.
    (C) was approximately 41%.
    (D) cannot be determined from the data given.

69. The least number of injuries to troopers occurred
    (A) on Monday.
    (B) on Wednesday.
    (C) on Friday.
    (D) on Sunday.

70. The greatest number of injuries to troopers happened on
    (A) Wednesday.
    (B) Friday.
    (C) Saturday.
    (D) Sunday.

71. The number of injuries that happened to prisoners on Wednesdays was approximately equal to the number of injuries that happened to prisoners on
    (A) Fridays.
    (B) Saturdays.
    (C) Sundays.
    (D) Mondays.

72. The ratio of prisoner injuries to trooper injuries on Wednesday
    (A) was about 2 to 1.
    (B) was about 3 to 1.
    (C) was about 4 to 1.
    (D) cannot be determined from the data given.

73. On what day of the week was the number of injuries to prisoners closest to the number of injuries to troopers?
(A) Monday
(B) Wednesday
(C) Thursday
(D) It cannot be determined from the data given.

Answer questions 74 and 75 based on the following legal rule.

Troopers are legally entitled to use physical force upon another person when and to the extent they reasonably believe to be necessary to defend themselves or a third person from what they reasonably believe to be the use or imminent use of unlawful physical force by such other person. Troopers may not use deadly physical force upon another person unless they reasonably believe that such other person is using or about to use deadly physical force against them or another.

74. Which of the following represents a violation of this rule?
(A) A trooper uses physical force against a prisoner who was assaulting another trooper.
(B) A trooper uses physical force against a prisoner who is assaulting him.
(C) A trooper uses physical force against a prisoner who threatens to get him one day.
(D) A trooper uses physical force against a prisoner who is about to assault him.

75. Which of the following is NOT a violation of this rule?
(A) A trooper shoots at a prisoner who is using his fists to beat another prisoner.
(B) A trooper shoots a prisoner who is about to attack him with a knife.
(C) A trooper shoots an unarmed prisoner who is threatening to have another prisoner shot.
(D) A trooper shoots an unarmed prisoner who is attempting to escape.

76. When a high-speed chase is in progress, there must be only one primary pursuit vehicle and one secondary pursuit vehicle. Caravanning of vehicles during a high-speed chase is prohibited. The primary purpose of this rule is to
(A) avoid vehicle accidents.
(B) guarantee the capture of the pursued vehicle.
(C) save manpower.
(D) simplify control of the pursuit.

77. The courts have ruled that a juvenile, someone under the age of 16, who has been accused of a crime, has the right to a lawyer. In turn, such juvenile can decide to waive the right to a lawyer providing the parents/guardians of the juvenile concur with that decision. The lawyer may be of the juvenile's own choosing or appointed by the court for financial or other reasons. Therefore, a trooper who finds it necessary to arrest a juvenile must give notice of the juvenile's right to a lawyer. Based on the statement, the most reasonable conclusion to reach is that
    (A) a lawyer must be assigned to represent a juvenile.
    (B) a 16 year old can waive his right to a lawyer without obtaining concurrence from a parent or guardian.
    (C) a trooper who arrests a juvenile must secure a lawyer for that juvenile.
    (D) the only time the court can appoint a lawyer for a juvenile is when there are financial considerations involved.

78. At the first sign of street violence, a trooper who is alone on duty must always
    (A) make an immediate call for backup assistance.
    (B) intervene in the situation.
    (C) use force.
    (D) retreat.

79. State troopers are prohibited by law from making random car stops. This means most nearly that a trooper
    (A) can stop cars at the trooper's own discretion.
    (B) must have a reason for making a car stop.
    (C) cannot ever make a car stop.
    (D) needs supervisory permission to make a car stop.

80. No trooper should allow any prisoner under 19 years of age to be transported together with adult prisoners in any state police vehicle. The main purpose of this rule is probably to prevent
    (A) disputes and confrontations.
    (B) escape attempts.
    (C) exposure of younger prisoners to the views of adult criminals.
    (D) possible assaults on younger prisoners by adult prisoners.

81. A trooper shall not authorize the use of a photograph of himself in uniform in connection with any commercial enterprise. The purpose of this rule is most probably to
(A) protect the identity of undercover troopers.
(B) prevent troopers from enjoying unethical commercial gain.
(C) maintain the image of the state police uniform.
(D) prevent the endorsement of substandard products.

Answer questions 82–89 solely on the basis of the following legal definitions. Do not base your answers on any other knowledge of the law you may have. You may refer to the definitions when answering the questions.

NOTE: The perpetrators in the definitions that follow are referred to as *he* but actually refer to either gender. However when the male and/or female gender is a factor in defining an offense or legal action, such distinction shall be made by the specific use of both pronouns *he* and *she*.

Definition: A search warrant is a court order directing a police officer to conduct a search of a designated premises or designated vehicle or designated person, for the purpose of seizing designated property and to deliver the property to the court that issued the warrant.

Property subject to seizure:

In addition to property designated to be seized by a search warrant, a police officer executing a search warrant may also seize:

1. Stolen property, or

2. Property that is unlawfully possessed such as contraband, or

3. Property used in the commission of a crime, or

4. Evidence that a crime has been committed.

When executable:

1. A search warrant must be executed not more than 10 days after the date of issuance and it must thereafter be returned to the court of issuance without unnecessary delay.

2. A search warrant may be executed on any day of the week. It may be executed only between the hours of 6:00 A.M. and 9:00 P.M. unless the warrant expressly authorizes execution thereof at any time of the day or night.

Execution of a search warrant:

In executing a search warrant a police officer must make a reasonable effort to give notice of the officer's authority and purpose to an occupant thereof before entry and show him the warrant or a copy of the warrant upon request.

However, if there are reasonable grounds to believe that the property sought may be destroyed or disposed of or someone's safety will be endangered, the officer executing the warrant may be given privilege not to announce the officer's purpose and authority before executing the warrant.

If denied access to the premises, the officer may use that force which is necessary to enter and conduct the search.

Disposition of property:

Property seized under the authority of a search warrant, along with an inventory of such property, must be returned to the court that issued the search warrant. In addition a receipt must be given by the officer seizing the property to the person from whom the property was seized. If the property was seized from a premises and no owner can be established, a receipt must be left in a conspicuous place in the premises by the officer seizing the property.

Larceny:

Petit larceny is committed when a person steals the property of another and the value of the property is $1000 dollars or less. Petit larceny is a misdemeanor.

Grand larceny is committed when a person steals the property of another and

1. the value of the property is more than $1000 dollars; or

2. the property stolen is a public record; or

3. the property stolen is a credit card; or

4. the property is stolen from the person of the owner regardless of the value of the property; or

5. the property stolen is a secret scientific formula.

82. Jay steals $999 from Bob's pocket while they are riding on a crowded bus. Jay has committed
    (A) a misdemeanor due to the dollar amount stolen.
    (B) a felony due to the dollar amount stolen.
    (C) petit larceny due to the fact that the property was taken from a person's pocket.
    (D) grand larceny due to the fact that the property was taken from a person's pocket.

83. Which of the following constitutes the offense of petit larceny?
    (A) the theft of a credit card
    (B) the theft of a deed from the county clerk's office
    (C) the theft of a ring worth $750
    (D) the theft of a secret formula used in scientific experiments

84. State Trooper Baker executes a search warrant and obtains the property named in the search warrant. Under such circumstances it would be most correct for Trooper Baker to return the property
    (A) to the troop barracks.
    (B) to her supervisor.
    (C) to the court that issued the search warrant.
    (D) to the nearest court.

85. Jay is a Highway Patrol Officer who is executing a search warrant. In addition to property designated to be seized by the search warrant, Jay may also seize all the following except
    (A) any property that anyone named in the search warrant may be carrying.
    (B) stolen property.
    (C) evidence that a crime has been committed.
    (D) contraband.

86. Today, April 1st, Trooper Weeks has just been issued a search warrant to search a certain premises. Of the following dates, which indicates the latest date that this search warrant may be executed?
    (A) April 6th
    (B) April 10th
    (C) April 15th
    (D) April 30th

87. Trooper Parks is recently graduated from the State Training Academy. She approaches Trooper Meadows and asks her when a search warrant can be executed. Officer Meadows would be most correct if she stated which of the following?
    (A) on any day of the week, but it must always be executed between the hours of 6 A.M. and 9 P.M.
    (B) only on weekdays but any time of the day or night
    (C) at any time of the day or night if expressly authorized as such
    (D) on any day of the week, but it must be executed between 9 P.M. and 6 A.M.

88. Officer Collars wishes to obtain a "No Knock" search warrant. That is, she wishes to be given privilege not to announce her purpose and authority before executing a certain search warrant. Officer Collars would be most likely to obtain such a search warrant if there are reasonable grounds to believe that
    (A) the property sought may be destroyed.
    (B) a person named in the search warrant may be alarmed by the officer making such an announcement.
    (C) the persons inside the premises have been arrested before.
    (D) the property sought is expensive stolen property.

89. After Trooper Day executes a search warrant and seizes property named in the search warrant, the trooper would be most correct if he
    (A) always left a note in a conspicuous place in the premises.
    (B) gave an inventory sheet of the property seized to the person in charge of the premises.
    (C) in all instances did not leave the premises until he personally gave a receipt for the property seized to the lawful owner of the property.
    (D) gave a receipt to the person from whom the property was seized.

DIRECTIONS: Answer questions 90–94 solely on the basis of the following map. The flow of traffic is as shown by the arrows. Where there is only one arrow, then the traffic flows only in the direction indicated by the arrow. You must follow the flow of traffic when moving from one location to another.

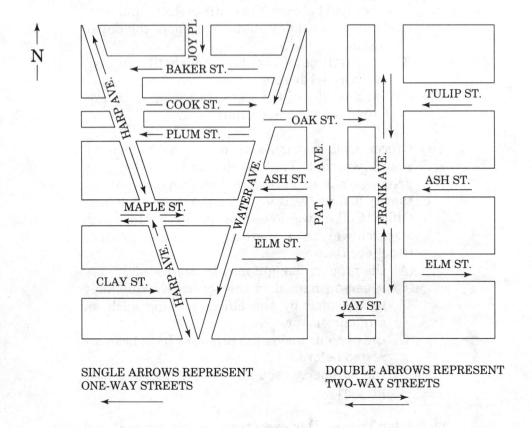

SINGLE ARROWS REPRESENT
ONE-WAY STREETS

DOUBLE ARROWS REPRESENT
TWO-WAY STREETS

90. Trooper Days is in his patrol car on Ash Street as he is approaching Frank Avenue. The dispatcher directs the trooper to respond to an accident on Clay Street and Harp Avenue. Which of the following is the most direct route for the officer to take in his patrol car, making sure to obey all the traffic regulations?
    (A) Turn onto Frank Avenue, head south to Jay Street, make a right onto Jay Street, and then continue west on Jay Street to the destination at Harp Avenue.
    (B) Head west on Ash Street to Water Avenue, head south on Water Avenue to Maple Avenue, make a left at Maple Avenue to Harp Avenue, and then make another left onto Harp Avenue to Clay Street.
    (C) Continue on Ash Street to Water Avenue, head south on Water Avenue to Maple Street, turn west on Maple to Harp Avenue, and travel one block south on Harp Avenue.
    (D) Head west to Pat Avenue, make a left onto Pat Avenue, continue on Pat Avenue to Elm Street, head west on Elm Street to Water Avenue, head north on Water Avenue to Maple Avenue, head west on Maple Avenue to Harp Avenue, and then make a left and continue south to Clay Avenue.

91. Officer Brooks is driving south in her patrol car on Pat Avenue approaching the intersection of Ash Street. She receives a call to respond in her patrol car to Water Avenue and Elm Street. In such an instance, which of the following should be the officer's first action while making sure to obey all the traffic regulations?
    (A) to make a left
    (B) to make a right
    (C) to head north
    (D) to head east

92. State Trooper Parks is seated in his patrol car on Clay Street west of Harp Avenue. State Trooper Pines is parked in her patrol car on Tulip Street east of Frank Avenue. They are both notified by the radio dispatcher that a fire has occurred in a jewelry store located on Elm Street between Water Avenue and Pat Avenue. The town police are requesting that the troopers assist them by blocking both ends of Elm Street where the fire has occurred. Which of the following actions would be most appropriate in attempting to fulfill such a request while making sure to obey all the traffic regulations?

(A) If Trooper Parks headed east to Harp Avenue, headed north to Maple Avenue, proceeded east one block to Water Avenue, and then headed south on Water Avenue to Elm Street.

(B) If Trooper Pines made a left onto Frank Avenue, headed south to Jay Street, headed west on Jay Street to Pat Avenue, and then headed north on Pat Avenue to Elm Street.

(C) If Trooper Parks turned onto Harp Avenue and continued north to Plum Street, made a right onto Plum Street and proceeded to Water Avenue, and then headed south on Water Avenue to the fire.

(D) If Trooper Pines headed south on Frank Avenue to Ash Street, made a left onto Ash Street, drove one block to Pat Avenue, and then headed south on Pat Avenue to the fire.

93. Trooper Carter is legally parked in his patrol car on Baker Street facing Harp Avenue. He is directed by the sergeant to respond to Jay Street at the intersection of Frank Avenue. Which of the following is the most direct route for the trooper to take in his patrol car, making sure to obey all the traffic regulations?

(A) Head east on Baker Street to Water Avenue, head south on Water Avenue to Oak Street, head east on Oak Street to Frank Avenue, and then head south on Frank Avenue to Jay Street.

(B) Head west on Baker Street to Harp Avenue, head south on Harp Avenue to Cook Street, make a right onto Cook Street to Water Avenue, head south on Water Avenue to Oak Street, head east on Oak Street to Frank Avenue, and then head south on Frank Avenue to Jay Street.

(C) Head west on Baker Street to Harp Avenue, make a left and head south to Maple Avenue, head east on Maple Avenue to Frank Avenue, and then head south on Frank Avenue to Jay Street.

(D) Turn onto Harp Avenue and proceed south to Cook Street, head east on Cook Street to Water Avenue, head south on Water Avenue to Oak Street, head east on Oak Street to Frank Avenue, and then head south on Frank Avenue to Jay Street.

94. An accident has occurred on Oak Street at the intersection of Pat Avenue. If Trooper Rivers is on Ash Street approaching Water Avenue and is directed to respond to the accident, then which of the following most accurately describes the trooper's first action in taking the most direct route to the accident, while making sure to obey all the traffic regulations?

(A) make a right onto Water Avenue
(B) make a left onto Water Avenue
(C) go east on Ash Street
(D) go north on Pat Avenue

DIRECTIONS: Answer questions 95–100 on the basis of the following sketches. The model face, the one appearing above the dotted line, is a sketch of a person who is wanted. Of the four comparison faces, the ones appearing below the dotted line, one of them is the way the model face looked after changing appearance. You are to assume that no surgical alteration of the wanted person's face has occurred. You are to select the face that is most likely that of the wanted person.

95.

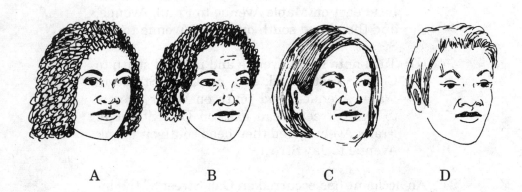

A   B   C   D

96.

A   B   C   D

97.

A   B   C   D

98.

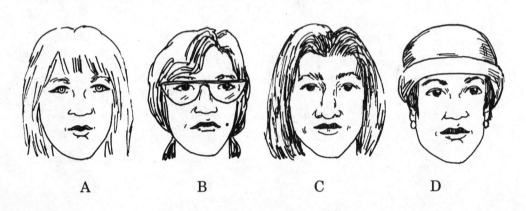

A   B   C   D

99.

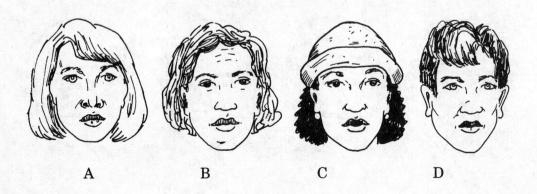

A   B   C   D

100.

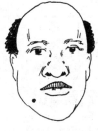       

    A   B   C   D

ANSWER KEY

1. A	21. C	41. A	61. A	81. B
2. B	22. B	42. C	62. D	82. D
3. A	23. B	43. A	63. B	83. C
4. B	24. B	44. D	64. B	84. C
5. A	25. C	45. B	65. C	85. A
6. B	26. A	46. D	66. C	86. B
7. B	27. B	47. B	67. A	87. C
8. B	28. C	48. B	68. B	88. A
9. A	29. C	49. A	69. A	89. D
10. D	30. C	50. B	70. C	90. C
11. C	31. D	51. B	71. A	91. B
12. C	32. B	52. D	72. A	92. A
13. B	33. B	53. C	73. C	93. D
14. D	34. C	54. C	74. C	94. B
15. A	35. B	55. C	75. B	95. A
16. A	36. C	56. C	76. A	96. A
17. C	37. D	57. B	77. B	97. B
18. D	38. C	58. C	78. A	98. D
19. A	39. A	59. B	79. B	99. C
20. C	40. B	60. B	80. C	100. B

Diagnostic Chart

INSTRUCTIONS: After you score your test, complete the following chart by inserting in the column captioned "Your Number Correct" the number of questions you answered correctly in each of the ten sections of the test. Then compare your score in each section with the ratings in the column captioned "Scale." Finally, to correct your weaknesses follow the instructions found after the chart.

SECTION	QUESTION NUMBER	AREA	YOUR NUMBER CORRECT	SCALE
1	1–8	Memory (8 questions)		8 Right—Excellent 6–7 Right—Good 5 Right—Fair Under 5 Right—Poor
2	9–28	Reading Comprehension (20 questions)		20 Right—Excellent 18–19 Right—Good 16–17 Right—Fair Under 16 Right—Poor
3	29–48	Applying State Police Procedures (20 questions)		20 Right—Excellent 18–19 Right—Good 16–17 Right—Fair Under 16 Right—Poor
4	49–57	Verbal and Math (9 questions)		9 Right—Excellent 7–8 Right—Good 6 Right—Fair Under 6 Right—Poor
5	58–65	State Police Forms (8 questions)		8 Right—Excellent 6–7 Right—Good 5 Right—Fair Under 5 Right—Poor
6	66–73	Interpreting Data (8 questions)		8 Right—Excellent 6–7 Right—Good 5 Right—Fair Under 5 Right—Poor
7	74–81	Judgment and Reasoning (8 questions)		8 Right—Excellent 6–7 Right—Good 5 Right—Fair Under 5 Right—Poor
8	82–89	Legal Definitions (8 questions)		8 Right—Excellent 6–7 Right—Good 5 Right—Fair Under 5 Right—Poor
9	90–94	Traffic Directions (5 questions)		5 Right—Excellent 4 Right—Good 3 Right—Fair Under 3 Right—Poor
10	95–100	Matching Sketches (6 questions)		6 Right—Excellent 5 Right—Good 4 Right—Fair Under 4 Right—Poor

How to correct weaknesses:

1. If you are weak in Section 1, concentrate on Chapter 6.
2. If you are weak in Section 2, concentrate on Chapter 4.
3. If you are weak in Section 3, concentrate on Chapter 9.
4. If you are weak in Section 4, concentrate on Chapter 5.
5. If you are weak in Section 5, concentrate on Chapter 7.
6. If you are weak in Section 6, concentrate on Chapter 8.
7. If you are weak in Section 7, concentrate on Chapter 10.
8. If you are weak in Section 8, concentrate on Chapter 11.
9. If you are weak in Section 9, concentrate on Chapter 13.
10. If you are weak in Section 10, concentrate on Chapter 12.

Note: Consider yourself weak in a section if you receive other than an excellent rating in it.

Answer Explanations

1. **A**   John Doe had eye drops so it is likely that he was experiencing some sort of eye problem.

2. **B**   Jane Roe had divorce papers. That fact supports the assumption that she is most likely experiencing marital problems.

3. **A**   John Doe had a pistol permit issued in his name.

4. **B**   Jane Roe had diet pills. That is a fact that supports the assumption that she is experiencing a weight control problem.

5. **A**   Jane Roe lives on 12th Road, and her address is 456.

6. **B**   John Doe lives on Park Drive, and his address is 123.

7. **B**   John Doe had a $10 bill, a $20 bill, and 60¢ in change.

8. **B**   Jane Roe had a student identification card.

9. **A**   Patrol is the one police function that cannot be eliminated. It is, therefore, essential.

10. **D**   This is a very difficult question because choices A, B, and C are all factors that logically have an impact on the effectiveness of any police division. But, they are not mentioned in the paragraph. Choice D, however, is as stated in the paragraph.

11. **C**   Most of the money in the budget is used to support the patrol function.

12. **C**   Mrs. James opened the door of her apartment and saw the two strange males at 3:30 P.M.

13. **B**   Mrs. James apartment, 13C, is directly opposite the elevator.

14. **D**   Credit cards were not mentioned anywhere in the passage.

15. **A**   Choice B is Mr. King's work address. Choice C is the King's home address. Choice D is not mentioned in the passage.

16. **A**   When times are given in the passage, they will most certainly be the subject of questions.

17. **C**   Mr. King is a foreman at the telephone company. If you picked choice D, you didn't realize the question was about Mrs. King. Be careful!

18. **D**   Note that all four numbers suggested in the choices appear somewhere in the passage. This is a very common trick of the examiner to see if you can pay attention to details.

19. **A**   The taller man was about 38 years old. The other man (the shorter one) was about 31 years old.

20. **C**   The second male, who was carrying a flashlight, was white, about 31 years old, 5'8", 140 pounds, with black hair and a scar on the right side of his face.

21. **C**   The taller man was described as having a tattoo on his left hand.

22. **B**   Mr. King is a foreman at the telephone company.

23. **B**   Mr. King left for work at 6:00 A.M. and his wife left 10 minutes later.

24. **B**   The troopers arrived on the scene at 9:15 A.M., and the accident happened 5 minutes prior to their arrival.

25. **C**   Only choice C fits the fact pattern in the story. If you picked choice D, you were tricked by the specificity of the choice. It sounds good, but it is wrong because the accident occurred 300 feet south of Exit 28 which, of course, is near Exit 28.

26. **A**   There were no personal injuries involved in the accident.

27. **B**   The driver of the station wagon was Mrs. Pat Crow, age 28.

28. **C**   The station wagon was dented on its left side near the rear door, and the van had a dented front fender.

29. **C** According to procedure, the first person to be consulted under such circumstances is the patrol supervisor.

30. **C** The minimum number is six.

31. **D** Miranda warnings are required if the suspect is to be interrogated before, during, or after the lineup. Choice A is correct because the suspect could, while still not under arrest, volunteer to be in the lineup. Choices B and C are as stated in the procedure.

32. **B** Prior to conducting the lineup, a detective supervisor will be consulted and will personally supervise the entire procedure and then after the lineup actually prepare the LINEUP REPORT form.

33. **B** If an attorney representing a client wishes to be present when the lineup is conducted, the lineup will be delayed for a reasonable time to permit the attorney to appear.

34. **C** The attorney may observe the lineup from any place where he/she cannot be observed. Choices A, B, and D are contained in the procedure.

35. **B** The first action is to inform the violator of the violation committed.

36. **C** The information suggested in choices A, B, and D are all required by the procedure in the entry made by the post command desk officer. The information suggested in choice C is strictly made up and is not required by the procedure.

37. **D** The action described in choice D is inappropriate because the first copy of a summons should be given to the violator. The information found in choices A, B, and C is found in the procedure.

38. **C** Pat is only 15 years old. The trooper should prepare a Youth Report Card for a violator who is at least 7 and less than 16 years of age.

39. **A** Because Spirits is intoxicated, he cannot receive a summons. He must, as suggested by choice A, be arrested. Choice B is incorrect because a summons may not be issued to an intoxicated person. Choice D is incorrect because the Youth Report Card is prepared only when the violator is at least 7 and less than 16 years of age. Spirits is 17 years old. Choice C is not found anywhere in the procedure upon which the directions state you must base your answers.

40. **B** It is the post command desk officer who has the responsibility to verify such an arrest. When answering procedure questions, you should imagine yourself as one of the persons in the narrative. This helps you understand the specifics of the situation that is being described more quickly.

41. **A** The arrest was made at 8:30 A.M. The chemical test of prisoners charged with operating a vehicle while under the influence of alcohol must be administered within 2 hours of the time of arrest or as stated in choice A by 10:30 A.M.

42. **C** The Alcohol Test Unit technician conducts the "Coordination Test" of the prisoner, in the presence of the arresting trooper.

43. **A** The actions suggested in choices B, C, and D are correct. The use of the word *always* in choice A makes it incorrect. Only in the event that the examination of the prisoner cannot be videotaped will the desk officer at the driver testing location supervise the examination. Any time limiting words such as *always* or *never* are used in a choice, particular attention should be given such a choice.

44. **D** The arresting trooper must notify the prosecutor if the prisoner has any previous convictions for the same crime within the past 10 years. A conviction is clearly not the same as an arrest. The need to read all the choices is obvious.

45. **B** Choices A and C are incorrect because the department's test must be completed before any test by a prisoner's personal physician may be conducted. Choice D is incorrect because the test by a personal physician will be allowed after the department testing has been completed.

46. **D** The first action to be taken is to interview the person. Then, if unable to direct the person, the person should be brought to the post command.

47. **B** The trooper in possession of the child is required to inform the Missing Persons Squad if the child is moved from the post command to another location.

48. **B** The actions of the trooper were improper because the procedure clearly states that before anything else is done, the trooper should notify the post command desk officer and the radio dispatcher.

49. **A** Choice B is incorrect because *implicit,* which means implied, was used; instead, *explicit,* which means expressed directly, should have been used. Choice C is incorrect because *moral,* which means virtuous conduct was used; instead, *morale,* which means spirit of a group, should have been used. Choice A is accurately and clearly stated.

50. **B** *Ingenuous* means open and frank, whereas *ingenious* means clever and resourceful. Therefore, choices A and C are incorrect; *ingenious* should have been in choice A, and *ingenuous* should have been used in choice C. Choice B is accurately and clearly stated.

51. **B** Choice A is incorrect because it should state "Wolf and me." Words such as *myself, herself, himself,* and *themselves* are known as reflexive pronouns. This type of pronoun such as myself cannot be used in place of *me.* Reflexive pronouns should be used to reflect back to the doer of the action such as I see myself, she shot herself, and they hurt themselves. Choice C is incorrect because it should state, "as good as she" (is). The word *is,* although not specifically written, is understood. Choice B is correct as stated. Remember that, as in choice B, remove the words you know and then read it as who committed the murder, which you should then recognize as correct.

52. **D** All the choices are clearly and accurately stated.

53. **C** Choice A is incorrect because *compliment* should have been used to indicate praise. Choice B is incorrect because *casual* should have been used to indicate informal. Choice C is clearly and accurately stated.

54. **C** Bello is 39 now and in 11 years will be 50 but will not be eligible for retirement because he will have only 20 years (11 + 9) with the agency. Dubs is 25 now and in 25 years will be 50 and will have 27 years (25 + 2) with the agency. Love is now 45 and in 5 years will be 50; he will be eligible for retirement because he will have 25 years (5 + 20) with the agency. Ling is now 33 and in 17 years will be 50; he will be eligible for retirement because he will have 28 years (17 + 11) with the agency. However, Officer Love will be eligible for retirement in only 5 years, reaching both the required age and time with the agency. Choice C is the answer.

55. **C** The combined ages of the two oldest officers, Love and Roe, is 45 + 40 = 85, and their combined time with the agency is 20 + 17 = 37. Doing the same type of calculations for the two youngest officers, Dubs and Barns, we arrive at 55 years with 10 years with the agency. Choice C is, therefore, the most accurate statement.

56. **C** The total of all the ages is 282 years divided by the number of officers, which is 8, yields 35.25 (²⁸%).

57. **B** The sum of all the time with the agency of all the officers assigned to Squad One is 92, divided by the number of officers, which is 8, yields an average of 11½ years with the agency.

58. **C**   The case number is 3356. This question was difficult if you did not note that caption 2 was the first caption on the form and asked for the case number. If instead you went directly to the second caption on the form, the date of occurrence, you incorrectly assumed that all the captions were sequentially numbered. You, therefore, probably selected choice A, which was April 7, the date of occurrence.

59. **B**   The captions ask for who towed each vehicle which is indicated as Bilecki Towing Service.

60. **B**   Mr. Sal Marini is the name of the only person who was injured and caption 43 asks for the name of who was injured. Choice A is incorrect because Sal Marini is driver two, not driver one.

61. **A**   Nothing in the narrative would call for the number 55 to be inserted in caption 28, the date of birth (D.O.B.), of driver two, which refers to Mr. Sal Marini, the owner of vehicle two. However, the number 55 should appear in caption 43A, the age of Mr. Marini, the person who was injured.

62. **D**   The word *Florida* should be inserted in caption 39, which calls for the state of registration for vehicle two, which is the Ford Explorer with Florida license plates.

63. **B**   Caption 43C asks for the injured person's vehicle number. The narrative indicates that Mr. Marini is injured and that he is from vehicle two, the Ford Explorer.

64. **B**   Choices A and D are incorrect because caption 9 asks for the sex of Driver #1, which in the narrative refers to Ms. Vivian Bianco, a female. Choice C is incorrect because caption 44B asks for the sex of a second injured person and in the narrative only one person, Mr. Marini, was injured. Caption 26 refers to the sex of Driver #2 and caption 43B refers to the sex of the first and only injured person. In both instances, it is Mr. Marini.

65. **C**   Caption 3 asks for the time the officer was notified, which according to the narrative was 10:35 A.M. This is another favorite area examiners like to ask form questions about, namely the time an officer is notified as opposed to the time the officer arrived.

66. **C**   During 1996, about 90 injuries occurred to prisoners on Saturdays.

67. **A**   There was no day of the week that had a higher average number of injuries to troopers than to prisoners. The closest day was Thursday, when there were about 40 injuries to prisoners and about 35 injuries to troopers.

68. **B** Concerning injuries to prisoners, there were about 40 on Monday, 48 on Tuesday, 60 on Wednesday, 40 on Thursday, 60 on Friday, 90 on Saturday, and 60 on Sunday. This is a total of about 398 injuries. Because there were about 90 on Saturdays, by dividing 398 into 90 it is determined that Saturday accounted for about 23% of prisoner injuries.

69. **A** For the whole year, only about 15 troopers were injured on Mondays.

70. **C** Approximately 60 injuries happened to troopers on Saturdays.

71. **A** There were approximately 60 injuries to prisoners on both Wednesdays and Fridays.

72. **A** There were about 60 prisoner injuries and about 30 trooper injuries on Wednesdays, which is a ratio of 60 to 30, or 2 to 1.

73. **C** There were about 40 prisoner injuries on Thursdays and about 35 trooper injuries on Thursdays.

74. **C** The rule allows troopers to defend themselves against the use or imminent use of force. It does not allow the use of force to defend against future threats such as, "I will get you one day."

75. **B** According to the rule, troopers may not use deadly physical force upon another person unless they reasonably believe that such other person is using or about to use deadly physical force against them or another. Choice B is the only example that satisfies this rule. All the other choices are violations of this rule.

76. **A** We have all seen those movies where a number of police vehicles become involved in a multiple-car accident among themselves. The no caravanning rule is to avoid such an occurrence.

77. **B** The passage defines a juvenile as being under 16 years of age. Choice B speaks of a person who is already 16 years of age.

78. **A** Whenever a trooper who is alone sees that violence is about to occur, the first step that trooper should take is to request backup assistance. One never can predict if and when violence will spread.

79. **B** Random car stops are made by chance and for no reason.

80. **C** The thinking behind this rule is that younger prisoners have a better chance of rehabilitation if they do not associate with hardened adult criminals.

81. **B** It is unethical for any trooper to use his uniform or any symbol of his public office for personal gain or profit.

82. **D** In this instance the offense is grand larceny because the property, regardless of its value, was stolen from the person of the owner.

83. **C** Choices A, B, and D indicate instances of grand larceny. Only choice C represents an instance of petit larceny where the property stolen is $1000 or less.

84. **C** Property seized under the authority of a search warrant, along with an inventory of such property, must be returned to the court that issued the search warrant.

85. **A** A search warrant does not allow the officer executing the warrant to seize anything someone named in the warrant may be carrying (e.g., a photo of one's child).

86. **B** The search warrant must be executed within 10 days of the date of issuance. Of the suggested dates, April 10th is the latest date on which the warrant could be legally executed.

87. **C** A search warrant may be executed only between the hours of 6:00 A.M. and 9:00 P.M. unless the warrant expressly authorizes execution thereof at any time of the day or night.

88. **A** If there are reasonable grounds to believe that the property sought may be destroyed or disposed of or someone's safety will be endangered, the officer executing the warrant may be given privilege not to announce her purpose and authority before executing the warrant.

89. **D** Choice A is incorrect because a receipt must be left in a conspicuous place in the premises by the officer seizing the property if the property was seized from a premises and no owner could be established. Choice B is incorrect because an inventory sheet should be returned to the court. Choice C is incorrect because, if no one is present, a receipt for property taken from a premises would then be left in a conspicuous place. Choice D is correct because a receipt must be given by the officer seizing the property to the person from whom the property was seized.

90. **C** Choice A is incorrect because it is not possible to take Jay Street directly to the accident. Choice B is incorrect because making a left at Maple Avenue would result in heading away from the accident. Choice D is incorrect because heading west on Elm Street would result in going against traffic. Also choice D requires heading north on Water Avenue, which is a southbound only street. Note that, even

though there could be more than one incorrect direction in a choice, one is all that is needed to rule it out and move on to examine the next choice.

91. **B** Following the directions given in choices A, C, and D would require the officer to go against traffic.

92. **A** Choice B is incorrect because it requires heading north on Pat Avenue, which is a southbound street. Choice C is incorrect because it requires making a right turn onto Plum Street, which is the same as heading east on a westbound street. Choice D is incorrect because it requires making a left turn at Ash Street, which would take the driver off the map. Remember that, in this type of question, it is quite important to put oneself in the driver's seat or, said another way, to always answer the questions as if you were actually driving the car. Such a technique helps greatly when right and left turns are directed. Also note that, although no one choice was able to fully comply with the request to block both ends of the block involved, choice A was the most appropriate action in attempting to fulfill the request while following the traffic directions.

93. **D** Choice A is incorrect because traveling east on Baker Street does not follow the traffic regulations. Choice B is incorrect because making a right turn on Cook Street is not only against the traffic regulations but also leads away from the required destination. Choice C is incorrect because it is not possible to head east on Maple Avenue to Frank Avenue. There are obstructions.

94. **B** Following the directions in choices A, C, and D would require going against the traffic.

95. **A** The nose of choice B, the chin line of choice C, and the eyes of choice D leave choice A as the only possible answer.

96. **A** The nose of choice B, the eyes of choices C and D leave choice A as the only possible answer.

97. **B** The facial line on the chin of choice A, the eyes of choice C, and the eyes and nose of choice D leave choice B as the only possible answer.

98. **D** The lips of choices A and B and the nose of choice C leave choice D as the only possible answer.

99. **C** The nose of choice A, the ears of choice B, and the eyes of choice D leave choice C as the only possible answer.

100. **B** The mole on the chin of choice A and the eyes of choices C and D leave choice B as the only possible answer.

A FINAL WORD

CHAPTER 19

The Final Preparation

Many students become anxious in the final days right before the examination. They ask, "Has enough preparation taken place? Is there anything left to do in these final days before the examination?"

While it is normal to feel some degree of anxiety, if you have used the book the way we have recommended, studied the various chapters dealing with the different question types, and taken the practice examinations, you should be prepared and do well. Each time you sat down and practiced the various question types with this text, you were helping yourself pass the actual exam. Your passing the exam actually began when you started learning test-taking strategies and practiced answering the various test questions. On the day of the examination, all you will be doing is appearing at the exam site to collect what is owed you for the hard work you have already done. You will be demonstrating what you have learned. The hard work is really over. Taking the examination should be seen as a reward for what you have already done.

However, to maintain your level of preparedness, we recommend that you do certain things in the week right before the examination.

Exam Day Minus Seven

Seven days before the examination take a look at the first practice examination, the Diagnostic Test. By reviewing the Diagnostic Test, you should be able to identify the types of questions that give you the most difficulty. Here is where you should be spending your preparation time in the days immediately preceding the exam. You should study the chapters explaining those question types you find difficult and practice questions in these areas.

In addition, a week before the examination take a trip to the actual examination site. For this trip actually use the same public transportation you plan to use on the day of the examination. Become familiar with the exact stop to get off at, how best to go from the public transportation to the site, and most importantly what the transportation schedule will be like on the day of the examination. Since the examination is often given on weekends when a reduced transportation schedule is in effect you do not want to be left waiting on examination day for a train or bus that never arrives because it does not run on weekends. You must get to the examination site on time and without the anxiety that comes from traveling to a location that you have never before visited. Your hard work and examination preparation is of no use if you don't get to the examination site on time and take the examination.

During the week that precedes the examination actually drive to the site if you intend to use a private auto on the day of the examination. Make sure that you are familiar with parking availability on the day of the examination. Check to see that your car is in good mechanical order. It is not a bad idea to have someone drive you to the site. If car trouble should then develop, the car can be left with the driver and you can proceed on to the site alone possibly via alternate public transportation. You should know where the site is, how to get there, how long it takes to get there, and, if driving, where to park your car safely and legally. There have been incidents reported where candidates have hurriedly parked their cars, entered the examination site, and begun taking the examination only to look out the window during the examination to see their cars being towed away from an illegal parking space. Being unfamiliar with an area and somewhat in a hurry, can cause someone to park in a No Parking area. To then continue to take an examination, knowing that, when finished, the unpleasant and expensive experience of getting your car back awaits you, can be extremely stressful. Taking an examination while you are unnecessarily preoccupied about your car certainly is not a good idea. Give yourself every advantage so that you can concentrate exclusively on your examination.

Exam Day Minus Six and Five

On the sixth and fifth days before the examination reread the chapters that explain those question types you have found to be difficult based on your taking of the Diagnostic Examination. Do not restudy those areas that pose no difficulty for you. For example, if handling state police forms is difficult but graph questions are easy, then you should concentrate on the chapter and any questions that deal with handling state police forms. Continuing to study the chapter on graphs and continuing to answer practice questions on graphs would not be most productive for you in the short time remaining before the examination.

Exam Day Minus Four, Three, and Two

On days four, three, and two before the examination, we recommend reviewing all the practice examinations that appear in the text. When you take these practice examinations, you should strive to take the examinations under conditions very similar to actual examination conditions. That means that you should take each examination in its entirety. Do not just answer a few questions and then stop and then go back and answer a few questions more later on. You will not be able to do that on the day of your examination, so get used to what you will be facing in just a few days. Sit in a chair at a desk or table. Time yourself and aim to finish each examination in the time allotted. Usually you will be required to bring and use a No. 2 pencil, so use one when taking these practice examinations. The goal is to take the practice examinations under simulated examination conditions. Therefore, when you finally do take your examination in few days, you will be used to sitting in one place and concentrating for a fairly long period of time without tiring.

Exam Day Minus One

On the day before the examination, review the chapter in the text dealing with test taking and how to maximize your test score. Give particular attention to the section dealing with strategies for handling multiple-choice questions. We do not recommend cramming. If you have used the text and learned our strategies for handling the different question types, your study efforts should be over. You should now begin to relax and mentally prepare to take the examination tomorrow.

We have been asked by students, "Should I eat anything special the night before the exam and how about getting extra sleep?" The key is to do nothing other than what you normally do. The night before the examination you should eat what is for you a normal dinner.

After dinner lay out what you will need the next day. This includes any admission cards, pencils, and other test-taking equipment. Regarding test-taking equipment, you should be prepared to bring anything that the testing agency requires, such as pencils, erasers, or a form of identification. In addition, we recommend bringing a sweater. If the room is too cool, wear it. If the room is too warm sit on the sweater. A sweater can serve to soften a desk seat, which after several hours can become quite hard and uncomfortable.

Also bring a serviceable watch to help you keep track of your time, extra pencils with erasers, a sharpener, and, if required, a pen to sign your name. An extra pair of glasses might come in handy along with something to clean them with. In order to refresh yourself while remaining in your seat, you might find it helpful to bring a few packets of alcohol wipes. Also, if it is allowed and it does not present dietary problems, you might want to bring along a snack of your choice as a quick source of energy during the examination.

Concerning a good night's sleep, get what is normal for you. Unless there is a bona fide medical reason and they are recommended by a physician, we do not recommend sedatives to help you get to sleep. It could be harmful to you the next day, examination day.

Remember that exam day is just the day when you demonstrate what you have learned during your many hours of preparation.

Exam Day Minus Zero

On examination day wake up with enough time to dress, have breakfast, and gather your test-taking equipment. Have a friend call you to make sure you are up.

Arrive at the examination site early enough so that you do not feel rushed. Follow the instructions you receive from those supervising the examination. When directed, proceed to your assigned room and seat. Examine your seat. If there are any problems with the room or seat that have been assigned to you, report them immediately to those supervising the examination. Follow all instructions exactly. If you do not understand any instructions, seek clarification of them. Get ready to demonstrate what you have learned as a result of your many hours of study and preparation. If you have faithfully followed what has been outlined for you in this text, you should be successful. Have confidence in your preparation effort and your ability to deal with the examination.

We will see you on the road on post. Good Luck!

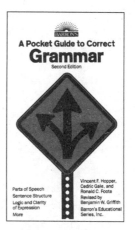